P29 – Massa.
153 – Onitsha people ran away first
196 – Human sacrifice when prince Odiri – died in Onitsha thraldom.
198 – Abokko, Idda, ~~Ata~~
200 – Atjai was the sun (wrist watch)
200 – Bonny prince with his 8 wives (son of King Wi[illegible] Pepple
201 – Bonny evil place of cannibalism. 120 miles of sea front is the bight of Biafra
206 – Iguana Lizard ceased to be worshipped by the ijaw in April 22nd 1867
207 – King William Pepple was crowned in ~~18[illegible]~~ 1835 at the age of 19.

ISBN 978-1-331-49948-0
PIBN 10198418

BV 3625 N6 C7 1909
UNIVERSITY OF CALIFORNIA, SAN DIEGO
3 1822 01080 4128

S. A. Crowther
Bishop, Niger Territory

THE BLACK BISHOP

SAMUEL ADJAI CROWTHER

BY

JESSE PAGE, F.R.G.S.

WITH PREFACE BY EUGENE STOCK, D.C.L.

LATE EDITORIAL SECRETARY OF THE CHURCH MISSIONARY SOCIETY

WITH 16 ILLUSTRATIONS AND MAP

FLEMING H. REVELL COMPANY

NEW YORK : CHICAGO

THE BLACK BISHOP

SAMUEL ADJAI CROWTHER

BY

JESSE PAGE, F.R.G.S.

WITH PREFACE BY EUGENE STOCK, D.C.L.

LATE EDITORIAL SECRETARY OF THE CHURCH MISSIONARY SOCIETY

WITH 16 ILLUSTRATIONS AND MAP

FLEMING H. REVELL COMPANY

NEW YORK : CHICAGO

WILLIAM BRENDON AND SON, LTD.
PRINTERS
PLYMOUTH, ENGLAND

TO

THE RIGHT HON.

SIR GEORGE D. TAUBMAN GOLDIE

P.C., K.C.M.G., D.C.L., LL.D., F.R.S.

THE FOUNDER OF NIGERIA,

WHO WAS A FRIEND OF THE LATE

BISHOP CROWTHER

AND IS THE EARNEST WELL-WISHER OF

THE WEST AFRICAN RACE,

THIS VOLUME

IS DEDICATED BY KIND PERMISSION.

PREFACE

WITH real pleasure I respond to Mr. Page's kind request that I should write a brief preface to his book. I knew Bishop Crowther well, and greatly appreciated the simplicity of his character and the devotion of his whole heart and life to the Niger Mission. It is a good and a right thing that his biography should be written; good and right also to dwell most fully upon the central parts of his long career as Mr. Page has done. The story of his rescue from the slave ship and of his early days, both before and after that decisive moment in his life, is tolerably familiar, having been told in speeches and lectures and books and magazines innumerable. Many amongst us have vivid recollections of the times of difficulty and controversy that caused his later years to be somewhat shadowed. What the author of this biography has mainly sought to do, and has done with skill and judgment, is to portray the missionary Bishop at work during the earlier years of the Niger Mission.

Samuel Crowther's career was unique. A kidnapped slave in 1821, a rescued slave in 1822, a mission schoolboy in 1823, a baptized Christian in 1825, a college student in 1826, a teacher in 1828, a clergyman in 1843, a missionary to the country whence he had been stolen in 1845, the founder of a new mission in 1857, the first negro bishop in 1864,—where is the parallel to such a life? And what a familiar figure he was to us at home! Ten times in seventy years he came to England. In his later years as Bishop he was in constant demand as a speaker all over the country, and his absolute unselfishness and cheerful readiness to be at everybody's service were an example indeed to "deputations." If he had accomplished nothing in Africa he would still have been a valuable helper of the missionary cause among ourselves. But, in fact, after all possible deductions, he accomplished much in Africa. Amid circumstances of almost unexampled difficulty he went steadily on his way; and if the Upper Niger in his lifetime bore little fruit, the Delta to-day, with its cannibalism and infanticide and horrible superstitions practically at an end—though not its sin, and who could expect *that?*—is a monument to Bishop Crowther's indomitable perseverance in a holy cause. He lived in an atmosphere of suspicion and scandal, yet no tongue, however malicious, ventured to whisper reproach against his personal character. Some might criticize his administration; no one ever questioned his sincerity and simplicity.

I heard of his death one Sunday morning while I was in Rome, in January, 1892. I was to address Signor Capellini's band of earnest Christian Italian soldiers that evening. I put aside the subject I had chosen and told them the story of Samuel Crowther. Never, surely, had an audience been more surprised and interested.

I commend Mr. Page's volume heartily to the reader of missionary books; and the Mission, with its modern developments under Bishop Tugwell, Bishop James Johnson, Archdeacon Crowther (the Bishop's son), Archdeacon Dennis, Dr. Miller, and others, to the prayers and sympathies of all Christian people.

Eugene Stock

AUTHOR'S FOREWORD

IT is a reminder of the flight of time that twenty years have passed since I saw Bishop Crowther and wrote a short sketch of his life in my series of missionary biographies published by Messrs. Partridge. Since then much has happened. The sickle of that great Reaper, who strews his swath with full ripe golden corn and frail young flowerets, has gathered this good old man Home. And now, after all these years, his son, Archdeacon D. C. Crowther, on behalf of the family and many friends, has asked me to prepare from the mass of papers and letters left behind by his father a complete biography upon a scale and with a fulness worthy of his character and career.

The task has not been an easy one, but it has been made possible by the kind co-operation of the Church Missionary Society, to whom I have been so much indebted in respect of my previous books, and in this particular instance they have rendered me a priceless service. I have had the privilege of perusing their Niger correspondence during the long period of

Crowther's career as student, schoolmaster, catechist, clergyman, explorer, and finally as Bishop of the Niger. It has been literally a labour of love to collate, with necessary care, not only this mass of valuable material in the archives of Salisbury Square, but the hundreds of letters and MSS. sent me from West Africa. I am grateful for the help also afforded me by some of the Bishop's old friends, amongst whom I would specially mention the Rev. Canon Henry Venn, a name to him so full of sacred associations; Archdeacon James Hamilton, who was with him on the Niger in those closing years; Bishop James Johnson, his old and true yoke-fellow, still in the field; and the Rev. J. Bradford Whiting, his commissary in England and greatly esteemed friend. Last, and certainly not least, I have to thank Dr. Eugene Stock for his kindness in looking over my proof sheets and for the Preface which he has so appropriately written for this work.

I will only add that it has been my earnest endeavour in these pages to allow the Bishop to speak for himself, and to reappear to his friends, old and new—enemies he has none—as a living personality, exercising those gifts of head and heart with which God endowed him for that great work to which He called him amidst his own kindred and people.

Nigeria has a future of great promise before it, although it may be some time before Lagos becomes the Liverpool of West Africa, and the lordly Niger the highway of a prosperous and developed Protectorate of the British Empire. Still, every mile of railway brings this consummation nearer, and, in a deeper sense, every Christian convert makes it more possible. There are difficulties to face, of which climate takes a second place to-day, and the resources of a wise and courageous statescraft will be taxed to the uttermost in their settlement. But if in the remaking of this nation we lay our foundations in righteousness, eliminating all those hurtful elements which give us trouble at home, it may be the lot of these Black children of our world-wide Empire to dwell in safety under the smile of Heaven. And assuredly all along the line of her coming history, however chequered it may be, the sons of Africa will never forget the memory of one who, sharing their sorrows as one of themselves, exalted their race in honour and lived and laboured for his country and his God.

JESSE PAGE

CONTENTS

CHAPTER VII

CHAPTER VIII

CHAPTER IX

CHAPTER X

CHAPTER XI

CHAPTER XII

ILLUSTRATIONS

CHAPTER I

A LITTLE SLAVE BOY

AFRICA is the mystery land of the world. It is old as the everlasting hills, and yet in a sense newborn, for the maps of a century ago had nothing to disclose of its vast interior but blank spaces, as undiscovered as the North Pole. Since then, however, explorers have penetrated these solitudes, and in the subsequent scramble for empire the flags of the foreigner have been busy in the partition by pinpricks of this immense anybody's land.

And yet the traveller thither often finds himself a modern trespasser on ancient landmarks, and discovers in the gloom of her forests vestiges of noble cities, the habitation of a people beyond the horizon of history. The Dark Continent, shadowed in more ways than one, is the tomb of a long past age of life and activity, for the dust of all the Pharaohs and the pomp and intellectual affluence of Egypt lie silent at the bottom of her sea of sand.

Imagination calls back to being again her glorious past, reminding us that she has been the mother of mighty sons. Once her ancient northern cities were the sanctuaries of learning, and amid the darkness shone the lamps of Divine truth where Christianity, still young, inspired its confessors and saints. Through the grey haze of centuries we seem to see again Tertullian busy with his parchments; catch a glimpse of the white-haired Cyprian followed by a wailing crowd to martyrdom; see Origen, defender of the faith; Athanasius, his face against the world; and Augustine, with eyes full of heartbreak: truly a vision of wonderful memories. Then the shadows creep up again and thicken, for days of wild declension came when the glory of that early Church gave place to darkness, her lights blurred with heresy and in blood outblown.

At first sight there seems a wide historical distance between the days of those primitive fathers and the African Church of our time, a far cry from Carthage to Calabar, for we often fail to realize that those great councils of the early centuries were crowded with African bishops, representing hundreds of native churches in the country northward. This fact establishes some link of association between those great ecclesiastics of old and the black prelate whose remarkable history these pages will endeavour to record.

While Africa has her history her children can boast of a lineage, and find no little gratification in tracing the branches of their genealogical tree. The negro can, of course, claim no title of centuries, and is destitute of those legal muniments which attest the ancestry of the white man. Tradition is good enough for him, and he is satisfied that sometimes his short line of "forbears" not only mingles with royal blood, but skirts relationship with distant deities. We may not be prepared to take their evidence too seriously, but the family records which trace the descent and parentage of Bishop Crowther deserve a brief mention here.

He was by birth a pure Yoruba of the great Yoruba kingdom, which, according to the *arokin*, or chronicles, was at the end of the eighteenth century ruled by Ajabo, a powerful monarch, succeeded in 1770, or possibly later, by a famous King Abiodun, who by the family tree is shown to be the maternal great-great-grandfather of the Bishop. Tradition ascribes many virtues to this potentate, whose name simply signifies "a child born during an annual festivity." His daughter Òsú became the mother of Olaminigbìn, the modest meaning of which is "all my joys, honour, and glory are laid low," who in turn became the husband of Omo-oga-Egùn and the father of Ibisomi-T'-Elerin-masà, the mother of the subject of this biography. She also possessed, however, a special dignity, being known among her people as Afàla, signifying the princess or priestess of the great god Obatala, or "Lord of the White Cloth," whose province was to bring order and beauty out of chaos, his supposed habitation being a sphere of absolute and dazzling purity. The distinctive honour of Afàla was that she was responsible to keep pure and clean the snowy raiment and unblemished curtains of this deity. Leaving these high latitudes of myth and mystery, it may be noted, in passing, that in African ancestry the maternal side has always a special importance and value.

On his father's side the Bishop belonged to the clan

"Edu," and his grandfather was the Bale or Duke of Awaiye-petu, who had migrated into the Yoruba country from Ketu. He appears to have been a man of great wealth, amassed by the trade of weaving a peculiar fabric, specially designed for the use of the King of Erin, and this "aso elerin" became the recognized production of the family looms.

It only remains to add a word as to the origin of his birthplace. Some of his ancestors, the ancient princes of Oyó-Ile, founded a colony to which they gave the name Iba-Agbākin, that is to say, "to pull through the course of life and keep on peaceful terms with the world one needs to be very careful." Notwithstanding this sapient title, rivalries broke out, and in due time another settlement was established and called Oshôgún, literally "It is not like medicine," the native explanation of which is that "wisdom being the gift of the gods, unlike medicine, is freely imparted from man to man." In Africa, it must be remembered, the names of persons and places have distinctive meanings.

It was in this little town, at a date which cannot be precisely determined, but was probably in the year 1806, the little black boy was born who was destined to a career of conspicuous honour and usefulness, certainly the most remarkable representative of his race in modern times. The name Adjai, which his parents gave him, was a significant title or proper name, only given to a child born with his face to the ground, a natal peculiarity very rare, and considered by the natives of the West Coast of Africa to forecast a remarkable future. Because of this, his parents, according to Yoruba custom, made their little boy a present of some white fowls and were, moreover, perplexed to know to which of the four hundred tribal gods he should be dedicated. They therefore repaired to the shrine of Ifâ, the god of divination, whose priest, called *baba lawo*, i.e. "father who has a secret," was always ready, for a consideration, to inquire of the oracle on behalf of the troubled and fearful of the people. In some cases a whitened board was employed, similar to those used as slates in Moslem schools, upon which strange figures were drawn and from which still stranger calculations were made. Or the priest would simply produce the carved wooden Ifâ bowl, in which thirty split palm nuts were shuffled and the decision of the god announced after counting the whites and the browns. In this particular case the oracle certainly gave remarkable counsel as regards little Adjai. The priest declared that on no account was the child to be a devotee of any idol worship, for he was destined to be an Alùja, that is, one celebrated and distinguished, to serve the great and highest God and no idol whatever. By this he implied the principal deity, spoken of as Olorun, the maker of heaven and earth, the great sky god, a sort of deified firmament. It is still usual on the Niger, in answer to the customary salutation, "Have you risen well?" to answer, "A yin Olorun," i.e. "thanks to Olorun."

His parents, however, were mightily disappointed by this flattering prophecy, for Olorun was specially honoured by the Mohammedan Foulahs, who also were the bitter enemies of the Yorubas. They seem to have paid the consultation fee of two or three heads of cowries, equal to one shilling and threepence of English money, and bade the priest an abrupt and dissatisfied good-bye. On their homeward way they mused in silence upon what they had heard, and inwardly resolved to carefully watch the tendencies of the growing mind of this little boy of theirs, who, all unconscious of his importance in the world, skipped along between them.

Adjai's father continued the family trade of weaving, and was, in a way, a well-to-do and prosperous man, owning a little property some seven miles from the town ; he was also one of the headmen or councillors, and in consequence of these responsibilities handed over his farm very much to the care of his elder son, Bola by name. Meanwhile Adjai grew apace, and became quite a successful breeder of poultry, finding a market for his fowls and becoming passing rich in the possession of a head of cowrie shells worth sixpence. He was still only a little boy, and at the age of eight years had secured for himself a piece of land near his father's farm, and after a period of training under his brother Bola, Adjai became quite clever in the cultivation of yams, the staple food of the people. Morning and evening the youthful gardener trudged seven miles to his work, cheering himself with one of the proverbs of his country, inculcating habits of industry—" When the day dawns every trader to his trade; the spinner takes his spindle, the warrior his shield, the weaver stoops to his batten [shuttle], the farmer arises with his hoe, and the warrior takes his bow and arrow," in other words, no one is idle. It was the custom for the boys and youths of Oshôgún to form themselves into little clubs to help each other in their small farms in case of need. Of such a club Adjai was made captain and president, and its forty members doubtless recognized in the boy with the auspicious name one who was going to make his way in the world.

In these memories of very early days we have another incident which shows the courage of the boy and his respect for the religion of his parents. The household gods of the Yorubas are many, and on one occasion the house caught fire and the father, having called his family from their perilous position, cried out, "O my gods, my gods! They are in the house and will be burned." Adjai promptly rushed through the flaming doorway and brought all the idols back in safety, amid the cheers of the neighbours, who cried out, "This child will be a great worshipper of the gods; he will one day restore the gods to our nation!"

A new home was, however, soon established; the family, gods and all, resumed their old places, and Adjai, now about thirteen years of age, was again busy with his poultry and his yams. Whether in those days of his boyhood he ever dreamed dreams of the future, or like Joseph of old had intimations of being a spiritual ruler in a greater kingdom than Egypt ever knew, we cannot discover. But to a youth of such alert mind, already taking precedence among his fellows, the talk of his parents and neighbours would scarcely fall upon inattentive ears. From the accident of his birth being under special circumstances he had acquired the name of "the lucky one"; possibly his scrupulous observance of religious rites would also enhance his reputation as one blessed by the gods. This much, however, is certain to us: in the light of that long and noble life, beneath that thatched roof under the bombax and palm trees of Oshôgún, a new era for the African race was being born. The spring of this young life, which was bubbling up amid the simple surroundings of this Yoruba town, was on the eve of a new impulse, a catastrophe which, like a fallen rock, should obliterate its peaceful meanderings and force it into new and tumultuous courses. To some lives the parting of the ways is reached much later on; it was given to this boy to suffer in his springtide, and to drink the cup of sorrow in a darkness which seemed to eclipse all his radiant morn. But he lived to see the silver lining of the cloud and to find, as we all must do, that God's ways are best, and not less so because in the time of trial our eyes are holden. In the breaking of the day, as in the breaking of the bread, we cry, "It is the Lord," and are satisfied.

A few years later, when the storm was over and gone, and

> God smiled back from the retreating cloud

Crowther sat down in the college room and wrote in a long letter the story of this experience which changed the current of his life, a precious scrap of autobiography. To his present biographer the story has a deep and tender interest, not only as a fragment written by a hand that can be clasped no more, but as recalling many sweet seasons of personal intercourse, when in that little upper room at Salisbury Square the venerable Bishop recounted those early griefs. His wonderfully expressive face all alight with emotion, the bright, searching eyes suffused with tears, ever and anon the recital was broken by fervent thanksgivings to God. And now, from his written and familiar testimony, let him tell his story once again.

I suppose some time about the commencement of the year 1821 I was in my native country, enjoying the comforts of father and mother and the affectionate love of brothers and sisters. From this period I must date the unhappy, but which I am now taught in other respects to call blessed day, which I shall never forget in my life. I call it unhappy day because it was the day on which I was violently turned out of my father's house and separated from my relations, and in which I was made to experience what is called "to be in slavery." With regard to its being called blessed—it being the day which Providence had marked out for me to set out on my journey from the land of heathenism, superstition, and vice to a place where His Gospel is preached.

For some years war had been carried on in my Eyó country, which was always attended with much devastation and bloodshed, the women, such men as had surrendered or were caught, with the children, were taken captive. The enemies who carried on these wars were principally the Eyó Mohammedans, with whom my country abounds, who with the Foulahs and such foreign slaves as had escaped from their owners, joined together, made a formidable force of about twenty thousand; which annoyed the whole country. They had no other employment but selling slaves to the Spaniards and Portuguese on the coast.

The morning on which my town Oshôgún shared the same fate which many others had experienced was fair and delightful, and most of the inhabitants were engaged in their respective occupations. We were preparing breakfast without any apprehension, when about 9 a.m. a rumour was spread in the town that the enemies had approached with intentions of hostility. It was not long after, when they had almost surrounded the town to prevent any escape of the inhabitants. The town was rudely fortified by a wooden fence about four miles in circumference, containing about twelve thousand inhabitants and producing three thousand fighting men.

The inhabitants not being duly prepared, some not being at home, but those who were having about six gates to defend, as well as many weak places about the fence to guard against —and to say, in a few words, the men being surprised and therefore confounded—the enemies entered the town, after about three or four hours' resistance. Here the most sorrowful scene imaginable was to be witnessed—women, some with three, four, and six children clinging to their arms, with the infants on their backs, running as fast as they could through prickly shrubs, which, hooking their blies (baskets) and loads, threw them down from the heads of the bearers. When they found it impossible to go with their loads they only endeavoured to save themselves and their children. Even this was impracticable with those who had many children to care for, as while they were endeavouring to disentangle themselves from the ropy shrubs they were overtaken and caught by the enemies, by a rope noose thrown over the neck of every individual, to be led in the manner of goats tied together, under the drove of one man. In many cases a family was violently divided between three or four enemies, who each led his away to see each other no more.

I was thus caught with my mother, two sisters, one infant about ten weeks old, and a cousin, while endeavouring to escape in the manner described. My load consisted of nothing else than my bow and five arrows in the quiver; the bow I had lost in the shrub while I was extricating myself, before I could think of making any use of it against my enemies. The last time I saw my father was when he came from the fight to give us the signal to flee; he entered into our house, which was burnt some time back for some offence given by my father's adopted son—hence I never saw him more. Here I must take thy leave, unhappy, comfortless father! I learned sometime afterwards that he was killed in another battle.

Our conquerors were Eyó Mohammedans, who led us away through the town. On our way we met a man sadly wounded in the head, struggling between life and death. Before we got half-way through the town some Foulahs among the enemies themselves hastily separated my cousin from our number. Here also I must take thy leave, my fellow-captive cousin! His mother was living in another village. The houses in the town on fire were built with wood, about twelve feet from the ground, with high roofs in square forms of different dimensions and spacious areas. Several of these belonged to one man, adjoining to with passages communicating with each other. The flames were very high; we were led by my grandfather's house, already desolate, and in a few minutes afterwards we left the town to the mercy of the flames, never to enter or see it any more. Farewell, the place of my birth, the playground of my childhood, and the place which I thought would be the repository of my mortal body in its old age!

We were now out of Oshôgûn, going into a town called Neh'i, the rendezvous of the enemies, about twenty miles from our town. On the way we saw our grandmother at a distance, with about three or four of my other cousins taken with her, for a few minutes; she was missed through the crowd to see her no more. Several other captives were held in the same manner as we were—grandmothers, mothers, children and cousins were all taken captives. O sorrowful prospect! The aged women were greatly to be pitied, not being able to walk so fast as their children and grandchildren; they were often threatened with being put to death upon the spot, to get rid of them, if they would not go as fast as others, and they were often as wicked in their practice as in their words. O pitiful sight! Whose heart would not bleed to have seen this? Yes, such is the state of barbarity in the heathen land!

Evening came on, and coming to a spring of water we drank a great quantity, which served us for breakfast, with a little parched corn and dried meat, previously prepared by our victors for themselves. During our march to Iseh'i we passed several towns and villages which had been reduced to ashes. It was almost midnight before we reached the town, where we passed our doleful first night in bondage. It was not, perhaps, a mile from the wall of Iseh'i where an old woman of about sixty was threatened in the manner above described. What became of her I could not learn.

The next morning, our cords being taken off our necks, we were brought to the chief of our captors—for there were many other chiefs—as trophies at his feet. In a little while a separation took place, when my sister and I fell to the share of the chief, and my mother and the infant to the victors. We dared not vent our grief in loud cries, but by very heavy sobs. My mother, with the infant, was led away, comforted with the promise that she should see us again when we should leave Iseh'i for Dahdah, the town of the chief. In a few hours after it was soon agreed upon that I should be bartered for a horse in Iseh'i that very day. Thus was I separated from my mother and sister for the first time in my life, and the latter not to be seen more in this world. Thus in the space of twenty-four hours, being deprived of liberty and all other comforts, I was made the property of three different persons. About the space of two months, when the chief was to leave Iseh'i for his own town, the horse which was then only taken on trial, not being approved of, I was restored to the chief, who took me to Dahdah, where I had the happiness of meeting my mother and infant sister again, with joy which could be described by nothing else but tears of love and affection, and on the part of my infant sister with leaps of joy.

Here I lived for three months, going for grass for the horses with my fellow-captives. I now and then visited my mother and sister in our captor's house without any fears or thoughts of being separated any more. My mother told me she had heard of my sister, but I never saw her any more. At last, one unhappy evening arrived when I was sent with a man to get some money at a neighbouring house. I went, but with some fears for which I could not account, and to my great astonishment in a few minutes I was added to the number of many other captives, fettered, to be led to the market town early next morning. My sleep went from me. I spent almost the whole night in thinking of my doleful situation with tears and sobs, especially as my mother was in the same town, whom I had not visited for about a day or two back. There was another boy in the same situation with me ; his mother was in Dahdah. Being sleepless, I heard the first cockcrow, and scarcely was the signal given when the traders arose, loaded the men slaves with baggage, and with one hand chained to the neck we left the town. My little companion in affliction cried and begged much to be permitted to see his mother, but was soon silenced by punishment. Seeing this, I dared not speak, although I thought we passed by the very house my mother was in. Thus was I separated from my mother and sister, my then only comforts, to meet no more in this world of misery. After a few days' travel we came to the market town of Ijahi. Here I saw many who had escaped from our town to this place, or who were in search of their relations, to set at liberty as many as they had the means of redeeming. Here we were under very close inspection, as there were many persons in search of their relations, and through that many had escaped from their owners. In a few days I was sold to a Mohammedan woman, with whom I travelled many towns on our way to the Poh-poh country on the coast, much resorted to by the Portuguese to buy slaves. When we left Ijahi, after many halts, we came to a town called Toko. From Ijahi to Toko all spoke Ebweh dialect, but my mistress Eyó, my own dialect. Here I was a perfect stranger, having left the Eyó country far behind.

I lived in Toko about three months, walked about and with my owner's son with some degree of freedom, it being a place where my feet had never trod ; and could I possibly make my way out through many a ruinous town and village we had passed I should have soon become a prey to some others, who would gladly have taken advantage of me. Besides, I could not think of going a mile out of the town alone at night, as there were many enormous devil houses along the highway, and a woman having been lately publicly executed —fired at—being accused of bewitching her husband, who had died of a long, tedious sickness. Five or six heads of persons who had been executed for some crime or other were never wanting to be nailed on the large trees in the market places to terrify others. Now and then my mistress would speak with me and her son that we should by and by go to the Poh-poh country, where we should buy tobacco and other fine things to sell at our return. Now, thought I, this was the signal of my being sold to the Portuguese, who, they often told me during our journey, were to be seen in that country. Being very thoughtful of this, my appetite forsook me, and in a few weeks I got the dysentery, which preyed on me. I determined with myself that I would not go to the Poh-poh country, but would make an end of myself one way or other. Several nights I attempted to strangle myself with my band, but had not courage enough to close the noose tight, so as to effect my purpose. May the Lord forgive me this sin ! I next determined that I would leap out of the canoe into the river when we should cross it on our way to that country. Thus was I thinking when my owner, perceiving the great alteration which had taken place in me, sold me to some persons. Thus the Lord, while I knew Him not, led me not into temptation and delivered me from the evil. After my price had been counted before my eyes, I was delivered up to my new owners with great grief and dejection of spirit, not knowing where I was now to be led.

About the first cockcrowing, which was the usual time to set out with slaves to prevent their being much acquainted with the way, for fear an escape should be made, we set out for Elabbo, the third dialect from mine. After having arrived at Ik-ke-ku yé-re, another town, we halted. In this place I renewed my attempt at strangling several times at night, but could not effect my purpose. It was very singular that no thought of making use of a knife ever entered my mind. However, it was not long before I was bartered for tobacco, rum, and other articles. I remained here in fetters alone for some time before my owner could get as many slaves as he wanted. He feigned to treat us more civilly by allowing us to sip a few drops of white man's liquor, rum, which was so estimable an article that none but chiefs could pay for a jar or glass vessel of four or five gallons. So remarkable it was that no one should take breath before he swallowed every sip for fear of having the string of his throat cut by the spirit of the liquor: this made it so much more valuable.

I had to remain alone again in another town in Jabbo, the name of which I do not now remember, for about two months. From hence I was brought, after a two days' walk, to a slave market called I'-ko-sy, on the coast, on the bank of a large river, which very probably was the Lagos on which we were afterwards captured. The sight of the river terrified me exceedingly, for I had never seen anything like it in my life. The people on the opposite bank are called E'-ko. Before sunset, being bartered again for tobacco, I became another man's. Nothing now terrified me more than the river and the thought of going into another world. Crying now was nothing to vent my sorrow. My whole body became stiff. I was now bade to enter the river to ford it in the canoe. Being fearful of my entering this extensive water, and being so cautious in every step I took, as if the next would bring me to the bottom, my motion was very awkward indeed. Night coming on, and the men having very little time to spare, soon carried me into the canoe and placed me amongst the cornbags, supplying me with an Abálah (a cake of Indian corn) for my dinner. Almost in the same position I was placed I remained with the Abálah in my hand, quite confused in my thoughts, waiting only every moment our arrival at the new world, which we did not reach till about four in the morning. Here I got once more into another district, the fourth from mine, if I may not call it altogether another language, on account of now and then, in some words, there being a faint shadow of my own.

Here I must remark that during the whole night's voyage in the canoe not a single thought of leaping into the river entered my mind, but, on the contrary, the face of the river occupied my thoughts. Having now entered E'ko, I was permitted to go any way I pleased, there being no way of escape on account of the river.

In this place I met my two nephews, belonging to different masters. One part of the town was occupied by the Portuguese or Spaniards, who had come to buy slaves. Although I was in E'ko more than three months I never once saw a white man until one evening when they took a walk in company with about six and came to the street of the house in which I was living. Even then I had not the boldness to appear distinctly to look at them, being always suspicious that they had come for me, and my suspicion was not a fancied one, for in a few days after I was made the eighth in number of the slaves of the Portuguese. Being a veteran in slavery—if I may be allowed the expression—and having no more hope of ever going to my country again, I patiently took whatever came, although it was not without a great fear and trembling that I received for the first time the touch of a white man, who examined me whether I was sound or not. Men and boys were at first chained together with a chain of about six fathoms in length, thrust through an iron fetter on the neck of each individual and fastened at both ends with padlocks. In this situation the boys suffered the most. The men, sometimes getting angry, would draw the chain most violently, as seldom went without bruises on our poor little necks, especially the time of sleep, when they drew the chain so close to ease themselves of its weight, in order to be able to lie more conveniently, that we were almost suffocated or bruised to death, in a room with one door which was fastened as soon as we entered, with no other passage for communicating the air than the openings under the eaves drop. And very often at night, when two or three individuals quarrelled or fought, the whole drove suffered punishment without distinction. At last we boys had the happiness to be separated from the men, when their number was increased and no more chain to spare, we were corded together by ourselves. Thus were we going in and out, bathing together and so on. The females fared not much better. Thus we were for nearly four months.

About this time intelligence was given that the English were cruising on the coast. This was another subject of sorrow to us—that there must be wars on the sea as well as on the land—a thing never heard of before nor imagined practicable. This delayed our embarkation. In the meantime the other troop, which was collected in Poh-poh and was intended to be conveyed into the vessel the nearest way from that place, was brought into E'ko among us. Among the number was Joseph Bartholomew, my brother in the service of the Church Missionary Society. After a few weeks' delay we were embarked at night in canoes from E'ko to the beach, and on the following morning we embarked on the vessel (a Portuguese ship called the *Esperanza Felix*), which immediately sailed away. The crew being busy in embarking us, one hundred and eighty-seven in number, had no time to give us either breakfast or supper, and we, being unaccustomed to the motion of the vessel, suffered the whole of the day with sea-sickness, which rendered the greater part of us less fit to take any food whatever. On the very same evening we were surprised by two English men-of-war, and the next morning found ourselves in the hands of war conquerors, whom we at first very much dreaded, they being armed with long swords. In the morning, being called up from the hold, we were astonished to find ourselves among two very large men-of-war and several brigs. The men-of-war were His Majesty's ships *Myrmidon*, Captain H. G. Leeke, and *Iphigenia*, Captain Sir Robert Mends, who captured us on 7 April, 1822, on the river Lagos. Our owner was bound, with his sailors, except the cook, who was preparing our breakfast. Hunger rendered us bold, and not being threatened at first attempts to get some fruit from the stern, we in a short time took the liberty of ranging about the vessel in search of plunder of every kind. Now we began to entertain a poor opinion of our new conquerors. Very soon after breakfast we were divided into several of the vessels around us. This was cause of new fears, not knowing where our misery would end. Being now, as it were, one family, we began to take leave of those who were first transported into the other vessels, not knowing what would become of them and ourselves. About this time we six intimate friends in affliction—among whom was my brother Joseph Bartholomew—kept very close together that we might be carried away at the same time. It was not long before we six were conveyed into the *Myrmidon*, in which we discovered no trace of those who were transported before us. We soon concluded what had become of them when we saw part of a hog hanging, the skin of which was white—a thing we never saw before, as a hog was always roasted on fire to clear it of the hair in my country—and a number of common shots ranged along the deck. The former we supposed to be the flesh and the latter the heads of the individuals who had been killed for meat. But we were soon undeceived by a close examination of the flesh, with cloven feet, which resembled those of a hog, and by a cautious approach to the shots that they were iron. In a few days we were quite at home on the man-of-war; being only six in number, we were soon selected by the sailors for their boys, and were soon furnished with dress. Our Portuguese owner and his son were brought over in the same vessel, bound in fetters, and I, thinking I should no more get into his hands, had the boldness to strike him on the head while he was standing by his son—an act, however, very wicked and unkind in its nature.

The youthful Adjai spent two months and a half on board while the man-of-war continued her cruise for slaves, and had time enough to get accustomed to his new friends; indeed, it is said that he became a great favourite with the sailors as a lad of exceptional quickness and intelligence. At length they reached Sierra Leone, and he has made a note that on 17 June, 1822, he set foot again on African soil, this time as a little liberated slave. With others he was sent to a missionary schoolmaster at Bathurst, a small town a few miles from Freetown, and in the wise and loving care of Mr. Davey and his wife, the best in the boy opened as the flower to the sun. He not only regained his health and strength, but received into his heart those deeper sources of divine grace which were to fit him for his future destiny of usefulness. His earliest lesson in the English alphabet was, however, given him by another native boy who had been there before him, and the story is told that after his first day's schooling Crowther was so delighted with his new taste of knowledge that he ran down into the town, begged a halfpenny from one of his countrymen, and with it bought for himself an alphabet card. At last the gate of knowledge was really open, and in six months from the day of his landing Adjai was able to read his New Testament. Those early days he never could forget, and was fond of recalling these scenes through a long vista of years. How he would sit with his books in the evening, a candle burning in the middle of the table, at the head of which sat the schoolmaster's worthy wife, and by his side another little sable scholar named Asano—a girl of his own tribe who had also been rescued from slavery, and of whom we shall hear more later on. Possibly she also felt a little gratified when Adjai was promoted to be a monitor and earned his first scholastic income of sevenpence halfpenny a month for his services.

But not alone was his mind being developed by study—the youth was also taught a trade; and in the care of another schoolmaster, Mr. Weeks, he attained a knowledge of carpentry, and from his wife more steps of reading. How little this good man imagined, as he taught this boy's black fingers the use of plane and chisel, that his pupil would one day wear the lawn as Bishop of the Niger, and he, in his turn, would direct the see of Sierra Leone!

The greatest incident of his life, and of any life, was when he met Jesus Christ and worshipped Him, saying, "My Lord and my God." To the boy's young heart there came the impulse of a new life and an undying love and that fuller "freedom wherewith He makes His people free." On 11 December, 1825, Adjai was baptized, and received as his new name Samuel Adjai Crowther, after a venerable clergyman, the Rev. Samuel Crowther, vicar of Christ Church, Newgate Street, London, and one of the first committee of the Church Missionary Society.

At this point we can safely leave him for the present and pause to look round with some interest upon his environment and the events which have led up to this first page of a unique history. With the following brief historical retrospect we shall better appreciate Crowther's character and career, not only as a rescued slave, but for the reason that when he landed from that man-of-war his feet touched one of the noblest battlegrounds of missionary conquest. In all the precious annals of missionary enterprise, rich as they are in brave deeds, there is nothing more magnificent than the costly valour which fought a good fight for God and man on the shores of Sierra Leone.

The story is inseparably linked with the emancipation of the slave. Perhaps it may be one of the penalties of our privileged age that we forget so soon, things as they are we want to know, as to how they will be we have no spirit of prophecy, for what they were we have ofttimes short memories. How difficult, for example, it is to rekindle that fire of national indignation which a hundred years ago freed the slave. The force of that moral impulse cannot be fairly measured by the purer and healthier public opinion of our own day, for English politics and morals were a mixed quantity at the dawn of the last century. The cup of our culpability as a nation in this unrighteous traffic was then full enough, and the sorrows of the enslaved seemed to be forgotten in earth and heaven. But justice was not left without a witness to prophesy against this sin, and there sprang forth men whose names are borne hither on the memories of that strenuous time.

The battle began when Granville Sharp gave shelter in 1765 to a suffering slave from Barbados, and on the simple issue of this man's wrongs won the famous dictum of Lord Mansfield that "as soon as a negro set his foot on English soil he was free." Then followed the faithful advocacy of the equal rights of man by Thomas Clarkson, a philanthropist of purest type, and William Wilberforce, with persuasive eloquence lit up with flashes of kindly wit, took the lead. The cause aroused bitter enemies, but it had also capable and loyal friends. John Wesley and George Whitefield, the two great evangelists of their age, denounced the traffic in burning words. The last letter Wesley ever penned, four days before he died at the house by the chapel in City Road, was addressed to Wilberforce, urging him to persevere in his "glorious enterprise." "Go on," he writes, "in the name of God and in the power of His might till even American slavery (the vilest that ever saw the sun) shall vanish away before it." It must not be forgotten, however, that the Society of Friends, lifting through the darkest hours of history always an unquenched torch, presented the first petition to the House of Commons praying that something might be done to ameliorate the shocking condition of the slave. By parliamentary speeches, leaflets, and addresses up and down the country the horrors of the middle passage, with its wholesale waste of human life, were made known, and it would seem amazing that any righteous or barely honest man could have opposed this merciful plea. But the history of all great struggles for the moral emancipation of men and women has taught us sufficiently that any conflict with evil, means storming the ramparts of self-interest with bloodshed, heartbreak, and tears. Was the slave trade attacked? Its representatives must be reckoned with. So they raised the commercial difficulty by predicting the downfall of Liverpool trade, that its honest proprietors would not submit to an act of confiscation so unconstitutional, that the public revenue would suffer beyond recall, and then, dexterously standing on another foot, they hunted up a Book they did not believe in, and pleaded the sacred antiquity of the traffic, and that, moreover, the slave was happy in his lot. Perhaps it were more charitable to human nature to forbear to awaken these echoes of obstruction which were lost in the acclamation of victory when on 25 March, 1807, the Bill for the Abolition of the British Slave Trade became law.

Even then, however, its opponents endeavoured to drive the proverbial carriage and four horses through the provisions of the statute. The penalties for slave trading were simply pecuniary, and to the dismay of Wilberforce and his friends the traffic went up by leaps and bounds, for it paid handsomely to square the penalties. Lord Brougham (then plain Mr.) tried to checkmate this by a further Act making the offence a felony punishable with imprisonment with hard labour, but it was not until the Act of 1824 was passed, declaring it to be piracy with a death penalty, that the law was duly respected.

But although the slave trade was condemned, the practice and system of slavery had yet to receive its legal death blow, and Wilberforce, now aged and weary, passed the sword to the younger hand of Mr. (afterwards Sir) Thomas Fowell Buxton. It was a glorious succession. The new leader declared war by moving the historic resolution, "That the state of slavery is repugnant to the principles of the British Constitution and of the Christian religion, and that it ought to be gradually abolished throughout the British colonies with as much expedition as may be found consistent with a due regard of the well-being of the parties concerned." To us there seems a superfluous modesty about the verbal drawing of the demand, but its opponents gathered its ultimate issue, and the eyes of Wilberforce glistened with delight as Fowell Buxton declared:

"The object at which we aim is the extinction of slavery—nothing less than the extinction of slavery—

in nothing less than the whole of the British Dominions." And then, replying to some taunts of enthusiasm, he exclaimed :

"There are such enthusiasts. I am one of them, and while we breathe we will never abandon the cause till that thing, that chattel, is reinstated in all the privileges of man."

It was soon seen that the second step in the emancipation of the negro was to invoke a bigger and more protracted struggle than the first. The Anti-Slavery Society was established, and the term "Abolitionist" was at once an honour and a reproach. But after years of conflict the victory was won. On 7 August, 1833, the Bill was passed; on 1 August, 1834, every slave was free, and four years afterwards the apprenticeships ceased throughout the Colonies, and slavery, root and branch, was ended.

And now from this glorious event, which may be called the Magna Charta of the black man's freedom, we pass to a land called "the white man's grave." While the friends of the slave were struggling for his emancipation in 1786, thankful when, as Cowper sang,

> Slaves cannot breathe in England; if their lungs
> Receive our air, that moment they are free—
> They touch our country and their shackles fall,

a practical difficulty presented itself. What shall we do with these slaves when free? Their altered circumstances were soon evidenced by hundreds of black beggars on the streets, and these naturally flocked to the door of Granville Sharp and their other friends for relief of their necessities. As a result of this a plan was arranged with this ancient title: "A settlement to be made near Sierra Leone on the grain coast of Africa, intended more particularly for the service and happy establishment of Blacks and People of Colour, to be shipped as freemen under the Direction of the Committee for Relieving the Black Poor and under the Protection of the British Government."

In pursuance of this, a little fleet of liberated negroes, with a fair proportion of European women (who might have been well spared), sailed for the West Coast of Africa in April, 1787, under convoy of a man-of-war, whose commander, on arriving, acquired a strip of coast in the name of King George. This, from the contour of its mountains, was called Sierra Leone, and identified as the spot where the slave-raiding vessels of Hawkins in the spacious days of Elizabeth captured their living cargo. Never was a merciful mission so ill-starred as this new settlement. Disease, disorder, mutinies, and aggressions of the natives soon brought the place to early ruin. Later on a fresh contingent of emigrants arrived from Nova Scotia, our black auxiliaries in the American War, and under the wise oversight of the new Sierra Leone Company, Freetown was built and a bright day seemed to have dawned. But the French, masked by English uniforms and flying the Union Jack, invaded the town, laying all waste and carrying off the trading vessels of the Company from the harbour as spoils of war. The Governor was Zachary Macaulay, father of the historian, and it was due to his discipline and zeal that order and prosperity were afterwards re-established. Sierra Leone became a Crown Colony, and from that date the men-of-war cruising in African waters brought hither their captures of slaves. The pitiful state of these poor creatures on landing, after the suffering of a slaver's voyage, may be imagined, and the gross superstition and low moral sense of the negro element of the Colony caused much trouble and uneasiness. Under the direction of the newly-formed African Association, composed of bishops and philanthropists, schools were opened, but it was not until a definite introduction of Christian teaching by faithful missionaries that the true prosperity of Sierra Leone began. What the law could not do however wisely administered, and the spread of education with its refining and humanizing qualities failed to accomplish, the Cross of Christ with its message of dying love was able to achieve. But from a human point of view the victory was dearly won. The bravest and the best came but to die. No sooner had a missionary reached the Colony and started his work than he was stricken with fever, and found a grave in the land he came to bless. The history of the heavy toll of precious lives is pathetic, but it is also inspiring. These early missionaries and their not less heroic wives did not labour long enough to win a name in missionary annals, but they are surely counted among those who have won the deathless crown. They came to the field with hearts beating high with faith and hope ; they spared not themselves when the fever began to consume their powers ; they pleaded with tears of love as they lay stricken with fever ; and when God drew the curtain, sometimes on land and often on the sea, the watchers whispered, "To die like this is gain indeed."

When they fell others rushed to fill the breach; in one year out of five missionaries who went out from Salisbury Square four died in six months; two years later out of seven brave substitutes six died in four months; during the first twenty years of the work fifty-three missionaries and their wives died at their post, and this mortality is not reckoning the large number of deaths in connection with the Wesleyan and other societies.

Not only was the climate a fatal hindrance, but other difficulties arose; the chiefs and headmen of the tribes up country refused to allow the Gospel to be preached; the Mohammedans were up in arms, and the degradation of the people made the soil very hard ground for sowing the good seed. There was, however, hope in the future of the young natives, and at quite an early stage of the work it was said, "Let us fervently pray that these children may become faithful disciples of our great Master, and that some of them may be raised up as instruments to proclaim the glad tidings of salvation throughout their native tribes. It is this way we may expect God will be pleased to work when His time is come for diffusing the Gospel widely through the nations, because it is in this way that He has usually effected His purposes hitherto."

The story of a remarkable revival among these people is associated with the name and work of the Rev. William A. B. Johnson, whose brief ministry in Sierra Leone is not unlike that of Brainerd among the

Red Indians. The life of this devoted missionary is full of the deepest interest; his conversion when a poor workman at a London sugar refinery, and his subsequent call to the foreign work, form the vivid history of a soul's awakening. His early experiences of his field of work were depressing enough; he made a note in his journal: "If ever I have seen wretchedness (on arriving at Regent) it has been here to-day; these poor depraved people are, indeed, the offscouring of Africa. And who knows whether the Lord will not make His converting power known among them? With Him nothing is impossible."

With incessant ardour Johnson laboured to this end, daily disappointed, but always, after hours of wrestling prayer, finding every morning radiant with the promise of the revival to come. He felt the preciousness of the flying hours. He notes that in one day in Sierra Leone, in 1816, more persons died than were born in a whole year; and he thanked God, looking over his little orderly town, so different now, that the prophecy of Isaiah xxxv. 1, 2 was literally fulfilled. But it is an entry in his journal of 6 September, 1817, which speaks of the shower of blessing having at last fallen. He entered his church.

> The vestry, the gallery stairs, the tower, the windows were all full; some of the seats in the passages were overweighted and broken down. When I entered the church and saw the multitudes I could hardly refrain myself. After evening service one of the boys wished to know if it were really true Jesus prayed for them. Many had been in the field to pray and did not know how. I spoke to them, and they went back with joy. It was a moonlight night, and the mountains re-echoed with the singing of hymns, the girls in one part praying

and singing by turns. The boys had got upon a huge rock with a light. One gave out a hymn, and when it was finished another engaged in prayer.

At morning prayers, though it was raining, with a tornado of wind, as he looked out the streets were crowded with worshipping people, and crossing over to the church he found it quite full again. It was not a condition of excitement merely, and he notes how the usual emotion of the race was suppressed, a solemnity as of the very presence of Jehovah pervaded the crowds. The next day Johnson and his wife listened to the children praying by themselves, and the supplications of one little boy of ten quite broke his heart with joy. He rushed in with streaming eyes, crying with a thankfulness too big for words. Falling on his knees, he could only cry amid sobs of joy: "O my God and Saviour, what hast Thou done? What shall I render to Thee?" A few days after Johnson baptized one hundred and ten adults, the result of this marvellous outpouring of grace.

His missionary zeal urged him to take journeys inland, and on one occasion he visited the Plaintains, a group of islands where the Rev. John Newton had planted some lime trees when wandering there as a slave trader sixty-five years before. Johnson found one still existing, and also discovered an old book of Newton's hymns, and here, in the language of the natives, he sang the song of triumph under the shade of the tree.

Any memorial of this remarkable man is worthy of note. Johnson discovered the very spot in which

John Newton in his captivity and wretchedness used to beguile his lonely hours with the solitary book in his possession, Barron's Euclid, tracing diagrams with his stick in the sand. It was, indeed, a miracle of mercy which lifted this miserable outcast, despised by the meanest slave, to become one of the most saintly and successful preachers.

The breakdown of the health of Johnson's wife and his own increasing weakness made it necessary for him to take a furlough to England. In parting, the people crowded the shore and cried, "Massa, suppose no water live here," pointing to the wide sea, "we go with you all the way till feet no more." When he returned, Johnson exclaimed, "Ah! who would not be a missionary in Africa? Had I ten thousand lives I would willingly offer them all for the sake of one poor negro." He found his work sadly neglected and that many, for want of tender shepherding, had gone back. One of the native converts thus expressed the position: "Suppose somebody beat rice, he fan it and all the chaff fly away and the rice get clean. Now, massa, we be in that fashion since you gone. God fan us that time for true."

Two years afterwards, in utterly broken health, he again set sail homewards, but it proved to be a voyage to the everlasting shore. His wife had already passed that way to England before him, and his longing was that he might be spared to see her again. Before he left Sierra Leone, where fever was raging, and all the day the mourners went about the streets, Mr. and Mrs. Düring, fellow missionaries, brought their only remaining child and begged Johnson to take it home with him to save its little life. As nurse to the infant he also took a young negress named Sarah Bickersteth, his first convert, and she told afterwards the touching story of his last hours. He had left Africa but three days when the fever seized him; sometimes he lay in deep stupor, at others crying aloud in delirium, always with his heart among his poor people. He asked the weeping native girl to read to him the 23rd Psalm, and then told her to pray—"I am going to die, pray for me." The poor black nurse, nursing the little white baby, knelt on the cabin floor and in simple words asked "that the Lord Jesus would take massa the right way." Then he sent a message to David Noah, his native assistant. "Tell him to do his duty—for if he say, 'because massa dead, I can do nothing,' he must pray and God will help him, and so we shall meet in Heaven." He turned his dying eyes upon his solitary watcher, clasped his hands and whispered, "I cannot live. God calls me, and this night I shall be with Him."

It is quite possible that among the crowd assembled to see this devoted missionary embark for his last journey would be a black youth of about fifteen years, with perhaps his school books and Bible in his hands; and who can tell but what the departing one may have spoken to him in turn and said, "Crowther, God bless you, my boy. Good-bye"? He, too, would doubtless mingle with the sorrowing people when the news came of this bereavement. They crowded the church like sheep huddled in distress, the shepherd gone, and one of the missionaries begged them to make no noise, knowing the African custom of loudly wailing for the dead. Not a word or sob was heard; this silence was more impressive than any grand funeral music could have been. After a time an African convert rose, his voice thrilling with deep emotion. "My dear brethren, I think God took him away because we looked more to Mr. Johnson than we did to the Lord Jesus. I hope that this trial will make us look more to the Lord Jesus, for He alone can save us, He alone is the Light of the World. Let us go to Him and beg Him to sanctify this trial to us, and then let us show our love to our dear minister by *doing what he told us.*"

Could any eulogy be more eloquent than these simple heartbroken words?

One of the most sacred spots on the West Coast of Africa, a veritable "God's acre," is the old burial ground on the Kissy Road, Sierra Leone. The author of "The Finished Course" takes us from grave to grave. "There lies the veteran missionary worn out by years of toil; and there the young brother struck down in the prime of youth and the height of his usefulness. There sleeps the young wife who rejoiced that she was 'counted worthy' to die for the name of the Lord, and there the little children, early blighted by that deadly climate—like the Babes of Bethlehem—'unconscious martyrs in the cause of the Redeemer.' . . . Volume upon volume might be filled with the record of the lives, work, and death of God's dear servants who laid down their lives for their Saviour in Africa; and whose bodies there lie 'sown as precious seed in God's garden ' around the churches they died to found—seed that in the Resurrection morning will doubtless spring up to new and glorious and unfading life.

Death hath not slain them; they are freed, not slain!
  It is the gate of Life, and not of Death,
That they have entered; and the grave in vain
  Has tried to stifle the immortal breath.

They are not tasting death, but taking rest
  On the same holy couch where Jesus lay;
Soon to awake, all glorified and blest,
  When day has broke and shadows fled away."

CHAPTER II

SCHOOLMASTER AND EXPLORER

A VISIT to London for the first time is an event in the lifetime of an English boy, but infinitely greater must have been the excited anticipation of young Crowther when his friends and guardians, Mr. and Mrs. Davey, told him that they were taking him with them on a short visit home to the white man's land. One can easily imagine the boy's delight at the prospect, for already he had by the key of knowledge opened some of the doors of English history in his reading books, and he had his day-dreams of that wonderful country from which the ships had come, where all the people had white faces, lived in houses of brick and stone, and were able to move quickly to and fro by steam. It is strange that in his diaries there should be no extended record of his impressions of this interesting visit in 1826; all he notes is by way of retrospect: "I had the privilege of visiting your happy and favoured land in the year 1826, in which it was my desire to remain for a good while to be qualified for a teacher to my fellow-creatures." But from other memoranda we find that he landed at Portsmouth on 16 August, and that during his stay of about eight months he attended the Parochial School in Liverpool Road, Islington, a building still standing, just behind the burial ground of the Chapel of Ease. He would probably be staying at the house of the Rev. E. Bickersteth; and it is stated that for a short visit he was taken to the country home of the same clergyman and mingled with the family circle of boys and girls as one of themselves. What a wonderland all this would be to him!

On his return to Sierra Leone he was appointed as schoolmaster by the Colonial Government in one of the villages at a salary of £1 per month, not a very munificent remuneration, but grateful enough to him, the first money of any consequence that he had earned since in the old home at Oshôgún he made a profit of a handful of cowries by the sale of his chickens. He notes in his diary about this time that he had never since met a dozen of his people from that devastated town, and had not cast eyes on his father, mother, or any of his relations. When the question was mooted of sending a likely native youth to England for training, Mr. Davey, who had just returned with him, wrote:

> The only lad I could at present recommend as fit to be sent to England is Samuel Crowther. He would, I have reason to believe, prove a very useful instrument for carrying on the work in Western Africa. He has abilities far surpassing any I have met with before, and added to this he appears to be truly pious. Our only fear respecting him might be that he should be lifted up too much by a second voyage to England. He has improved very much under the assiduous care of Brother Haensel, and gave great satisfaction in the examination the other day.

This letter, dated Christmas Day, 1827, makes a

reference to new developments of much importance, for it was a day to be remembered when Crowther entered the doors of the African Institution, afterwards known as Fourah Bay College. The history of this place also marks a point in the story of the Colony and missionary work. Its establishment was the result of that appalling death-rate which hitherto had decimated the ranks of European missionaries sent to the West Coast of Africa. The committee of the Church Missionary Society felt that if Africa was to be evangelized it must be through native agency; for her own sons would not be stricken down by fever as the white men were, and it was therefore imperative that such should be trained, intellectually and spiritually, for this high vocation. It was in the nature of an experiment, and there were those who then almost distrusted the capacity of an African to discharge the functions of a responsible ministry. At this juncture the Society was particularly fortunate in sending out the Rev. Charles Haensel to start the Institution. He was a young Lutheran missionary, of German birth, from the Basle Seminary, and proved to be the man for the post. The site selected for the future Alma Mater of the negro student was an old disused slave house, an undesigned coincidence as a starting point of spiritual freedom, with extensive grounds overlooking Fourah Bay. It was far enough away from the surrounding villages to ensure the privacy and quiet of the students. The building, as adapted to its new occupation, was of the plainest character, really an ordinary dwelling-house, where the young fellows were boarded and lodged on the ground floor, the principal and his wife occupying the floor above, and the verandah doing duty for classroom and lecture hall. It was a simple and unostentatious beginning. Mr. Haensel felt the responsibility of organizing such a work, which would lay down a new principle in missionary enterprise, for the committee told him on leaving for his sphere of work that they had "come to a fixed determination of prosecuting by all means in their power and in any place, whether in Europe or Africa, which may ultimately prove most eligible, the education of intelligent and pious natives with a view of their becoming Christian teachers among their countrymen." It may not be out of place to record, in parenthesis, the subsequent development of this germ of native higher culture.

In 1840, with twenty-five students, a new building was erected of laterite stone on a proper plan, with library, lecture room, college chapel, and dormitory. The architect, with a touch of unconscious humour, fitted up every room with an English fireplace, a needless provision for a climate generally 90° in the shade! The college was in 1876 affiliated with the University of Durham, so that its students could qualify for English degrees without leaving Africa. That this privilege has been justified is seen by the fact that since then from the latest calendar fourteen hold the licence in theology, twenty had degrees of B.A., twenty held both L.Th. and B.A., five have taken M.A., and two B.C.L. To two others Durham has granted the honorary M.A., and two more the honorary D.D., and

FOURAH BAY COLLEGE

the principals and tutors have also borne University honours. These facts will be a sufficient answer to those critics who, even in Crowther's early days as we have seen, shew a disinclination to credit the African brain with much intellectual capacity. As a matter of fact, given the same advantages, the negro proves himself second to none in the acquisition of knowledge. In addition to these academic details one is tempted to add that they have a capital cricket team (they play on matting), football and hockey clubs, and a debating society and missionary parliament, where they discuss up-to-date problems on House of Commons methods with, it is hoped, an equally profitable result. The spiritual standard of the college is kept in view; they are trained to be manly Christians, and are ever ready to engage in evangelistic work. They are good linguists and soon pick up other dialects, so that, without any official compulsion, the Gospel is preached for six months of the year every Sunday in four languages, other than English, by students of Fourah Bay. One word more as to the destination of the fine young fellows. Many work as missionaries in the interior until God has evidently set His seal on their labours, when they are ordained for service at the front or the pastorate of the three native churches in Sierra Leone, Lagos, and the Niger Delta, besides which they do duty at the grammar schools, others becoming doctors and barristers-at-law on the West Coast. Some enter the Civil Service, of which two are now heads of departments; two more are appointed by His Majesty to seats on the Legislative Council of the Colony, one has been three times mayor of Freetown, eight have been canons of the cathedral, one of whom, the late Henry Johnson, was a Hebrew, Greek, and Arabic scholar, and Honorary M.A. Cambridge; two others Archdeacons of Sierra Leone, and four to the Episcopate. Of these last mentioned, the most distinguished, of course, is Crowther. This record generally is strong evidence of the progressive possibilities of the African mind and character.

Returning again to those early days, we find Crowther was the first student to enter the doors of Fourah Bay College. He made some sacrifice of present interest to do this, for he had, although still a youth, obtained an independent position as a schoolmaster, and he would, by taking this step, leave teaching to become a scholar again. From some old letters of Mr. Haensel, the principal, we get a few curious little details of the daily round and the rather common but salutary tasks of those youthful students, with occasionally a glimpse of Crowther himself, well worth rescuing from oblivion. Mr. Haensel is evidently exercised in his mind lest his students part through high-mindedness.

It has been my endeavour (he writes) to prevent any sudden rise in the outward condition of the youths. Coming out of Government schools, or out of menial employ, they have mostly brought scanty clothing with them—a couple of shirts, a pair of trousers, a hat and perhaps a jacket, with a book of Common Prayer, and in some instances a Bible, constitute their entire possessions. I have, in the first place, where necessary, added a Bible to their stock, a pair of trousers, and a shirt after a little while, a jacket, if necessary, after a month or two, and another pair of trousers some time after that.

This for their full dress on Sunday and other particular occasions; at home they always go barefooted. Even Samuel Crowther does so at home, though his visit to England has raised him to the height of white stockings, a suit of blue cloth, a waistcoat, and a beaver hat on Sundays!

Their food consists of rice and yams (a sort of potato), plain boiled, with some meat or fish occasionally and palm oil, which they eat out of tin pans. The youths are their own servants; they sweep and scrub the schoolroom and sleeping room, clean the table, and wash their clothes. I send occasionally one or other on errands, just to remind them that they are not above carrying a basketful of rice or anything else on their heads. From Samuel Crowther I require only the inspection of these services. I have, however, pointed out to him the necessity of example accompanying precept in this as in all other branches of our work, and he follows my suggestions. When Samuel Crowther first entered the Institution he brought with him a mattress with which he had been presented when in England, but as this was too great a luxury I at once forbade its entrance, to which he readily consented. I wish for the good of his own soul to see him in that state of lowliness of mind which Africans so easily lose by visits to England.

This picture of the future Bishop appearing at the college portals with a mattress on his shoulders is a touch of nature worth preservation. What grace he must have had to take his treasure back again and leave it behind! Now we will have the opinion of the pupil upon the principal, written by Crowther after a lapse of forty years.

Mr. Haensel was a peculiar person altogether; we could never find one to match him. He was so venerated by all the merchants, they would all tremble at his presence if they did not act straightforwardly or honestly. He would tell you in language which was not offensive, but which you could never forget, and next time you saw him you would tremble to act in the same way, either by speaking inadvertently or by acting contrary to Christian principles. He was a man of very penetrating qualifications.

Between the lines of this neatly-worded recollection, peering through the bars of memory's lattice, we discern the dour countenance of this faithful dominie, "a peculiar person altogether," with a Teutonic tendency for discipline, sternly but sincerely striving to make something out of this native material for the glory of God. A deeply sensitive man, too, under that strong exterior, carrying his crosses without a murmur, for all his boys did not turn out so well as Crowther. He was overburdened also with many secular duties as secretary, responsible for other schools. There is something very pathetic in this paragraph from an old letter, laying bare his heart, overtaxed and self-condemned in its anxious concern for his black boys :

> The regularity (he writes) of proceedings in the Institution has been a good deal interrupted during the quarter by those duties of an official character which have so frequently called me from home and have at home also confined me to the secretary's table, more than the schoolroom could well spare me. Formerly I had some time to enter into my children's little concerns. I could help them to bind a little book, to paint a lion, and to sew on a button ; of late I have been generally in too great a hurry to attend to them as I desire. To my great regret I now miss that affection which I think I formerly possessed, and as my mind becomes distressed on that account I feel more keenly the absence of spiritual fruit. Perhaps this is sent by the Lord in judgment because I was too easily contented when I had the affection of the youths, and was not zealous enough that their hearts should be given to Him. I do not say that they make no progress in learning, even in Scriptural knowledge. I believe they advance to a certain degree, but in spiritual attainment there does not seem to be any growth ; and how insecure is the foundation of all my work so long as this blessing is withheld !

Faithful servant of God, a truce to these misgivings ; thou didst thy part valiantly and well !

It is worthy of note that in a letter written a few months after Crowther came into the Institution, Mr. Haensel speaks well of his pupil and clearly discerns special ability in him.

"He is a very clever lad," he writes, "and it is a real pleasure to instruct him. He advances steadily in knowledge." Later on he writes: "He is a lad of uncommon ability, steady conduct, a thirst for knowledge, and indefatigable industry."

But the youth was already on the threshold of manhood, and it is not surprising that on these Sunday walks, arrayed in the blue suit and beaver hat, this good-looking young African of promise should find a life companion. It has been already hinted that soon after he landed there was also a little girl named Asano, who learnt her letters at his side. She, too, was a rescued slave, having been captured by His Majesty's ship *Bann*, Captain Charles Phillips, on 31 October, 1822, and was landed at Sierra Leone in the same year as Crowther. She in her turn had grown up, and so far made her mark that at this time she was acting as schoolmistress, and had changed her name at baptism to Susan Thompson. His old and candid friend, Mr. Haensel, drew attention to the existence of this young lady at the very time when Crowther was first entered as a student, showing that this attachment was no hasty one. The principal, in sober terms, is reporting to his committee in March, 1827:

You will see by the minutes that Samuel Crowther is to be admitted into the Institution as a probationer for the present. This is owing to the information which is received of an attachment entertained by him towards a girl who is schoolmistress at Bathurst. He says he will not let it interfere with his education, and I am ready to trust in his sincerity, but it is to be doubted whether he knows himself sufficiently; and it will be easier to let him withdraw during his period of probation if he should feel it too hard to be separated from her than after his full reception as a student.

Crowther had by this time been appointed assistant master at Regent at a salary of £24 a year; and now comes this very interesting and significant minute passed at a meeting of the Missionaries in Council:

> An application from Samuel Crowther, schoolmaster of Regent, for leave to enter into holy matrimony with Susan Thompson, of Bathurst, having been submitted and a satisfactory account being received of the girl's suitableness for a fellow-worker with him, it was resolved that this meeting consent to the marriage of Samuel Crowther with Susan Thompson taking place.

No time seems to have been lost by the happy couple, for they appear to have been wedded on the same date as this minute was passed! Thus began a united happiness which, in the providence of God, extended over half a century until his wife's death at Lagos in 1881, leaving three sons, one being the Venerable Archdeacon Dandeson Coates Crowther; two were laymen, and the three daughters all married African clergymen. This good wife and mother was spared to see her children's children to the third generation, to whom the promises of blessing are assured.

In this first year of his married life Crowther was associated with his old friend Mr. Weeks, who mentions him in a letter thus: "I have now a good assistant in Samuel Crowther; he promises fair to be very useful; the Lord give him grace and keep him humble."

But in 1834 we find him going back to Fourah Bay College, this time as a regularly appointed tutor, working hard at his Greek and Latin during his leisure hours and doing good service as a parish assistant under the Rev. G. A. Kissling (afterwards Archdeacon in New Zealand), who had succeeded the Rev. C. L. F. Haensel as principal. He also did useful work in conjunction with two other native students who were under instruction by him, named George Nicol and Thomas Maxwell, who both afterwards became Government chaplains, and the former the husband of one of Crowther's daughters. A Sunday-school, especially in the care of Crowther, was held in an old building called Gibraltar Chapel, afterwards destroyed by fire.

Fortunately he put in writing some of his impressions at this time, and shall now speak for himself. He is writing a letter to England:

As I doubt not it will be acceptable to you to know a little how part of my time is employed, I hope it will not be looked upon as ostentation. When I briefly mention the effect of Mr. Kissling's advice on my study, I thankfully accept the offer of improvement held out to me by my being stationed here. At my coming to the Institution the second time I look on myself as a student rather on the one hand, while I endeavour to assist the pupils on the other, and I may humbly say through the ministry and private assistance of the Rev. G. A. Kissling I am greatly improved in many respects. My views of many things, which were dark, are set in a much clearer light, and when any difficulty arises in my course of study I always endeavour to avail myself of the opportunity of a living teacher, for which I sometimes prove troublesome to him. My studies, which before were loose and unconnected, have been more stated and regular. When plans of a regular study and its consequent effects have been pointed out to me, I immediately endeavoured to follow the experimental direction. I chose Doddridge's "Family Expositor," with which the paternal desire of the Rev. C. L. F. Haensel, for my improvement, has furnished me, and which was pointed out to me by Mr. Kissling as indeed a worthy book. I commenced reading it regularly at six o'clock for one hour, in the school-room, before our morning devotion. Though it was with some difficulty before I could bridle myself down to this plan, yet in a few weeks, when I began to see the thread of the Four Gospels harmonized, at the same time comparing it with what was expounded at our morning devotion by Mr. Kissling, I soon began to perceive the privilege of a regular and stated course of study and the beauty of the history of our Lord and Saviour. When I had gone through that book I was very much delighted with it, and being so poorly and scantily supplied with its rich and excellent contents, especially the epistolary part, I hesitated not to give it a second regular perusal, which I am now doing as far as the Revelation, with clearer views and greater delight than formerly. Thus I began to experience what is quoted of Bishop Horne in the "Companion to the Bible," when he said, with respect to the Psalms, "These unfading plants of Paradise become, as we are more and more accustomed to them, still more and more beautiful; their blooms appear to be daily heightened; fresh odours are emitted, and new sweets are extracted from them; who hath once tasted their excellencies will desire to taste them yet again, and he who tastes them often will relish them best." I hope I may pursue the study of the Holy Bible without much mixture of weakness and weariness, which I often experience in so doing. May the Lord pardon my infirmities, rovings, and instabilities in the use of His Holy Word! That the time may come when the heathen shall be fully given to Christ for His inheritance and the utmost parts of the earth for His possession.

About this time Crowther wrote another letter dated from Kissy 3 July, 1840, in which he gives a glimpse of his own climbing of the ladder of learning:

I have begun (he writes) to study the Greek language. I learned some time ago, through the aid of Mr. Schlenker, the declension of nouns and adjectives and the conjugation of verbs ; the only books I have are Parkhurst's "Greek Lexicon" and a Greek Testament. I hope, by God's blessing, that I shall soon be able to understand the Word of God in that language, in which it was first written by the evangelists and apostles.

But Crowther found that the education of these natives and their Christian teaching was no easy task, although he felt it such a labour of love. The peculiar temperament of the negro race, their impulsive emotionalism, the groundwork of superstition and ignorance which had to be drastically dealt with, that natural lightheartedness which led them to almost childish vanity and frivolity—all these, recognized by Crowther so readily, being of one blood with themselves, were real difficulties to be overcome and reckoned with in his work. And yet the wonderful change which had come over Sierra Leone since the Gospel had been preached there gave great hope of future progress. As was his wont, he quietly set down his thoughts upon this matter at the time, and the following quotation from an old letter expresses his hopefulness :

That state of our people (he writes) some years ago, compared with what is at present, affords a delightful scene. Our country is greatly improved and benefited by the labours of the servants of the Church Missionary Society. The private feeling of individuals with whom we are conversant, as well as the great stir which is seen amongst the liberated Africans at present, who seemed to be awakened from their foolishness and superstition to serve God, greatly shows that they are becoming another people. Twelve years ago, hundreds of men and women, who now fill our Sunday-schools, and many of whom we see through that privilege are now able to read for themselves the wonderful works of God, thought they were too old to learn ; they used to say that book-learning was for white people, and was rather boyish employment. There were some few, indeed, who used to attend the evening school which was then kept, from motives of desiring to improve; but a greater part of them used to attend merely to please their missionary, who was also their manager. For often when school was opened with a hundred or more scholars, it was not often closed with many above fifty; for many of them, under pretence of going out, slipped away to their homes. Some there were who openly expressed their displeasure at school by an artifice most ridiculous in its nature. These were the inhabitants of Wellington. Upon agreement they soon assembled at the call of the bell, but before school was opened they all, with one accord, simultaneously rushed out of the grass chapel, through the doors and windows, in the utmost confusion possible. To crown the whole, they shouted in their country language, as soon as they got out, with an expression of their victory over the schoolmaster. But, blessed be our God! these are the very people who have willingly contributed and built a chapel which is by far too small for the attendants on public worship on Sunday mornings and for the Sunday scholars.

There were some others who gave a greater part of their time to drumming and dancing. At that time this was a favourite amusement, with which they would not part, at any rate. I well remember the time when the Rev. J. W. Weeks spoke to one of the head dancers, a man of understanding, on the folly of so doing, especially as he could read his Bible, but instead of being thankful for this kind admonition he looked at Mr. Weeks as an intruder on their peace. He immediately applied to the manager for permission to play, and that being granted he retired with his company, with singing, clappings of hands, dancing and performing somersets [*sic*], in spite of their kind admonition. Though the working of the Gospel leaven be slow, yet wherever it touches it will prove effectual in converting the lump to its nature. This very individual, after many years, was brought to see the real state of his danger. He was under Mr. Weeks' instruction as a candidate at Bathurst for some time, and was one of the five baptized by the Rev. J. F. Schön. How many instances of former follies, ignorance, and superstition may be mentioned when the individuals have been brought to see their real state and condition and have become followers of the Lamb! Was not the former conduct of these individuals cause of great discouragement to the missionaries? When such reports as these were made, did it not seem as if all that was doing for Africa was to no purpose? But Christian perseverance will have its fruit at last, success will crown their labours, and with joy they will bear the sheaves of the seeds which they had sown in tears.

Throughout his long and eventful life Crowther never failed in his grateful appreciation of all that the Church Missionary Society had been to him, especially its tender and generous care of him during these early days of his career, when his mind and heart were receiving impressions from the missionaries and schoolmasters which so much influenced him for good. A special interest therefore attaches to his first letter to the secretaries at Salisbury Square. This has happily been preserved, and is a rare and self-revealing document which must find a place here. It is written from the Christian Institution, Fourah Bay, and bears date 19 January, 1829.

Rev. and Dear Gentlemen,—Your most humble and obliged servant addresses these few lines to you and hopes that all what he says is directed by his God, in whose vineyard he desires to labour and be useful. I thank you for all the privileges which I have had, by and through you, in learning those good things which are very useful and pleasant in this life, and most of all in learning to know that one needful which none can take away from me.

When I was brought to England by my honoured master, Mr. Davey, my chief desire was to learn something which may be good for me and my fellow-creatures. When I was to be sent back home again, I begged very hard, not for anything else, but that I might remain there and learn something, that when I came back to Africa I might be a little help to the Mission. But when I found that it was not God's will that I should stop there any longer, I cast myself upon Him, because He knows best. He has not forgotten, He has sent a faithful servant of His to impart to me those good things which I was in need of, and not to me only, but to those to whom He sees fit to be employed in His vineyard.

I am very glad to say I am now engaged as the assistant to my faithful master Mr. Haensel, in the Christian Institution, yet this is not my chief desire, for I am desiring to be instructed by God's Holy Spirit that I may soon rise up and become a teacher to the others. I have hope that Africa will soon stretch forth her hands unto God, and that joy and gladness shall be found in her, thanksgiving and the voice of melody. I hope I am not forward in saying I can and do bear all things if Jesus strengthens me. My earnest prayer is that my four brethren, who are yet with you, may have the same desire and pray with me and those that are here in the Spirit, that in future we may join in Africa as Christ's faithful soldiers, who come forth to fight for the souls of their fellow-creatures under the great Captain of our soul's salvation. Pray ye for Africa, that many natives may come forth and give themselves unto Jesus, to employ them in what He wants them to do.

My kind respects to all who care for the Africans. And I would comfort them that they need not be in despair that Africa shall not return. Though how few we natives may be that profess to be teachers, we shall try, perhaps God will hear our prayers and help us. Elijah was the only prophet that remained, as it is said in the 1st Book of Kings, chapter xviii. v. 22, in the days of Ahab; and the prophets of Baal were four hundred and fifty, yet God answered him, though he was the only one that remained, and his life was sought to be taken away.

Pray for Africa is the prayer of your most humble, thankful, and obliged servant,

SAMUEL CROWTHER.

In the year 1841 a new sphere of usefulness opened to him unexpectedly; indeed, the step he took had a great influence in shaping his future course of life. It brought him out of the narrow limits of his work as a schoolmaster, and this incident gave him an opportunity of testing and developing those qualities of practical wisdom which distinguished him. He was still a young man, with any amount of brimming energy and not a little laudable ambition; he probably recognized that God had called him to a wider and more important field, and it was for him to watch every way which led upward and onward, to what goal he knew not. But it will be seen that the humble spirit so much desired by his old tutor was not wanting as he sought how best to be a means of grace to his native land and people. Africa was written on his heart. There never was a truer patriot than Crowther, and as such he looked hopefully for the day when her great waterways might become, not only crowded with commercial vessels, but the highways of salvation, along which the message of peace and goodwill should travel into the interior. His letters show that his reading and his own personal conviction alike convinced him that if Africa is to be won for Christ it must be by the service of her own sons. An unlooked-for honour now came to him through the Church Missionary Society.

Ever since the abolition of the slave trade the West Coast of Africa had retained a special interest in the eyes of the British nation. What might be called the Experimental Colony of freed slaves at Sierra Leone, with its trials and disappointments, had nevertheless demonstrated the capacity of the African race under proper training and supervision to be a dependable factor in missionary work. The spread of Christianity and its striking effect in bringing order out of chaos, and flourishing towns where revolution and crime had been rampant heretofore, had its due effect upon the faith and confident hope of the Christians at home, and the minor chord of sorrow and bereavement had made the work still more precious.

And the British Government were also not behind

in reading the signs of the times. Probably that important work by Sir Thomas Fowell Buxton, entitled "The Slave Trade and its Remedy," had pointed out to politicians that the extinction of the accursed trade should open a door for commerce and the development of a new world. It was therefore decided to fit out an expedition of discovery to ascend the Niger and obtain valuable information for the use of the Government. Lord John Russell, then acting as Colonial Secretary, addressed a letter to the Lords of the Treasury on 26 December, 1839, in which he explained the objects of the proposed expedition:

> The Queen has directed her ministers to negotiate conventions and agreements with those chiefs and powers, the basis of which conventions would be, first, the abandonment and absolute prohibition of the slave trade; and, secondly, the admission, for consumption in this country, on favourable terms, of goods, the produce and manufacture of the territories subject to them—of those chiefs the most considerable over the countries adjacent to the Niger and its great tributary streams. It is therefore proposed to dispatch an expedition, which would ascend that river by steamboats as far as the points at which it receives the confluence of some of the principal rivers falling into it from the eastward. At these, or at any other stations which may be found more favourable for the promotion of a legitimate commerce, it is proposed to establish British factories, in the hope that the natives may be taught that there are methods of employing the population more profitable to those to whom they are subject than that of converting them into slaves and selling them for exportation to the slave traders.

Such an expedition could not fail to attract the attention and sympathy of the Church Missionary Society, who obtained permission for two of its representatives to accompany the ships, so as to obtain information with a view to establishing a Christian mission among the natives of the Niger district.

The committee wisely selected for this duty the Rev. J. F. Schön, a very able missionary, who during his ten years at Sierra Leone had acquired a special knowledge of native languages; and as his companion they chose the young catechist, Mr. Samuel Crowther, of Fourah Bay College. This would be deeply interesting news to both, but one can imagine the palpitations of delight with which the younger man would hasten home to tell his wife what had happened that day. With that sincere and ever-present humility of his nature, Crowther felt keenly his unworthiness of such a distinction, and doubtless he prayed without ceasing that it might prove a real service to his beloved Africa.

This event also brought him into intimate touch with Mr. Schön, the commencement of a life-long friendship. It was a little disappointing to both that they could not travel on the same ship together, Mr. Schön being appointed to the *Wilberforce* and Crowther to the *Soudan*. In saying good-bye to wife and children, they little thought how disastrous would be the issue of their journeyings and how many valuable lives would be sacrificed.

The journals of Mr. Schön are very graphic, and his experienced eye evidently took in the situation and saw the difficulties and possibilities alike of future work, as they pushed slowly up the river. His proficiency as a linguist also enabled him to take notes of the languages of the people, of which afterwards he made good use. The story of his sufferings, as one by one the fever laid them low, until scarcely any Europeans save himself survived to manage the vessel, is a recital sad enough.

But our immediate interest is with Crowther, who also diligently kept a journal, full of word pictures of a vivid and personal nature. It was his first experience of the world beyond and behind the coast; and it was working, all unconsciously to him, in preparing him for the government of a huge diocese in the days to come. The tears of separation from Mrs. Crowther and his family are still upon his cheeks as he takes up his pen to make the first entry in his diary on board:

> To-day about eleven o'clock the *Soudan* got under way for the Niger, the highway into the heart of Africa. She was soon followed by the *Wilberforce*, which took her in tow in order to save fuel. When I looked back on the colony in which I had spent nineteen years—the happiest part of my life, because there I was brought acquainted with the saving knowledge of Jesus Christ, leaving my wife, who was near her confinement, and four children behind—I could not but feel pain and some anxiety for a time at the separation. May the Lord, who has been my guide from my youth up till now, keep them and me, and make me neither barren nor unfruitful in His service!

He begins to work on his vocabulary of African languages, but gives it up, as sea-sickness has made him feel so ill; but we find him down in the steerage, joining in a Bible-class. He soon meets with a little misadventure which might have been serious:

> July 10. While we were at dinner to-day the glass called "the bull's eye" fell from its fastening on my head and then on two plates in which I was taking my dinner, and dashed them to pieces. Providentially this heavy glass, weighing about five pounds, did not fall perpendicularly on me. At night also my hammock, in consequence of its not being properly fastened, gave way at the foot, when I fell and got

a slight stroke on the head. Had the lash given way from the head of the hammock I should have suffered seriously. I mention these trifling circumstances, as without God's watchful care over us how soon may we, by such small accidents, be humbled to the dust.

Arriving off Cape Coast Castle they went ashore, and here he was fortunate enough to meet with that able Wesleyan missionary the Rev. T. B. Freeman, who received him with marked kindness, took him into his library, telling him that he might use what books he liked. A great treat to Crowther!

Wandering among the monuments in the graveyard of the Castle, he made a note of the tablet erected to the Rev. Philip Quaque, a native who was sent to England by the Society for the Propagation of the Gospel in 1754, baptized at St. Mary's, Islington, 7 January, 1759, and returned fully ordained as chaplain to the factory, and died, after many trials and disappointments, in 1816. This tablet was naturally of enthralling interest to Crowther. When the expedition was over he referred to the incident in a letter, in which he says:

Who the individual was I know not, neither have I ever heard anything of him, except from this monument. What attracted my attention was that he was a native of that place —sent to England for education, received Holy Orders, and was employed in his own country upwards of *fifty years!*

A few days afterwards they were on board again, crossing soon the dangerous bar of the mouth of the Niger, and found the other two vessels waiting their arrival. We take up his journal and read:

Aug. 15. *Lord's Day.* This day we had the pleasure of commemorating the death of our Lord and Saviour Jesus

Christ by receiving the Sacrament of the Lord's Supper administered by the Rev. J. Müller, the chaplain of the expedition. Seven officers, three coloured men, and the captain himself, eleven in number, surrounded the Table of the Lord, in deep humility, contrition for sin, and earnest desire for amendment of life. *He that humbleth himself shall be exalted.*

We always esteemed our captain and his officers as honourable, but we did much more so when we saw them humbling themselves before the Lord. May this refreshing feast strengthen us to serve the Lord our God more actively than we have done before!

They soon got under way again, and steaming up the Niger discovered that they were surrounded on all sides by thick mangrove trees. He tells us significantly that while everybody seemed pleased that the navigation of the river had actually begun, some could not help also remarking that they believed they were going to their graves. Here is a view of the Niger as Crowther saw it for the first time:

Aug. 21. We were gradually introduced from the mangroves into a forest of palm and bamboo trees, embellished with large cotton trees of curious shapes, interspersed among them on both sides of the river, and with other lofty trees of beautiful foliage. All hands were invited on deck by this new scenery, and the day was spent with great interest at this novel appearance. We passed on both sides of the river several plantations of bananas, plaintains, sugar cane, cocoa, or *Kalabe*, as called by the Americans, and now and then some huts with natives in them. The natives were so timid that they several times pulled their canoes ashore and ran away into the bush and peeped at the steamer with fear and great astonishment. We got opposite a village containing about seven or eight huts, where the inhabitants, in very great earnest, armed themselves with sticks and country billhooks and ran along the bank to a neighbouring village, to apprise the villagers of the dreadful approach of our wonderful floating and self-moving habitation. These villagers also followed the example of their informers. Having armed themselves in like manner, they betook themselves to the next village to bring them the same tidings. When they were encouraged to come on board, it was difficult to find persons brave enough to do so. Those who ventured to come near took care not to go further from shore than the distance of a leap from their canoe, in case there should be cause for it. The captain, perceiving some of them inclined to come off, stopped the engine and persuaded them to come near us. In the meantime we had come opposite to a large village, into which all the former villagers had collected themselves.

There was a little boy who acted as their interpreter because he understood two English words, "Yes" and "Tabac," which he had picked up at some place. They constantly told him something to tell us, but he could not say anything else besides his "Yes" and "Tabac." After much hesitation, a large canoe came off with no less than forty-three persons in it. My expectation was greatly raised when I found among them a Yoruba boy of about thirteen years of age, from whom I thought we could get some information about the people; but the poor little fellow had almost lost his native language through his lonely situation among them. He could not even understand me very well when I asked about his father, mother, and his own town. He must have travelled hundreds of miles before he got into this secret part of Africa.

As they proceeded up the stream they met with other natives who had, apparently, been in touch with the white man before, seeing that they were dressed in old soldiers' and drummers' coats, wearing battered black hats, but no shirt or trousers. From another village the natives came in their canoes, laden with fruits to exchange for rum, for which they frantically called "Vlolo! Vlolo!" and applying their hands to their mouths to show what they wanted. As the captain would not comply with their demand they paddled back again in high dudgeon.

Here is Crowther's account of a visit to a native potentate, who was interviewed by Mr. Schön in the other steamer. He seems to have been a rather remarkable personage in his way, and no doubt exercised considerable influence in the district.

Aug. 28. I had the opportunity of seeing Mr. Schön on board the *Albert*, where the treaty was making with King Obi, who was on board very early this morning. I did not see the King in his best dress yesterday, the day he introduced himself. He is a middle-sized man between the age of forty and fifty, his countenance is soft, and he appears to be of a peaceful temper. To-day his dress, as I was told, was very plain. He appeared in calico trousers of a country make, and an English-made jacket of the same stuff; it would have been more respectable had they been cleaner, especially as he had no shirt on. He had on his neck three strings of pipe coral, as large as a man's small finger, two of which were short and close to the neck, while the third extended to the navel. As far as we could count, from the feet of his trousers, when he moved, each of his feet about the ankles was ornamented with eight strings of coral, a dull old brass button closing each string, and two leopard's teeth attached to the strings of coral at each foot. He had on a red cap, over which was a marine's cap decorated with brass scales and other pieces of coloured cords. His Majesty was not a little proud of this equipment from the commander of the expedition. He marched about the quarter deck, with apparent satisfaction at having white men for his friends. He consented to the treaty, and made a proclamation the same day among his people for the abolition of the slave trade in his country.

One of Crowther's characteristics was a saving sense of humour. He could always enjoy a joke, and many of these entries in his journals show how he relished the ridiculous aspect of these natives in their nondescript European costume, and their strutting self-importance. The beauty of natural scenery always appealed to him, and though these villages under the palms and mangrove trees were, in a sense, the common objects of his country, they gladdened his eye as the boat pursued its way up the Niger. But from time to time the gross ignorance and spiritual darkness of heathenism presented itself to his mind: its prevalent misery suggested many grave thoughts. All this we find reflected in some entries which he made in his journal at this time.

> There was another circumstance which damped my spirits and tarnished my amusement at the pleasing sight of the villages above mentioned. Among the spectators of our steamers was an old woman, who was bowing down to the ground, kissing her hands and then looking up with great seriousness, as if asking for some protection from the gods. Whether she was performing this act of worship to the figure in front of the ship or to the steamer itself was not certain; however, it sufficiently shows into what degree of superstition these people are sunk. Moreover, we had to witness the naked bodies of our fellow-creatures floating along one side, or washed about the banks of this splendid river. This is the third time we have seen such unpleasant sights since we have entered this river. If they were slaves whose circumstances could not allow them a burial, it is much more to be lamented.

Soon after these words were written the expedition sustained a severe loss in the accidental death of their Ingalla interpreter, upon whose services they had chiefly to depend in dealing with these people. He had fallen overboard, and was carried away by the stream and drowned before any help could come. This sad event, coupled with the sickness which began to prevail, had naturally a depressing effect upon the crew, and Crowther did his best to hearten the sinking spirits of his fellow-travellers. We find him reading to the sick men, and under date 9 September he makes a note that in his presence the steward of the ship breathed his last, he hoped "trusting in Jesus," whom Crowther had kept continually before his eyes as his only refuge. In the forenoon the poor fellow was buried on a small island in the river. Day by day their troubles were increasing, and whenever they got a chance of exchanging notes with the other vessels it was to tell each other a rather woeful tale.

This morning the *Albert* and the *Wilberforce* came up to us where we were getting wood. Captain B. Allen immediately came to his ship. He took all his unexpected afflictions with Christian resignation. I went with Mr. Sidney, one of the officers, to a village on the top of the hill, below which we were wooding. These villagers are refugees from the town of Addu Kuddu, on the right side of the river at the confluence, having been driven away by the Fulatahs. From the top of the hill you may see three other villages at the foot. The one on the top of the hill contains two hundred inhabitants, the four together contain eight hundred, at an average. The people are Kakandas. As I could understand a little, I mentioned to them the design of the expedition, at which they were transported with joy. One of them was so confident that he wished to go with the white men altogether. I asked them whether they would like me to stay among them and teach them about God. They all answered in the affirmative.

The chief of this village, an old man about sixty, had been sacrificing a fowl to his idol this morning. The blood he sprinkled on his forehead, to which were attached a few of the fowl's feathers. His idol is rather difficult to describe, as it was a mixture of some sort of grass or palm leaves, clay, and broken pieces of calabashes, to which feathers of fowls were fastened by means of blood. I shook my head, indicating that it was not good, at the same time pointing my finger to heaven, directing him to worship the only true God. He did not pay much attention. They all took fright at Mr. Sidney's instrument to take the distance, but their fears soon subsided. Their huts are built in the same form as those of Iddah—a circular form, and they are so low and close to each other that if a fire should break out in one, the whole village of about sixty huts would be consumed in a moment.

It would appear that the expedition kept constantly in touch with the natives on the banks of the river, in order to keep up the supply of fuel for the stokeholes of the ships. They sent men ashore and cut the wood, where it was possible giving some consideration to the inhabitants, and especially when they showed themselves willing to help in supplying this indispensable requisite. It may be mentioned here that Crowther afterwards attributed the terrible loss of life on board, in this particular expedition, to the practice of storing green wood in the hold of the vessels, which in progress of rapid decomposition soon filled the ship with malarial germs of fever. Doubtless this hypothesis was a correct one; at any rate, on future expeditions the suggestion of Crowther that a supply of dry wood for the engines should be towed after the ships in barges evidently prevented a recurrence of the fever.

The payment of the natives was, of course, made in cowries, the current coin of the country, and in the circumstances of so much illness being on board Crowther had to take these business details in his charge. As an instance we take the following:

As I was busy purchasing for the purser, who himself is now laid up with fever, I was robbed of some handkerchiefs with which I was bartering, for there were many people about me in the ships. I must say that this people, speaking generally, are honest, and I rather wonder that such acts of dishonesty were not more common with them, as they were exposed to many temptations on board the ship, where many things were lying about. We buy of them by certain measures of cowries, which we told them contained a certain number; but as they would take the trouble of counting thousands of cowries, placing them in heaps of one or two hundred, they very honestly returned the overplus, which, of course, we never took from them. They count by fives with the same quickness as we count by twos. Under a pretence of distrust, we counted these heaps of one or two hundred after them, which we always found to be quite right. If there should be found one dishonest person among these people, that should not be the reason of charging the whole with guilt. For their articles they charge most extravagantly ; for what they want a thousand cowries—the most reasonable price—they will at first ask seven or eight thousand, and if anyone is not aware of this trick he will soon empty his shipload of cowries for their canoe cargo. So fond are these people of cowries, that when they would not take a handkerchief of fivepence value, they would readily take one hundred and fifty cowries, scarcely valuing twopence farthing, at the rate of eight hundred and sixty cowries for a shilling. They love to give presents because they expect to receive twice as much. They are very fond of looking-glasses.

It strikes one that these characteristics are extremely human, and that there are white men and women with all the accomplishments of civilization and some of the benefits of Christianity who would have to confess to a share of the same weaknesses. These simple black folk little dreamed that both cowries and looking-glasses were quite as much sought after in the wonderland from which the ships came.

At this point the vessels were getting so full of invalids that it was resolved that the *Wilberforce* and *Soudan* should carry this precious cargo of sick folk back to the sea ; but Captain Trotter in the *Albert* decided to push on a little further, and here Crowther was able to join Mr. Schön, to their mutual satisfaction. When they reached a place called Gori they went ashore, and Crowther, in describing an interview with the chief, draws attention to the curious custom of " the King's mouth."

We were led to the house of the chief, where the gentlemen of the expedition were seated on mats in the courtyard, about

SOME OF THE BISHOP'S OLD FRIENDS

Rev. J. F. Schön
Rev. J. Boyle
Mr. Sydney Gedge

Rev. J. Bradford Whiting
Rev. Henry Venn
Dr. R. N. Cust (*Photo, Russell & Sons*)

Bishop Weeks
Archdeacon Henry Johnson
Sir Thomas Fowell Buxton

To face page 61

twelve feet by eight, and formed by five huts in the shape of casks placed in an oval form.

The chief is about seventy years of age. He appeared to have been so frightened at the sudden appearance of the white men that he could not speak a word, and was thought to be deaf and dumb. There was one who acted as his mouth (or speaker), who answered with great reserve every question put to him, especially such as related to the slave trade. He denied knowing the number of slaves brought to market to-day, or that they were the Attah's subjects. The heat from the crowd by which we were blocked up in this narrow spot was suffocating; besides, the noise was so great, not only from the spectators, but the headmen themselves, that it was almost enough to deafen anyone else. When one headman calls out for silence, it takes him nearly five minutes to complete his palavering with the people, and when he is on the point of holding his tongue he is never in want of three or four seconders who also must scold the people, so that instead of obtaining quietness both the headman and the people make more noise and create greater confusion than ever, till perhaps after a quarter of an hour there is silence for a time.

Negotiations under such circumstances were not easy, and especially when almost all the visitors are absolutely ignorant of the language. Mr. Schön was, of course, a good linguist, and during the expedition was able to reduce to writing and grammatical form some of the dialects of the Niger tribes; but it is evident that Crowther had to be the principal spokesman, and his kinship as a negro no doubt gave the people a certain confidence in listening to him.

When they reached Egga, an infragrant spot, the captain and officers had an important interview with Rogang the chief, a person of great authority, and Crowther took some pains to explain to this black ruler the objects of the expedition, from a commercial and religious standpoint. He tells us:

After a long walk through narrow and crooked streets we came to Rogang's palace, and in about half an hour's time he made his appearance. After a hearty salutation, by shaking of hands in the name of the king of the ship, and telling him the reasons why the ship could not then come near, I commenced my message:

That the Queen of the country called Great Britain has sent the king of the ship to all the chiefs of Africa to make treaties with them to give up war and the slave trade—to all their people in the cultivation of the soil, and to mind all that the white people say to them, as they wish to teach them many things, and particularly the Book which God gives, which will make all men happy. I added likewise that there are many Nufi, Haussa, and Yoruba people in the white man's country who have been liberated from the Portuguese and Spanish slave ships, that they are now living like white men, that they pray to God and learn His Book, and consequently are living a happier life than when they were in their own country, and much better off than their country people are at present. To this many of them said that they could judge of their happy state merely by my appearance. I added, moreover, that our country people in White Man's country had written a letter to the Queen who lives in Great Britain, expressing their wish to return to their country if she would send white men along with them; but the Queen, who loves us all as her children, told them to stop till she had first sent her ships to the chiefs of Africa, to persuade them to give up war and the slave trade; and if they consented to her proposals she would gladly grant the request of our country people.

The result of this elaborate palaver seems to have been that, although the astute Rogang was on the whole favourably impressed, he took Crowther aside and confided to him that nothing final could be arranged, as he himself was only a vassal of Sumo Sariki, the Fulatah King of Rabba, who must be consulted. Clearly Rogang stood in terror of his superior. After several more interviews Crowther, with much diplomacy, obtained a mass of useful information, and subsequently had a private consultation with Rogang on his own account. This interview throws some light upon the importation of strong drink into Africa, a practice which has been such an unspeakable evil ever since. It was, he observed by these entries in his journal, that Crowther found these poor natives were not only being drugged with vile stuff, but were cruelly deceived by those who traded upon the alcoholic craze they had created.

As I wished to buy some articles for curiosity, and the people were generally so much about me that I could scarcely move, I sent the interpreter to ask Rogang if he would permit me to buy what I wanted in his porch—an entrance leading from the street to his yard—where only a few persons might be admitted. He sent word back that he would not have had the least objection to do so, but he was afraid lest the Fulatahs should say that he had given his house for a market to the white men. In private conversation Rogang asked the interpreter if he had rum to sell—a bottle or two of which he would be very glad to buy. He said that the rum which comes to them from the coast is almost converted to water, yet they paid four to five thousand cowries a bottle. My Yoruba visitors, being Mohammedans, were surprised to see me, as they considered me an English Mallam, drink country beer made of Guinea corn—a stuff which is held in great abhorrence by the Mohammedans, yet they think it not contrary to the precepts of the Korân to drink any kind of spirits. When they came on board they asked me to give them some rum to drink, if it were but a small drop. As I took no grog, I told them that I had none. At leaving, my Mohammedan friends did not forget, among many other things, to remind me, when we came this way again, not to forget to bring plenty of dollars and a large quantity of rum.

I have just one account of this kind to relate. As we were lying near the village of the refugees on the hills a Nufi Mohammedan, who was returning from Keri market, came alongside. He spoke a little Haussa. As he made himself very friendly, Mr. Waters, the purser, treated him and his wife with great kindness. He took them down to the gun room, gave them biscuits, and set a decanter of wine before them. Whether the woman had taken any wine before I came in or not I could not tell. Her husband placed the biscuits before her, and he himself took possession of the wine. He had taken some before I went in. As it was time for them to go, he was desired to do so. He then took a glass of wine and asked me if Mr. Waters could not supply him with some for his journey. He was answered in the negative. He again took another glass. When he was upon the point of rising, still squeezing the decanter as tight as he could, he took another glass. Mr. Waters and the woman had gone up and I was upon the ladder, thinking as there was no person in the cabin he would not stay any longer. When he was rising he took another glass. As I was going up, the servant who stood on the ladder said, "Mr. Crowther, he is taking another glass; he will finish the wine."

After he had taken this he came up to us. It is difficult to say in what state of mind this man left the cabin, whether with gratitude and satisfaction for the kind treatment, which he greatly abused, or with regret that he could not get a supply of wine for his journey. He said he belonged to Kattam Karifi, a village on the Niger. He was told to go and get plenty of wood ready against our coming, so he left the ship that evening quite warm at his canoe crew. He had two slaves on board. Early next morning, contrary to our expectation, this man was seen alongside, and he soon found his way into the ship, but to-day he met with an ill reception, as he was not allowed to stay on board five minutes.

The fever now began to claim its victims on board with such rapid strides that the journal is a succession of sad records of sickness and death. That brave, high-spirited officer, Captain Trotter, has at last taken to his cabin, and Captain B. Allen is also lying in a most dangerous condition. The only officer left to navigate the ship is Mr. Willie, the mate. Dr. Stanger has had to take charge of the engines. At ten o'clock at night the captain's clerk takes advantage of the darkness to fling himself overboard in his delirium. A black sailor, however, swims after him and brings him back to be roped down in his hammock; this precaution has also now to be taken with the second engineer, who is fast losing his wits. Next morning, however, the latter struggles free and leaps into the stream and is seen no more. Dr. McWilliam, in this emergency, takes control of the vessel. Mr. Kingdom dies suddenly, and is buried by Mr. Schön by the marshy bankside, and then drifting dangerously down the river they meet with the *Ethiope*, an emergency craft bringing news of the terrible mortality on Crowther's old ship, the *Soudan*, which has included all three of the medical men and Mr. Waters, the purser. But the toll of precious life is not yet exhausted. A few days afterwards a marine named Cole dies, and is buried immediately; Mr. Willie follows, and the purser's steward expires in an hour. Then Captain B. Allen passes away, and is carried to his grave by the weak remnants of his ship's company. Within the space of a week three other officers and a marine die and are buried.

This return of the *Albert*, running almost unguided down the swift current of the Niger, amid risks on every hand, its decks strewn with dead and dying men, the overworked doctor managing the engines from a book on machinery he finds in the dead captain's room, having to desert his levers to rush where some poor fellow is screaming in delirium: was not this homeward voyage a tragedy indeed? As a matter of fact, Crowther seems to have been the only man untouched by the fever, and he kept his head as well as his health through it all, working anywhere, and at anything to save the situation. Poor Mr. Schön, with his own temples throbbing with fever, scrawls these words in his journal:

> Pain of body, distress of mind, weakness, sobbing and crying surround us on all sides. The healthy, if so they may be called, are more like walking shadows than men of enterprise. Truly Africa is an unhealthy country! When will her redemption draw nigh? All human skill is baffled, all human means fall short. Forgive us, O God, if on them we have depended and been forgetful of Thee, and let the light of Thy countenance again shine upon us that we may be healed!

This piteous cry of a brave man is not to be wondered at, when we read that on a Sunday morning, while conducting service on the quarter-deck, he had the body of a dead sailor behind him, in front of him the carpenters were busy making a coffin, and in the forepart yonder seven men were lying delirious with fever! Out of a complement of one hundred and fifty Europeans, the expedition lost forty-two within two months.

When the news reached England there was universal grief; such a disaster came as a shock to the people, and it is not surprising that public opinion would not risk a repetition of the attempt for twelve years. And yet something had been done, and the expedition had not been all failure. The expenditure of human life was heavy indeed, and for this reason the ships had to return perforce without reaching their destined point. But the project had paved the way for other pioneers; its very sufferings were the school in which the lessons of experience had been painfully but usefully taught. It led to a better knowledge of the native tribes and the future establishment of the Niger Mission; it enabled Mr. Schön to compile a valuable vocabulary of the different tongues, and it added some fresh geographical knowledge of one of the waterways of the world.

But in addition to this, these journeyings had an immense influence on the life and character of Crowther. We have watched him closely from the slave market to the schoolmaster's desk; we have seen him pursuing his studies with eager thirst for knowledge, and across the dim memory of many years his earnest, thoughtful face seems to look at us, with that longing gaze of his, as though yearning to discern the finger of God in his life history. That direction came, as we have seen, to what at first seemed a pleasant voyage of discovery, but proved ere long to be a furnace of affliction to all concerned. And yet the anguish of that experience, when in sight of other woes the iron verily entered into his own soul, was not unprofitable to one who was destined to bear such heavy burdens and to be a succourer of many.

CHAPTER III

FROM COLLEGE TO MISSION FIELD

WHEN the Rev. J. F. Schön wrote his long report to the Church Missionary Society on the expedition up the Niger he made a strong point of the importance of a native ministry. In his opinion one of the lessons which that ill-starred enterprise had taught was the needless waste of European life, instead of utilizing Africa's own sons in preaching the Gospel to their countrymen. He then gave these suggestions a practical shape by recommending the society to send for Crowther to England for ordination. Mr. Schön had known him intimately, and his experience of his character and capacities under the trying ordeal of this expedition supplied ample evidence to justify this strong recommendation. It is worth while to transcribe here the opinion of this experienced missionary respecting his young and promising companion. On 26 June, 1841, just before their sailing for the Niger he writes:

> The association of Samuel Crowther with me has proved beneficial to both. He becomes much interested in our labours and rendered me great assistance. I have no hesitation in saying that I fully believe that, by God's grace, he will render to the mission great service.

Again, writing from the *Wilberforce* at the mouth of the Nun River on 11 August, 1841:

> I have just seen Samuel Crowther from the *Soudan*, and am happy to say that he is very well and anxious to get into the heart of Africa. I find him a very useful man and wish much to have more of his company, especially when we once get into the interior. He only regrets, with myself, that he cannot pursue his studies as much as he wishes; he has, however, lost no time. He copied our translations and reads the Greek Testament, which will always be of much use to him.

Still more to the point is another letter, addressed to the secretaries in London on 10 September, 1841:

> I have thought much about the propriety of Samuel Crowther's returning to England with me and receiving ordination, and should be happy to learn what opinion the Parent Committee may form of this plan on my return to Sierra Leone. Of his decided piety I have no doubt; his studious habits and anxiety to improve himself would, after a few weeks' attention, qualify him in other respects. He is highly esteemed by all who know him, and his love to his country and for his people would prevail on him to lay himself out for their good. The committee in Sierra Leone was ever in favour of the measure, and his excellent conduct in this expedition can only raise our opinion of him.

A testimony from another source was given by the Rev. F. Bultimam, one of the missionaries at Sierra Leone. It is dated 13 October, 1841:

> There is no one more fit to be entrusted with the ministry of the Gospel, among his own brethren, than Samuel Crowther. However rarely the solid knowledge of Samuel Crowther is found among his brethren, it is so far more rarely combined with such *modesty* as his; and while I am convinced that he would do honour to our Society, if presented by them as a candidate for Holy Orders to the Bishop of London, I sincerely wish and hope that on his return from the Niger this opportunity of evincing the innate prowess of an African mind will be afforded him, though I am sure his modesty will not allow him to ask for it.

In response to these high testimonies to his life and capabilities, it is not surprising that the committee summoned him to England, and we find him stepping ashore once again on 3 September, 1842. He would have vivid memories of his former visit as a boy, and how earnestly he had pleaded to be allowed to stay longer. But God knows best, and His best for Crowther was to mould him by these intervening experiences, so that he might present himself a more fit vessel for the Master's use. He looked around him now with the eyes of a man, and from the standpoint of a knowledge of human nature, also with the benefit of the culture of those studious days at Fourah Bay. But above all there burned in his heart the inextinguishable passion for the spiritual enlightenment of his own people. He yearned that Africa might be saved. While others had discerned in him gifts and possibilities of future service, he was conscious of that secret and inward call of God to that great work.

He brought with him in manuscript a grammar and vocabulary of Aku, the Yoruba language, which he had compiled during his leisure hours on board on his way to England. This was of practical value, and showed that in this direction he could be of special utility in the mission field. After several interviews the committee placed him at the Islington Church College in Upper Street for a few months' preparation. Here he was under the direction of the Rev. C. F. Childe, whose daughter wrote that touching account of West African missionary martyrs called the

"Finished Course," already referred to, now quite out of print, and a rare little record in more senses than one. It is difficult to get any memories of his stay in this college after so long a time, but we can well imagine that he worked hard during this short term and fully appreciated the training he received there, and is now counted one of the brightest in its roll of honoured names inscribed upon its walls. While there the annual examination was conducted by the Rev. James Schofield, Regius Professor of Greek at Cambridge, who had often discussed with others, holding the common idea that the mental capacity of a negro is always deficient as regards the logical faculty. But after conducting the examination on Paley's "Evidences of Christianity," he made the following significant remark to the principal of the college:

> I should like, with your permission, to take young Crowther's answers to those Paley questions back with me to Cambridge, and there read a few of them in the Combination Room to certain of my old Trinity friends. If, after hearing that young African's answers, they still contend that he does not possess a logical faculty, they will tempt us to question whether they do not lack certain other faculties of at least equal importance, such as common fairness of judgment and Christian candour.

Some of the men who shared lessons with him have also left their mark upon the world to some good purpose. Two especially may be named—Henry Baker, who did such splendid service as a missionary among one of the hill tribes of South India; and James Hunter, who carried on a like noble work among the Indian tribes of North-West Canada.

On Trinity Sunday, 11 June, 1843, Crowther received his deacon's orders, and was invited, with another candidate, afterwards Prebendary Newell, to breakfast at Fulham Palace, and to the latter the Bishop remarked, directing attention to Crowther: "That man is no mean scholar; his examination papers were capital, and his Latin remarkably good."

Years afterwards, when the Prebendary and Bishop Crowther met at a meeting the incident was mentioned. It greatly amused Crowther, who perfectly remembered being taken to Bishop Blomfield by Mr. Venn, and that he was thereupon examined pretty smartly. After he retired Bishop Blomfield said to Mr. Venn, "He'll do, he'll do, only polish him up a bit," which brightening process Crowther thought must have been the work of Islington, for his chief education he owed to Fourah Bay. In the October following the same Bishop ordained him as a presbyter of the Church in full orders. This occasion, when the first African was to be so ordained in connection with the Church Missionary Society, was looked upon as one of the events of the year. When Bishop Blomfield preached the anniversary sermon he referred to this when he said:

What cause for thanksgiving to Him who hath made of one blood all nations of men is to be found in the thought that He has not only blessed the labourers of the Society, by bringing many of those neglected and persecuted people to a knowledge of a Saviour, but that from among a race who were despised as incapable of intellectual exertion and acquirement He has raised up men well qualified, even in point of knowledge, to communicate to others the saving truths which they have themselves embraced, and to become preachers of the Gospel to their brethren according to the flesh!

It was a remarkable coincidence that his ordination was twenty-one years less one week after, as a little liberated slave boy, he had been put ashore from the *Myrmidon* at Sierra Leone. It is also worthy of note that soon after his ordination Sir Thomas Fowell Buxton, now full of years, heard Crowther preach in the pulpit of Northrepps Church. How that brave and faithful worker for the oppressed must have felt his heart warmed at the sight of a negro clergyman, a rescued slave, preaching the Gospel!

Soon after his ordination Crowther set sail to return to his native land. That voyage home must have filled his mind with many thoughts and expectations of what awaited him, now that under due authority he was to commence his ministry amongst his countrymen. As we have seen from his letter, addressed to the secretaries at Salisbury Square, while at Fourah Bay College, he was fully convinced that it would be by the ministry of her own sons that Africa was to be blessed with Christianity. Beyond that he felt his own personal call to this responsible privilege, and his heart was gladdened with the prospect of going to his own people. He watched the lessening shores of England, the land to which he was indebted for both personal and spiritual liberty, and then turned to watch wistfully for the first glimpse of his own homeland over the sea.

His coming was already exciting a flutter of expectation. A few months before Mr. Davies, one of the missionaries, wrote in a letter home, dated 10 August, 1843:

This morning one of the male communicants called to see me with an apparent degree of concern. I asked him what he wanted to say to me. He replied, " I wish to know, sir, if Mr. S. Crowther is crowned a minister, for I long very much to see him back again so that we poor black people may look to him as our Black Minister."

On 2 December he arrived at Freetown, and was heartily welcomed by troops of friends. The missionaries were delighted to grasp his hand and wish him God-speed, and afterwards to hear all the news from the dear home country, and to receive messages from London. The natives were, of course, full of joy, and one, an old catechist, exclaimed in the spirit of ancient Simeon :

Happy am I to see that the saving knowledge of the truth, as it is in Jesus, is spreading far and wide in the world, that even Africans, who were bowing down to images, are receiving the sacred scriptures as the very Word of God. Truly may one say that the Lord is now opening a way into the interior of Africa by choosing an African, the Rev. S. Crowther, to be a minister to bear his name among his countrymen. Now many of the sons of fallen man will hear the glad sounds of a Saviour's Name! May the Lord give His blessing to His servant, that he may be useful in turning many souls to glory! May the Lord raise up many more after him to become faithful ministers of His Gospel to the world!

On the following day, being Sunday, Crowther preached his first sermon in Africa to an immense congregation of natives in the mission church at Freetown. This was delivered in the English language, of which he was already a perfect master, and would be quite understood by all his hearers, as it had become the common tongue of the Colony, and was taught in the schools as well as used in the churches. He took for his text Luke XIV. 22: " Lord, it is done as Thou hast commanded, and yet there is room." The preacher made a note afterwards of this memorable gathering:

> It was Sacramental Sunday. I had the pleasure of hearing once more, from the lips of my African brethren, the hearty and loud responses of our excellent Liturgy. The singing was performed with solemnity, and I doubt not was *with the Spirit and with the understanding also*. The novelty of seeing a native clergyman performing Divine Service excited a very great interest among all who were present. But the question, "*Who maketh* thee to differ?" filled me with shame and confusion of face. It pleases the Disposer of all hearts to give me favour in the sight of this people. Wherever I go they welcome me as a messenger of Christ. After service I assisted the Rev. E. Jones to administer the Lord's Supper. It was a very solemn season. The Lord was with us. In the evening I preached to a large and attentive congregation from 2 Cor. x., parts of 15th and 16th verses.

He also remarks that at the end of each service, after the Benediction had been pronounced, the whole church rang with the cry of "Ke oh sheh"—"So let it be."

This is a most interesting stage in his career, the beginning of that great work, henceforth his devoted and lifelong care. His spirit will be best expressed in his own words, and therefore we will quote again a few extracts from the journal which he had begun to keep, and continued so faithfully to do for many years. It will be seen from the date that he had hardly been in Africa a fortnight when he penned these lines:

> Dec. 13, 1843. Being desirous of carrying out, as far as possible, the instructions of the Parent Committee—preaching in the Yoruba language in the Mission Church at Freetown—I began making some translations during the voyage; and

thinking that the sooner I began to prepare myself the better and easier so as to drive my business, and not let my business drive me, I translated the first three chapters of St. Luke's Gospel with less difficulty than I at first anticipated, always leaving what appeared insufficiently translated until revisions, when new words and thoughts would present themselves, which is generally the case in revising translations. I also translated the first two chapters of the Acts of the Apostles to see how that also would go, and it answers equally well. Thus have I prepared myself with some portions of the Holy Scriptures, although at present some verses require great consideration before the sense is fixed, that I might not be without some sort of provision for my countrymen.

But it was not only his public services which called for attention, but he began a diligent visitation of his countrymen in the district, and here we have a record of his first visit to a Mohammedan, who had evinced a great desire to see the black minister from over the sea. Crowther always took a deep and intelligent interest in the followers of the False Prophet, of which more will be seen later on. This, however, is worth notice, as his earliest recorded conversation with one of the Moslem faith:

Dec. 17. On Lord's Day morning the Mohammedan headman in the neighbourhood of Fourah Bay sent four men to Bathurst, about seven miles distant, to ask after my health and to learn for certainty whether I was going to the Yoruba country. On Monday I saw him. He is a clever Yoruba man, a very strict Mohammedan, and has a very great influence over those who profess Mohammedanism. He speaks Haussa like a native. I told him and his people who were present, in the Yoruba language, of the influence of Christianity on the people of England, referred them to the proceedings of the Friends of Africa in the late Niger expedition, and remarked that it was the religion of Christ which taught them to love all men and to do them all the good they could. I told them of the importance of yielding to the religion of the white man's Bible, because it led to the sure way of happiness, that the

Bible had already been translated into many languages and also into the Arabic, a copy of which I gave him some years ago; that I was instructed to translate the same into the Yoruba language, that the people may read this Bible for themselves in their own tongue; and that I should open a service in the Mission Church, where I should read and preach to the people from the Holy Scriptures in the Yoruba language. I did not raise any objections to their faith nor attack it, but endeavoured to show them the great blessings Christianity bestowed on mankind wherever it was embraced. To my great surprise they gloried at one of their countrymen being the first clergyman of the Church of England among the liberated Africans in the colony of Sierra Leone.

This dates his commencement of services in his native tongue. If he had been impressed with the effect of his first sermon in English, how much more he felt these, his early ministrations to his own people in their native Yoruba.

As the people were expecting me to open the Yoruba service in the Mission Church, I fixed the 9th January at half-past four in the afternoon, and requested the Rev. H. Rhodes to notify the same at church on Sunday, the 7th. After the morning service of that day I visited the people in their houses, especially those who never attended Divine Service, and invited them to the Yoruba service on Tuesday afternoon.

Jan. 9, 1844. *Monday.* Was visited by the headman of the Yoruba Mohammedans, who is living in the neighbourhood of Fourah Bay. In our conversation I told him, among many other things, that I should commence a Yoruba service on the 9th, and should be very glad to see him and his people there.

Jan. 9. This afternoon at half-past four o'clock I opened the Yoruba service in the Mission Church in Freetown. As might be expected, the novelty of the thing brought a large number of people together—Yorubas, Ibos, Calabas, etc.—to witness the reading and preaching of the Gospel of Christ in a native language in an English church. Although the language is my native tongue, with which I am well acquainted, yet on this occasion it appeared as if I were a babe just learning to utter my mother tongue. The work in which I was engaged, the place where I stood, and the congregation before me were altogether so new and strange that the whole proceeding seemed to myself like a dream. But the Lord supported me. I opened the service in English, when I read those of the prayers which were not translated and a portion of St. Luke's Gospel in Yoruba. In the congregation I observed three of my young Mohammedan friends, sent by their headman to attend the service, according to promise. The text from which I preached was taken from the lesson I had read to them—Luke i. 35. I was glad to hear the people express their satisfaction at my feeble attempt to express this doctrine. After service the Mohammedans followed me to my house and expressed their satisfaction at what they had heard. They apologized for the non-attendance of their headman, a stranger having called on him upon a visit, when he was making ready to come to the service. They wished God to help me in this important work I had commenced.

This must have been an encouragement to Crowther, and shows that his tactful and no less faithful treatment of this Mohammedan had met with a measure of success. He was naturally deeply moved at the sight of the heathenism around. Even in Freetown, where the Gospel had been preached for so long, the people in many cases were still in the dense darkness of paganism. He tells us himself:

A great portion of them are gross idolaters. My visits caused some stir among them. Generally they received me with great respect, and always acknowledged the worship of the only true God as superior to any other; but they cannot resolve to give up their gods, whom they believe were created by the great God for the good of mankind, and ought therefore to be worshipped. I told them that none of these things are true, but are the devices of Satan to keep man from God and in darkness and superstition.

Feb. 23. This day (Friday) is sacred to Shango, the god of thunder and lightning. At seven o'clock this morning I visited a party of the worshippers of Shango, when I was received rather to be thundered upon than to be listened to. On my entering the yard I found the drummers sitting opposite the representation of Shango, which was placed in a conspicuous part of the house. The seat of Shango was a bank of earth, raised a few inches above the ground in a semi-circular form, about two or three feet from the centre to the circumference. The banks of earth were streaked with two broad bands of red clay and white chalk. Within the other circle was another smaller one, in which was placed a wooden mortar bedaubed with blood, and on the top was a large calabash, washed with white chalk and covered up. By the side of this were placed many smaller calabashes, country pots, bottles, etc., and a club with which the thunder does execution, completed the whole. Every Shango worshipper has his house thus furnished. They commence their worship on Thursday night, and drum and dance till Friday morning. Occasionally they offer a ram—an animal particularly dedicated to the god. On entering the yard I asked for the master of the house, when one of the drummers presented himself to me. I was offered a seat in the house, and no further notice seemed to be taken of me. Some were busy and in great bustle, while others were drowsy. I called to the pretended master of the house, saying that I wished to speak to him, when he told me to wait a little and he would come. My coming had thrown them into confusion. At last a person came to me, fell on his knees trembling, and said that he was master of the house, and he hoped there was no matter why I came. Kneeling is a mark of great respect among the Yorubas. I told him not to kneel, but to sit down ; that I had come to say something important to him and his friends, but no harm ; and that I wished him to call them all in. As they were coming the head drummer, who seemed to be deeply sunk in superstition and debauchery, made use of most indecent language.

Having entered and taken their seats, I drew their attention to the character of their worship from the lewd expression which had been shamelessly uttered in my hearing. This was sufficient to inflame the whole assembly. The man rose up with wrath and indignation at my rebuke, and with eyes vivid as lightning spoke like thunder. He instantly referred me to nominal Christians, who he said were the greatest adulterers that could be met with in the Colony, and that he himself was formerly one of the churchgoers, but found no benefit from his connection with the religion of the Bible. To my great mortification, shame, and regret I was silenced—the charge was too true.

This is the effect of the inconsistent lives of nominal Christians, and occasion is thus given to this people to speak reproachfully. I asked only for a few minutes' silence just to say a few words to the owner of the house, but even this was hardly granted. However, as he was inclined to hear me, I turned and spoke to him. No sooner did they perceive that he was yielding than they pulled him in every direction to draw him away from me, but he did not go, and I continued speaking to him. When they could bear this no longer they brought their drums and, sitting on the bank where Shango was placed, commenced drumming to drown my voice and cried out in honour of their god. This I did not mind. Finding that I was making impression upon the man, they left their drums and actually dragged him away. They asked whether my forefathers were not idolaters, even to the thirtieth generation, whether I was not born and preserved through their gods, and said if my forefathers had gone to hell I must go there also.

The only weapons I used on this occasion were patience and an even temper, which the Lord has pleased to grant me. I was calm and steady without any notion of anger or indignation ; all my expressions went to show that I sought their welfare. When I had obtained a few moments' silence I affectionately addressed myself to the head drummer, and then left the house, promising to call at another time when they were more sober. When I had got into the street two of them ran after me to express their wonder at the command I had had over myself all the time I was insulted, and that, instead of revenging, I had spoken kindly to them. I told them it was the religion of Christ only which could make the temper of man sweet and amiable.

Feb. 25. According to promise, I repeated my visit to the house of the Shango worshippers in Circular Road. Unfortunately the master of the house was absent. However, I took the opportunity of speaking to his wife, two other women, and a man, who were present, of the folly of worshipping thunder and lightning. To speak of the principles of electricity is to speak of a new god. I, however, explained the subject to them as well as I could. A small electrical machine would be very useful to this colony and in our Abeokuta Mission towards opening the understanding and enlarging the minds of this superstitious people. The exhibition of experiments by such an instrument would, I think, go to abate the fears of the people, if not do away with the worship of this god of terror, especially if a few of the worshippers were to be electrified. The votaries of this god are obliged to go out, whether at day or night, when it rains, lightens, or thunders, however awfully, and run about the streets crying out in praise of their god to appease his anger. If any person, or his house or property, should be struck by lightning, they believe it is because he has sworn falsely by Shango, who revenges it.

As Crowther was now about to start on his first missionary tour, it is necessary to glance at that page of Yoruba history which covers the score of years and more since he was captured as a slave.

The devastating raids of the Foulah or Fellatah tribes had depopulated vast areas of the country, and Crowther's town of Oshôgún had been rebuilt and again destroyed, and it is difficult now to identify the site of the place associated with his happy childhood's days. The Yoruban king was now an exile, his capital was in the hands of the enemy, and he retreated to the town of Aggo-oj-a with diminished authority, for all the inferior chiefs had thrown off their allegiance to the fallen sovereign, each fighting for his own hand.

The scattered natives, running hither and thither to escape the slave hunters, at last found a place of refuge in a huge heap of stones, on a hill near the river Ogūn, in the south-western district of their country. It was a primitive fortress, for its huge porphyrite rock called Olumo had provided a hiding-place for a band of robbers. The large rounded stones formed a considerable cavern at the base, and here in 1825 a few poor frightened fellow-countrymen of Crowther's, finding the robbers departed, were glad to take up their abode. Others joined them, sharing their hardships as well as their safety, for they dare not show themselves, living for a time on the leaves of the pepper plant and the carcass of any animal which might come within reach. Little by little they grew more brave; one would steal down to the nearest village and buy a little seed corn, and in time tiny patches of growing crops appeared at the foot of the boulders of Olumo. Other stragglers found this refuge, the remnant of at least one hundred and thirty towns which had been destroyed by the slave raiders, and in the course of a few years a large community, comprising a number of tribes and clans, each with its own war captain, judge, and code of laws, in many cases naming their little village, fondly, after the town of their better days now destroyed. Prosperity waited upon security, and soon they gave their new dwelling-place the name of Abeokuta, i.e. Under the Stone. These people belonged to the Egba tribe of the Yorubans, and were all under the government of a brave and enlightened chief named Shodoké, who arranged for each town to have its civil governors or mayors called *Ogbonis*, and war chiefs or generals, called *Balaguns*. Then they had a sort of general council or parliament, of all these at Aké under the personal leadership of Shodoké. This unity of interests gave great strength to the new settlement, and they were able to defend themselves successfully against several serious attacks from their enemies.

As might be expected, news was brought them from the coast of the settlement of liberated Africans at Sierra Leone, of English ships with big guns cruising on the sea off the coast and capturing slave vessels, and that at this place, under the British flag, many of their own tribe were living. On both sides there arose fervent longings to meet again, and to those in Sierra Leone it seemed as though the Promised Land of a restored nation was before them at Abeokuta. They determined to start trade relations with the Yoruban settlement, and in 1839 they bought an old slave ship from the Government, and set sail, laden with goods, for Badagry, the nearest port to their destination. Other spirited adventurers landed at Lagos, at the mouth of the Ogūn, which, however, was the Popos' land, and these only welcomed the emigrants with their goods for what they could get out of them, and sent their hapless visitors into the interior without food or guidance to perish by the way.

Those who settled at Badagry fared better; the town was already in part occupied by Yorubans, and their chief, Wa Wa, was friendly and willing to help the newcomers. The great exodus of the Egba tribe to Abeokuta soon began in real earnest, and their return had many touching incidents. After their arrival at Badagry they would travel for many miles through a flat alluvial country, here and there swampy or covered with thick jungle. Then they would reach the undulating region bright with flowers and shaded with groves of palm trees, along which the clear shining stream of some river would invite them to rest and refresh themselves. But the pilgrims would also see the blackened ruins of the towns which the enemy had destroyed; in one day's journey they passed no less than twenty of these sad scenes of wanton destruction. And now as they approached Abeokuta they would notice signs of cultivation and industry, farms with poultry, and men busy everywhere and happy. Then following the noble river Ogūn along its beautiful banks of luxuriant foliage they caught sight of to them the glorious city for the first time. They raised their hands and greeted the city with shouts of joy. Soon they had passed its gates and were eagerly inquiring for their relatives and friends; they clasped each other with kisses of recognition, and each had a wonderful story to tell of suffering and escape to the sheltering rock of Olumo, of the kindness of the English at Sierra Leone, and the strange marvels of civilization there. And amongst other things the visitors were not slow to tell of the missionaries who had taught them out of the book of God, and preached how Jesus Christ came to seek and to save those that were lost.

To the minds of the missionaries at Sierra Leone this wholesale exodus of their people suggested some grave fears. Withdrawn from the guidance and restraints of Christian life, these natives might possibly relapse again into the dark practices of heathenism, and, in spite of promises to continue in the good way, it was felt that the new situation was fraught with danger. Indeed, many of those going away shared

CAVES OF OLUMO ROCK, ABEOKUTA

To face page 84

this feeling too, and a petition was sent to the Church Missionary Society in London, asking for spiritual leaders to accompany them. As a result of this Mr. Henry Townsend, a very promising young missionary, was dispatched on a visit of inquiry to Abeokuta. He had an eventful journey, not without many hardships and difficulties, meeting happily with the Rev. T. B. Freeman, with whom he took helpful counsel. But at every step of the way he found many opportunities of preaching the Gospel. At one place where they had stopped for the night, and he had held an evening service, with his party from Sierra Leone, a large crowd of natives gathered and listened attentively. Mr. Townsend in his journal tells us:

> I said, "Do you know the true God who made us all and preserves us day by day?"
>
> "No; but we heard about ten years ago that white men knew Him, and we have wished they would come and teach us."
>
> "Do you want to know Him?"
>
> "Yes."
>
> "Then you must ask God to send you teachers, and He will send them to teach and lead you in the right way of God."
>
> They arose, and lifting up their hands said, "O God, send us teachers to teach us about Thee."

On reaching Abeokuta at last, Townsend was received with great kindness and welcomed by the chief, Shodoké, who allowed him to hold services in his palace yard, and promised that if a number of missionaries were sent he would give them places of worship and his full support. Townsend returned to Sierra Leone and came to England in 1843, where he was ordained by Bishop Blomfield and sent again to establish a mission at Abeokuta.

This proposal created great interest in Sierra Leone ; offers of help in money and men flowed in from all sides. Mr. Fergusson, the Governor of the Colony, was fully in sympathy with the undertaking, and invited Townsend and his fellow-missionaries to breakfast with him on the morning when the expedition was to start. All the missionaries within reach gathered to say good-bye ; they sang :

Guide me, O Thou Great Jehovah,

and Mr. Schön, with many memories of the Niger expedition, committed them to the safe keeping of God in prayer.

The missionary party embarking was a large one—two Europeans—the Rev. C. A. and Mrs. Gollmer and the Rev. Henry and Mrs. Townsend—also the Rev. Samuel and Mrs. Crowther, with their two little children; Mr. Marsh, a catechist, with his wife and two children; Mr. Phillips, a schoolmaster; Mr. Mark Willoughby, the interpreter, with his wife and three children; four carpenters, three labourers, and two native servants. They sailed on 18 December, 1844, spent Christmas Day at Monrovia, and reached Badagry on 17 January, 1845.

On landing, where they were very kindly entertained by the Rev. W. Annear, the resident Wesleyan missionary, they received the disappointing news that Shodoké, the friendly chief of Abeokuta, was dead. They had built so many great expectations on the promises of this strong and wise leader, and although messengers arrived soon afterwards with welcoming words from the chiefs at Abeokuta, they were warned against going, especially as the roads were infested with robbers. They had, therefore, no alternative but to stay in Badagry for a time until the way was opened to take the journey to Abeokuta. Their present position, indeed, offered plenty of opportunity for mission work. The natives were Popos of the Dahomian type, steeped in degrading and cruel superstition, and in addition utterly demoralized by the vile rum which the slave ships had been in the habit of supplying in exchange for the captives. Human sacrifices were common, and it was no strange thing for some poor woman, suspected of witchcraft, to be dragged through the streets by her feet until death terminated her sufferings, and her body was thrown into the fetish grave. Just after the party had arrived Kosoko, the nephew of the King of Lagos, had conspired against him, and fled to Badagry, while this man, a cruel and merciless slave dealer, who was responsible for many massacres, tried to gain possession of the town, and threatened Abeokuta. But these troubles did not affect the purpose and conviction of these brave missionaries in their work. They were prepared for suffering in their Master's cause, and they had been in the place scarcely three months when Mrs. Gollmer passed away suddenly, and they laid her body to rest with much solemnity and mourning.

Crowther writes thus about this sad event :

This is the first Christian funeral that has ever been publicly performed in this country. Many of the natives out of curiosity accompanied us to the church and to the burial ground, to witness the burial of a Christian. Though our dear sister is dead, yet she speaks to the natives around, and shows the difference between the death of a saint and the death of a heathen. The scene of this day will not soon wear away from the minds of those who were present—about 150 persons. The chiefs having been informed of our mournful bereavement, sent their messengers to express their sympathy with us. Although no worshippers of the great God who made all things, yet they invariably ascribed this afflictive visitation to the providence of God, who knew and ordered all the events of life in His secret wisdom. Truly, although they knew Him as God, " they glorify Him not as God," but become vain in their imaginations, and their foolish heart is darkened.

Mr. Townsend took the opportunity of acquiring more perfectly the Yoruban language, while Crowther and the bereaved Gollmer visited the people, and from time to time preached the Gospel under the shade of an ancient tree, between the two busy markets. On 9 March they opened their first little church on this very spot.

Crowther, in his journals, makes some interesting notes of a visit to the chief Ogubonna's house:

At the entrance to the square we met him sitting on a mat spread on the ground, a fine stout, tall, clean, and noble-looking man, and his pet daughter, really her father's image, about ten years old, but quite naked, sitting close beside him. He soon obtained a chair and two empty powder kegs for our seats. As the drums continued beating and the horns blowing, the noise was so great that we could scarcely hear ourselves. Many of the chiefs came, and were introduced to us by Ogubonna. As the noise was still very great he conducted us to the square and into his room, where he lodged us. Here we were glad to rest awhile and to be quiet from the noisy multitude. He asked whether we had brought our house (tent) with us ; we answered in the negative on account of our haste in leaving Badagry. Ogubonna not being accustomed to provide for white men, was at a loss what to do on this occasion, but we soon made him easy by ordering one of our men to assist in boiling a fowl and some yams for our dinner and supper. Before supper was ready we passed the time in conversation, lying on a leopard skin, which was sometimes used for a chair and at other times for a sofa, as we wished to change our position. Supper being ready, after a blessing had been asked, every one took his plate on his lap or placed it on the leopard skin, as it suited him best. We asked Ogubonna to partake with us, but he declined because he did not know how to eat as white men eat. We took some tea without milk and asked Ogubonna to take a cup, to which he consented. To make it agreeable to his taste Mr. Gollmer sweetened it well with sugar, and the chief seemed to enjoy it very much.

When it was about nine o'clock we expressed our wish to have family prayer, and said we should be glad if he and his household would join us. He instantly ordered all in the square to assemble, when I read Acts xvii. 16–31, and expounded it to them and prayed in their native tongue. After prayers we told him that it was our custom to read a portion of Scripture every morning and evening and to pray to God with our people, and that not only had I been taught in the white man's country thus to read the Word of God, but many also of our country people in Sierra Leone. To prove this Mr. Thomas Puddicomb, a liberated African of the Yoruba nation, who is our head carpenter, and Mr. Mark Willoughby, Mr. Gollmer's interpreter, were each requested to read a portion of Scripture and to translate it to the chief, and Mr. Willoughby read the miracle of the widow's son at Nain, which they both translated to the astonishment of Ogubonna. Mr. Willoughby was liberated at the same time with me, and Mr. Puddicomb at the same time with my wife. We were all taught to read the Word of God at Bathurst school, superintended at that time by Mrs. Weeks.

It was very remarkable that these natives who were giving evidence and witness in the presence of this chief should all have been as boys together at the same school after their liberation. The services under the umbrella tree, to which reference has already been made, were a great success, and the formation of a Sunday-school of forty children, the first ever seen in Badagry, became a very popular feature of their work. Crowther had always a tender place in his heart for the children, and could hold their attention and touch them as few were able. One is not surprised, therefore, that he mentions them in his account of such a service on 13 April:

> I preached to a congregation of sixty-three adults and forty children. The children seemed to be peculiarly delighted with the service, and were heard distinctly joining in the Confession, the Lord's Prayer, the Creed, and the Responses to the Ten Commandments in the Yoruba language. Last Lord's Day I sighed that we could not as yet get any of these children to school, but to-day I brought with me a few letters of the alphabet, thinking they might amuse them and that thus they could at the same time be initiated, though but slowly, into the mystery of speaking their own language out of books, as they see me do every Lord's Day. The simple-hearted children were quite pleased with this new art, and soon blocked me up in their midst to see me point to the moon-like O and the serpent-like S. Although the men and women were at liberty to go away after service, yet they remained to see these wonderful letters. When I was about to return home some of the poor children fell on their faces to thank me for teaching them the White Man's Book. This mode of showing respect I hope hereafter to alter to the more convenient English custom.

After several months' stay in Badagry, Crowther had made great progress in his translation of the Scriptures in the Yoruba tongue, and had also translated the Liturgy, so that the congregation could now join intelligently in the service. This work was of permanent value to the mission, and with the new accomplishment of learning to read, the natives were filled with delight. Especially were they struck with the prayers in the service;

they evidently were able to appreciate, as all must do, the comprehensive scope of these petitions. "Ha! ha! ha!" exclaimed the chief. "So they pray to Olorun (God) for everything, for all people, for their enemies even—we never heard of the like before."

Crowther always had the deepest affection for the Liturgy of his Church, and it will not be out of place to quote here a few words from his journal, relating an incident which illustrates this:

> When I was spending a few days with a pious officer in the army at Woolwich in 1843 I came in contact with a gentleman of the Plymouth Brethren, who used all the arguments he could to get me into his persuasion. When he found that he could not succeed, he gave me this one solemn advice—not to make use of the Liturgy among my country people. In reply I begged him to consider for a moment the propriety of the conduct of a son who has been cared for, nursed up, and taught to pray upon the lap by his kind mother from his infancy, till he attained the years of discretion, and then because the prayers of his mother did not suit his fancy to kick against them. How ungrateful! I have considered the Church as my mother, which has taught me to pray, as it were, upon her lap by the Prayer Book, when I knew not how to utter a word. After having been thus taught to express my wants, shall I now kick against it?
>
> My attachment to the use of the Liturgy has not in the least abated since that time, but, on the contrary, since I have been sifting various portions in translating them into my native tongue, I have found its beauty sparkles brighter and brighter; it is scriptural in its language, and very well adapted for public service, and I can find no substitute for my countrymen.

Their progress to Abeokuta, so long retarded, was providentially expedited by the interposition of an enemy. Domingo, a notorious slave dealer of Porto-novo, had sent presents to Sagbua at Abeokuta, promising to clear the roads of robbers if he would allow a traffic in slaves to be established; but the missionaries at Badagry had managed to send with this embassy a private appeal to Sagbua, saying how urgently they wished to come to his city and commence missionary work among his people. Ignorant of this, Domingo had taken the precaution to give a scandalous report of the missionaries, knowing full well that if Christianity became strong in Abeokuta, his slave trade would suffer. When the messengers arrived and had given Domingo's account, Sagbua soon showed them that he was not going to be so easily deceived.

"We can ourselves," said he, "tell who are our best friends—those who rescue our children from captivity and send them freely to us again, or those who bring goods to purchase them for perpetual slavery and misery. The English are our friends, and you people at Badagry take care, for if any wrong is done to them in your town, you must answer to us for it." So, far from his intention, this slave owner opened the way for the progress of Christianity, instead of his inhuman traffic. They started on 27 July, 1846, in the rainy season, but, fearing that any delay might give Domingo a chance of blocking the way after all, they resolved to push forward. It proved to be a terrible journey of misfortunes and difficulty. Nothing but the indomitable pluck and faith of these devoted men and women could have survived such a struggle with the opposing elements. Crowther wrote in a letter to a fellow-missionary at Sierra Leone after their arrival at Abeokuta, in which he tells something of their woeful plight on this march through jungle and rain. It is dated 12 November:

The first day we travelled about twenty-five miles, with an escort of twenty-five men from Badagry to accompany us till we had passed the most dangerous part of our journey. Being pelted by rain all day, we were glad to rest ourselves in our tent, which we pitched, after we had cleared away the bush, in the middle of a large forest on the bank of a stream, which we had to cross in a bathing-tub the next morning, because it was unsafe to carry anyone across the stream. The tub was brought with us all the way to Badagry, that this stream might not be an obstacle to prevent our proceeding to Abeokuta.

The next morning we crossed the stream with safety in our bathing vessel, navigated by two men as they waded to the middle in the water, the bottom of which was full of roots of trees which grow in it. Our second day's journey was still more difficult than the first, because the road was so badly cut by rain that our horses could scarcely go on, and there was no way to turn on either side, which was high, bushy, and slippery. There were also many trees which fell across the path, around which travellers must go if it cannot be crossed, in doing which our horses and carriers found it very wearisome. Mrs. Crowther was nearly thrown down by her carriers, because they could not keep on their feet on account of the slipperiness of the path; she had to walk nearly all the way to Abeokuta, which completely knocked her up. Our children, Juliana and Dandeson, were carried on the back according to African fashion; there was not much trouble on their part, but the poor little children did not like travelling in the dark forest, besides which they were beaten by rain, the path even not admitting the use of an umbrella. When we halted in the forest the second day we were obliged to catch rain-water for our use, there being no water near where we could pass the night with safety.

A few days later they were gladdened to meet some messengers from the chiefs to welcome them to the town, which they reached at last in pouring rain, wet to the skin, but compelled by their enthusiastic friends to go all round the town to see the sights before being introduced to Sagbua, the King or principal chief. The day previously had been occupied by a long discussion among the chiefs who should have the honour of receiving the English visitors, and the town-crier, a wild-looking person in striped garments of bright colours, with a head-dress of monkey skin, a bell in one hand and a suspicious-looking axe in the other, warned all and sundry of the consequences of interfering with the safety and comfort of Sagbua's guests.

When the missionaries were in due time introduced to this great man Sagbua, they presented him with a large mirror, which had miraculously survived this travelling, but he, with rare tact, made it over to the Town Hall or Council Room, where it might excite the envy, but not the jealousy, of the chiefs. A public meeting was summoned, and Crowther gave a speech in Yoruba, describing the events which had led to their coming, and what the purposes of the mission would be. Contributions were not wanting towards the new premises required for the work, everybody gave at least one thousand cowries, equal to two shillings and sixpence English (which would have broken the record in any missionary meeting in the white man's land), and Sagbua, with a chairman's generosity, gave 20,000 cowries and a sheep into the bargain. Crowther shrewdly remarks that this copious collection did not strike him after all as so remarkable. "No wonder; some of the chiefs had liberated relatives of their own, sitting by them at the very time."

A piece of land having been allotted, the missionaries began to enlist their friends in the task of building a house for the Lord. Women fetched the clay with which to make the walls, and to these helpers they gave threepence each. The labour difficulty with them was, however, just the reverse of its common complaint in the white man's land. So many offers of assistance came that they reduced the pay to twopence, but nearly four hundred applied. To thin their ranks the rate was again reduced to one penny, when six hundred and seventy offered, and even then a huge crowd of willing but unemployed stood all day lost in admiration at the way the women worked, exclaiming, "God is great, white men have sense." The result of all this industry was a quite respectable church with glass windows, smooth boards for flooring, and generally, considering it was native handiwork, good workmanlike finish.

During this visit to Abeokuta Crowther had received intelligence that his mother was still alive with his sisters at the neighbouring town of Abake. He therefore lost no time in sending for them, and the news seemed so incredible that the sisters would not act on it. But the old mother's heart had more faith, and in the company of one of Crowther's half-brothers she started for Abeokuta. The meeting, so sacred and wonderful, must not be described in any words but those of Crowther himself:

The text for to-day in the Christian Almanac is "Thou art the Helper of the fatherless." I have never felt the force of this text more than I did this day, as I have to relate that my mother, from whom I was torn away about five-and-twenty years ago, came with my brother in quest of me. When she saw me she trembled. She could not believe her own eyes. We grasped one another, looking at one another in silence and great astonishment, while the big tears rolled down her emaciated cheeks. She trembled as she held me by the hand and called me by the familiar names which I well remember I used to be called by my grandmother, who has since died in slavery. We could not say much, but sat still, casting many an affectionate look towards each other, a look which violence and oppression had long checked, an affection which twenty-five years had not extinguished. My two sisters, who were captured with me, and their children are all residing with my mother. I cannot describe my feelings. I had given up all hope, and now, after a separation of twenty-five years, without any plan or device of mine, we were brought together again.

The story she had to tell her son was full of very sorrowful remembrance. After he had been taken to the coast she and her daughters regained their liberty, and went to live with the half-brother, who had redeemed them. They could hear nothing of the lost Adjai. The sisters married, and after a time of peace and safety, one day when the mother and her eldest daughter were going to market, they were kidnapped, and the daughter had to be ransomed by her husband. But the poor old mother was dragged from place to place, exposed for sale in the market place, and being so aged was made a domestic slave. She was sent by her mistress to Abeokuta, and, again captured on the road, sold into hard and bitter bondage, until her daughter collected cowries sufficient and bought her back for £4 10s.

There is something inexpressibly touching in this reunion between mother and son, and also that she should become his first convert in Abeokuta. She, of course, accepted his filial offer to come and stay with him, but he was pained at heart often to see how she was still without knowledge of the true God and in heathen darkness of soul. This happy event of meeting her son once more she attributed to the influence of his deceased father in the unseen world. But one bright day she accepted Christ as her Saviour, and was able to mingle her weak and quavering voice with the prayers of her son. Her change of heart was in part due to an illness, and it was an abounding joy to Crowther when she quietly told him, "Had I been left alone I should have attributed my sickness to this or that deity, and should have made sacrifices accordingly; but now I have seen the folly of so doing, all my hopes are in the Lord Jesus Christ, whom now I serve."

She was baptized with the appropriate Christian name of Hannah by her son Samuel on 5 February, 1848, and lived to be over a hundred years old.

The work at Abeokuta made so much progress that Crowther, in a letter home, dated 3 August, 1849, wrote:

> This mission is to-day three years old. What has God wrought in that short period! We have 500 constant attendants on the means of grace, 80 Communicants, and 200 candidates for baptism.

Mr. Townsend had to return home on account of his wife's ill-health, and the Rev. J. C. Muller and Crowther were joined in May by the Rev. D. Hinderer, a most valuable helper. At this time Crowther and his family had made their home at Abeokuta, the children still young in years. An interesting incident, with its personal touch, then occurred. The mission had already attracted much attention in England, and a little girl in the West of England made some childish sacrifices in order to send a few picture books for Crowther's little ones in their African home. This youthful helper of the missionary cause is an old lady now, but she has preserved as a precious memento the letter from Crowther's daughter Julianna, written by her father's hand, but evidently at the dictation of his tiny girl. It is dated from Abeokuta, 11 June, 1849, and gives us a peep into the home life of the Crowthers at this time:

My dear Ellen,—My papa read your kind letter to me and Dandeson, and gave us the little books which you denied yourself the pleasure of sweet sugar plums in order to purchase for us. We like them very much, and as we cannot understand all that they contain yet, our papa has kept them in good order for us till we can read them through and understand all in them. He carefully put them up in envelopes, but we like now and then to look at them and return them to him for safe keeping. I remember the time very well when we were crossing the river on the backs of our carriers, but Dandeson, being much younger, almost forgets all about it; the journey of four days in the bush on the backs of men was very tiresome. I have seen the picture of our crossing that river, called Mojuba.

My papa has a great deal to do. As I myself cannot write a good letter yet, he has kindly done it for me. I am learning to write in copy-books which papa gave to me, and I hope by and by to be able to write myself, as my elder sister, who is now in England, can do. Miss Lanfear saw her. My mamma teaches me to sew and to mark on canvas, and I shall soon be able to master all my letters. I have some native school companions living with mamma; they knew not a letter when they first came, and did not know how to hold needles, but since mamma has taken pains with them they can now hem and make stitches, and they learn to read very fast in the school. Four of them have been baptized by papa at the earnest request of their parents.

I hope you will pray for us all that we may grow up good children and love the Lord Jesus Christ from our childhood.

My mamma desires her kind love to you and your kind aunt, who wrote your letter.

Dandeson is gone to bed, but I am sure he would also send his love to you. Our grandmamma is quite well; she has been baptized.

I remain,

Yours affectionately,

JULIANNA CROWTHER.

But news of the approach of a Dahomian army soon plunged the devoted city into wild excitement and dismay. Everybody, including the missionaries, knew that the miscreant who called himself the King of Dahomey had determined to utterly make an end of this Abeokuta, which stood so much in his way as a slave trader. At first it seemed as though they were helpless and at his mercy, and that the city built up with such patriotism and patience, and the mission work with its peaceful success, were to be wiped out amid a wholesale slaughter of the inhabitants. At the outset the Egbas failed to hold back the enemy at the ford, and retreating, waited on the walls to repel the assault. For a long time both sides exchanged musketry fire, much to the advantage of the defenders, who were partly under shelter, and then, after resisting many attacks, the Egbas made a sortie, and the Dahomian army turned tail and fled. Some of the famous Amazons were captured, but many of the enemy fell in battle. It was a glorious victory, and a merciful deliverance for Abeokuta, to the Egbas akin to the defeat of the Spanish Armada. On the day following Crowther picked his way over the battlefield, and was grieved to notice on the side of the enemy almost as many women slain as men.

This occurred in March, 1851, and soon afterwards Crowther came on his third visit to England, reaching London on 13 August of that year. Before going, however, he had the opportunity of explaining to the chiefs and people a very gracious message which had arrived from the Queen of England. This was in answer to a letter which they, on their own initiative, had addressed to her, and sent by the hand of Mr. Townsend. In it they spoke with gratitude of the missionaries. "We have seen your servants the missionaries, whom you have sent to us in this country. What they have done is agreeable to us. They have built a house of God. They have taught the people the Word of God, and our children besides. We begin to understand them." But the burden of their letter was the sorrows of slavery, and to implore the good white Queen to deal summarily with the people on the coast at Lagos who still thrived on the traffic in flesh and blood. The gracious reply of Her Majesty, sent through the Earl of Chichester, was delivered at a great gathering of chiefs, and at the same time Sagbua was presented with some gifts which accompanied it, two beautifully bound Bibles and a steel corn mill from Prince Albert. Crowther translated the kindly letter in these words :

> The Queen and people of England (he explained) are very glad to hear that Sagbua and the chiefs think as they do upon the subject of commerce. But commerce alone will not make a nation great and happy like England. England has become great and happy by the knowledge of the true God and Jesus Christ. The Queen is therefore very glad to hear that Sagbua and the chiefs have so kindly received the missionaries, who carry with them the Word of God, and that so many of the people are willing to hear it.

The reading of this message created a profound impression upon the King and his great warriors as they sat in the outer court of the Council House at Ake. Crowther then proceeded to show them the two handsome Bibles which had been sent to them, and he took the opportunity of reminding Sagbua that in reading therein he would see that King David, Jehoshaphat, Hezekiah, and Josiah had prosperous and glorious reigns because they feared God, and led the people in His worship and service; on the other hand he pointed out that when Israel rejected God and turned to idolatry and sin, they were punished with severe judgments.

After this Crowther brought forward the wonderful steel mill which Prince Albert had sent for their use. The whole crowd watched with eager eyes full of curiosity, and when some Indian corn was put in, the handle turned, and fine flour poured forth, their delight knew no bounds. An incident a few days later showed that Sagbua, however impressed by the words of the missionaries and the message of the Queen, was still at heart a heathen. Crowther was talking to him when he solemnly asked whether he ought not to offer some sacrifice to the beautiful things which he had received. Astonished, Crowther asked, "What things? the corn mill or the Bibles?" "The Bibles," was the prompt reply. After reading from Scripture some passages about idolatry, it was explained to the chief how such an offering would be at variance with its teaching. Ogubonna, however, seems to have taken the matter much more to heart, for he spoke to Crowther of the deep impression the meeting had made on him, and gave it as his firm persuasion that in six years Christianity would become the national faith of Abeokuta.

During Crowther's brief stay in England he had an interview with Lord Palmerston, to explain to the Foreign Secretary the political position on the West Coast, and especially Abeokuta, and how that the King of Dahomey was not only an unscrupulous slave trader, but was injuring the interests of commerce and civilization on the coast. On 18 December, 1851, Lord Palmerston addressed a letter to Crowther, expressing his pleasure at having had this interview; he added:

> I am glad to have an opportunity of thanking you again for the important and interesting information with regard to Abeokuta which you communicated to me when I had the pleasure of seeing you at my house in August last. I request that you will assure your countrymen that Her Majesty's Government take a lively interest in the welfare of the Egba nation and of the community settled at Abeokuta, which town seems to be a centre from which the lights of Christianity and of civilization may be spread over the neighbouring countries.

It was an honour to receive this letter, but a still greater distinction was in store. One day Lord Wriothesley Russell asked Crowther to accompany him to Windsor, where he was very kindly received by the Prince Consort, who discussed with interest the position of affairs on the West Coast of Africa, following the story by reference to a large map. Presently a lady came into the room, and entered into the conversation, and it was only by a word dropped by Lord Russell that Crowther knew that he was in the presence of the Queen herself. For a moment he was quite overcome, but she soon put him at his ease again, and the gracious lady listened with deep interest as he spoke of the steadfastness of the native Christians in his country under such cruel persecution and trial. This interview with Her Majesty Crowther never forgot. Indeed, it was his practice, when his children were young, to relate to them this wonderful story of their father's life, and even wrote it out for them to read. This graphic and most interesting narrative has happily been preserved, and is here given, word for word, just as Crowther told it:

"Through the kind recommendation of the then Hon. Secretary of the C.M.S., the late Rev. Henry Venn, on the slave trade question agitating the minds of the Members of Parliament at that time, on 18 November, 1851, at 4.30 p.m., Lord Wriothesley Russell kindly took me to the Palace at Windsor. On our arrival there Prince Albert was not in; the servants in waiting went about to seek him. While we were waiting in a drawing-room I could not help looking round at the magnificence of the room glittering with gold, the carpet, chairs, etc., all brilliant.

While in this state of mind the door was opened, and I saw a lady gorgeously dressed, with a long train, step gracefully in. I thought she was the Queen. I rose at once, and was ready to kneel and pay my obeisance; but she simply bowed to us, said not a word, took something from the mantelpiece, and retired. After she left Lord Russell told me that she was one of the Ladies-in-waiting. 'Well,' I said to myself, 'if a Lady-in-waiting is so superbly dressed, what will be that of the Queen herself!' Soon we were invited to an upper drawing-room, more richly furnished than the first. Here we met Prince Albert standing by a writing-table. Lord Russell made obeisance and introduced me, and I made obeisance. A few words of introductory remarks led to conversation about West Africa, and Abeokuta in particular. The Prince asked whether we could find the place on any map, or thereabouts. I then showed the position in the large map from the Blue Book, and brought out from my pocket the small one which Samuel [his eldest son] had made on the section of the slave trade influence, with the different towns and seaports legibly shown. About this time a lady came in, simply dressed, and the Prince looking behind him, introduced her to Lord Russell, but in so quick a way that I could not catch the sound. This lady and the Prince turned towards the map to find out Abeokuta and Sierra Leone, where the slaves are liberated. All this time I was in blissful ignorance of the Great Majesty before whom I stood, was conversing freely and answering every question put to me about the way slaves are entrapped in their homes, or caught as captives in war. On inquiry I gave them the history of how I was caught and sold, to which all of them listened with breathless attention. It was getting dark, a lamp was got, and the Prince was anxious to find and define the relative positions of the different places on the map, especially Lagos, which was the principal seaport from which Yoruba slaves were shipped; and when the Prince wanted to open the Blue Book map wider, it blew the lamp out altogether, and there was a burst of laughter from the Prince, the lady, and Lord Russell. The Prince then said, 'Will your Majesty kindly bring us a candle from the mantelpiece?' On hearing this I became aware of the person before whom I was all the time. I trembled from head to foot, and could not open my mouth to answer the questions that followed.

"Lord Russell and the Prince told me not to be frightened, and the smiles on the face of the good Queen assured me that she was not angry at the liberty I took in speaking so freely before her, and so my fears subsided. I pointed out Lagos, the particular object of inquiry, and told them that I with others were shipped from that place, and showed the facility which that port has, beyond all the other ports, as a depot, being much nearer, and the port of the highway to the interior Yoruba countries. The Prince said: 'Lagos must be knocked down, by all means; as long as they have the lake (lagoon) to screen themselves, and the men-of-war outside, it is of no use.'

"The Queen was highly pleased to hear this. Lord Russell then mentioned my translations into the Yoruba language, and I repeated, by request, the Lord's Prayer in the Yoruba, which the Queen said was a soft and melodious language. Lord Russell informed the Queen of my having seen Sir H. Leeke, who rescued me and others from the slave ship many years ago, which interested her very much. She was told that Mrs. Crowther was recaptured in the same way that I was, and she asked whether she was in England, and was told no. She asked after Sally Forbes Bonetta, the Yoruba African young girl rescued from Dahomey. After these questions she withdrew with a marked farewell gesture."

Before he returned to his native land Crowther addressed a large audience composed of the students of the University of Cambridge, and appealed to them with touching earnestness for missionaries, who would preach the Gospel to his people on the West Coast of Africa. His closing words were:

> St. Paul saw in a vision a man of Macedonia, who prayed him to come over to his assistance. But it is no vision that you see now; it is a real man of Africa that stands before you, and on behalf of his countrymen invites you to come over into Africa and help us.

On 5 December, 1851, the old parochial schoolroom in Church Street, Islington, was the scene of a very interesting gathering, to which Crowther and his wife, with another missionary, said good-bye on their leaving for West Africa. The Earl of Chichester, the President of the Church Missionary Society, presided, and amongst many well-known friends of the cause was the Rev. Daniel Wilson, the excellent Vicar of Islington. The speeches were not many, chiefly the Rev. Henry Venn, clerical secretary, conveying the wishes of the committee; but the reply of Crowther, who with his wife attracted the greatest attention, sitting there with their bright eyes suffused with emotion, two black faces amid a concourse of white men, is happily preserved to us.

Presently the secretary arose, and thanked God for all that had been done since the Yoruba mission eight years ago, and how very merciful He had been in delivering Abeokuta from the hordes of the King of Dahomey. Then in earnest tones he gave many discreet cautions to the outgoing missionaries that they might be "harmless as doves" in the midst of the people. He congratulated Crowther upon his tactful dealing with the chiefs, and urged him to be careful in dealing with their enemies, the slave traders, the Mohammedans, the native priests, and the ignorant heathen. And then he turned to the future, and seemed to see already the dawn of those days of blessing which were to follow. He begged them to remember that the future character of the Christian Church in West Africa was at stake, and their policy and individual action would influence it. Their sphere of labour was very different from India or New Zealand, where other missionaries had been on the ground before; but here on the Niger they would have not only to spread Christianity, but fix its character, organize a native Church, create a Christian literature, and lay plans for days to come.

He asked them to aim at self-government and self-support, to put the Bible in the hands of the people, and said how much they were already indebted to Crowther for his translation into Yoruban of a great portion of the Holy Scripture and the Liturgy. They were recommended also to start an educational institution at Abeokuta for young men and young women. He then turned to Mrs. Crowther, and told her how heartily England welcomed her as the help-meet of her husband, and how important they all felt her position was as the first Christian mother in Abeokuta, and they rejoiced that her own children were also an example to others:

> May she return with a double blessing to her country-women! May she indeed be a mother to that spiritual Israel in the wilderness of Africa! And may the native Church, once confined to the house of Samuel Crowther, become a national Church, but still retaining its character as an aggregation of Christian households, bound together by one common tie of love and union with Christ, in whom all the families of the earth are blessed!

When Crowther arose to speak his heart was very full, and amid a deep and impressive silence he reminded the audience that eight years ago, in company with a great company of missionaries, he first received his commission with much fear and trembling. He feared because he had a doubt in his own mind whether it was possible to obtain an entrance into a country which the slave trade had rendered so difficult of access; but the promise of Him who said, "Lo, I am with you alway, even unto the end of the world," had been fulfilled. He drew attention to the importance of the time he had been able to use in translation, so that the Word of God, at any rate a part of it, was now in the hands of their converts, and they made it a topic of conversation in their homes and on their farms, and its influence had also been felt in the war camp. With a fervent optimism he spoke hopefully of his nation. They were an industrious people, anxious for trade and commerce. They were weary of the slave traffic and sighed to be relieved from it. This was their great enemy, and when this was removed there was nothing to disappoint the expectation that Christianity would extend rapidly to the Niger.

These native Christians (he said) are quite ready with a reason for the truth as it is in them, and can stand their ground bravely. When during the fierce days of persecution at Abeokuta they were required to renounce Christianity, they were enabled to reply: "You elder chiefs admitted the teachers without consulting us. When you did so, they told you what they were going to teach, and that they had no cloth, no tobacco to give. You gave them admission. Then why do you now hinder us from going to them? The Book and the religion which they teach we consider this as our share. When they came we had no part of the gifts which you received from them. When you promised them that they should have children to teach, we had no share of the presents. Now this instruction is our share."

These natives (pursued Crowther) are quite ready for employment in the cultivation of cotton in the country, of which I have hopes that a real trade will be one day established.

Brethren, believe me, these Christian natives of Abeokuta do not wish to keep the Gospel to themselves. Already they have promised that teachers should be sent to other towns; nor do they fail, wherever they go, to speak of what they know. I am going back to my own land with great hope in my heart, feeling much blessed and encouraged, and have only to ask that my many kind friends in England will continue to pray for me and for the salvation of my people.

At the close of this meeting many crowded round Crowther and his wife to wish them God-speed, and a few days afterwards they had set sail, and were once more on their way to their native land.

CHAPTER IV

UP THE NIGER AGAIN

WHEN Crowther arrived at Sierra Leone he was heartily welcomed by many old friends. In many respects it was a homecoming, for it was here that he first experienced the blessing of Christian love, and his young mind had begun to lay in store those firstfruits of knowledge for which it hungered. He was a boy then, and ran these streets barefoot with his slate and books; then as a young man he was student and afterwards tutor of the College on the head of Fourah Bay; here, too, he asked the schoolmistress at Bathurst to become his wife. What memories were awakened by these familiar scenes!

Although Abeokuta was his destination, he remained some time at Sierra Leone, and whenever he preached the churches were crowded to hear him. In some cases he spoke in English, but the people were always anxious to hear him in his own tongue, and afterwards he would often give them a little discourse in the Yoruba language to their pleasure and profit. In some cases where he would be preaching to the people in English, and there occurred any text of special difficulty, he would drop into his native tongue, so that he might more perfectly explain it to his countrymen. Before leaving Sierra Leone he attended a missionary meeting which was crowded with people, who listened with profound attention as he told the story of the work at Abeokuta, how the converts stood the fire of persecution, and what a grand future appeared to be in store for this famous city, the rallying-point of his scattered nation. Many who listened to this address recognized the names of places and people, and all were proud to think that one of their own nation should have been so honoured as to become a clergyman.

On 14 June he reached Lagos, and here again the site of a never-to-be-forgotten event awoke many thoughts. He was able to point out to Mrs. Crowther the very spot from which, in 1822, he had been forcibly shipped as a slave boy. He remembered so well his trembling at the unaccustomed sight of so much water, and his simple and unfounded fears when on the safe deck of the English ship of war. Walking over the old places again, he stopped to take off his hat and reverently thank God on the very bit of shore where he with others was chained to the slave hut. In after years he often said, "What hath God wrought!" but he felt his own personal history the greatest miracle of mercy. One of the reasons for his thankfulness at this time was the sight of so much change and improvement and civilization showing itself everywhere. Crowther was an ardent patriot, the love of country and tribe beat in his bosom, and he rejoiced that instead of degrading

MARKET PLACE, LAGOS

To face page 112

slavery on all hands were to be seen the peaceful pursuits of trade. He writes:

> I could well recollect many places I knew during my captivity, so I went over the spots where slave barracoons used to be. What a difference! Some of the spots are now converted into plantations of maize or cassava, and sheds built on others are filled with casks of palm oil and other merchandise, instead of slaves in chains and irons, in agony and despair.

When, in due course, Crowther reached Abeokuta, a large number of Christian natives came to welcome him, and the other missionaries there were equally glad to have him back again. He found the work going on apace, and during his next two or three years he was enabled to make progress with translating the early books of the New Testament. In the course of this labour he found many of the laws and customs of his own nation in harmony with those given to ancient Israel, and he noted that many Yoruba words were related to the Hebrew. These Yoruba countrymen of Crowther's were a wideawake and intelligent people in many respects. He relates an interview with one, upon whose attention he was urging the claims of Christianity:

> One man, an Ifá priest, spoke very sensibly. "Softly you must go with us," was his first answer, "or you will spoil the whole matter; stretch the bow too much and it will break. Remember how deeply we are rooted in heathenism. We cannot get out of it all at once." I thought, and said: "If you would even make a beginning at once on the 'new road,' as they call it, you would still leave us scope enough to exercise patience." His answer was: "Some time ago, in a conversation with your servants, I was, among other things, told that a man who serves God could no more steal, no more deceive, no more commit adultery. These words we have as

we remember, but our eyes are watching your hands also, to see what they do. Only have a little patience. After some time we shall see if the works of your hands agree with the words of your mouth; then we shall consider again if this new way will suit us also."

It will be remembered that the early history of the Crowther family was in past times associated with the Kingdom of Ketu, and on 5 January, 1853, we find him making a journey from Abeokuta on a visit thither. Here he had some striking experiences.

He tells us that on reaching the old town of Ilogun he heard that the white men crossed through there some years before; these he believed to be the travellers Clapperton and the Landers. Arriving at Ketu, he lodged with Asai, the Prime Minister, who gave him a warm welcome, shaking him by the hand, and saying: "Crowther, I have at last seen you face to face. I am very glad to see you." Next day he had an interview with the King in a large room, with holes, as in a pigeon house, perforated in the walls, through which his Majesty looked upon his people when they came to plead their wrongs. He was wearing an old pair of red carpet slippers, which had been sent by Crowther by the hand of Captain Trotter years before. Over his cotton patchwork gown he had draped himself with a piece of red damask, and on his regal brow he wore a crown studded with coral beads. Presently all his audience humbly prostrated themselves, crying, "Reverence, reverence." Crowther, however, preferred to remain standing on his feet and dignity, and then the King, after narrowly observing his visitor, his hand shading his eyes, said with cordiality:

"Crowther, friend, long known by mutual understanding only, here at last we see each other." He then politely spread a handkerchief for Crowther to sit on by his side, drew attention to his old slippers with graceful remembrance, saying: "This is your doing. I have heard of you for a long time, and had almost despaired of seeing you."

After a long talk about nothing particular, Crowther held his Bible in his hand and showed it to the inquisitive King, telling him that this was the book which God had sent down from heaven to mankind to teach us His mind and will, that this book had been received by hundreds of heathen, who are now walking according to its instruction and doctrine. Also how God had been pleased to send this book to this country, to him and his people, that he, Crowther, was a preacher of that word, and as he had now come on a visit, he proposed its reception by both King and people. The King was evidently really touched, and replied with quiet dignity: "Hitherto I have had no helper; now I have found one, I will hold it fast."

The next day being Sunday, Crowther read a few prayers and the Litany, and preached in the morning from St. Paul's sermon at Athens, and in the evening on the parable of the Prodigal Son. Next day the gratified monarch told him to walk round the town and select a spot for building mission premises. In exchange for these courtesies Crowther presented him with a beautiful silk patchwork quilt, made by a lady in England, and two silk and velvet caps decorated with feathers and flowers. The King of Ketu was simply captivated. For a time he could find no words, and when Crowther put on the quilt and exhibited its rainbow tints in the sunshine, his Majesty clapped his hands with delight:

"Ketu is entirely left open to you; do whatsoever you like in it, and bring whomever you think proper. We will receive them with both hands."

On leaving the town a number of natives came to Crowther and begged for more words about the subject of his preaching. He inquired what religion they professed in their country, and they said: "Heathenism and Mohammedanism, mostly heathenism."

> I told them I was a Christian. I showed them my Bible, and said this was the best of books, which God would have every nation to receive and hold. I asked whether the worshippers of thunder and lightning ever grumble with the worshippers of the god of palm nuts, whether the worshippers of their numberless gods do not live in peace with each other, though they worship different deities. They said: "Certainly they do not trouble each other, but each one worships what he thinks good for him."
>
> I then told them that when Christianity should be introduced into their country the same tolerance ought to be observed as in other countries.

On his return he found that for the present his work at Abeokuta was to be suspended, and he must take to exploring again.

Another expedition up the Niger had been arranged, thanks to the public spirit and enterprise of Mr. Macgregor Laird, who had been long identified with the commercial developments of Western Africa. It was proposed to send a single vessel up the river

Nun and the Niger to the Confluence, and then explore the Tshadda as far as possible. Dr. J. Baikie was invited to accompany it for the purpose of making fresh observations and notes of geographical value. Mr. Laird made an offer to the Church Missionary Society of a free passage for Crowther, which was gladly accepted. This voyage was, unlike the previous one, a complete success; the explorers were able to penetrate two hundred and fifty miles beyond the limit of any other explorations, and it was conspicuously fortunate in preserving a clean bill of health, returning without the loss of a single man. Of this very interesting journey Crowther kept again an admirable journal; his habit of indefatigable industry and careful observation of every important detail makes such a record bright and instructive reading. On this expedition he brought to bear the advantage of his later study and training. He had developed very much during these last ten years, and his visits to England had enriched his mind. These words of his are valuable in themselves as conveying information about the country and people which at that time was specially useful, but they have also a peculiar interest as revealing very much the practical turn of the writer's impression of things. They are absolutely devoid of that introspective faculty which is so common to many diarists; these deal with facts alone, describing in clear, vivid language incidents; we seem to see it all through Crowther's eyes, rather than being permitted to look down into Crowther's heart. And beneath and behind all these notes of things seen and heard, there is the true missionary spirit, watching for every opportunity of bringing the Gospel to these far and isolated regions where heathenism reigns supreme. It is easy to imagine the "good-byes" at the gates of Abeokuta, the journey down to Lagos, in which he tells us, with his practical instinct:

I took about seven hundredweight of clean cotton down with me to be shipped to Manchester.

Reaching Fernando Po he waited for the arrival of the *Pleiad*, the exploring vessel, and while staying on shore he makes a reference to one who, as British Consul and as an intrepid explorer, had been of great service to West Africa.

The people were very glad to see me, and expressed their regret for the loss of Mr. Beecroft, for he had made full preparation for the expedition and had engaged many intelligent natives who had been used to go up the Niger with him, and who were ready to go anywhere with him, they being mutually attached to each other, for he treated them as a father. It will be a long time before his place can be supplied by another who will take the same interest in the country and her people as he did.

After breakfast visited Mr. Beecroft's grave, which is on the point of the cliff of Clarence under a large cotton tree, where he himself had directed he should be buried. Thus ended the life of this useful person, after twenty-five years' stay in Africa, during which period he had won the affection of many who knew his worth in the countries he had visited, and could not but greatly regret to hear of his removal by death. The chiefs of Abeokuta had sent salutations and messages to him by me, which he did not live to receive. As long as this generation lasts the name of Mr. Beecroft will not be forgotten in this part of Africa.

The voyage began with a few mishaps, a breakdown in the machinery, a rather awkward crossing of the bar outside the Nun river, and a mistake in choosing the channel, through which they ran ashore on Sunday Island. Nobody on board, however, seems to have been the least disconcerted by these vicissitudes, and we found Crowther conducting Divine Service with all hands on deck, preaching from the text: "Then said they unto him, Who art thou? that we may give an answer to them that sent us. What sayest thou of thyself?" A number of canoes presently came alongside, asking significantly, "Are you slave ship or oil ship?" to which they were able to give a satisfactory reply. In a few hours they got away, and Crowther, watching the banks of the great river, began to make notes of the changes which had taken place since his last visit. There was little enough trace of the hand of civilization then.

Soon after we had cleared Sunday Island traces of cultivation began to appear, together with land about three feet above the water's edge. As the water has not yet risen to its full height, it gave an entirely new appearance to the river from that it bore in August, 1841. At that time only a few spots near the water's edge were under cultivation, and the whole was covered with water, as the river overflowed its banks. Not only old plantations showed a continual industry of the people of the Delta, but many newly-cleared spots in the midst of which numerous lofty palm trees stood, which were carefully preserved for their rich and valuable produce, showed further the improved state of the banks. About three hours from Sunday Island we came to inhabited villages; we induced two canoes to come off, from whom we learnt that the people between Brass and Aboh are called Uru. One of the people who came off, and who spoke the Ibo language, was so confident that he offered to go with us to Aboh; and the people on shore never showed the least sign of opposition, but folded their arms and gazed at the steamer as she glided on.

Fewer traces of cultivation were observed during the day till we came to the village of Angiama. Brass people came up here to buy palm oil, with large casks in their canoes, some of which they land as they proceed upwards. There is another striking change in the habits of the people themselves. In 1841 very few of them were to be found with any decent articles of clothing. I spied to-day, among a group of about forty people, fifteen who I could distinctly see had English shirts on. This is an evident mark of the advantage of legal trade over that of men. The chief of Angiama, or Anya, came off and expressed his regret that we did not wait at his village as Captain Trotter did, and it was with some difficulty we could satisfy him by our excuses, but we hoped to be able to stay on our return. Dr. Baikie gave him a red cap and a looking-glass ; but I could read in the countenance as well as by the temper one of his men manifested that if they had had it in their power they would have detained us in Oru, to reap all the benefits of the trade to themselves instead of allowing it to pass through their waters to the people of the interior beyond them.

At the commencement of the voyage Crowther made the suggestion, to which reference has already been made, that the fuel should be kept in attendant canoes, and not in the ship's hold, which, no doubt, saved the expedition from fever.

When they reached Aboh (formerly written as Ibo) they were sorry to hear that the old King Obi was dead. He had for years waited for the English vessels which never came, and now a weak son named Tshukŭma reigned in his stead. But they found the Aje, a younger and more energetic man, was the real governing power. He was absent when the *Pleiad* cast anchor, but we have a striking sketch of the weak and elder brother from Crowther's pen :

July 22. Took an early breakfast, and about eight a.m. we started for the town of Aboh, which lies about one mile in length along the western bank of the creek, very thickly populated. We landed close to Tshukŭma House, which is very small and confined, his old house having been lately burnt. He had been worshipping his god that morning, which we saw on his piazza in a calabash placed in front of the wall, covered with a white sheet. We waited about ten minutes before Tshukŭma made his appearance, dressed in a pair of thin Turkish trousers, a white shirt, a white waistcoat, and a string of coral beads about his neck; he is smaller in size and stature than Obi, his father, is very soft in his manners, and seems not possessed of much energy. He shook us all heartily by the hand, and in a short time the little square was crowded to excess, so that there was no room to move, and the place became so thronged that it was difficult to keep one's seat on the mat spread for our accommodation. Tshukŭma used all his efforts to command silence, but to no purpose. Obi's daughter and the chief's wives took their turn to command silence, but it only increased the noise. At last Tshukŭma requested us to frighten the people away, which, of course, we did not do. As it was impossible to obtain perfect silence, I suggested to Dr. Baikie to begin business, as we could manage to keep close enough to hear each other.

The substance of Mr. Baikie's interview with the chief was that the Queen had desired him to visit them and see how they did, that we were sorry to hear of Obi's death—we hoped his successor would be of the same mind as the late king—and that they still adhered to the treaty he had signed with Captain Trotter, who acted in the name of the Queen; and that trade was now come to the Aboh country, about which Dr. Hutchinson would speak fully with him.

Tshukŭma replied that he was very glad to see a large ship come to Aboh again, and that he and the other headmen were particularly charged by Obi before his death not to deviate from the path he had trod respecting his friendship with the white men, and that they would act accordingly; but as Ajé was absent from home in Igara with a great number of headmen, to settle some matter in that place, he expressed a wish that we should wait till he returned, as he expected them in three or four days' time, and he would send a slave to hasten their return. . . . I now thought it time to introduce the subject of a missionary establishment among them. I told him that we had come to see what we could do to make a missionary station at Aboh, as we had done in my country at Badagry, Lagos, and Abeokuta, and had been done also at Calabar and the Camaroons.

One of Obi's daughters replied that they could not conceive why white men should build houses in Bonny and Calabar, and not in Aboh.

I told them our superiors had been thinking of it a long time, but now they were in earnest, and we were very desirous of sending some Ibo teachers to Aboh, to reside there and teach them many things if they are willing to learn. Tshukŭma said my words were too good for them to hope that they will be realized, and that he would not believe anything until he had seen us do what we proposed; that there was no difficulty on their part, nor need we fear any unwillingness to receive those who may be sent to them or learn what they may be taught, but that the fault rests with us in not fulfilling what we had promised to do.

This interview shows how keen these people were for teaching, and how disappointed they felt because in times past the white man had not kept his word with them. In this case a little irritation existed in consequence of tribal jealousies and fightings among themselves; indeed the absence of the younger and more energetic brother from this palaver was due to settlement of a quarrel. But the tact of the white man did excellent service. A visit on board the ship by the chief, his wife, the head wife of Aje, and three of Obi's daughters, with luncheon in the saloon, had a wonderfully soothing effect, and after Dr. Baikie had given these sable dames some glittering presents, the whole party returned home highly gratified. The day following Crowther went ashore to pay a visit to the chief, to get an opportunity of talking to him on religious subjects, and introducing such Christian doctrine as might be profitable.

The quickness with which he caught my explanation of the all-sufficient sacrifice of Jesus Christ, the Son of God, for the sin of the world was gratifying. I endeavoured to illustrate it to him in this simple way. "What would you think of any persons who in broad daylight like this should light their lamps to assist the brilliant rays of the sun to enable them to see better?" He said: "It would be useless; they would be fools to do so." I replied: "Just so." That the sacrifice of Jesus Christ, the Son of God, was sufficient to take away our sins, just as one sun is sufficient to give light to the whole world; that the worship of country fashions and numerous sacrifices which shone like lamps, only on account of the darkness of their ignorance and superstition, though repeated again and again, yet cannot take away our sins; but that the sacrifice of Jesus Christ, once offered, alone can take away the sin of the world. He frequently repeated the names "Oparra Tshuku! Oparra Tshuku! Son of God! Son of God!"

As I did not wish to tire him out I left my discourse fresh in his mind. The attention of his attendants, with the exception of a few, was too much engaged in begging and receiving presents to listen to all I was talking about. I gave to Tshukŭma a Yoruba primer in which I wrote his name, and left some with Simon Jonas to teach the children or any who should feel disposed to learn the alphabet and words of two letters.

They were now approaching the Confluence, and Crowther records in his journal how on the right bank of the Niger, from opposite Adamugu, there is scarcely a village to be seen, while on the left-hand bank there are new and extensive towns, which had no existence on his previous visit in 1841. This is accounted for by the warlike raid of Dasaba, who had swept down with his warriors to avenge the death of Mr. Carr, the Atta of Mgara having urged him to punish the people of the Delta who had, without reason, killed a white man coming to establish trade with the upper country. About a hundred towns and villages were destroyed. As some of the exploring party wished to make sketches and observations from the top of Mount Patteh, they started from the ship early in the morning of 5 August in high spirits, and full of expectations.

Mr. May wished to sketch from that elevation of about twelve hundred feet the juncture of the Kowara and the Tshadda, but owing to the desolated state of the country the valley was so overgrown with wood and high grass as to be impenetrable, except where we came upon the track of elephants, now the undisturbed possessors of these once thickly populated districts. As we could not go on because of the thick grass and swamps, we returned to the boat and pulled further up till we came to a landing-place, where a small canoe was seen under the trees, belonging to a little village of eight or ten huts, a scanty remnant of the once secure villages of Mount Patteh. This village is built on the first cove, about a third part of the way up Mount Patteh, where very old persons only were living. We asked them the way to the Mount, but they told us there was no way thither at this time, as Dasaba had driven or carried all the inhabitants away. The sight of these villages was truly pitiable. They pointed to the site of the model farm below, which is now covered with trees and grass, and asked if we were coming to rebuild it. I told them it might be taken up again in due time. They entertained us according to their means, with country beer and clear, cool water, which they fetched from the side of Mount Patteh. We promised to give them some presents if any of them would come on board, and then we returned to the ship about 10 a.m.

Ama-Abokko, the chief, had come early on board, and Captain Taylor had been talking with him about trading affairs till our return. Dr. Baikie called him into the saloon and gave him some presents from Government, with which he was much pleased. We tried to get him to forward letters to the coast for us by way of Ilorin, Ijaye, Ibadan, and Abeokuta, but he made so many excuses that I saw he was evidently afraid to do it, though he did not like to say so, for fear of committing himself, because people might accuse him of sending a bad book or charm through Ilorin, as Dasaba, their common enemy, has taken refuge there, and he did not sufficiently know us or our footing on the coast. We reminded him of the person he promised to send with us, and told him also that we would pay some of his canoe men if he would let us have some, to which he consented and raised our expectation as to his readiness. Ama-Abokko styled himself the king of this part of the country, and I tried to ascertain whether he was independent of the Atta, but could receive no satisfactory reply to my question. I dare say he did not like to tell us. That we might see more of the town and collect information we went after lunch to Igbégbe, each one in a different direction except that Mr. Richards and myself walked together. Ivory was shown us, as well as trona (salt packed up in grass bags from the coast), horses, and two slaves. I offered to purchase one of the owners herself instead of the slaves, but she shuddered a little at the idea. I left her to infer from that the propriety of dealing in our fellow-men. Some slaves were in a canoe alongside the ship to-day. It is not to be wondered at that many slaves are to be seen about at this time, for many unfortunate persons who have suffered in the war between Dasaba and his brother, and such as have fallen a prey to the Filatas at the destruction of Panda, are now scattered about the country in all directions by their captors. Fortunately they must remain in the country, as there is no place known in the Bight of Biafra for exportation of slaves, the only foreign slave markets being Whydah and Porto Novo, in the Bight of Benin.

Sunday, August 6. Had service on board at half-past ten; preached from 2 Timothy i. 7 on the former part of the text, "God has not given us the spirit of fear," and applied it to individual members of Christ's Church; but I preached in much weakness. May the Spirit of God carry His Word home to the heart and conscience of those who heard it!

As regards Mr. Carr, already mentioned as having met with his death on the Niger, Crowther adds a footnote from Mr. Schön, that this Englishman was one of the expedition of 1841, and having been invalided at Fernando Po, he wished to return to the Confluence on his recovery. He set out in a canoe with some natives, but was never heard of again, and the probability is that he was murdered for the sake of plunder. Some articles of his clothing were afterwards found, and for a time suspicion rested upon the old chief Obi. Mr. Carr was originally intended to superintend the model farm at the Confluence, and while he remained there did good work.

At every point of their journey up the Tshadda inquiries were made of the natives whether they had seen a white man, Dr. Barth, about whom some sinister rumours were common in England that he had lost his life also. The quest of this eminent traveller, to whose valuable works on West Africa we are so much indebted, was one of the reasons for this expedition being promoted. At one time hopes were aroused by information that two white men were not far off in a town called Ksana, four days' journey north. Crowther and his party hurried forward, and met with a native of the place, who said that the white men had been there a month ago, and on being shown the portraits in the frontispiece of Petermann's Atlas of Central Africa, pointed to that of Dr. Barth and then to the picture of Vogel as his companion. This messenger was dispatched in hot haste with a letter in his hand to Dr. Barth, written by Dr. Baikie, and the greatest excitement was felt in expectation of his reply. This, however, never came. Whether the man was misinformed, or for the sake of possible gifts had misled the inquirers, never transpired. As a matter of fact, Dr. Barth was at this time at a considerable distance in the interior, and happily returned to Europe some time afterwards. Some characteristics of the native mind are revealed in the following extract, in which Crowther pictures the easygoing life on the Niger, the fear everywhere of being attacked either by gods or men, and also the innate love of those presents which count for so much in transactions with Europeans.

The wants of the people are so few that they are content to sit down the whole day smoking their pipes, instead of going to cut wood to sell, although they are very desirous of getting many things by begging.

Sunday, August 27. Had service at half-past ten as usual, and read the third part of the nineteenth Homily on Prayer. Having been informed that the people were running away from the village of Ojogo, we went on shore after service to ascertain the cause and quiet their fears. During two previous nights Dr. Baikie and Mr. May had been on shore to take lunar observations, and of course had lights with them. The bull's-eye lamp seems to have made them afraid. The chief was previously apprehensive of something when he saw Mr. May measuring the beach, and thought that he did this because the white man had it in mind to take his country from him. When we got on shore we desired an interview with him. His heart was throbbing with fear, but I tried to explain to him how, from ignorance of the depth of the river, our ship was grounded very near his village, where we remained a part of two days ; that Mr. May's measuring the beach was to ascertain the breadth of the river and how much it has risen since we have been here ; that their looking at the moon and stars in the night was to ascertain how far we were from our own country ; that he himself must have taken notice that the moon does not remain stationary, but rises higher every day, so by looking at either the moon or stars we also know how far we are from home ; that God has commanded us to do good to all men and never to do evil, for if we do them harm God will not be pleased with us.

With this explanation both he and his people appeared satisfied. I asked him if there were anything of which he wanted further explanation, as we were ready to give it. He replied that he had nothing more to ask but for some red velvet, a stool, and a basin.

When Crowther arrived at Ijogo he found the people very shy of coming to the *Pleiad* for the purpose of trade. This he believed was owing to the false reports which had reached them, and also because the slaves were still sold in the neighbourhood. In the meantime he was doing his best to acquire a knowledge of the Doma or Arago language, although the natives whom they had taken on board at the last stopping-place made but sorry teachers. He speaks of his difficulties in this respect in dealing with men who refused to sit still for long together or give any steady attention to the questions put to them. And yet Crowther had to manage them very carefully, lest they should lose their temper, and perhaps give him the wrong word for his pains. Some men from the interior came down to the shore, among them being a poor fellow named Asaba, from Rogankoto, one of whose legs had been bitten off by a crocodile; but the wound had since healed, and it was pitiable to see the man hobbling about with the aid of a long stout stick. As soon as the two doctors on board noticed the poor fellow they set about to find some way of improving his locomotion, and with the assistance of Mr. Guthrie, the chief engineer, a wooden leg was made. At the prospect of such kindness the man hobbled back to his town to tell the people the marvellous news that the white men were going to give him a new foot. A large crowd returned with him, and amid their wondering plaudits Mr. Guthrie fixed on the wooden leg, and the man was proud enough of his new limb, as might be imagined.

When they had pushed on to Abitsi, they found a safe anchorage nearly opposite Mount Ethiope. Here Crowther made careful notes of the geographical situation, the easy navigation in consequence of the absence of those islands which had hitherto been such peril to them, the picturesque scenery and high banks, and that the appearance of the river-side exceeded in beauty the group of mountains they had seen between Idda and the Confluence of the Tshadda and Kowarra. Here the high hills are quite close to the water's edge; in some cases when the river rises it runs just under the overhanging mountains, as when it makes its way between Mount Herbert on the right and Mount Adams on the left. Small farms and fishing villages are seen on either hand, and they passed a little group of huts where the people were busy making pottery. After a time, making headway against a very strong current, they reached more open country; for miles not a creature or village was to be discerned on the flat land. At last they reached a fishing hut, but no one was in it. Suddenly they met a fresh tribe of natives, whose fear and hostility were disarmed by the confidence the visitors showed. Crowther tells us:

At four o'clock we spied a group of houses at a great distance before us. This was something delightful, and about 5 p.m. we anchored off the villages of Gandiko, whose chief was Ama, and Gaukera, whose chief was Garike. Before the ship came to an anchor, intelligence had reached the chiefs of the villages, and all hands were up in arms. Their weapons were bows and arrows, and some men also carried three or four of the latter, poisoned. Our boat was ready for us, and we pulled toward shore in search of the landing-place. There were some plantations of maize and guinea corn along the water's edge, and some of the farmers were near; three women stood very close to the bank with seeming confidence. We addressed them in Hausa, to which they replied, and asked them for the landing-place, but they gave us no satisfactory reply. A little way higher up we saw a man on the bank, who drove the women away. We addressed him in Hausa, and he replied. We told him we were from the white man's country and wanted to see the chief. As soon as he saw the Europeans he cried out lustily in Hausa: "Bature Anasara maidukia na gode allah!" ("White men, the Nazarenes, men of property, I thank God!") many times over. He took the lead through old cultivated grounds, but overgrown with grass and bushes, through which we had to beat our way to the footpath leading to the town. Our leader, either from excitement or intoxication, became louder and louder in his cry: "Bature Anasara maidukia na gode allah!" We soon came to a juncture of two paths and where the Galadima, a war chief of the first rank, with a small party of about twenty-four men, armed with bows and arrows and spears, were stationed, and our leader, with his boisterous cry, introduced us to them as men of peace and trade. In the meantime we were lost in the midst of the soldiers; Dr. Baikie was in one direction, Dr. Hutchinson in another, and Mr. May in the midst of the soldiers.

We had not a single weapon about us, offensive or defensive, but the confidence with which we went among such an armed party was enough to prevent their doing any mischief. During our whole progress the few instances where hostility was shown arose out of nothing else but want of mutual understanding. On the present occasion, as soon as we came together, we shook hands with the Galadima, and he led us to the town. The path was full of soldiers coming out to join the Galadima, but seeing him return with us they all fell back on both sides of the path which brought us to the entrance to the town. The place was fortified with a wooden fence and a ditch around it, and in the midst of the town and under a kind of fig or banian tree, planted for the sake of its shade, we met the chief Ama, also armed with a bow and arrows, as were about two hundred men with him. We were introduced to him by the Galadima, and after shaking hands conversed briefly with him respecting our visit to the country. He appeared quite satisfied, and requested us to return to the ship and wait till to-morrow before entering into particulars of the object of our journey.

After this experience Crowther makes some reflections upon the common report of the hostility of the natives of Africa towards Europeans. He points out that they are always in such a state of alarm by reason of the tribal and marauding wars, that any stranger coming makes them fly to arms. He thinks that European explorers often overlook the fact that the natives are in constant fear of the treachery of their enemies. This makes them carry their weapons, to be in readiness for any attack.

> Though travellers fear nothing themselves (he says) yet they should endeavour to take due precautions to allay the fears of those whom they intend to visit, by previous communication, which will soon be circulated in the neighbourhood, and then all will be right. A prudent man will not consider an hour or two wasted to effect this purpose, rather than risk the painful result of misunderstandings which may never be remedied. As far as I know, there is no place in Africa, uncontaminated with European slave dealers, which Europeans have visited with the intention of doing good, where such an event has not been hailed as the most auspicious in the annals of the country. Every chief considers himself highly honoured to have white men for his friends.

This good advice, from one so eminently fitted to give it, will never be out of date. Their visit to Zhibú brought them in contact with a wary chief, who so little understood the character of his visitors that he called the interpreter aside to tell him he had a little boy to sell, and asked him to buy him. He was soon undeceived, and eventually brought ivory and maize to the ship for trading. Here Crowther noticed that as the men were so much engaged in marauding expeditions, the infirm male and female slaves tilled the ground. No fruits were cultivated or eatables hawked about the streets by girls and women, or refreshment places arranged for the sale of food; in short, it was the only town without a market they had met with on their journey. One night while anchored off this point the expedition had a narrow escape. They had some sheep as well as wood in the canoe attached to the ship, and while Dr. Baikie and Mr. May were standing on shore with their instruments, taking observations of a star's altitude, a low growl was heard, and a leopard, no doubt attracted by the smell of the sheep, made its appearance. Some fowling pieces were fired off, and this unusual sound no doubt frightened the creature away; but it was perilously near the two scientific observers.

Their need of constant replenishing of their fuel was a great inconvenience, and sometimes without steam they were helpless to proceed or even keep their position without careful anchorage. At one point the current was running three knots an hour against them; at another time they were involved in a submerged herd of hippopotami; again they found themselves in a gorge where the Tshadda became extremely narrow, the depth not less than five fathoms, and the whole volume of the Binue having to rush through. Here they had to set up two sails to help them, and soon afterwards reaching the broad bed of the river, they found nothing but green and useless wood growing in the soft and swampy marshes.

As there was no alternative, a look-out was kept to capture the trees floating down the stream, and two were secured before breakfast, the chase affording us no little amusement. About ten another was chased and captured, so large that it pulled the boat a considerable way down the river, but it was secured and greatly added to our little stock to enable us to get to Tshomo. In the meantime Imoru, the mallam of Zhirù, came on board with the leg of a buffalo killed last night for a present to Dr. Baikie. The doctor would have bought the head, but the superstition of the people was so strong against selling it that they begged him not to be vexed at their denying him that request; nor could they be persuaded to sell the skulls of hippopotami which were piled up before the fetish in the town of Zhirù. I asked the mallam whether the people are willing to embrace Mohammedanism. He said they were not. Imoru very earnestly told Alihebi to ask me if I would pray for his wives, as they had no children. I at once called for my Bible and read Psalm cxxvii., which I tried to explain to him, and showed him my arms and neck to prove that we never used charms for any purpose, telling him that we resign all our affairs to the hand of God, who knows better what is good for us. He was quite satisfied with my explanation, though he felt disappointed of his hopes.

Crowther had a great desire to visit Mohumma, the King of Hamaruwa, to whom indeed he had already sent a message saying that he was coming. This man was of some influence, and held a sort of independent position under the Sultan of Sokoto. One evening from the masthead of the *Pleiad* they could see this town at the foot of the chain of the Muri Mountains, and when they arrived at Little Isumo they met with a native trader named Ibrahim, who became very friendly. This man promised to be their guide. They landed at Tshomo, where the people were, in the opinion of Crowther, the most degraded he had met with since leaving the Bubis of the island of Fernando Po. Destitute of clothing and very dirty, the men getting a livelihood by killing hippopotami, the women carrying their children on their backs with the hands of the infants under their arms, by which they were held fast, Ibrahim explained that it was not their fashion to wear clothes. Crowther, of course, made inquiry for their chief, and was referred to an old grey-bearded man, standing under a tree by the water-side, with a dirty cloth about his waist. This, they told him, was the Sariki of Tshomo. In some cases they found a difficulty with their Krumen, who did not relish the hardships and risks of the expedition. Crowther gives us an instance of this in relating his experiences on his way to Hamaruwa, when he was undoubtedly led astray by his guide; not Ibrahim, but an improvised leader who did not certainly inspire much confidence. A word picture of travellers' troubles!

The creek which divides Tshomo had not enough water for our boat, so we had to pull through the flooded cornfields to get into the main creek; but as the whole was overgrown with grass and corn-stocks Ibrahim was obliged to get one of the canoe-men to take the lead. Our Krumen did not like either the appearance of our guide or the passage he was leading us through. As a fisher and hunter of hippopotami he had with him five or six harpoons or spears, and pulled through the grass with his narrow canoe like a snake, while the grass was so thick that we could not see him ahead of us nor perceive the track of his canoe. However, we followed in his direction till we met him under a tree, where he waited for us. We had here to stoop beneath the low branches, but a short distance brought us to the main creek. The bank being only partially covered with water, the men jumped out and carried the boat across, and our pilot then left us to ourselves. I called the attention of Friday, the head Kruman, to mark the direction of the tree that they might not miss the way on their return ; but Captain Friday and his crew did not seem to relish the idea of returning alone among these rude and apparently ferocious people. We followed the creek, thinking we should soon come to the landing-place, but, contrary to our expectation, we did not land till one o'clock p.m., four hours after leaving the ship, our progress having been down with the stream since we came into the creek, which runs parallel with the river. From all the inquiries we had made Hamaruwa did not appear to be more than six or seven miles from the river, and, considering the distance we had made down the creek, I thought we must have been at least three or four miles nearer than if we had landed immediately on the bank of the main river. It seemed to me that if the Krumen had to return with the boat against the stream in the circuitous creek they would not get to the ship before dark ; and under the impression that an hour or an hour and a half would bring us to Hamaruwa, and we might be back by five and return to the ship together, especially as there was no other conveyance for us except the miserable patched canoes, used to fetch corn from the plantations, I ordered the boat to be pulled up, and, leaving it and all belonging to it to the care of the headman of the village of Wuza, we started for Hamaruwa. An hour's walk brought us within sight of the first farm village, which I at first took to be the capital or its suburbs, but I was mistaken, and was told the town was yet before us. Another hour brought us to a second farm village, and our way led almost direct west towards the furthest mountains we had left westwards. By the time we had travelled three hours the Krumen, who were as much deceived as ourselves, became very much dissatisfied and expressed regret that they had not returned to the ship instead of going such an unpleasant journey in which they had no interest. Truly it was unpleasant, inasmuch as we were deceived as regards distance, and the road was by no means enviable to walk in. We had not left Wuza half an hour before I was obliged to take off my shoes and roll up the legs of my trousers, as did Mr. Richards, to wade through the continual splash of water and mud we met with more than one third of the way.

They reached it in due time, and Crowther gives us a fine description of the town and its people. It was beautifully situated on a hill, from which a grand view of the river and scenery around is obtained, the stretches of light green grass by the water's edge, then the darker green of the tree foliage, and beyond the blue ranges of Fumbina, with the lofty Mandranu mountain in Adamawa, and the Muri mountain in Hamaruwa near at hand. The houses with their conical roofs and long public street, with luxuriant trees, are characteristic of most African towns. If it had been laid out with any European direction, it would have been a delightful place, for it is built on a rock, and rapidly dries after heavy rains. The people were poor and ill clothed; very few goats or sheep were seen, and the slaves do all the cultivation of the corn in the lowlands. The travellers received a hearty welcome from the King, and were liberally supplied with food, as the following note will indicate from Crowther's pen:

The King sent five sheep and lambs with a kid, six in all, and a large pot of plum honey for our entertainment, but unfortunately before the honey was delivered the pot broke and the whole was spilled on the ground, to the great grief of all present. Ibrahim came with much sorrow to tell me of this great misfortune, and I must say I felt the loss myself, because it would have been a very acceptable present to all the ship's company, considering that since the fourth instant we had been out of sugar. Butter and milk had been all consumed long before, and a pot of honey would have been an invaluable substitute. But travellers must take things as they come, and be content with such things as they have.

The Filanis use no lamps in their houses in the evening; we had therefore to remain outside the house where we were lodged, seated in the dark, as they themselves did, till bed-time, when a few sticks were kindled, which gave out much smoke and little light, to enable us to ascertain the position of our bed, which was rough enough. Before we turned in Ibrahim requested me to take care of my sheep and goat in our room for fear of the wolves, with which the country abounds. I told him it was impossible to admit five sheep and a goat into a room already filled with eleven occupants, and he promised to take care of them until the morning. Ibrahim's yard was full of visitors going and coming, to whom he was relating the wonderful news of the Anasara's ship made of iron and moved by fire. Being tired with our journey, we left them to enjoy the story, and rested ourselves after we had offered a prayer of thanksgiving to God for our protection.

After some disagreeable experiences on the journey home, which Crowther seems to have taken in a happy and philosophic spirit, they got back to the ship. They arrived on a Sunday morning, and Crowther preached from the not inappropriate subject of "the fall and misery of man."

The river was now sinking rapidly, and it was felt that the prow of the *Pleiad* should be turned homeward, if a safe return was to be counted on. Dr. Baikie and Mr. May took a boat to go three days further up the river to make additional observations. Crowther confesses to a good deal of fear and heart-searching at leaving these two in such dangers, among an unknown and perhaps hostile people. The *Pleiad* shot down the stream like a home-coming horse, but next day ran aground, and was detained until loud cheers announced the return of the boat, with its two occupants whom they had left behind.

Of this return journey Crowther makes many interesting notes, and revisiting the various chiefs, was able to make arrangements for opening mission stations at several points. At Oboh, for instance, he tells us how he fixed upon a spot of land at the entrance to the creek on the bank of the main river for the establishment of mission work, and got the chief Ajé to faithfully promise that no one should interfere with this claim. A little lower down the stream he met with a young chief, Agbekun, who, being childless, had been paying a visit to Aeò, where Tshuku, the great god of the Ibos, resides, to make inquiries of a domestic character. He went through many ceremonies, and performed many sacrifices, and subsequently returned home with a favourable answer communicated to him through the priests. He also brought with him several small representations of the god. When he showed these to Crowther he wanted to know what the Anasara thought of his Tshuku.

This gave me the opportunity (the journal records) of speaking to him about the true God, to whom I endeavoured to turn his attention to look for blessings both temporal and spiritual. He wanted to know how to pray to the Great God, whom he knew to be greater than Tshuku. I told him to do so just as a little child would ask his father for what he was in need of. Agbekun was very shy in speaking much about the Tshuku of the Ibos, as a great mystery is connected even with the place of his residence. Since this young chief's return he has been going through some ceremonies, and cannot be seen or spoken to much in public till the time allotted to them has expired, which will be in about two days. In consequence of this he did not attend market, but he was told that as we were from the white man's country his ceremony could not be spoiled by his conversation with us. He replied: "There is no hatred in white man's country as in black man's country." I told him to look at me, a Yoruba by birth, Simon

Jonas, an Ibo, and Dr. Baikie, an Englishman; though of different nations, we live together as brethren, and so our God teaches all men to love one another. I expressed my hope that we should soon be able to teach them this love, which he was glad to hear.

On 6 November the *Pleiad* crossed the bar, and Crowther held Divine Service, expressing the devout thanks to God of all those on board for such a good and favourable journey, and preached from Joshua iv. 6, 7. He closes his journal with this note of praise:

May this singular instance of God's favour and protection drive us nearer to the Throne of Grace, to humble ourselves before our God, whose instruments we are, and who can continue or dispense with our services as it seems good to His unerring wisdom.

In reviewing the results of this expedition Crowther draws attention to several points, which are very encouraging. One is the remarkable absence of sickness as regards Europeans, and that not a single life has been lost on the voyage. This, in contrast with that of 1841, was satisfactory. He was convinced that the time was come for the introduction of Christianity on the banks of the Niger, for the people were evidently willing to receive teachers, and he greatly regretted the loss of time since the ill-fated expedition of 1841 had discouraged any ascent of the river for twelve years. He laid great stress on the importance of utilizing native agency. Let such workers go back to their own countrymen as a renewed people, superior now to others, and whose walk and conversation would do so much to commend Christ and His Gospel in these regions. The converted African was a special value in his testimony:

It takes great effect when, returning, liberated Christians sit down with their heathen countrymen and speak with contempt of their former superstitious practices, of whom, perhaps, many now alive would bear testimony as to their former devotedness to their superstitious worship, all of which he can now tell them he has found to be foolishness and the result of ignorance, when he with all earnestness invites them, as Moses did Hobab, " Come with us, for the Lord hath promised good to Israel," and all this in their own language, with refined Christian feelings and sympathy, not to be expressed in words, but evidenced by an exemplary Christian life.

From the standpoint of commerce the expedition undoubtedly demonstrated great possibilities. Crowther took much personal interest in the encouragement of cotton growing, and the subsequent development of trade in this direction was largely due to his initiative and persistency. A meeting of the friends of Africa was convened shortly after the return of the *Pleiad*, and it was resolved to urge upon the Government the importance of establishing a regular service of trading steamers between Fernando Po and the Confluence of the Niger and Tshadda rivers.

Crowther took advantage during this voyage to ascertain the various languages of the tribes, and in a valuable appendix to his journal he gives their vocabularies and a comparison of their grammatical construction. Dr. Baikie, at the conclusion of the voyage, addressed a very kind letter to him, in which he gives the following well-deserved commendation :

After having been together for upwards of four months, closely engaged in exploring Central Africa, I cannot allow you to depart without expressing to you in the warmest manner the pleasure I derived from your company and acknowledging the information I have reaped from you. Your long and intimate acquaintance with native tribes, with your general knowledge of their customs, peculiarly fit you for a journey such as we have now returned from, and I cannot but feel that your advice was always readily granted to me, nor had I ever the smallest reason to repent having followed it. It is nothing more than a simple fact that no slight portion of the success we met with in our intercourse with the tribes is due to you.

Once more the people of England began to turn their eyes from the strain of worry and weeping over the Crimean War to the West Coast of Africa and to the Niger, that noble river which may be called the Nile of the West. The last expedition had been a very successful one, and all felt, whether they regarded the question from a commercial or missionary standpoint, that this great waterway was the gate to the heart of Africa, and wonderful possibilities had been revealed. Crowther had always a practical mind, and served efficiently the State as well as the Church in his travels. He saw a future trade in palm oil, an almost unlimited reserve hardly touched yet by European requirements, and he foresaw that this trade would in time eliminate the slave traffic, with its accursed train of evils.

"The advantage of the increase of palm oil trade," he writes, "over that of the slave is so much felt by the people at large that their head chiefs could not help confessing to me that they—aged persons—never remembered any time of the slave trade in which so much wealth was brought into their country as has been since the commencement of the palm oil trade, the last four years; that they were perfectly satisfied with legitimate trade and with the proceedings of the British Government."

He saw also that there was a large store of ivory waiting the touch of commerce, and that cotton, as proved by his experiments at Abeokuta, might be cultivated to a very considerable extent, and, adopting the prophet's mantle, he anticipated no reason why the present export of two millions from West Africa "might not quadruple itself in the next twenty years, if it be only protected until it has struck its roots a little deeper in the soil of Africa." He pointed out that up to the present he had touched the coast only, and if by pushing up the Niger he might strike those great caravan routes of the interior, a new world for investment, both in a business and a spiritual sense, would be opened up. Crowther recommended a visit being paid to Kano, that rich province with its large and prosperous town to which Dr. Barth had already drawn attention in his travels. This was the seat of a most valuable cotton cloth industry. These reports, of course, gave hope at home, and the Government of the day were not slow to confer with Mr. Macgregor, the enterprising African merchant, as to what should be done. But an impulse of deeper import was given to the minds of those whose higher aim was to bring the light of the Gospel to Africa. The Church Missionary Society conferred with Mr. Laird, who again offered Crowther a free passage up the Niger, thankfully accepting the opportunity thus given of establishing a Niger Mission, where the services of converted Africans from Sierra Leone and elsewhere might find a useful sphere. They expressed their intentions in a letter to Crowther, which filled him with joy, and he replied thankfully accepting the position, and giving many valuable suggestions in the matter. He freely discussed the commercial side, and says that "the first five years the contract was to last should be the seedtime for introducing Christianity and civilization. When trade and agriculture engage the attention of the people, with the gentle and peaceful teaching of Christianity, the minds of the people will gradually be won from war and marauding expeditions to peaceful trade and commerce."

Everything seemed favourable, and Crowther had spent some time in conferring with his old friend of bygone days, Bishop Weeks, and the valuable missionaries Messrs. Beale and Frey. It was arranged that a number of native teachers should be sent up the Niger from Sierra Leone. While Crowther was away on his journey it was felt that while he was placing these European missionaries in their new spheres of work, Bishop Weeks, of Sierra Leone, at the base of operations, would be able to support and advise. But once more this African climate, with its insatiable toll of human lives, claimed all three as its latest victims. The story of the passing of these good and faithful servants is indeed very pathetic.

The first to fall was Mr. Beale, a man full of faith and of the Holy Ghost, who was struck with fever while at his post of duty at Lagos. He was such a brave man, and when he found his strength ebbing away towards the eternal sea he summoned all his powers to bring back to God some poor Sierra Leone emigrants, who had fallen away sadly, and brought discredit on their profession. The Bishop reached the harbour of Freetown on the evening of 14 March, and his chaplain hurried on board the ship *Candace* to find him lying utterly prostrate in his hammock, too weak to move. With loving care they carried him ashore, and laid him in his own quiet bed. Mr. Frey, who had exerted himself to bring the Bishop home, then fell sick, and lay in another room, the two grief-stricken wives, Mrs. Weeks and Mrs. Frey, quietly ministering with hearts full of foreboding. On the Sunday afternoon the Bishop's chaplain stepped to his side, and with a sweet smile of recognition the sufferer whispered: "Mr. Pocock, if there is a time when Christ is more especially precious, it is when we have death before us. I am very weak. Pray for me." At three in the morning he was with him again, and to the question put by one of the ladies, "Do you find Christ precious now?" the dying Bishop spent his last breath in slowly spelling out the word, "P-r-e-c-i-o-u-s," and fell asleep in the Divine keeping. A month afterwards his colleague in labour and sickness, Mr. Frey, followed him; his end, too, was peace. Those who watched him during those last days speak of the calm serenity of his mind. The day before his call came he took the Sacrament, and was able to say farewell to his weeping wife and friends, and shortly afterwards crossed the river so quietly that none quite knew the moment when he reached the other shore. The news of all this plunged Crowther into the deepest distress. It was not only that he grieved over the loss as a drawback to the mission which he was on the eve of founding, but he mourned for the departure of those whom he personally loved, especially of Bishop Weeks, to whom he owed so much for kindness and training in boyhood.

Writing from Fernando Po on 29 May, 1855, he expresses his grief over these troubles:

> The late floods of affliction upon the West African mission are overwhelming. The removal of our good Bishop Weeks, and that of the Rev. Mr. Frey so soon after, both just on their return from their visit to the Bight of Benin and the Gold Coast, calls for prayers to and humiliation before our God, who is the disposer of these painful dispensations. Perhaps we have been sacrificing to the nets and the drag instead of to Him, who has said, "Cast the net on the right side of the ship." May our sins be forgiven and our errors corrected in judgment and not in anger!

CHAPTER V

THE MISSION PLANTED AND FIRSTFRUITS

THE year of grace one thousand eight hundred and fifty-seven was a memorable one in the annals of our Empire. It is marked in our history with a crimson stain. On the horizon of the Far East was the glare of the Indian Mutiny; across the sad and silent sea were wafted the dying shouts of brave and defenceless men, the shrieks of women in terror, and children's cries of pain. The heart of the nation throbbed with indignation and grief, fed by the stream of tearful tidings which daily reached our shores. But out of the travail of that great sorrow a new India was born, more loyal, better and more wisely governed, and an open door and effectual was given to the missionary with his message of redeeming love.

When Crowther heard the news he immediately wrote a letter of sympathy from an encampment at Zeba, dated 4 January, 1858:

I deeply sympathize with you on account of the sudden mutiny which has risen in India, with the unparalleled barbarities attending it. The news burst upon us all of a sudden like a dry tempest, which threatened destruction everywhere; but I believe the Lord will never allow such afflictions to arise without intending to teach us something thereby ; the wrath of man will praise Him, and the remainder of wrath He will restrain.

The reputation of the unjust disparagement on the missionary work as being the cause of this barbarous mutiny in India will open the eyes of those who opposed the conversion of the Sepoys, to see what advantage it is to any community to have converted natives mingled with it, who are like salt in the midst of a mass of corruption. May it be the fervent prayer of the Church to God to remove this heavy affliction from us and to make known what is her duty to the Sepoys as a Christian nation, as she has been showing to the long-oppressed children of Ham, whose cause she has warmly taken in hand for their liberation not only from the bondage of man, but also from the power of Satan.

But in other respects the time was fraught with great issues. Lord Elgin, with his fleet, was breaking down the barriers which shut in the mighty Chinese Empire from Western contact, and Japan, the youngest child of the nations of the world, had also yielded to the kindly pressure of Commodore Perry, and was thereby taking the first step on her unique and swift progress to power and influence. The missionary field all over the world was witnessing fresh conquests. The Isles of Fiji laying aside the idols, their cannibal King converted, were in a state of spiritual revival. Under a new Queen the breath of persecution was fanning and sifting the Christian flock in Madagascar, men and women going cheerfully with hymn-singing to torture and death. In England Livingstone, just about to start upon his last journey, was speaking at Cambridge University, turning his toil-worn face with its eyes of fire on the listening students with the words: "I go back to Africa to try and make an open path for commerce and Christianity. Do you carry out the work which I have begun. I leave it with you." From our shores had just sailed the Rev. J. N. Gordon for Erromanga, where, like Williams before him, he met a martyr's death; and on 29 June, in that same year, a small but well-appointed vessel left Fernando Po for the Niger, with Crowther on the deck, amid cheers from ships and shore. This was the beginning of a new era in the commercial history of West Africa; but as he stood there, with his Bible clasped to his heart, he saw in the voyage a higher purpose, that of laying with prayer and faith the foundations of that missionary work which should for all time be associated with his name.

It was a peculiar satisfaction to him that his old friend and fellow-traveller, Dr. Baikie, was appointed as the responsible head and leader of the expedition, and although through the lamented death of Bishop Weeks and the two missionaries Messrs. Beale and Frey, he could not have them and some native helpers from Sierra Leone included in the plan, he had with him the Rev. J. C. Taylor, a native clergyman, born in Sierra Leone, but the child of liberated slaves from the Ibo country. In addition he took with him Simon Jonas, who had already done good work in connection with the previous expeditions.

But Crowther had also provided himself with another companion, besides the two or three native catechists which made up the party. The objective of the voyage was the great Foulah kingdom, with its im-

VISIT OF MOHAMMEDAN CHIEFS

portant towns of Kano, Rabbah, and Sokoto. He therefore took precautions which in his judgment were very necessary under the circumstances. He knew he would have to face a Moslem people. Here are his words on the point :

> I have thought it advisable, with a view of making favourable impressions on the minds of the Mohammedan population through whose country we shall have to pass to Sokoto and Ilorin, to engage Kosomo, a Yoruba Mohammedan and liberated African, who has been an Arabic teacher for many years, to accompany me on my travels. Kosomo has ever appreciated the benevolence of the British Government on behalf of Africa, nor less so the labours of the Church Missionary Society in converting the heathen from idolatry to the worship of the true God. Such a man will do a vast deal in softening the bigotry and prejudice of men of his persuasion. The beginning of our missionary operations under Mohammedan government should not be disputes about the truth or falsehood of one religion or another, but we should aim at toleration, to be permitted to teach their heathen subjects the religion we profess.

This action on the part of Crowther indicates the attitude which in his opinion was a wise one to take up in future dealings with these Mohammedans. It will be admitted that such a course was on the line of least resistance, and, moreover, created friendly allies where the work might have made bitter foes. He was eminently a man of discretion, and it never seemed his habit to undertake anything or embark on any step in life, however simple in itself, without looking all round the question and estimating probable consequences. Crowther was not the man to be carried away on a mere wave of impulse, if the phrase may be used he never lost his head, and it is equally true that with his indomitable spirit of perseverance he never lost his heart. In all these journeys, travels, toils, and sometimes sufferings, one great ideal, like an undimmed lamp, glowed in his very soul. It was, as we have seen from his earliest letters, the establishment of a native Church in Africa; a native clergy, duly trained and equipped, ministering to their own people. It is said that wherever the Japanese go, their alert mind estimates everything from one absorbing patriotic standpoint, "How will this benefit Japan?" In a nobler sense than this was Crowther's attitude, not only the welfare of his country, but the conversion of his people. He had already gained experience, and the native churches of Sierra Leone, Lagos, and Abeokuta supplied him with reliable data upon which to form his conclusions as to future possibilities and difficulties. Through the cloudy sky of many disappointments the sun of hope and success still cheered him; he had such faith in his people and in his God for them. These, then, were the thoughts which stirred him as he looked once more upon the broad expanse of that lordly Niger, whose hurrying waves seemed to bring with them the cry of Macedonia from afar.

The *Dayspring* was now well on her way. She had touched at a village of the Brass country, where the inhabitants were found to be of a very degraded type. It was indeed in this neighbourhood that Mr. Carr and his servant so mysteriously disappeared. The chief town Nembe they had not time to visit, and pushed on until they reached Angiama. In the meantime Crowther was busy with his pen on board, sketching out divisions of the Bights of Benin and Biafra to be occupied by different societies. He had a horror of so much overlapping. Each society its own sphere of labour was his idea, and he makes a strong note of his convictions at this stage of the work. He was always in brotherly union with the missionaries of other communions, but he lamented the fact that with the best intentions the missionary societies were fostering the evil of competition with each other.

> At Sierra Leone (he writes) this unavoidable evil has gone to a great extent, and it has been unhappily introduced into the newly-established Yoruba Mission, where it has already begun to cause strife and disparagement of one another's church connection among the newly-converted natives belonging to the different missionary societies. This does no good in a new mission field either to the new converts or to the unconverted native population, and has caused us many sorrowful days and weeks.
>
> It is of the utmost importance that timely measures should be adopted by the great societies, whose sole and benevolent object is the conversion of the heathen to Christianity, and to do this effectually and with greater success than hitherto they should, and ought to, work separately for the extension of the Church of Christ. Why should not this generous-hearted proposal be as applicable to Christian missions as to the settlements of Abraham and Lot?
>
> Is not the whole land before thee? Separate thyself, I pray thee, from me. If thou wilt take the left hand, then I will go to the right; or if thou wilt depart to the right hand, then I will go to the left.

He was surprised and delighted to find such improvements in the appearance of the natives of the Delta; the men were wearing shirts of Manchester make, the soil was being cultivated, and he counted one hundred native Brass canoes, laden with palm oil, evidently for trading purposes. Reaching Abo, they had a visit on board from Aje, with his twelve spouses, but Crowther was sorry to find so little improvement in this self-important young ruler. He only asked for rum, and because it was liberally diluted expressed his dissatisfaction, and his cool insistence upon having his presents at once was firmly declined.

Aje manifested his covetous propensity to-day beyond description; his conduct on board disgusted everybody, his own attendants not excepted. His familiarity with Europeans from his youth, and the kind indulgence he has ever met with from them as a son of Obi, have completely spoiled him. His tenacity in keeping his attention fixed on any object he cast his eyes upon or which entered into his brain to ask for was beyond conception. My pair of shoes first attracted his observation, which he took without asking any permission and tried to put one on, but fortunately for me my No. 8 shoe could not admit his enormous foot of the size of No. 11 or 12.

Before he departed he tried to get Mr. Taylor's shoes, wanted to carry off the cushion kindly placed at his back, made a clutch at the handbell which was being rung to give notice that dinner was ready, and generally displayed his cupidity all round, until, to the relief of his hosts, he got into his canoe and paddled back home. Crowther has serious thoughts as he watches this young ruffian disappear.

These trifling details would have been unnecessary if they have not intended to show what kind of man Aje is and how careful one should be in entrusting goods to such a person, who has no control over his covetous propensity. I have observed this failing among the Abo people more than in any other with whom we have had communication in the upper parts of the river. Presents from the people should be avoided or refused as much as possible, otherwise one is placed in the painful position of an insolvent debtor; if a sprat be received, a salmon is sure to be required in its stead.

After many subsequent interviews with the grasping Aje, Crowther went to the headman of another part of the town and secured land whereon the new mission premises might be built. Passing on they landed at Ossamare, where they were received with much civility, and here also the site of a mission station was arranged. When they arrived at the important town of Onitsha, the people took sheer fright at the appearance of white men, the first they had ever seen, and it took some time to persuade them to lay aside their weapons of defence and agree to a friendly palaver. Eventually one of them acted as guide through groves of bombax, cocoanut, and palm trees, and some plantations to the town itself, which was finely situated one hundred feet above the level of the Niger. Their interviews with the King and chiefs were most promising. Dr. Baikie and Captain Grant were soon arranging for a factory to be built, and the King addressed the crowd of people in his courtyard, asking whether they concurred in this proposed trading with the white people. This democratic step met with a quick response, and the agreement was concluded by firing of muskets, and then one man stepped forward and said on behalf of the crowd that it was felt that the King's wishes were for the good of their country. Then Crowther mentioned his own particular mission, and introduced Mr. Taylor as the religious teacher who was to live in Onitsha, to show them the Word of God, and to teach the children to read, and that if they paid attention to him, many more would be sent to live with them, and all this they promised to help and further if they could. Afterwards the party repaired to the town in search of a house in which Mr. Taylor should live till the mission premises were built. The houses they found were mere oblong squares of mud, without rooms or windows, and they finally selected a little square at the price of six pieces of romal handkerchiefs at five shillings a piece. Leaving his Sierra Leone catechists and Simon Jonas to clear this mud mansion and make it habitable, Crowther makes a further tour of discovery, to estimate the extent and value of this new sphere of work, and notes his impressions as follows :

While they were doing this we took a stroll about the town, to know the extent of it, as well as to make acquaintances. We paid a visit to four groups of houses, the chiefs of which expressed their great joy at our establishments among them. The town of Onitsha is about one mile in length, if not more, which is divided into two sections. On either side are groups of houses, a little remote from the high road, ruled by heads of familiar or inferior chiefs. Both sides of the road are either covered with bushes or plantations till you come to an open road leading to a group of houses further back ; but some of the groups are close and open to the high road, where also a market is held occasionally. In the afternoon we returned on board, thankful for the success God had granted to us, though we felt fatigued after a few days' exertions. The whole of yesterday and to-day was a very busy time about Onitsha ; goods were landed, bushes were cleared, and sticks cut for the construction of the factory shed ; the botanist and naturalist took their departments in the fields ; while some of the naval gentlemen, not content to go out in the dawn of the morning to lie in wait for the hippopotami in their hitherto undisturbed haunts, pitched their tent in the immediate neighbourhood of these amphibious quadrupeds, if possible to shoot one of them at the same time they were pursuing their nautical observations ; but the mosquitoes, the universal pest of the rivers, did not leave them unmolested during their nightly watch.

During their stay at Onitsha, although they were treated with great kindness, and on every hand there seemed a willingness to receive the Gospel, they had abundant proof that heathenism and superstition had a strong hold upon the people. On one occasion as they were going through the town to their temporary lodging, Crowther noticed a number of people dressed in their best, and in one of the square houses was a crowd of men and women excitedly dancing to the beat of drums and firing of muskets. When they reached the door they inquired of a headman what was the cause of all this jubilation, and were told that it was in honour of the burial of a relative who died six months ago. Simon Jonas, who had remained on shore the night before, had also heard that a human sacrifice was to be made. This roused the indignation of Crowther, and in the presence of a crowd of people he protested against this cruel act. It appeared that the victim, a poor blameless female slave, was already waiting for execution, and she was not a little astonished to find the Christian teacher chivalrously standing betwixt her and death. The headman then proposed that Crowther should buy the woman, and they would kill a bullock instead; but this he refused to do. However, afterwards it was discovered that the poor creature was loosed from her bonds.

Better times were now at hand. Not only the mission premises began to put in an appearance, but in due time a number of native workmen were busy building the factory, and at a solemn council of the King and his headmen protection was guaranteed to the houses, the work, and the persons employed; also they promised to abolish human sacrifices and to absolve all visitors from the white man's country from the native law which permits no stranger to sit on any mat or seat in the King's court. Crowther then left Mr. Taylor, Simon Jonas, and three young traders from Sierra Leone to make Onitsha their future home, affectionately saying "Good-bye," and praying that the blessing of God might be their joy and stay. It is worthy of note that this was the first stage in planting a purely native mission as an off-shoot of the colony of Sierra Leone, and having a purely native ministry was a move in advance of the Yoruba mission, which was under the guidance and teaching of Europeans. Crowther rejoiced in spirit. He writes at this time:

Mr. Taylor has to break open the fallow ground and to sow the seed of a future bountiful harvest among the people of his fatherland. May this be the beginning of a rapid over-spread of Christianity in the countries on the banks of the Niger and in the heart of Africa through native agents! In parting with his colleague Crowther gave him much valuable advice. "Though we are about to separate," says he, "for a season, dear brother, yet you are not alone. 'Lo, I am with you alway,' is the faithful promise of the Lord of the harvest to His disciples; this will also be realized concerning us. . . . Your ministerial duties will be very simple and plain. You will have to teach more by conversation when you visit the people or they visit you, at the beginning, than by direct service. Be instant in season and out of season. May the Lord give you wisdom to win souls to Himself! You will need much patience to bear and forbear with the ignorance and simplicity of the people, they are like babes. . . . Be not disappointed if you find the people do not act as to their engagement; it is rather a matter of surprise that they do so much. They must be taught the lesson of justice and truth, and that by your own example."

With these and many other admonitions of a very practical character Crowther left Onitsha, fully convinced that he could not have selected a better place as the headquarters of the Ibo mission establishments, for health, goodwill of the people, and facilities for holding communication with the interior.

As the *Dayspring* drew near to Idda they heard that the old Ata was dead, and that two rivals were fighting for the throne. A little difficulty was experienced when the ship drew near the shore, and Crowther landed for the first time.

At the dawn I heard the gougon at the landing-place, and the town crier said something about the Oibo which I could not understand. At 7 a.m. we landed on English Island, where we met Ama-Abokko, our old friend, who had come from the Confluence some time ago on political business. He had heard of our arrival at Abo and had been expecting us. Having entertained us as usual, he was requested to send a messenger to announce our arrival to the Ata and our intention to visit him in the course of the day; he would not tell us, when asked, whether the old Ata was alive or dead. His reply to that question was, "King never dies." We returned on board for breakfast. Before noon we landed to pay our respects to the Ata, and were conducted by Ama's messenger first to Abeya, where we were kindly received and entertained according to custom. After a considerable delay we were conducted to the house of our old friend Ehemodina, who embraced me and Dr. Baikie with open arms to express his joy at seeing us again. Here we sat, and were entertained as usual.

But this hospitality was interrupted by the entrance of the head eunuch, and difficulties were promptly placed in the way of an interview with the

King. In a tone of insolence this man told the visitors they might sail away if they liked, as the river was open for everybody, but the Ata should not be seen that day. In like manner Captain Trotter had been treated sixteen years before, and Mr. Beecroft, the consul, fared no better, and on the last occasion Crowther found himself stopped at all points when he desired to see the Ata. It was felt that this swaggering official must be taught that the white man was not to be played with, so the whole party rose and returned to the ship without a word. This had the desired effect; a string of royal notables came on board next morning to apologize for the affront, and after much palaver the King was finally visited, a new young Aṭa in the place of the old, who promised to follow in his father's footsteps as regards his friendship with white men. Before leaving Idda a learned mallam, who had been there four years, was introduced to Crowther. He had a full copy of the Korân, and from him some slight information was gathered respecting Sumo Zaki and Dasaba, whom Crowther was hoping to see at the end of the journey. A few days later a number of Mohammedans were also interviewed, and portions of the Korân were read aloud; one of these men not only read with great fluency, but shutting up the book he repeated chapter after chapter from memory, to the great surprise and admiration of all. Crowther's comments are:

The further we go the more convinced I am of the necessity of introducing the study of Arabic into our institutions at Sierra Leone. What advantage it would have given if any one of the Christian teachers could also have stepped forward and read a few verses out of his Arabic Bible! Such capability would place the teachers of the Anasaras in a much more prominent position among these self-conceited people. Beside this, I believe in this part of Africa, where the knowledge of Arabic is so imperfectly known, the use of the Arabic character, combined with teaching in Roman or italic characters in the native tongues, would be the means of counterbalancing the rapid spread of Mohammedanism among the rising generation. But so long as the use of the Arabic character is excluded from our schools and left to the use of the ignorant followers of Mohammed alone, they will take advantage of this to continue their deception upon the ignorant heathen by holding these letters as more holy than any others in the world; but by these characters being brought into common use their artful cheat would be laid open.

In this town of Ghebe Crowther arranged for mission premises to be erected on the north side of the town, while the site of the factory had been settled on the south. Some rather awkward situations were caused by a misunderstanding with the farmers, who thought their land was being confiscated, and stopped the workmen accordingly. This fortunately quieted down, and Crowther gives an interesting word picture of a meeting he had when he had gone ashore after conducting a service :

After service I went on shore to make a beginning of public Christian instruction in the town of Ghebe. Mr. Crook, the disbanded soldier of the Nupé nation, interpreted for me in Nupé, there being a large number who speak that language there. Besides my English I took an Arabic Bible and Schön's translations of St. Matthew and St. John into Hausa, and an Ibo primer, out of which to teach the alphabet. Taking my seat in the Galadima's ante-hall, which is the common resort of all the people, holding from forty to fifty persons, a number of both sexes, old and young, soon entered, as usual, to look on. Having carefully placed my books on the mat, after the custom of the mallams, Mr. Crook sitting on my right, and

Kasumo on my left, I commenced my conversation by telling them that to-day was the Christian Sabbath, on which we rest from our labour, according to the commandment of God. The Galadima came in, and to him I read some verses from the third chapter of St. John in Hausa, in the hearing of the people, which he understood and which, by further explanation, became more intelligible to him. In the meantime some Mohammedans walked in and desired to see the Arabic Bible, which I delivered to Kasumo to read and translate to them. The Galadima, who reads Arabic, expressed a wish as soon as the school opened to learn to read Hausa in Roman or italic characters. There was an intelligent young man present who could read Arabic, who was also very anxious to read our translations in the italic character. After a long talk I ran over the alphabet from the Ibo primer several times with the Galadima and the young man, at which they showed much quickness and intelligence. I then gave an Arabic copy of the Bible as a present to the Galadima. This was so unexpected that he did not know how sufficiently to express his gratitude in words; and, contrary to the usage of the Mohammedans, he actually was going to throw dust on his forehead as a token of the value he placed on this gift, when Kasumo stopped him by saying it was not our custom to do so. He said his father would be able to read it fluently. May the Lord bless this small and feeble beginning of an attempt to introduce the religion of Christ into this benighted part of Africa! May the prayers of the Church be heard on its behalf!

Throughout Crowther's journals one is continually reminded of his reverent regard for the Sabbath Day. It always gave him pain and much heart-searching when upon these voyages he found the sailors busy with getting and storing fuel, and working in other ways which defrauded them of their day of rest. And we see him here in his service on board, under date 23 August, preaching a practical and fervent discourse on the well-known text, Exodus xx. 8, "Remember the Sabbath Day, to keep it holy."

When going ashore to teach the people he frequently took with him one of the officers of the ship, and these would appreciate the difficulties which the missionary must encounter, and which would scarcely be likely in a place of worship at home. As an instance of this, here is an extract from the record of a Saturday afternoon preaching:

> When a sufficient number was collected I began to address them from Matthew vii. 12: "Therefore all things whatsoever ye would that men should do to you, do ye even so to them, for this is the law and the prophets," to which they paid very great attention. I read the text from the Hausa translations as occasion required; and as the Galadima was present I made Kasumo read the verse from the Arabic Bible, to assure him that the Hausa translations agreed with the Arabic text. Lieut. Glover took his seat on one side of the raised floor to witness our mode of teaching. Every attention was paid to all that was being said, when a little interruption took place among the hearers. As the people stood thick against the doorway, a respectable looking man who was present desired a girl of about thirteen years of age to move a little out of the way to give him room, but she abused the man by calling him a dog. The man, being indignant at such an insult, proceeded to punish her with his long pipe-stick, which caused such a disturbance just at the moment I was telling them of the dying legacy Christ left to His Church, "Peace I leave with you," etc., that I was obliged to stop and pacify the man, while the girl made her escape through the opposite passage. This circumstance directed my discourse to the duty of obedience which children owe their parents and inferiors to their superiors. I kept them long until I perceived they were beginning to be weary, when I ceased speaking and employed the remainder of the time teaching from the Ibo primer till half-past three, when I closed altogether.

While anchored opposite Little Fojo the mate died, and the sorrowful party of the ship's company followed his coffin to the place of burial on a small island near the right bank of the river. They laid their comrade to rest under a little tree, opposite the lower corner of the Rennell Mountains, cutting a cross on the bark with a chisel, together with his initials and the date. Crowther says the day was very hot, the thermometer standing at 112°!

On 9 September they reached the town of Murégi, at the Confluence of the Kowarra and Lafun or Kadúna, and as the latter appeared to be a navigable stream, the *Dayspring* steamed up, passing the villages of Nupeko and Bajofu on the right bank, and Nku and Abogi on the left, and at sunset they anchored off the ruins of Gbara, the former capital of the Nupé country, now reduced to a village of potters, standing at the foot of Mount Barrow, called by the natives Kpaté Gbara, or Gbara Hill. This happened to be the old home of Mr. Crook, their Nupé interpreter, who was naturally very excited on visiting the place after an absence of forty-five years. As they approached Wuyagi, the landing-place for the camp at Bida, Crowther looked forward with keen anticipation to seeing the great Fulani king, Sumo Zaki, and Dasaba, upon which interview so much of the future of the mission depended, at any rate in that wide district. As an act of courtesy some horses had been sent for their use, and at dawn they entered the huge Mohammedan camp, hearing all round them voices of the faithful at their devotions uttering the "Allahu-akbaru," although seeing as yet no man. Presently they passed a blacksmith's shop, where a man was making knives and beating out a sword blade; then they saw the carpenter cutting shoes and stools, and the whitesmith in his shop repairing the royal brass trumpet. At this point the rain came down in a steady drizzle, and the visitors took refuge in a shed, where a number of natives were sitting round a fire. The weather clearing up, they crossed to the market place, with its slaves, a woman with her infant just being sold for 70,000 cowries, equal to £7.

Finally, pressing through a crowd of princesses, courtiers, and other persons of high rank, they were ushered into the presence of the king, Sumo Zaki, a man about forty years old, and of an exceedingly cordial manner. His Majesty shook hands all round, begged them to sit on mats prepared for their use, and in his profuse expressions of joy and welcome told his visitors that he believed it was not for his own goodness, but it was God who directed them to visit him. This interview was of so much importance that Crowther himself shall take up the narrative, and thereby show again, from his point of view, the relative position of Christian mission work and the Mohammedan religion. He also gives here an amusing picture of a rather volatile leader of armies, who could hardly be credited with the grim qualities which led to the devastation of the Niger country. But behind the smile of an African heathen there may be a ferocity which spares nothing when aroused.

After this (writes Crowther) I introduced myself to him as a mallam sent by the great mallams from the white man's country to see the state of the heathen population and to know the mind of the rulers, whether we might teach the people the religion of Anasara and at the same time introduce trade among them. To this he at once gave a full consent, saying that it was all one—we might teach them, and that he would give us a place for a station at Rabba on their return after the rains. He also gave free consent to trade in all parts of the river, with his protection as far as his influence extended. He then entertained us with a large calabash full of kola nuts, some of which he first took himself, and after dividing them gave the parts to Dr. Baikie as a token of great friendship between us. After his presents were given him, with which he was well pleased, he requested us to visit Dasaba in his department, which was about half a mile distant from Sumo Zaki. The doctor had tried to get them both together before the interview took place, but it was not practical. Dasaba is half-brother to Sumo Zaki on the father's side, who was Mallam Deudo, but his mother was a Nufei. We met him dressed in a fine white silk tobe. He is between forty and fifty years of age, and appears to be a person of very lively disposition and humorous in his manner. After the usual salutations we took our seats on the mats and hides spread on the ground for us. When the Doctor repeated the object of his coming to this country it pleased him so much that he rolled on his mat for joy, and in such a jocular manner that it excited us all to laughter. He was quite agreeable to anything which his brother agreed to, as he gave the first place to him and made his brother's wishes his own. After the kola nuts were passed he presented the Doctor with a cow; but when he had received the Doctor's presents he was so pleased that he added a sheep, lots of yams, and a pot of palm oil.

On our leaving he accompanied us to the street and saw us mount in safety, and we returned to our lodging. When once bad principles are raised in the mind, especially in a bigoted people like the Mohammedans, whose religion does not teach them to put charitable constructions on what may be said of other people, how absurd and unlikely soever it may be, it is a most difficult task to overcome such prejudice in any other way but by showing the reverse in our own dealings with them. It had been circulated about the country and believed that as the Anasaras do not belong to the religion of Mohammed they cannot be friendly with the people of that faith, and that they cannot bear the sight of a Mohammedan praying in the name of Mohammed, whom his followers believe to be the true prophet of God. But the appearance of Abdul Kadu, the Foota Toro interpreter, and Kasumo, a

Yoruba, both of them Mohammedans and tolerable Arabic scholars, in our company, excited some inquiries respecting our situation and the treatment they received from us on board. Sumo Zaki himself was not behind in having his curiosity gratified in this respect. They were not a little surprised to hear from these men of their own persuasion that we treated them with the utmost kindness and did not in the least put any obstacle in the way of their performing their religious exercises. This was certainly unexpected tidings to a people shut up in the interior of the country, having no intercourse with the civilized world. Those who brought them news from the coast were not such as had opportunity of disarming themselves of the prejudice they had imbibed by mingling with Christians of sound principles and of friendly disposition. A Mohammedan can never be brought round by his religion being quarrelled with and abusively charged with falsehood and imposition, but by kind treatment he may be led to read and study the Christian's Bible, which by the blessing of God may lead him from the error of his way.

This advice is a counsel of perfection, and will possibly, after all these intervening years of experience, be confirmed by missionaries to-day who are labouring amongst Moslem people. A visit to the ruins of Rabbah, from which the highlands of Yoruba were seen, was a point of some importance, because it was found that this place was directly on the caravan route between Kano and Yoruba, and the halting-place for Ilorin, a great stronghold of Mohammedanism. Here at this spot one of the native crew, Joe from the South Sea Islands, going ashore after an illness, ate some roots which he mistook for cassava, which is eatable in this country. In a few days he died, self-poisoned by misadventure, and was buried by Crowther on the high cliff. Next day they were fortunate enough to meet with some Borgu traders, whose business is with Ashanti, and Dr. Baikie's servant, a Fanti, was able to speak to them. Others of the party, who were Yorubas, were brought on board to see over the ship, and said they knew the very spot where Mungo Park's boat was wrecked, which their fathers used to tell them was built of brass at the bow and the inside was full of sharp irons, against which they used to be warned, when diving in that direction. Crowther, therefore, entertained the hope that he might see this place, associated with this great traveller. Steering carefully between the steep rocks which made a narrow channel of the river beyond Jeba Island, the *Dayspring* struck and drifted, leaking rapidly, broken upon some rocky islets partly under the water. In a few moments their devoted vessel became a total wreck. They had only time to collect what was possible, and carry it to the shore, by the help of friendly canoes, and had to pass the nights, a tornado of wind and rain sweeping over them, with hardly any shelter, except rain-coats and umbrellas. When the day broke they saw their vessel rapidly disappearing, and the captain, seeing there was no hope, decided to abandon her. Friendly natives again brought them food, and a messenger was sent down to the Confluence to look for the *Sunbeam*, which vessel was expected to follow, and there report the woeful plight they were in. Meanwhile their visitors from the outlying villages were quite prepared with a theory in explanation of the disaster. They said that Ketsa, the god of the peak, had a dislike to red clothes, and having seen that colour among the shipwrecked party, had broken up the ship.

This gave an opportunity to obtain considerable information about this sensitive deity, whose worship had such a hold upon these poor people. And then he began to declare unto them the true God. He told them that the day of their sudden visit was the day of Soko (the great God), who made of one blood all nations of the earth, and (taking the hand of Mr. Glover and of the Nupé interpreter, being of different nations) yet God made us all alike as are the members of one body (pointing to each separately), and the great God who made these great waters on which they had come in their boat, and also the high hill of Ketsa, which stands in the midst of the great waters, is the God whom the white men worship, fear, honour, and love, and nothing else. This enforced delay was utilized to advantage, Crowther making many excursions into the interior, sometimes running no small risks in dealing with chiefs of a treacherous and unprincipled character.

One day a strange voice was heard in the crowd of natives, saluting Crowther with "Good morning, sir!" and the speaker, dressed in an old cast-off tobe and Turkish trousers, proved to be Henry George, a Sunday scholar at Abeokuta. He had a very sad story to tell of experiences in the Nupé country, as one of Dasaba's warriors. He then showed that he had not quite forgotten his reading and writing, and with his finger he forthwith scratched his full name on the sand. As Crowther's interpreter had been sent down to the coast with the mail, and his Hausa servant had been promised to Lieutenant

Glover, he engaged this young fellow to continue with him.

Another even more agreeable surprise was when an American missionary, the Rev. M. Clark, paid them a visit, having heard of their misfortunes, and brought with him some sugar, tea, and coffee, which were real comforts to Crowther and his companions, who had been living on parched Indian corn, sweetened with honey, for many weeks past. The visitor also brought them news of the outer world, of the Indian Mutiny, and also some old newspapers, which were eagerly scanned. Christmas Day was spent with as much decoration as was possible; the Union Jack flew at the head of the tent, a string of ship's flags and some branches of green shrubs were arranged over the doorway, and at the proper time in the morning Crowther conducted service and read the Homily on the Nativity and Birth of our Lord and Saviour Jesus Christ. At twelve o'clock seven guns were fired, echoing along the valley of the Yoruba hills opposite, and the purser, with much ingenuity, made a plum pudding out of Indian flour and a few currants, to follow the fowl which took the place of the usual turkey. If this Christmas was spent in somewhat Crusoe fashion, it was none the less a happy one. The little lonely group thought of wives and children and loved ones far away, and Crowther remarks, with his common-sense way of looking at things: "To me it was a matter of much satisfaction and thankfulness to the Giver of all good things that the party continued in such good health in a place believed to be most deadly in its influence on the European constitution." A week afterwards he makes some notes in his diary, bearing date 1 January, 1858:

"A happy new year to you!" was the salutation and wish which passed from one to the other early this morning. Last night we all kept up till twelve o'clock and the old year passed away and the new one commenced. Two large guns were fired to welcome this new round of time. How many recollections of the past were brought to mind, and how serious the thought of what the new year may bring forth! May God prepare us to meet every event as faithful soldiers of Christ.

Kasumo, the Arabic interpreter, having returned, came one night to Crowther with the Futa interpreter, and held a long conversation on the Christian religion until one o'clock in the morning. They had some doubts in their mind which they wished cleared up, whether it was Christ Himself who suffered death upon the Cross, or whether another person was substituted in His place, to save Him from that ignominious death, which they had been taught to believe God would not suffer Christ to endure, out of the great honour put upon Him. This naturally led to a long explanation and an account of Christ's passion, and Crowther says he put it to them thus: "that if Christ Himself had not died, then we were found false witnesses, because then He had never shed His blood, which is the price of our redemption; that if anything were kept back from Christ's ignominious death from a desire to honour Him, by so doing we deduct from the great dignity He obtained by His sufferings and death." So much were these two inquirers impressed with the truth of Christianity that both of them admitted that their knowledge from the Korân alone was very scanty and weak.

Crowther obtained permission from one of the chiefs to secure a piece of ground for mission premises; five conical huts were to be erected thereon. He had a desire to acquire also an adjoining portion of land upon which a huge pile of hippopotamus bones had been erected, but this was a fetish arrangement, and could not be disturbed. But he purchased a native boat and fitted it up with seats for six passengers, and then, in the sight of an admiring crowd, he launched it with the name of the *Mission Canoe*. Amongst the Mohammedans Crowther discovered a keen spirit of inquiry, and scarcely a day passed without some question being put to him, comparing their religion with Christianity. It was the fast of Ramadan.

During the fasting days the constant question was: "Do not the Anasaras fast?" My reply was: "Yes, they do fast; but the fast of the Anasaras is of a more private and conscientious kind than your public one. Thousands of the Anasaras may fast to-day and their neighbours know nothing of it, but their fast is known to God and to themselves; just so is their prayer in secret, as Christ has taught us." The answer I always received was: "*You are true persons; your religion is superior to ours.*" But be it remembered, this acknowledgment is made by the people, who only follow as they are led, and who embrace Mohammedanism because it is superior to the religion of the heathen; but from those who profess to be leaders and teachers of that religion we cannot expect such a ready acknowledgment, but rather opposite.

Several events, incidental to travellers, occurred to Crowther at this time, such as the discovery of a huge snake among the meal bags in the tent; a visit one dark night from a leopard, attracted by some young goats which, disappearing without touching them, came back again in the morning, and sprang upon one of the best milch goats. Every native seemed anxious at these times of danger to show a clean pair of heels, and as the party was destitute of firearms, it was only the shouting and general uproar of the camp which frightened the creature away, and saved their lives. Sickness began to make its appearance; the good health for which Crowther had been so thankful was no longer the rule, and Mr. Howard, the good purser, who had so deftly prepared the Christmas pudding, died after a few days of dysentery, much to the special grief of Crowther, who had an affection for him.

As might be expected, the only enemies of the proposed mission were the slave dealers, and these circulated false reports of the aims and conduct of the white men, doing their utmost to poison the minds of the kings and chiefs against them. Crowther had at one time, as a consequence of this, the greatest difficulty in dealing with the chief eunuch of the King N'deshi, who had fomented a strife about the building of the mission huts, and all these questions, especially relating to the holding of land, Crowther realized must be settled before he left, or it would entail endless trouble on the mission afterwards. The condition of the native women enlisted his sincere sympathy. They were the most industrious part of the population, but had to suffer most, as well as work the hardest. The picture he gives of their position, and the curious system they have of pawning their children to escape slavery, is worth quoting from his journal:

A great deal of labour is entailed on the women; on them solely devolves the care of the children, to feed and clothe from childhood until they are able to render their mothers a little assistance if they are females, or if they are boys, till the fathers claim their help in the farms if they be farmers. With such a charge upon them, without help, having to labour hard in bearing burdens—for they are the chief carriers of loads, grinding corn upon the millstones many times till late hours of the night, beguiling the tedious labour by their mill with songs, which labour is resumed at an early hour of the morning, preparing the flour into meal, retailing the same in the market, or hawking it about the town from house to house, and providing their husbands with provision from it—it is no wonder that they are soon worn out, and a female of thirty years has an appearance of forty. The most distressing part of the whole is that in time of war, when these poor women are unfortunate enough not only to lose their own liberty, but also that of their children, the additional care of procuring a ransom for themselves and their children adds tenfold more to their already heavy burdens. During the war which terminated in the subjugation of Umoru thousands of families had been brought into slavery by it, which added not a little to their painful toil. Very little is done by the husband to ransom so many wives and children; the consequence is every woman must see after herself and her children the best way she can to prevent their being sold into foreign service. Hence they have no other means but to have recourse to the system of pawning, as it is done in Yoruba. One example here will suffice. Fatuma, the aged mother of our good friend Dagenna, the Galadima at Ghebe at the Confluence, was met here living in the village of Kawura, about a day's journey from Rabba. She had the misfortune to have three nieces under her care, who were caught during the Umoru war. Her son being afar off at the Confluence, she had no help; there

OPOBO WOMEN AND CHILDREN

To face page 172

was no alternative; these children were to be sold northward by way of the desert, or westward down to the coast, if they were not forthwith ransomed. In this dilemma she could not do otherwise than sell all she had that was saleable, and then have recourse to a loan of cowries to make up the amount required. Two of the children were put in pawn for 20,000 cowries each—their labour was taken for the interest till the principal could be paid—and she herself was pawned for another 20,000, for which she had to pay the interest of 30 cowries a day, making 210 cowries per week. Since we had been cast up here she had been actively at work, selling yams, rice, rice flour, and such articles as were needed, and by small helps from us she had almost cleared up her debts when I last saw her. We should have been glad to release her at once in consideration of the assistance we had so many times received from her son if our means could have admitted of so doing.

There is something very pathetic about the spectacle of this brave, good soul, not even the mother, but the loving aunt of these little children, and one hopes that her self-denying labours were not in vain, and that the ransom was fully paid. It is noteworthy also that in a place which the usurious Israelite had not yet discovered, his dark-skinned representative, in exacting over fifty per cent on mortgage of this poor woman, displayed considerable business instincts. But the organ of acquisitiveness is never wanting in the children of Ham. Even so astute and watchful a mind as that of Crowther had all its time taken up in preventing abuses through the system of giving presents. He points out that it is established and practised by all throughout the country, and one cannot interview a chief for the first time with any prospect of success unless you bring a present in your hand. It is this chiefly by which the status and importance of the visitor are estimated; his character goes for little, but his gifts are talked about and valued everywhere. And, on the other hand, if they give presents to the visitors, it is in sure expectation of a similar return of the courtesy. A woman one day brought Crowther ten balls of a country meal called sondokoria, in exchange for which he gave her a paper containing twenty-five needles, which she promptly returned with contempt. Afterwards, however, finding the game of bluff did not pay, she repented and accepted the needles, asking pardon, and begging him to accept the meal, as she gave it him as a pious mallam, as her father was too.

At length, in October, 1858, the long looked for relief vessel, the *Sunbeam,* arrived, and Crowther, with the other members of the party, were taken on board. Before leaving the place of his enforced residence for two years, he said farewell to the chiefs, and completed all the arrangements for establishing a post of the mission there. The time had not been lost; indeed, he recognized the opportunity it had given him of gaining a knowledge of the natives which he could not have otherwise acquired. Not a slight advantage was his proficiency in their language, and the influence his name now possessed at a spot where the caravans crossed to and fro. On his way down the river Crowther stopped at Onitsha, and did not return to the coast. In the meantime Mr. Taylor had been working hard with marked success. He took Crowther to the mission stations, introduced him to the converts, and related what wonderful victories had been won at Onitsha. Many of his stories were full of encouragement. There had been a real spirit of inquiry manifested. Obi Ij'oma, one of the chief men, in the course of a religious conversation was asked if he had a soul. "Yes," was his reply. "But how is that soul to be saved?" "I do not know," was the sad answer. Then the way of salvation was pointed out to this poor dark mind. With a bright light in his eyes he exclaimed, "*Jesu Opara Tshuku Tun uzo oma?*" "Jesus, Son of God, show me the good way?"

Sometimes, however, they betrayed great caution, and made many curious comments upon the new teaching. At morning service one of the chiefs was present, and after a closing ejaculatory petition, the minister asked what he thought of it all. The old half-enlightened heathen gave answer in an idiom: "*Okuko ohunru obia na ata ona uku na ala ona na me wayo ele udo sia.*" The interpretation of which is as follows: "A new fowl when brought into the yard walks gently and looks steadily on the old ones, to see what they do." So the ministers and teachers, being experienced and mature in Christianity, are "the old ones"; but they being the new fowls, brought into the garden of Christianity, must necessarily walk gently and look steadily at their walk and conversation. Often in the market place one thousand people would listen to the good tidings of the new religion. Mr. Taylor had found the use of the Ibo tongue a great attraction in his services. On one occasion, while speaking of the folly of idol-making and the superstitious rites of fetishism as compared with the truths of Christianity, a spirit of genuine conviction seemed to possess the hearts of the hearers, and they confessed that they felt the power of those words, "Deliver me, for Thou art my God." Their black faces underwent an extraordinary change, beaming with delight and satisfaction, and they seemed quite carried away with the glad tidings. It brought to mind the prophetic words of Crowther's friend, good Bishop Vidal, who said: "The time will come when Tshuku (the gods) of Abo and the Ibos in general will fall down before the Gospel as Dagon fell before the ark. Their multifarious shrines shall give way for the full liberation and introduction of the Gospel to their forlorn, degraded, long-bewitched, but ransomed people of God."

On Advent Sunday Mr. Taylor preached in the King's quarters on the goodness of God in sending His only Son into the world, and illustrated his text by speaking of the capsized canoe on the river, and how readily the King would throw a cable to save his people's lives. Such an act would be what is called salvation. The world was in peril, and God sent His Son to save it, and only through Him can we have life. The old King listened with rapt attention, and then quietly rose with deep feeling, and lifting his hands and his eyes to heaven, slowly repeated these words: "*Opara Tshuku biko napu ga'm, Opara Tshuku biko napu ayi nile.*" "Son of God, save me; Son of God, save us all."

After a short stay at Onitsha Crowther started

back to the Confluence in a native canoe, with a crew which he found difficult to manage, sometimes threatening him for more passage money, and it was a relief when after these complications he reached Idda. Here he found his old friend Ghemodina ill, and Olumene, the owner of the canoe, took the opportunity of begging for almost everything he could lay his hands on. Finding, however, that Crowther's means and intentions gave him no hope, he begged for something as a charm to make people fear and respect him. He was told that Christians never made such things, but trusted in God, and prayed to Him morning and evening to preserve them. Crowther eventually gave him a small piece of Windsor soap, with which he was highly pleased, and possibly at some future time this unknown toilet requisite would be displayed to the admiration of his friends, if not their adoration too.

This little voyage to Rabbah was quite an eventful one, and occasionally really dangerous, and Crowther's tact and courage stood him in good stead. With most grateful feelings he at last found himself enjoying the shade and comfort of the mission huts at that place. Sumo Zaki was reputed dead; Dasaba was now King of Nupé, and was fighting for his throne against the Gbari. After a brief rest Crowther started for an overland expedition on foot from Rabbah to Abeokuta. He was ill with dysentery to begin with; this he attributes to the long exposure and constant worry in the open canoe on the journey to Rabbah. But he pushed on, nothing daunted, and reached

Ilorin, where the King and chief mallam cordially welcomed him. And at a large public meeting he was requested to address them on the all-important subject of Christ being the Son of God, leaving them afterwards with kind expressions of God's peace and blessing to rest on him. At last, after a weary and protracted journey, he came in sight of Abeokuta, and was there welcomed by the Bishop and Dr. Baikie, who had just arrived from Lagos. He expresses his heartfelt feelings in these words:

> I was thankful to meet all the members of the mission, tolerable in health, and the work of God prospering in their hands. Many new faces were seen among our old communicants and candidates who came to salute me on my arrival; these have since my absence been gathered from the scattered sheep among the thousands who are yet wandering from the fold of God. I hope and trust many more yet will hear the call of Christ through His faithful servants by the preaching of the Gospel. . . . My hearty prayer is that not only at Abeokuta, but in all other places where we have been permitted to have stations, obstacles may be removed out of the way, that many who are at present ready to join the Church, but kept back through the fear of man or through the influence of sin, may be released from their bondage, hear the call of Christ, and join His Church.

He could, however, only spend a short refreshing time with his friends here, for he soon made his way to Lagos, after being absent from his wife and family for two years and a half. He did not stay very long, however, for in the summer of 1859 he was going up the Niger again on board the *Rainbow*, but suffered a great disappointment on finding the passage stopped at the Confluence, a message having been sent down by Dr. Baikie that no missionary work could be undertaken at present. There was, therefore, no help for it but to return to the coast. On its way back the *Rainbow* was fired on by some natives at the Delta, and two men on board were killed. This unfortunate incident closed the Niger for two years, and during this long period of seclusion the native workers at the various mission stations which Crowther had established were left to themselves. He stayed at the mouth of the Nun for a long time, waiting in vain for the gunboat which was to be sent by the English Government to punish the villages. Early in the year 1861, through the lamented death of Mr. Laird, the pioneer of West African trade, the various factories on the Niger were closed, and no more vessels were sent for commercial purposes; and it was not until July of the same year that H.M.S. *Espoir* entered the river and destroyed the places from which the firing had come. Crowther was on board this vessel, and took with him two fresh native helpers to replace some on the Niger. A fresh mission station was opened at Akassa, at the mouth of the Nun river, and during the following winter he prepared a large party of thirty-three native teachers, with their wives and children, for the Niger. These, slightly reduced in numbers, were taken on board another gunboat, H.M.S. *Investigator*, which reached Onitsha on 5 September, 1862. Here, however, Crowther was not permitted to land, as the vessel proceeded up river in a few hours, much to his disappointment that he could not visit the mission station and see the people from whom he had been separated so long. When he reached the Confluence he went ashore at Ghebe. It was a memorable morning when the Christian converts and heathen gathered in the mission church to meet the kind and faithful minister who had first spoken to them of the Christian faith, and now met them with thankfulness as the firstfruits of his labours. This chapter will close with his own account of this remarkable scene, which naturally meant so much to him after so many trials and disappointments :

Sept. 14, 1862. This day at the morning service, though with fear and trembling, yet by faith in Christ, the great Head of the Church, who has commanded, "Go ye therefore, and teach all nations, baptizing them in the name of the Father, and of the Son, and of the Holy Ghost," I took courage and baptized eight adults and one infant in our new chapel in the presence of a congregation of one hundred and ninety-two persons, who all sat still with their mouths open in wonder and amazement at the initiation of some of their friends and companions into a new religion by a singular rite, the form in the name of the Trinity being translated in Nupé and distinctly pronounced as each candidate knelt. These nine persons are the first-fruits of the Niger Mission. Is not this a token from the Lord to the Society to persevere in their arduous work to introduce Christianity among the black population on the banks of the Niger, and that they shall reap in due time if they faint not? More so when the few baptized persons represent several tribes of large tracts of countries on the banks of the Niger, Tshadda, Igaru, Igbira, Gbari, Eki, or Bann, and even a scattered Yoruba was amongst them. Is not this an anticipation of the immense fields opened to the Church to occupy for Christ?

The newly-founded mission was, however, destined to pass through more trials, largely owing to the instability of authority vested in the ruling powers in native towns. As a king or superior chief exercises autocratic sway, it rarely follows that on his decease the same favour which he showed to the mission can be counted on from his successors. Crowther had always been successful in winning the confidence of these native potentates. He always made a point of impressing upon them that the visit of the Christian missionary was not with warlike intent, or from any desire to forcibly appropriate territory, but simply to teach them the truths of Christianity, and to encourage them, for their own advantage, to engage in trading relations with the world outside.

As an instance of this, while Crowther was staying at Ghebe one of the messengers of King Masaba, who seems to have cherished suspicions of the peaceful intentions of the mission, was entertained by Crowther at the mission station, and was taken round the premises, shown the schoolroom, the cotton gins, and the press and bales which were produced out of it, greatly to the astonishment of the visitors.

> I asked him (writes Crowther) to deliver this message to the King, that we are Anasara; there, pointing to the schoolroom, we teach the Christian religion; pointing to the cotton gin, I said this is our gun; and to the clean cotton puffing out of it, that is our powder; and I said the cowries which are the proceeds of the operation are the shots which England, the warmest friend of Africa, earnestly desires she should receive largely. The King was to judge from the messenger, who had seen of our proceeding here, whether the efforts of England were injurious to the prosperity of a nation or favourable to its peace and welfare.

To prove what an excellent impression was made by this tactful treatment of the position, it may be added that when Ama Abokko, the King of Ghebe, was on his deathbed, and was giving charge to his head chiefs about his children and the government of the town after his death, until a successor should be elected, he did not forget Crowther and his fellow-helpers in the mission, saying, "Suffer nothing to harm Oibos; they are my strangers." But unfortunately, when he had gone the country was thrown into confusion and anarchy, and in the midst of these revolutions the mission premises were entirely destroyed, and the Confluence station had to be removed to Lokoja.

CHAPTER VI

CONSECRATION AND AFTER

THE work on the Niger had now reached a point when it became absolutely necessary that some steps should be taken to ensure its consolidation and thorough supervision. Amid many hindrances and delays through the uncertainty of ships going up and down the Niger, and in spite of occasional hostility from native kings, the mission had obtained a permanent hold upon the country; but experience had shown that the climate was still a deadly barrier to European missionaries. At that time the origin and conditions of the malarial fever were not so accurately known as they are to-day, and this was a point of importance in determining the future support of the work by Englishmen in West Africa. But altogether apart from this consideration, the advantage of utilizing the native qualities of grace and ability was clearly demonstrated. Crowther's fond idea of Africa for the African as regards the foundation of a native Church seemed within sight of realization. In an important and ably written article which appeared in the "Church Missionary

Intelligencer" in May, 1864, the position was clearly defined, and shows the steps which were leading up to the new departure of creating a native Bishopric in West Africa. The writer, who evidently discusses the question from an official and authoritative standpoint, after adverting to the evils of the slave trade and the grave dangers of the climate in West Africa, says:

But these difficulties have been, in a great measure, overcome; the power of the slave trade is broken, and although it still lives, yet, like a venomous serpent which has received a mortal injury, it is in its death throes. The insalubrity of the climate no longer presents the same hindrance that it used to do to the progress of missions, and that because the European missionary is no longer alone in the work. A native Church has been raised up on the peninsula of Sierra Leone, with its well-ordered congregations and its native ministers effectively discharging the high responsibilities imposed on them. This native Church, in a great measure self-supporting and self-ministering, is now girding itself up to enter upon its duties as a missionary church and send forth its evangelists into the heathen and Mohammedan countries which lie around it. Already the African Christian has been tried in this service. He has shown himself not only capable of understanding and receiving the truth of Christianity, but of communicating it to his fellow-countrymen. On him the African climate exercises no malign influences, to him the languages of Africa present no impediment. Although few in number, compared with the multitudinous inhabitants of that great continent, yet the first-fruits of Africa to Christianity is in a remarkable degree multilingual, and thus the services of a large proportion of the tongues of Africa are clearly placed at the disposal and are ready to be engaged in the service of Christianity.

The opportune moment thus appears to have arrived when the native Church should be still further empowered to go forth and with a holy freedom do the Lord's work in Africa, and as the native Christian has been raised to the ministry so the native ministry be permitted to culminate in a native episcopate. The question is, can one among the African clergymen be found to whom so great a responsibility can with safety be trusted? and this question the Church Missionary Society has ventured to answer in the affirmative. Nearly twenty-one years have elapsed since the Rev. Samuel Crowther was ordained a deacon by the late Bishop of London. The Lord has given him grace during the period which has since elapsed to continue humble, consistent, and useful. He has made full proof of his ministry. The new missions on the Niger imperatively require episcopal superintendence. They are so remote from the Bishop of Sierra Leone as to be placed entirely beyond his reach. The native catechists who have been instrumental in raising up congregations at Onitsha and Ghebe require prompt admission to Holy Orders, that they may duly minister to their flocks and, as well by the teaching of God's Word as by the due administration of the Sacraments, promote their growth. Our Christians on the banks of the Niger need to be as quickly as possible brought forward into activity and be utilized in missionary effort among their countrymen. To delay any longer the native episcopate would be unduly to retard the development of the native Church.

These words will sufficiently indicate why a bishop was wanted on the Niger, and that Crowther must be the man called to fill that office. They are also an indication, one had almost said a vindication, not only of the capacity of the negro for full orders as a missionary clergyman, but of the success which had already attended his labours among his own people. Whatever trying vicissitudes the work might afterwards be called to suffer, the foundation of the native Church had by Crowther's earnest endeavour been well and truly made. Pioneers, like inventors, often miss the historical credit of their labours, and the man who cleared the ground and spread the base secure is generally forgotten in the acclaim when the flag flies over the completed structure. Crowther was being called to a diocese which he had himself created. He introduced by his discoveries these places in his country which have since become such familiar names in the missionary field. He had done more. He had in a quiet, unostentatious, and yet unmistakable way proved in himself the latent qualities and capacities of the African, and, in a lesser degree, it was also demonstrated in the native agents he employed at his stations. Therefore the selection of such a man to the highest honour the Church can bestow was amply deserved and appreciated, both in Africa and England. It was the culmination of a unique career.

The grey old cathedral at Canterbury has witnessed many wonderful events, but St. Peter's Day, 29 June, 1864, will rank as a red-letter day in its annals. There are those living who have interesting memories of that scene three-and-forty years ago. It was no ordinary occasion. Special trains were run from London and elsewhere, and as early as eight o'clock an unusual crowd were present at morning prayer. The cathedral never looked more beautiful, bathed in summer sunshine, a bright augury of the new epoch in missionary polity and enterprise. Among the thousands filling those seats with expectant faces were many friends of Crowther, but we will only notice two who had a special interest in the service. One in naval uniform is Admiral Sir H. Leeke, who was the young captain on board H.M.S. *Myrmidon* to first take in his hands the little rescued slave boy, palpitating with fear and wonder, from the captured slaver off the coast of Lagos. This boy, who was soon to be consecrated as Bishop, had never lost sight of his friend, who now, with many thankful memories, forms one of the congregation.

An elderly lady slowly makes her way to a front seat, where she might easily see and hear; but one of the churchwardens reminds her that this place is reserved for a distinguished lady who had a ticket. She turns round and quietly says in answer: "I think I have a right equally to this seat, because that black minister to be consecrated Bishop this morning was taught the alphabet by me." The Dean and the lady referred to, hearing this, at once begged the visitor to retain her seat. She was the widow of Bishop Weeks, of Sierra Leone.

When the Archbishop and other prelates had taken their places, the Bishop of Lincoln read the Epistle and the Bishop of Winchester the Gospel, and the sermon was preached by the Rev. H. Longueville Mansel, Professor of Philosophy at Oxford, from 1 Peter v. 2, 3, on being "ensamples to the flock." Then the choir, with those exquisite boyish trebles, sang Mendelssohn's "How lovely are the messengers," while the two Bishops-elect walked to the vestry to put on their rochets, and on their return, among the others, was this letter patent read:

"We do by this our licence, under our Royal signet and sign manual, authorize and empower you, the said Samuel Adjai Crowther, to be Bishop of the United Church of England and Ireland, in the said countries of Western Africa beyond the limits of our dominions."

It had been arranged that Crowther should be led up to the Communion Table by the two Colonial Bishops present, but the Bishop of Winchester, with kindly thoughtfulness, stepped forward, and waving aside Bishop Nixon, took his place beside Crowther, so that on such an occasion a double honour should be rendered to the African prelate, and he walked up with him to introduce him to the Archbishop. Such a graceful act was noticed by many present at the service. At this point the choir again sang Wise's anthem, "Prepare the way of the Lord," and while the Bishops-elect were kneeling with bowed heads, the "Veni Creator Spiritus" was beautifully sung to Tallis' music. Then, with hands outstretched, the Archbishop, in a clear voice, gave the apostolic charge: "Remember that thou stir up the grace of God which is given thee by this imposition of our hands, for God hath not given us the spirit of fear, but of power and love and soberness." At this solemn moment Crowther took from the hand of the Archbishop his consecration Bible, with the words: "Take heed unto thyself, and to doctrine, and be diligent in doing them: for by so doing them thou shalt both save thyself and them that hear thee. Be to the flock of Christ a shepherd, not a wolf; feed them, devour them not. Hold up the weak, heal the sick, bind up the broken, bring again the outcasts, seek the lost. Be so merciful, that you be not too remiss; so minister discipline, that you forget not mercy: that when the Chief Shepherd shall appear you may receive the never-fading crown of glory; through Jesus Christ our Lord."

At the conclusion of the consecration service the new Bishops took their places within the altar rails, and the Communion Service, to which a great number of the congregation stayed, concluded this impressive event. The crowd melted away, and the cathedral grew empty again, but this crowning incident in the life of Bishop Crowther would never be forgotten. Throughout all this solemn function, the impressive prayers, the pealing music, the cadence of the singing, the hush of the consecration vow, and the moment of sweet communion, the heart of this man turned to Africa, his own dear land, and the little flock of his black brethren, and beyond that larger multitude in spiritual fetters for whom Christ died.

This public event was commented on by the Press as a good and promising step in the right direction; a few thoughtful sentences from a leading article in the "Record" will sufficiently represent this

We might dwell on the practical refutation afforded by Dr. Crowther's merited elevation to the episcopate to the taunts of certain professors who maintain that the cerebral development of the negro shows that he is disqualified for intellectual pursuits, and that he cannot be lifted out of his congenital dullness; but we pass on to entreat the prayers of our readers for him and his diocese. He will need much wisdom, peculiar grace, and constant strength. Humanly speaking, the future of the native Church depends on the manner in which its first Bishop shall administer its polity and organize its laws. It will be necessary also for him to exercise great discrimination in conferring Holy Orders on his brethren, and to take heed that he magnifies his office in the estimation of all by the exemplary consistency of his life and the holiness of his conversation. That he will do so we are assured of past experience, but the slightest consideration proves how much he needs to be supported by the sympathy and prayers of the Church.

The new Bishop, amid many congratulations from friends, lost no time in getting to his field of labour again. On 24 July he left England, and arrived at Sierra Leone on 10 August, where he met with a most enthusiastic welcome. When the *Macgregor Laird* reached the harbour of Freetown crowds were waiting to witness the wonderful spectacle of a liberated African, an Aku man, the trophy of missionary teaching at Sierra Leone, coming as Bishop back to their shores. There was no lavish display of bunting or roar of cannon; the delighted faces of his own people, and the chorus of "God bless you," which met him everywhere, were to Bishop Crowther more than enough.

After a day's rest he was escorted to Fourah Bay College, where all the clergy, catechists, and schoolmasters had assembled in one of the lecture-rooms to give him a joyous reception, and express their congratulations. Two addresses were signed and duly handed to him amid applause, one by the whole body of the Church Missionary agents and native pastors, the other by the authorities of the College, upon whose history he had shed such lustre by his name. The first, which bore over thirty-six signatures, was full of brotherly love, as the following extract will testify:

We regard your consecration as a token of God's favour to the Church in Africa, and would unfeignedly rejoice with you in this mark of His distinguishing love, believing it, as we do, to be an earnest of richer blessings which are yet in store. In reviewing your whole past career in this colony, and subsequently at Abeokuta and the Niger, we thank God for the abundant grace bestowed upon you and for the measure of success granted you in your missionary work, and we trust that the same grace may be vouchsafed to guide and comfort, to strengthen and support you through all your future course in the high office to which you have been called.

It will be a source of comfort for you to know that prayer-meetings were held in every district in the colony on the day of your leaving England that God would protect you from the dangers of the deep, and you may rest assured that prayer will constantly ascend, that under your wise and judicious culture the thorn and thistle may be uprooted and the Rose of Sharon and the Lily of the Valley may be seen along the whole banks of the Niger. May the Spirit of the Lord rest upon you, the spirit of wisdom and understanding making you as a chief pastor of the flock of Christ in Africa, of quick understanding in the fear of the Lord, so that you will judge not after the sight of your eyes, nor reprove after the hearing of your ears, but ruling and superintending all things according to truth and love.

During the reading of this address Bishop Crowther was evidently under deep emotion, and when he rose to reply his voice thrilled with feeling. He very earnestly thanked them for all their loving expressions towards him. Reminding them of old times, he said :

When we look back to the commencement we find the mission took its beginning among a heterogeneous mass of people, brought together in the providence of God from many tribes of this part of Africa, out of whom, through the zealous, faithful, and persevering labour of the early missionaries, arose devout congregations of faithful and sincere Christians. After a time the mission produced a native ministry, then a self-supporting native pastorate, and latterly, out of the native ministry, an humble step outward was taken in faith to introduce a native episcopate in missions beyond Her Majesty's dominions. Here we pause and raise our Ebenezer to God's praise. Hitherto the Lord has helped us.

This onward progress seems to be an indication from God, beckoning to us to come forward, put our shoulders to the wheels, and ease our European brethren of the great work which they have so nobly sustained alone from their predecessors for fifty years, many of whom had sealed the testimony of their zeal with their lives. Their graves at the burial grounds are existing monuments of their faithful obedience to their Master's command: "Go, and teach all nations."

Whether called to their rest or whether beaten back from the fields of their labour through ill-health and forced to retire, or whether still labouring among us, it is our bounden duty in gratitude to remember and esteem them highly in love for their work's sake, of which we are the fruits.

We must exhibit a missionary spirit ourselves, and encourage it among our congregations, if we are imitators of missionary enterprises; if, like as Timothy knew Paul, we also have known their zeal, we should endeavour to preach the Gospel in the regions beyond the colony.

To extend our line of usefulness we must seriously impress on our Christian countrymen the necessity of exhibiting a spirit of liberality, after the example of the mother Church, whose spirit we should imbibe, not only to support their own pastors and school teachers, keeping in good repair their churches and other buildings made over into their hands, but also contribute, according to the means God has blessed them with, to send the Gospel into countries beyond them which are yet destitute of the blessings of its light.

But, above all, we must be followers of Christ, the Great Shepherd of His flock and the example of His apostles, in the habit of prayer for help from above. This is the weapon which prevails most in the work of the ministry. When we feel our weakness and insufficiency for the work to which God has called us, we must constantly go to the Throne of Grace for divine aid. We are better fitted when we feel our incompetency to change a sinner's heart. This will drive us to apply to the Fountain Head for a quickening spirit from above, which He has promised to all who ask Him; then we shall be encouraged to go on in this our might. Has He not sent us?

It was now the turn of the College, and the address they presented, signed by principal, tutors, and students, was not a whit behind in cordial appreciation of the honour laid upon the Bishop, in which they also shared. The words are preserved, but it will be enough to make a brief extract from the greeting of his Alma Mater:

> We thank God for the grace bestowed upon you, enabling you to labour so faithfully for the past thirty-five years in His service. This Institution at one time enjoyed the benefit of your instruction, but of late years the Yoruba and the Niger missions have been the fields in which you have laboured. Notwithstanding this, we have not been unmindful of you; your name has been familiar as a "household word" among us, and you have ever been held up as an example to our youth.

When he got up to reply he was received with that boisterous applause which is the peculiar attribute of old college comrades. When quiet was restored the Bishop excused himself from any set speech, seeing that since he landed every moment had been taken up with pressing engagements. But he naturally grew reminiscent, and urged them to avoid that spirit of worldliness and self-interest which had so decimated the sixty students of Haensel and Kissling's regime, that scarcely a dozen were now workers in the mission field.

> He left the college (he said) in 1841 to join the Timmanee Mission, which was then established under the superintendence of Mr. Kissling, but was shortly afterwards detached from that field of labour to join in the Niger Expedition. He then entered into a narrative of bitter taunts and ridicule from his friends, some of whom styled him a fool for joining the expedition without any guarantee of good pay like the Europeans. He told them, in reply, that the Society had promised to supply him with necessaries, and consequently he should not want. He was subsequently connected for ten years with the Yoruba mission, where had gathered, under God's blessing, a

very promising and much attached congregation. He dated his connection with the Niger since 1854, from which period he had been literally moving to and fro. To a friend inquiring at the same time whether he did not mean to rest, he answered: "I shall only rest when I have no more work to do." It was his firm conviction, from what he had witnessed from travelling to and fro along the coast, that the difficulties, hardships, and deprivations of missionaries are nothing in comparison with what many a merchant suffers for a paltry gain. A missionary should be jack-of-all-trades, one ready to put his hands to work and to do in a legitimate way anything that might tend to advance the cause of Christ. In conclusion, he called the attention of the students of the college, who were all present, to the fact that though they were but six in the reopening, yet that number was greater by two than what they were when the college was first established in 1827. They had all the brethren before them as an encouragement, whereas he and his fellow-students then had none to look up to.

He trusted that he had succeeded in his attempt to deepen their hearts in the work, and prayed that every one enlisted under the banner of Christ should never fail to prove himself a good soldier of the Cross.

The Bishop then recommended in prayer his brethren to the God of Christian missions, and pronounced the Benediction. Soon afterwards we find him starting for Lagos, which he reached on 22 August, and where he held his first ordination service, admitting Mr. Lambert Mackenzie to deacon's orders. He then took a passage on board the *Investigator*, and went up the Niger again. Bishop Crowther was a man of unresting activity, and a born traveller. This was one of the qualifications which marked him out as *the* Bishop of the Niger. The wide extent of his diocese "beyond the limit of our dominions," with an ever-retreating horizon inland, through which the lordly Niger and its tributaries flowed, demanded a man of almost inexhaustible energy. This was an impossible condition to a European constitution. Devoted missionaries with grand ideals had found themselves perplexed and baffled by the growing need of the work and their physical incapacity to do anything more. Either they died in the field with a vision of what might have been before their closing eyes, or returned sick and unfit, with a haunting sense of unaccomplished aims. But not so with Bishop Crowther. A little man, with nerves of steel, upon whose constitution neither lagoon nor mosquito could leave any deadly germ, whom incessant work did not seem to wear, intellectually alert and vivid, spiritually so optimistic and full of hopeful faith. He was always on the tiptoe of new achievements, and yet no man had more native dignity or common sense.

On reaching Onitsha he held another ordination service, and much interest was excited by the strange spectacle of a native being admitted by a native Bishop. The people gazed in wonder ; the like had never been seen before or thought to be possible. But if they were so much impressed, how much more was the Bishop's mind moved by it. He makes this note of his thoughts :

The native converts did not fully understand what it was, but our mission party entered into it with heart and soul. There was nothing grand in it, but a peculiar solemnity pervaded the whole service. The place of ordination, the congregation among whom it took place, the candidate for ordination, the assisting priest, and the officiating bishop, presented such a novel scene, as if a new thing was taking place in Africa. Can this be real? Is this the way Christianity spread to remote countries in the first centuries of its promulgation? In the nineteenth century, the time when "many shall run to and fro, and knowledge shall be increased," when "the wilderness and solitary place shall be glad for them, and the desert shall rejoice and blossom as the rose"?

But the shadow behind all this was the hold which the evil native customs still had upon Onitsha. While a few were rejoicing in their happy deliverance from this thraldom, there was around a cruel darkness, for on the death of Prince Odiri human sacrifices were made. The native missionary tried his best to stop this, and offered with money to redeem the victims, but without success. Amongst others who were buried alive in the grave of this dead prince was a little innocent girl of eight years of age, with a knapsack hung over her shoulder, containing a piece of mutton, some kola nuts, and a snuff-box, for the use of the spirit of the dead man in the next world. The Christian converts were roused to indignation, and at the risk of their lives they hurried into the King's presence, expressing their horror at what had been done. One cried passionately: "The Gospel, which we have never known before, has appeared in your day. Prize it! Prize it! Prize it! You have to give an account to your Maker and Judge! Do not shed blood!" Another man confined himself to a word of simple and heartfelt testimony. He uttered the following words before the King: "I am now a baptized convert, and one of your subjects. The Gospel teaches me to obey those in authority. I have been ridiculed by all my townsmen. I am glad to tell you this day, as my earthly King, that I am a scapegoat of Jesus Christ."

Some of their ways of expressing their real spiritual experiences are pathetic in their sweet simplicity. For instance, the native pastor had called upon a poor father whose girl, the very apple of his eye, had just died. After a word of condolence on the loss of his daughter the pastor asks his convert: "Do you wholly trust in the Lord?" The bereaved man clasped his hands and replied: "I do calmly resign all my afflictions to Him. I myself live and move by Him. God forbid that I should distrust my Lord and Saviour Jesus Christ. Look what afflictions and sufferings He undertook on my account. He rescued me from hell." So speaking, he rushed out in the front of his yard, raised his eyes to heaven, gazed long, then fell down on his knees, put his face to the earth with profound humility, and exclaimed, "Good Jesus! Good Jesus! Good Jesus! Give me heart to bear, give me heart to pray!"

When the Bishop reached Ghebe he held a confirmation of five settlers from Sierra Leone and sixteen native converts. This again was a new rite in this far-away outpost, and proved a solemn and impressive time. Next day we find him taking the Sunday-school. He was always such a favourite with the children. And after dismissal he had an earnest talk with the teachers about their work. Then he made his way up the river to Idda to see the Ata, in spite of the opposition of the chiefs or the rapacious demands of the canoe men, who found their match this time.

"I say at once," he remarked, "that they intended to make as much of me as possible by this intended trip to Idda, so I determined to listen to no such story."

When he arrived Abokko, the great chief, of whom we shall hear more anon, said he was glad to see him, and told him that he, the Bishop, was a true man, because his promise to come was not believed by the King, and to disappoint his royal master by the fulfilment of his promise was delightful to him. This fussy sable functionary took care to be liberally treated in the matter of presents, and the gift of a fancy border white sheet, damask cushion, and smoking cap, worked by the Reading Ladies' Working Association at home, had evidently a gratifying and profitable effect. The Bishop, in his journal, makes a note here:

> These articles being select, suitable for a king, and being ladies' handiwork, I purposed to make the best use of them, to convince the people and the King how superior civilized nations are through knowledge and the reception of Christianity, and how low and inferior the condition of those who are without them, and what they, both male and female, may also be if they receive the Gospel.

In this place he was solemnly informed that it was their belief that when their King or great chiefs died they go to the white man's country and became like him, travelling like a white man, and therefore they regarded the Bishop as one of their own countrymen from the spirit world who had died. Abokko was very anxious to know whether the white man's country was not in the neighbourhood of God's residence (Paradise), and therefore much nearer God than the black man; also whether it is not true that when the white man sees a person of note he puts him in a book and carries him back to his country, which perhaps was not altogether a bad guess at the truth!

The Bishop had a very interesting interview with the Ata or King, after many excuses and much rather clever diplomacy on the part of Abokko to keep them apart. The reason for this was found to be a feeling of terror lest the white man should take his photograph, with dire results, as depicted by the wise men of the court! In dealing with this crafty old heathen the Bishop had not only taken pains to specify the objects of his visits, but to tell other people during his enforced delay, so that the King might be fully impressed and prepared to consider them. The last of these applications was to this effect:

> That as we intend establishing ourselves at Idda, I should be glad if the Ata would take the ruinous state of a large portion of his town into consideration and act as a king ought to do, by calling together the elders of his country and consulting to put an end to the quarrel between him and the Abokko's family, recalling them to rebuild their houses, in consideration of the good services to his country of their grandfather, who was a worthy friend to the white men, for our sake who now interpose; but, above all, for God's sake, who might never forgive us if He were to keep His anger for ever.

It is really remarkable what influence the Bishop had with these people; how, for example, in this particular case the Ata entertained these rather weighty demands for favour, and at once gave every facility for the erection of mission premises and the furtherance of Christian work among his people. Doubtless the fact of the Bishop being a black man and understanding so much better the native mind and customs added much to his success. The inevitable present also had its share in keeping the royal mind in a good and peaceable humour. In his turn he loaded the Bishop with gifts of kola nuts, yams, and a sheep and goat, which were gladly accepted and were valuable, not so much perhaps for their intrinsic worth as the expression they manifested of friendly feeling. This interview ended with a little talk over this gift business, which the Bishop thus notes in his journal :

> I was thankful so far the Lord had given us success as to enable us to see and gain the confidence of the Ata and his people. But the King had been told that I had the sun (i.e. the watch) about me, which he should like to see. I got up and opened the watch, which I held to his ears that he might hear it ticking plainly. I then opened the case that he might see the working of the spring. The Ata had also been told of my glass lantern, and he would be very glad if I would order one like it for him, also a pair of long boots, with a pair of spurs, and a large umbrella. I wanted to see the size of his foot, and he immediately took off his sandal, which articles I promised to order for him.

The curiosity of these great men in Africa knows no bounds. On one occasion a king wanted to know whether the great white Queen wore leather boots, and in order to outshine her he told the Bishop to order him a pair of boots made of brass, which his visitor promised should be done when he had discovered in London a maker of brass boots.

BONNY CHIEF AND WIVES

On his arrival back at Ghebe the Bishop preached to the people, and afterwards administered the Sacrament, also baptized ten adults and seven children. The journey over, the Bishop visited Bonny, in the Bight of Biafra, and founded the first Delta station there. It was an important opening, and destined to become one of the most flourishing stations of the native work. He recognized the great necessity of dealing with that large and scattered population inhabiting the swampy and malarial region of the Delta, where the great river Niger loses itself in twenty-six branches, spread out like a gridiron, and intersected continually by other smaller streams stretching from the lagoons of Lagos at one end to the mouth of the Old Calabar River on the other. This territory of dark superstition, with its one hundred and twenty miles of sea front, and a depth landward of one hundred and forty miles, was to be the immense parish of the Delta mission.

Bonny had an evil reputation. Whilst its position gave it natural advantages for trade in palm oil, its people were most repulsive and degraded. Within a few years of this visit of the Bishop cannibalism was a common practice, human sacrifices were freely offered on the death of a chief, the juju temples were the scene of the most revolting customs, and were paved and decorated with the skulls and bones of their victims. Everywhere devilry and cruelty still abounded, and the town was infested with huge crawling lizards, which had been created into deities, and must not therefore be destroyed.

However, to this, one of the vilest spots on earth, full of the habitations of cruelty, the light of the Gospel was to come. Its King, William Pepple, paid a visit to the white man's land, and was actually in England shortly before the consecration of the Bishop. This king was so struck with the results of Christianity and civilization that on his return he addressed a letter to the Bishop of London, which document was handed by him to the Church Missionary Society. Fitting in with this remarkable chain of providential events, this was the means of directing the Bishop on his return to answer its requirements in person. He gives us a good picture in his first impressions of Bonny at this time :

The town of Grand Bonny is situated on the east side or left bank of the river which bears its name, Ubain, on a triangular point of a creek running eastward from the main river. The chief part of the town is built on the bank of the creek for the convenience of working and securing their canoes, because the agitation of the waves is not so much felt here as on the beach of the main river ; but the creek is very muddy, for which the people seem to care very little. All the ships and hulks lay as near the point of the town creek as possible, and consequently the chief scene of business.

The town being so flat, and almost on a level with the flow tide, is very seldom perfectly dry, and when it rains it is very soon saturated ; but, bad as it is, it can be improved. There are a few good houses owned by chiefs. I had to walk over the town many times to find an open dry space for a temporary schoolroom between three choices. After a little acquaintance with the localities I pitched upon the most suitable, it being somewhat good for our purposes. Here the temporary schoolroom, fifty feet by twenty feet, is put up of native materials. Near the schoolroom is a house hired for the use of the mission agents, and thus the preliminary arrangements to commence our operations are completed till we can erect a permanent mission station outside the town, where we shall have sufficient room, sea breeze, the comforts of dry and healthy ground, and of being separated from the irregular habits of the population. About ten minutes' walk from the town of Bonny I found a nice dry, sandy land, overgrown with woods, four feet elevation above the spring tide. Here I have chosen for the erection of a permanent mission station.

This was, of course, written after the Bishop had been received by King William Pepple and the chiefs. He was cordially welcomed, and obtained signed agreements for the establishment of the mission. After a short absence, visiting other places, the Bishop came back to Bonny, bringing with him two lay agents, who were lodged in an old hulk, *The Bahiamian*, opening a day-school and preaching in the streets and market place of the town. But the Bishop insisted on having a proper abode on shore, and an old chief known as the "Admiral" offered two houses, which were promptly cleared of rubbish, cleaned, and made suitable for habitation. The next step was to build a big mud and wattle school-chapel, capable of holding two hundred people, and finally the Bishop discovered a good place for mission premises to be permanently erected, and obtained the needful permission. But the natives were aghast at the choice, for it was what they called "a bad juju bush," being a place which had been used for the bodies of victims killed for sacrifice, also the rubbish heap where twins were, according to their custom, flung away to die. Cries were accordingly raised that if the missionaries took this place the gods would be angry. One could hardly imagine this horrid hovel to be a sacred shrine, and that these very trees were invested with a mysterious character and power for evil. The Bishop, however, was not the man to be frightened away by these terrors, and when, in spite of this public remonstrance, he was allowed to have the land, it was grudgingly granted at his own risk, and the powers would not guarantee the consequences.

"Give us the ground," he said, "and leave us and juju to settle the remaining palaver."

It was, however, no slight matter to get the evil place cleared. The horrified people would not touch a leaf of this sacred and yet infamous grove, and King William Pepple sent his son with ten obedient men to cut the bush; but even this young prince, when he arrived at the spot, asked to have a portion of Scripture read, and somebody to kindly pray, as there were so many evil spirits about to be disturbed. At last, not without misgivings, they commenced to hew down the branches, and meeting nothing of a supernatural sort, grew bolder, and the place was soon made fit for building purposes. When the mud school-chapel was at last finished and opened with prayer and thanksgiving, attention was drawn to a large copper bell, three and a half feet in diameter, which for many years had been lying on the ground in Bonny town. How such a huge import from the white man's country could have reached this place could only be explained by the inscription which the Bishop deciphered as follows: "*William Dobson, founder, Downham, Norfolk, England. This bell was cast for Opooboo Foobra, King of Grand Bonny, in the year* 1824." Here, then, was an opportunity of utilizing this old bell—once possibly half worshipped by the heathen, perhaps used in their dreadful practices—for the service of the new school-chapel erected for worship of the true God. Chief Oko Jumbo, a name strangely familiar, came forward, and, at his own expense, in English fully twenty-four pounds, transferred it from its resting-place in the mud to the roof of the mission chapel.

One of the happiest days in Bonny, a direct result of the preaching of the Gospel, was Easter Day, 1867, when the worship of the lizard or guana was formally and for ever renounced by the King and people. The Bishop wrote the news home with a gladdened heart, a remarkable story indeed when it is remembered what a firm hold these creatures had upon the superstitious fears of the natives. Sir H. H. Johnston, in his lecture before the Royal Geographical Society, gave his invaluable testimony to this, when he was pointing out that the animal worship was so real at this time that the British authorities on the Oil Rivers were compelled to afford it a certain recognition. He goes on to tell us:

> At Bonny the monitor lizards became a sickening nuisance. They devoured the European's fowls, turkeys, ducks, and geese with impunity; they might lie across the road or the doorways of houses with their six feet of length and savagely lash the shins of people who attempted to pass them with their whip-like serrated tails, and if you wounded or killed one of them there was no end of a to-do. You were assaulted or robbed by the natives, harangued by the consul on board of a man-of-war, and possibly fined into the bargain. For its effectual abolishment, which has been of the greatest benefit

to the well-being of Europeans and natives alike, we owe our thanks, not to the intervention of naval or consular officials, nor to the bluff remonstrances of traders, but to the quiet, unceasing labours of the agents of the Church Missionary Society.

Now let the Bishop tell the story of the extirpation of these privileged pests :

April 22, 1867. You will be glad to hear that yesterday, at the mutual consent of myself and chiefs, the geedee or guana, Bonny juju, was declared to be no longer Bonny juju, and many of the townsmen are killing them.

No sooner was this renunciation made and orders given to clear the town of them than many persons turned out in pursuit of these poor reptiles, which had been so long idolized, and now killed them as if it were in revenge, and strewed their carcases all about in open places and in the markets by dozens and scores ; fifty-seven were counted at one market-place, where they were exposed to public view as a proof of the people's conviction and former error, and that they were determined to reform in good earnest in this respect. Everywhere one went the carcases of the guana met the sight. There was another decision made respecting the removal of the guanas. Lest any should hereafter say he had not had some share in the extinction of the sacred reptile, it was decided that some of the blood should be sprinkled into all the wells in Bonny town to indicate that they had concurred not only in its destruction, but also in its use as food. Many soon after began to feed upon the flesh, roasted with fire. This reminds me of the passage: "And he took the calf which they had made, and burnt it in the fire, and ground it to powder, and strawed it upon the water, and made the children of Israel drink of it" (Exodus xxxii. 20).

The Bishop adds, however, that it could not be expected that the people would have the same courage and resolution as the King and his chiefs. Superstition dies hard, and after this it is not surprising that the wells of water were shunned from a superstitious fear rather than disgust. The water girls were sent to the mission premises for supplies of water from the only well unpolluted, and they came in large numbers, their pitchers upon their heads, and many in a state of nudity. The Bishop determined to make a protest against the habits of the people in this respect, and refused to allow any to draw water unless decently clothed, and this had the desired effect. Not only had the people suffered by these reptiles killing their chickens, but, as we have seen, many persons had been beaten, and even put to death for destroying these creatures heretofore. It seems that having been protected for so many years, these lizards had become quite tame, and treated as domestic creatures, and it was, of course, firmly believed that any injury done to them would incur the wrath of the gods. It was useless to argue against this idea; the answer invariably was, "Your country fashion be good for you, my country fashion be good for me." Had it not been by the command of the King and chiefs, the renunciation of the juju worship would have been almost impossible. It was the desire of the old King, William Pepple, to carry out this drastic measure of reform in favour of Christianity, but he did not live to accomplish it; but his son, a worthy successor, was not slow in fulfilling his father's wishes. After the old King's death his son wrote to the Bishop to acquaint him of his sad loss, and this letter, so very honourable to its writer and very interesting, may be snatched from oblivion:

His life has been one of the most extraordinary and remarkable kind for an African king. He was King in 1835 at the age of nineteen, and after reigning between nineteen and twenty years he had a misunderstanding with the chiefs, which made him go to Fernando Po, from thence to the island of Ascension, and from thence to London, where he landed in June, 1856, and resided there till June, 1861, when he set sail for his native land, arriving in Bonny in August, and by God's grace again ascended his rightful throne. Having seen England, and having had even before his visit a wish to bring the missionaries into his dominions, he instructed me to write to the Bishop of London, who handed the letter over to you, which made you visit Bonny in 1864, and the agreement was drawn. The rest you know as well as I, and even better than I do. I therefore do not repeat it. I am very glad to hear of your prosperous visit to and return from the Niger, and that the kings of the different countries down that river are upholding and introducing Christianity into their countries. As for me, the work which my father has begun I will never (D.V.) deny or desert.

Among many old records of this period of the mission is the story, quite simply told, of the death of a poor old woman known as Mammy Hagar, who was converted under the ministry of Mr. Johnson, the old missionary at Sierra Leone, to whom reference has been made in an earlier chapter. Possibly she was known to the Bishop; in any case, she, like himself, was a liberated slave brought into this haven of freedom by British cruisers about the same time as he. She was very poor, ignorant as regards this world's knowledge, but wonderfully wise in the grace and knowledge of God, dependent upon a Government allowance of twopence a day, supplemented by the willing gifts of loving friends. Her life was one of sweet and humble consistency, and not only a regular attendant at the church, but in her poverty she practised the grace of giving, and contributed her widow's mite, literally so, to the Church Missionary Society, the Bible Society, and almost every object pleaded for. She had a long and dangerous illness, from which she returned shaken, but sufficiently recovered, to the joy of the congregation. Then once more the Divine Hand was laid upon her, and she sickened unto death. Her faithful black pastor shall tell the rest:

It was now that Jesus was glorified in His servant. Reduced to a mere skeleton, there she lay on a mat near the ashes—literally so—the picture of a dying saint. Her sick chamber became the scene of great encouragement. She said to me on one occasion: "Heaven, sir, is not far; heaven live here," pointing to the palm of her hand. "I want to go to rest."

Then she began to repeat, although she could not read a letter of the alphabet (and this, by the way, shows how the memories as well as the hearts of our people are well stored with Bible knowledge), that beautiful text: "Come unto Me, all ye that labour and are heavy laden." "Heavy laden," she repeated. "Me, Hagar John, have rest, glory be to God." All who were present, with myself, burst into tears. But she turned round and said to me: "Master, my son, why do you cry?" I replied: "We all envy you. We would rather say, like Paul, 'To be with Christ is far better.'" "No, no," she said. "My son, my master, you have work to do. I am going home; mind your work. See Jesus near you"—pointing to the feet—"hold on, patience. Without patience no man can see the Kingdom of Heaven."

After a short pause I replied, in her own words: "Heaven, it is true, is not far; it is quite near." She turned round and said, with a feeling I shall not soon forget: "Master, it be far, far from the wicked, but near, very near, to the righteous," pointing to her palm again.

On another occasion when I visited her I read those beautiful words of our Saviour: "Let not your heart be troubled." As soon as I began she took it up, and repeated in broken bits, if I may so speak, the first verse and part of the second, then the latter part of the third, exactly like one who never learnt to read, but who could repeat bits of Scripture by rote. When she got to the end of the third verse she said, with a consciousness of being perfectly correct: "That in the 14th of St. John, 1st verse, not so?" I replied in the affirmative. She said: "Jesus prepares fine, fine room for poor Hagar and fine, fine clothes; no trouble, no pain, no crying, no sin, for ever and ever. Amen."

After this noble testimony to the value of Christ's Gospel she spoke but very little. She rather wished not to be disturbed, being in constant communion with God. Thus, after a few days of weariness and suffering, she fell asleep—for it was a falling asleep—in Jesus.

CHAPTER VII

THE BISHOP KIDNAPPED

A SUNNY day of success in the mission field often precedes a storm cloud, and showers of suffering. God holds the fan, and when He wills it He winnows the chaff from the grain. He knows best when and how to treat His people. Sometimes it is, as we guess at it, the premature snatching away of a brave and capable young life, just gripping its work with promise of success, or perchance the call home of a veteran whose priceless experience and influence we must sorely miss. But at other times the blow falls upon the flock; some traitor leads in the enemy, and heathenism, cruel, merciless, and fanatical, sweeps in like a flood, and the cry of martyrdom is heard, amid smoking sanctuaries and plundered homes. It seems as though the toil of years was all in vain. The field once golden with promise is bare, still the scythe which reaped was held by a Hand of mercy; it is mown that it may bring forth more fruit. It is said that after the forest fires of America there springs a carpet of fair flowers which are never seen anywhere but in this blackened ground. So from the ashes of a consumed church, with its martyrdoms, grow other saintly and valiant lives. This is true not only of the mass, but of the individual, for in the heart of every man is mirrored, as on the glistening sphere of a trembling dewdrop, the same experience of shadow and shine, the sleep of sorrow and the dream of joy.

These reflections introduce us to an epoch in the history of the Bishop and his beloved mission which lies in the path of persecution. It will be remembered with what pains he had laid the foundations of a mission station at Ghebe, which from its position near the Confluence was likely to make a useful place, not only for mission work, but for purposes of trade up the Niger. This town was not only adjacent to a confluence of rivers, but it was a veritable confluence of languages. The tribes from all parts met here; in its streets and markets might be heard Igara, Igbira, Nupé, Kakanda, Yoruba, Doma, and Djuku—quite a confusion of tongues, especially when several in a loud key are talking at the same time. In his journals the Bishop has spoken of the bright little congregations, and the readiness of the people in this flourishing town to hear the Gospel. It will be imagined what dismay and disappointment filled the minds of the readers of a letter from a native catechist, writing from Lokoja, to say that the town of Ghebe and its mission premises had been utterly destroyed. One of those fierce tribal wars, which break out often with little warning and as little excuse, brought the combined forces of the Basses and Akaias party to its gates. A battle was fought at a place called Obu; the men of Ghebe were defeated, and at once deserted the town, which was soon committed to the flames. The British Consul, Mr. Fell, hastened to protect the Christians, and saved their lives. Some managed to get into the canoes which he sent for them for crossing to Lokoja, others hurried into the bush and found safety in flight over the surrounding country. Everything was plundered, and, says the narrator, "Ghebe is now a ruinous heap, and this important town is swept away from the face of the earth."

The Bishop lost no time in visiting this scene of desolation, noting how the natives had stolen whatever the fire had spared; and confronting the two rival chiefs in turn, he protested very strongly.

> I made it a point (he writes) to show them what they were doing to themselves and the people at large; that God had brought the way of peace to them, but they have chosen war; God had brought blessing and prosperity to them, but they have abused it and did not appreciate these things; that they have deprived Ghebe, our first station at the Confluence, of all the advantages it had above all other places—the privilege of a place of worship, of civilization, and industry and trade, all of which were introduced at great expense for the general good of the country; but they regarded them not. How could they expect to prosper under such circumstances?

This plain speaking seems to have had a good effect; at any rate the Bishop retired, as he says, leaving "both parties under deep impression" of their misdoings and the consequences.

About the same time a fierce fire broke out at the mission premises of Onitsha. Some one had set fire to a dry field of grass across which a strong wind blew, in the direction of the mission buildings, which speedily were enveloped in flame. Scarcely anything remained, but it was a relief to know that no lives were lost.

But the most serious circumstance in these trying experiences was the violent and disastrous change in the situation at Abeokuta, although so far away. Of course not strictly a part of the Niger mission, the early establishment of Christianity in the city "under the stone" had been so intimately associated with the Bishop that the misfortunes which befell the work interested him naturally very deeply.

The seat of the trouble seems to have been our occupation of Lagos, and the subsequent Government of that colony appears to have been unfortunate enough to have excited the jealousy of the chiefs, and especially of the Egbas, whose hostile action had made the Government of Lagos take retaliatory measures. It is needless at this point of time and in this place to discuss the grounds of this contention; suffice to say that the Egba people, having gained the support of a man from Sierra Leone, who seems to have played a double game, found themselves in open opposition to the policy of the Lagos authorities. Mr. Townsend, the missionary for whom they had such a deep regard, had returned to England for his health, and during his absence things went from bad to worse, when the brewing storm, which had apparently a cause purely political, broke over the Christians at Abeokuta. On a Sunday morning, 13 October, 1867, the town crier went through the town prohibiting any native from assembling in any churches or Sunday-schools, and, in spite of the protests of the missionaries, representing the Wesleyan and Baptist, as well as the Church of England Society, some minor chiefs gathered a mob and commenced to ill-treat the Christians. They rushed into a prayer-meeting of elderly women and stripped them, dragging them round the room with blows; they broke into the mission premises, smashed the iron safe to pieces, and distributed the money. On every side was plundering and cruel outrage. The missionaries were ordered to leave at once, and seeking an explanation from the chief Akodun, were roughly told that Christianity had brought them wars and trouble, and that the English at Lagos had treated the Egbas badly. In the end the missionaries, a forlorn and sorrowful group, leaving their plundered houses and ruined homes behind, slowly left the town.

It is not easy to realize, through the cool retrospect of history, what all this meant to these faithful men. They had been building up, bit by bit, what they hoped would be a veritable city of God. Everything seemed to promise so much, and from the bells of their sanctuaries, and through the windows and open doors the song of praise and thanksgiving had been heard in Abeokuta. Now, carrying their sick, scoffed at, robbed, their Bibles burnt, the blood of their converts spilt, their hearts might indeed have fainted within them, had it not been that their hope was in God.

A few years later a wave of persecution reached Bonny, and the converts began to suffer very bitterly at the hands of their heathen masters. One or two instances will show how fiery was the ordeal, and how faithfully these poor native Christians witnessed a good confession, and laid down their lives for the faith. The protomartyr of Bonny was Joshua Hart, whose only offence was that he had renounced his idols and worshipped the living God. It appears that he was arrested and punished for the crime of attending church on the Sunday, but he endured the cruel treatment he received with patience and grace. Then he was requested by his tormentors to participate in some heathen rites, and to eat of things offered in sacrifice to the gods, and this he refused to do. Four men then caught him and flung him up in the air, so that he might fall with heavy force to the ground. This was done again and again, but Joshua still refused to abjure Christ. Two other chiefs then came forward and tried to reason with him, then to offer him bribes, then to browbeat and threaten him. But it was of no avail. In fearless words he answered: "If my master requires me to do any work for him, however hard, I will try my best to do it. If he even requires me to carry the world itself on my head, I will try if I can do it. But if he requires me to partake of things sacrificed to the gods, I will never do it." They then left him to the tender mercy of his master, who took the poor fellow, bound him hand and foot, into his canoe out on the river, to drown him. All this time Joshua was praying, calling upon Jesus to forgive his enemies. But this only enraged his master the more. "See," said he to one of the chiefs looking on, "see the person whom I am about to kill continues in doing the same thing against which we are speaking." Then turning to his helpless victim he shouted: "You be praying again? Then I will show you what prayer be!" Thus saying he flung him into the water, but he did not sink. So he was hauled out again, shaken, and asked if he would recant; but Joshua, like his great namesake, recalled the promise, "Be not afraid, neither be thou dismayed, for the Lord thy God is with thee," and refused to deny his Lord. Once more his body was hurled into the river, his head barbarously beaten with a paddle, and as a finishing stroke he was thrust through with a sharp-pointed pole.

It would be easy to enumerate the cases of many other martyrs, not always suffering such an open and violent death, for some of these ruffians began to get a wholesome fear of English interference, and therefore when they caught their Christian prisoners, they secretly hurried them away into the solitary bush, far from any chance of their cries being heard, and left them, stripped naked, exposed to the torment of the sand flies and mosquitoes which infested the place. In some instances it was slow starvation, as in the case of a poor canoe man, who, refusing to eat meat offered to idols, saying, "My master, I am on God's side, therefore I cannot eat things offered to idols," was carried away, with strict orders to his guards that not a drop of water or morsel of food be given him, so he died in six days. It is possible that some may think these converts might easily have saved their lives had they taken a more liberal view of things, and not sacrificed their safety on the turning of a text, for thus men may miss martyrdom in the white man's land. But this was the test upon which their whole loyalty was tried, and, like the Diocletian martyrs, who would have scorned to put a pinch of incense at the foot of Diana, they preferred to die rather than deny the Christ.

> They climbed the steep ascent to heaven
> 'Mid sorrow, toil, and pain;
> O God, to us may grace be given
> To follow in their train.

While the flock suffered the shepherd was not to go unscathed. Although, happily, the Bishop escaped with his life, the incident of his being forcibly kidnapped for ransom by the treachery of his pretended friend, Abokko, a chief of whom we have heard something already, was an exciting and perilous event in his career. After his usual fashion he kept a private diary of these dangerous adventures, and the story cannot be told better than in his own vivid words. He was travelling up the Niger on one of his missionary journeys in September, 1867.

Being assisted by the sail, he made a pleasant passage of fourteen miles against the current of about six hours, when he arrived at Oko-Okien, where Abokko has stationed himself. A canoe preceded us and halted at the landing-place. The headman of it told me this was Abokko's place, so I put in and landed, accompanied by one of my boatmen, to pay the chief my respects. The path led through a high dawa (native corn) farm in a winding direction, till we came to the group of huts which formed the farm village. I met him in a miserable low hut, dark and gloomy as a prison. He looks as cross as if he had suffered from serious disasters. We being old friends, I saluted him, but his reception was repulsive; the tone of his answer betokened something wrong. I asked after his health, to which he replied. The first question he asked me was: "Where are my presents?" I replied: "What presents?" While we were thus exchanging words I heard a rush outside of men running up towards the boats; the boatmen had all been apprehended to be put in irons. He at once went out of the hut and I after him down to the water side; his men had already commenced plundering the boat. He ordered the boat to be cleared of everything in her. Resistance on my part would be of no avail among a lot of strong, rude slave men, so I ordered Dandeson, my son, and Mr. Moore, the bricklayer, out of the boat, and thus let them do as they pleased. The boat was cleared of everything, sail and mast, and was conveyed to the creek in charge of keepers; the packages were conveyed into his new hut to be examined at his leisure. As he was in a state of anger and passion, I said nothing to him till towards the evening, when all the confusion was over. He had been busy in examining every package, parcel, and provision box, to see their contents and what would profit him most. Our personal luggage consisted of my small tin box containing some wearing apparel, my surplice, some accounts, papers, and books, and fifty pounds in gold and silver coins to wind up the salaries of the agents at Lokoja; Dandeson's portmanteau, containing his wearing apparel and sketches he had made in the river; the provision box and our bedding, and 16,000 cowries to buy provisions on the way. These constituted our chief luggage, having taken the precaution to take only what was really necessary to prevent serious losses in case of an accident, as above stated.

When he was tired he went and lay down on his mat outside the hut to rest himself. I took the opportunity of his quietness and addressed him: "Abokko, what was my offence that you served me so strangely to-day?" He replied: "You have committed no offence whatever." I replied if I had committed no offence I could not account for his hostility against me, in seizing my boat and plundering all my luggage in such an unexpected manner, especially when I put in to pay him my respects as a friend. Then Abokko poured forth a long string of complaints which had moved him to act as he did.

(1) That he, although superintendent of the board of trade in this part of the river, was not recognized by the English merchants; that he was slighted by being made only small and paltry presents, unworthy of high rank; neither would

the ships open trade with him; that he went on board last year, as also this year, but they would not trade with him.

(2) That three ships had visited the river this year (taking the *Thomas Bazeley's* two trips to be two different ships), yet none would recognize him. Although the small ship (*Investigator*) stopped at Idda and gave handsome presents to the Atta, yet he who owns the river and all the Oibos who travel on it was contemptuously overlooked; that as I knew all things about him, I ought to have represented them to the gentlemen of the ship's property; that as I had not done so he would not let me go till such a time as large presents were given him and trade opened with him.

No explanation that I could give would satisfy Abokko. In vain I assured him that it was beyond my power to control trading affairs or arrange with other departments what presents to give or where or with whom to trade. Abokko said he knew well that I possessed the establishments at Lokoja, Idda, Onitsha, Bonny, etc., and he believed that I owned the ships also and could direct them as I pleased. All my attempts to explain to Abokko the wide difference between mission stations and trading establishments belonging to a company of merchants were of no avail. He demanded three boatloads of goods for each of the three ships to effect my release. I referred him to Idda station, where there is not as yet a trading establishment, as a specimen of my other stations at Lokoja and Onitsha. In that station I saw no traffic going on but the simplicity of missionary work, but that would not satisfy him.

I can well account for such erroneous, perhaps wilful, attributing of such power and influence over the ships and training establishments to me. It arises from my being the oldest visitor known in the river. Since 1841 I have been always seen on board, whether in a man-of-war or a trading ship, as a passenger among the natives. To visit the river every year, and yet not to own the ships or the trading establishments, was what Abokko could not be easily made to believe.

A pure missionary object, unconnected with any selfish object, is beyond the comprehension of such avaricious men as Abokko, although there are hundreds of persons who could warmly support my statements as correct, having visited all our mission stations and seen the line of demarkation between them and training establishments as marked as light from darkness. I enter into such a statement to excuse Abokko, if, indeed, he were under a misapprehension after what he attributed to me; but if this were a mere pretence, and his purpose were to make me a bait to satisfy his cupidity, I can only pity the man, because he shall have to answer for his conduct to a higher power, except he repent before God.

To proceed. The night came on; no impression could be made upon Abokko to change his tone or soften his treatment. He sent me and party to take our quarters in an open shed, occupied by his canoe boys, on a mat laid on the damp ground, which served us for a bed for the night, without a morsel even of yam or corn to satisfy the cravings of nature. When I sent to ask for some of my own yams which had been plundered in the boat, Abokko said he was not aware before that Oibos were in the habit of eating late in the evening, and so we had to go without. We passed the night just as we jumped out of the boat; one of Abokko's slaves, pitying our condition, offered me his country cloth for a covering. I admired his tender feelings and self-denial, thanked him, and begged him to keep it for his own use. One of my boatmen took off his tobe and gave it to me for a pillow, as he had another cloth to cover himself with. I accepted that for Dandeson, whose head was on bare ground, I having a small raised earth under my head, softened with my cap. Thus we passed the night; I need not say sleeplessly, for my thoughts were full of these unexpected trials and the difficult situation into which I so ignorantly but innocently walked, without the least apprehension of treachery from such a quarter. But the God of mercies will interpose.

Abokko is practically known as an insatiable, covetous, greedy, grasping person; he is vindictive, cruel, and treacherous. On these accounts all his younger relatives, who ought to have supported his influence, deserted him, because he always took away from them, while he gave them nothing in return. In money matters he is shunned by all, no one having any confidence in him. What he receives from one and all are empty compliments, which could not better his outward circumstances. On account of some arbitrary conduct of his he incurred the King's displeasure, so he quietly deserted the town of Idda and stationed himself here at Oko-Okien.

Since my detention here I have been told in confidence that Abokko had planned an attack on the *Thomas Bazeley* while she was aground in this neighbourhood, but could not carry it out for want of men to support him ; that his visit to the ship was a mere one of inspection to satisfy himself of the possibility or otherwise of the attempt. This opened my eyes as to what was concealed under his pretended kindly invitation to me to come on shore to see his new house ; it was that he planned to entrap me.

Sept. 20. The boat sail was ripped into pieces from its cordage ; a part of it has become Abokko's verandah screen against the rays of the afternoon sun. All our packages have been examined and their contents plundered. Abokko was so anxious to receive the three boatloads of goods before my release that he readily accepted the proposal of one of the boatmen to take a letter to Lokoja in a small canoe to apprize our friends there of our situation. That I might be able to represent the matter properly he gave me access to my tin paper-box, which, however, he would not allow me to carry away from under his eye ; so I wrote to the consul from the threshold of his hut to hasten the message. I wished to take my Bible away from the box ; he refused, and demanded my keys.

In the evening I returned to ask for a pair of strong shoes for Dandeson, as he had on but a thin pair of slippers in the boat when travelling. I succeeded in getting two pairs, one for each of us, as well as our bedding. We were particularly thankful for the blankets. What he had already plundered from us, and what he was in expectation of receiving from Lokoja for our release, seemed to put him somewhat into good humour to-day, so that he easily let me have the shoes and bedding.

Sept. 21. Abokko was rather out of temper to-day ; he repelled me in everything I asked of him, even although it was a portion of our own luggage, so I left him alone. Many of his slaves censured their master's treacherous acts to me, his acknowledged old friend. They not only confessed their feelings of the wrong done to me, but showed them by kind actions. One presented us with two fowls and restored one of Dandeson's shirts plundered in the boat ; others brought eatables and beer, brewed from dawa corn, to present to us ; some, again, would fetch yams and Indian corn, and soap for us to wash with ; while their master was as unfeeling as a rock. That these little acts of kindness were very much to our relief I need not say, considering that the chief only sent us yams at times, and he cared not how we ate them, broiled or roasted or raw, whether with salt or not. I often told

Dandeson that these slave boys and tender-feeling females were our ravens which brought us daily food as it was needed. Should it please God to give me the opportunity, these small acts of kindness of these poor oppressed slaves shall not pass unrewarded. *A help in need is a help indeed.*

Sept. 22. *Lord's Day.* No Bible, no scraps of any book whatever in hand to read, I felt what it was to be deprived of the means of grace. I did not like to ask Abokko for any more things so soon after the refusal of yesterday. However, we took comfort by repeating such passages of God's Word as were applicable to our case. I waited till about noon, and then went to salute Abokko. I met a Mohammedan visitor with him. I told him to-day was "Aladi" (Sunday), when the people of God throughout the world met to read, sing, and pray to God, but here I was, having no scrap of book in my hand to perform my parts and duties of this day. Abokko appeared startled, and said: "Why did you not come for your books early in the morning?" I replied as he was out of temper yesterday he might think me too troublesome in asking for too many things; but he said he never put a hindrance in the way of worshipping God. That would be acting against his own life; so saying, he immediately ordered my tin box to be brought out with the keys, which I opened, apparently untouched; so I took out my Bible, Prayer Book, and Johnson's pocket dictionary and a blank pocket-book to write notes in during the week. The Mohammedan visitor could not refrain from begging me to sell him some paper. Although stripped of everything as I was, to satisfy him I tore a leaf out of the book and presented it to him. I returned to our shed with these books as new treasures. How strikingly appropriate were many portions of Scripture, which we opened and read here, to our situation. It appeared as if a door of communication with the Comforter were just opened to refresh us in a weary land.

Sept. 23. Four of my boatmen being restless and suspected of planning an escape, were put in irons. Abokko intended, no doubt, to make as much as he possibly could of this oppressive and treacherous seizure.

Sept. 24. Abokko sent me some yams this morning for our meal, and with them two small pieces of smoke-dried fish, for the first time in the way of a meal since the 19th; but God has provided for us otherwise through his slaves, who always gave us such necessaries as their scanty means allowed.

He had made an offering of fish to his idol to-day, and was generous enough to send me some bits of it soaked in palm oil as my share. I returned it with the message that I never ate anything offered to an idol as sacrifice; that I was thankful and satisfied with the unprepared pieces he had sent in the morning. He then said it might be given to some of my boys to eat, but as none were disposed to partake of such a thing it was pitched into the bush by one of them.

To-day was Dandeson's birthday, the twenty-fourth year of his age. How different was this to his former birthdays, kept among his relatives and friends, who congratulated and wished him many happy returns; but it took place this time in a shed on the bank of the Niger, where we are detained by a covetous chief to satisfy his greedy desire to get money in order to force goods from the merchants at our expense. Far away as he was from home and relatives, except myself, and friends and from all comforts, my wishes for him on this occasion were that he might be permitted to see many a return of the day, to which this of his captivity in his first career of missionary life might be the beginning of a new era. We were thankful that what has befallen us met us in the path of duty in our Master's cause.

Sept. 25. Visited Abokko, as I had not done so yesterday. He seemed sobered down a good deal in his high expectation of receiving the boatload of goods by the non-arrival of the canoe from Lokoja. Of course, I had written to the friends there not to send anything in an open boat or canoe, because they would be sure to be plundered on their way down, and there would be no end of buying and paying.

I feel convinced that the time wasted here, together with the losses and inconveniences we have suffered, will be more than counterbalanced by the good which will result from the treacherous conduct of Abokko. As he never gave me cowries, I asked for a loan of 2000 to buy some little articles, such as palm oil, salt, and pepper for our meal, which I promised to pay as soon as matters were settled. He readily lent them on that condition.

Towards the afternoon the Atta's messenger made his appearance by land on horseback to ascertain whether the news which had reached him about my detention and plunder by Abokko were true. The messenger had a long talk with the chief all night till about the first cock-crowing, the result of which I could not tell. However, he used his influence, and got a plate, a spoon, and a fork from Abokko for my use, a luxury which I had not enjoyed during the last seven days. The messenger's plan was to wait and send the Atta another messenger to inform the King of the state of things, but he changed his mind.

Sept. 26. Having ascertained what things were plundered from me, he left early for Idda to inform the King personally. The Atta's messenger had scarcely left about three hours when Abbega, the consul's messenger, arrived in a canoe from Lokoja with a kind and encouraging letter to me and some handsome presents and a letter to Abokko, requesting him to let me go up to Lokoja, which Abokko positively refused to listen to unless I purchased my life at the value of two hundred slaves. I had no voice in the matter, as others had taken it in hand. Since my detention I made him no promise to pay him anything for my release, nor did I show any anxiety about my painful situation, so he could have nothing to allege as being promised by me. After much long talk with Abbega and party he determined to take no less for my release than one thousand bags of cowries, equal to £1000, the value on the Niger; and he was thinking of charging another £1000 for Dandeson's release as he was my son, and I was able to pay the amount. However, the mediators over-ruled this, and he agreed for £1000 for the release of all the party. This amount he wanted to be paid in coral beads, velvets, white satins, and cowries. At the return of Abbega I wrote the letter to the consul, which Abbega took away next morning, promising to be back on Tuesday, 1 October (D.V.). It was then proposed that Dandeson and Mr. Moore should go to Lokoja with Abbega to lessen our number, but he, in a filial manner and as a dutiful son, would not leave me to remain alone, so I sent Mr. Moore with Abbega.

Sept. 28. The *Thomas Bazeley* very unexpectedly arrived early this morning with W. Fell, Esq., under the consul's flag, having met Abbega on the way with my letter to the consul, and anchored opposite the village. Mr. Fell landed, accompanied by W. V. Rolleston, Esq., late of the 2nd West Indian Regiment, being passenger on board, together with my two sons, Abbega, and some of Masaba's men. They immediately communicated with me, and told me their already prearranged plan to take us away without paying anything for our release. I advised that Mr. Fell should see Abokko and hear for himself what he really wanted, that he might satisfy himself as regards the price charged ; at the same time to assure the chief that I have no influence over the merchants, the chiefs, or trading affairs, my simple business being to teach the people God's Book, in the which work I was engaged when he seized my boat, plundered my luggage, and detained me. Mr. Fell did so, and promised the chief handsome presents if he let him take me on board with him ; but Abokko was stiff and insolent, and refused to let me go a foot till the value of £1000 was paid down. Mr. Fell having satisfied himself as to the extravagant nature of the charge demanded, determined not to give such a covetous rebel against his own King encouragement to do worse in future, the more so as men of like stamp with himself would be encouraged to act in like manner ; boats employed in communication between one trading establishment and another would be seized upon, and the plunderers' next step would be to set any value they might fancy on the crew of such a boat for their release, which would be, indeed, another kind of slave traffic in the persons of British subjects. He urged me to go at once into the boat. As others had thought for me and had deliberately arranged their plans, I yielded, and we ran into the boat. During the excitement of shoving off the natives fired muskets and shot poisoned arrows after us, at which time Mr. Fell received a mortal wound from a barbed poisoned arrow, which I very much regretted. Mr. Rolleston took direction of the boat, which was covered by firing from the ship. On our arrival on board the ship immediately weighed, while every attention possible was paid to extract the arrow from Mr. Fell's side. When the ship was within a very short distance from Lokoja poor Mr. Fell expired. It would have been more satisfactory to me, had such been the will of God, had I been shot and my dead body taken to Lokoja instead of his. But Mr. Fell had acted gallantly, zealously, and praiseworthily in his determination never to lower the honest character of British merchants by paying a covetous rebel the sum of £1000 to encourage a treacherous breach of confidence, friendship, and hospitality. This is not the first time that I have travelled in an open boat. I never shrank from the pursuit of my duty from mere personal exposure to dangers common to all travellers by land or by water, but I never expected such treachery from a professed friend ; against this I could not guard.

The Bishop never failed to express his gratitude for any kindness, and an old letter has turned up in which he thanks Colonel Rolleston for his brave part in his rescue at this time:

RIVER NUN, 15 *Oct.*, 1867.

H. V. Rolleston, Esq.,
Mission House, Akassa.

My dear Sir,—Permit me to express my feelings of unfeigned gratitude for your kind and active assistance rendered to deliver us out of treacherous Abokko at Oke-Okein. The more I think of your succour, covering me with your person, and hastening me into the boat to our middle in water, the greater obligation I shall ever feel for the sacrifice you had made by thus defending me; you exposed yourself to personal dangers such as had happened, to my great regret, to our much lamented friend, Mr. W. Fell.

I feel persuaded that if I had offended Abokko in any way you would not have hesitated to make apology on my behalf to appease him or to subscribe towards making satisfaction for such an offence; but as you were perfectly aware of the covetous, treacherous motives of that rebel chief for seizing my boat, and detaining me when I unsuspectingly landed to salute him as a friend, to be charged to pay such enormous sum as a price of his breach of confidence and friendship, and more than enough to arouse in your mind just feeling of high indignation against his unbounded avarice.

Had you not from pity acted in such a decided manner, in all probability our liberations would have been long delayed, and the committee of the Church Missionary Society would have been left in long and anxious suspense as to what has become of us in the hand of piratical Abokko unless the amount charged was paid.

May your life be long spared, and in God's all-wise Providence you may be an instrument, directly or indirectly, by devising plans, to do much good for the improvement of the tribes of these large and populous parts of Africa.

I remain, my dear Sir,
Yours thankfully,
S. A. CROWTHER,
Bishop, Niger Territory.

To show how deeply the children of the Bishop cherished the memory of this good friend, here is a letter from his married daughter, addressed to Mrs. Rolleston :

Lagos Grammar School,
16 November, 1867.

Dear Mrs. Rolleston,—I would not have taken the liberty of writing to you, being a perfect stranger, had I not been asked to do so by your dear husband, to accompany a few trifles I send for your dear children. I trust Mr. Rolleston has reached you safely and mentioned to you the invaluable service he has done for our family in the rescue of our dear father from the hands of wicked Abokko.

Mr. Rolleston's name is immortalized in our family, and is mentioned every day.

I send you one of my bracelets as a curiosity, and all to put you in mind of the same event. It is the palm nut carved, and may have got discoloured before it reached you ; a little oil rubbed on will give it its black colour again.

Trusting you are enjoying good health with your family, and with respects to Mr. Rolleston and yourself,

I am, dear Mrs. Rolleston,
Yours respectfully,
Abigail Crowther Macaulay.

It might be naturally expected that the Atta, King of Idda, with whom the Bishop was on such good terms, and whose father was a friend of the work, would have taken some steps to punish this traitor who had kidnapped the Bishop. But, unhappily, Mr. Coomber, who was in charge of the mission station at Idda, discovered that the Atta had been quite bought over by Abokko, and, probably at that all-night sitting in the hut, when his messenger came to discuss the situation, it was arranged that the ransom of £1000, when received for the Bishop's release, should be divided between them. Already when Mr. Coomber went to see the Atta, he had recognized in his hut some of the plundered property which had been received, the Bishop's tea-kettle, a pair of elastic-side boots, and a cap. Later on this crafty ruler showed his hand more clearly by telling the missionary that Abokko was coming to plunder and destroy the mission, and he could promise it no protection after the *Thomas Bazeley* had arrived. When the Bishop came and learned the state of affairs, he saw no alternative but to abandon the station, and without delay the workers, with their wives and children, were got on board, having had to leave all their furniture, books, and belongings to the rapacity of the people, who were only waiting, fully armed, to seize the spoil. So in sorrow the mission station at Idda was relinquished with the keenest regret.

A very touching letter was written to the Bishop by the native pastors at Lokoja, expressing their sympathy with him in his forcible and cruel detention by the chief Abokko, which with one common feeling both heathen, Mohammedans, and Christians decried with indignation :

Be assured, Right Rev. and dear Sir, that in your suffering fervent prayers were offered up at the throne of Grace on your behalf, and none were more glad than we in observing that our prayers had not been in vain. We are hereby encouraged in our reliance on the promises of God: "When thou passest through the waters, I will be with thee: when thou walkest through the fire, thou shalt not be burned; neither shall the flame kindle upon thee . . ."

In your patient endeavour of the distress in which you were placed we have a bright example of suffering all things for Christ's sake, and whenever we are called upon to suffer any like calamity for the Cross of Christ our Master we shall inevitably think of your sufferings and take courage. And, oh! may we have the measure of grace which has hitherto characterized your deportment under the most painful circumstances. And we do not fail here to convey our sympathy also with your dutiful son, who, though young and unaccustomed to privations, yet braved them when called to do so in order that you might not be too much anxious for his sake, and so add sorrow upon sorrow.

One of the great obstacles in the way of Christianity in the mission field is the dark and superstitious customs which are part and parcel of the lives of the people. For generations these practices have taken hold on the consciences of the heathen, who are priest-ridden and live in daily mortal fear. In some instances, as regards animal sacrifices, there is much that is akin to the Levitical usage among the ancient Jews, and the Bishop notices this fact as a foundation to work upon in preaching the doctrine of sacrifice and substitution "through the precious blood of Christ as of a lamb without blemish and without spot." He refers to this in giving his clergy some valuable advice in his first charge:

Whoever observes the rite of animal sacrifices as performed by the heathen in this country cannot but be struck with the similarity, in many cases, though rudely done, with the Levitical Institution. For instance, the application of the blood of the victims on the person of the offerer, or on his forehead, with a tuft of the hair of the beast or feathers of the bird, most frequently of the pigeon, attached to the blood on the forehead, which must remain on him till it dries and falls off; the application of the blood on the door and doorposts and on the lintels; the share of the priests; and the parts which must be taken out into the highway to be exposed to the evil spirits, intended to be pacified or propitiated, remind-

FETISH HOUSE AT ANGIAMA

To face page 230

ing one especially of the portion of the burnt offering whose ashes must be conveyed to some place without the camp, and as we have lately discovered at Onitsha, the yearly human sacrifice for the sin of the nation. All these cannot but lead one back to conclude that these rites must have their remote origin from imitation of the Levitical institution of sacrifices, which have degenerated as they were handed down from the tradition of the fathers.

But it may be said of some of their customs that they have no relation whatever to such a sacred principle, but are merely the outgrowth of cruel ideas, springing apparently from most trivial grounds, but none the less disastrous to human life and happiness. Take, for example, the destruction of twin children, which practice, however, varies in different localities, from the Brass and Idzo districts, where it is usual to spare the firstborn and destroy the second; the Bonny and Ibo districts, where both children are relentlessly killed, and the district of Old Calabar, where not only are both children destroyed, but the mother is banished from her native village, and never allowed to return. And yet, strange to say, in the Yoruba country, of which the Bishop was a native, twins were the object of worship and reverence.

This frightful custom became a very serious difficulty at the Bonny mission station. The missionaries were made aware of it by seeing numbers of women coming to the mission yard to take water from the well. On inquiry information was given that a birth of twins was the occasion when all the water in the pots during that night or day in town is to be poured out, and even the food cooked is to be thrown away.

Hence "a horrible thing is committed in the land." The poor unfortunate mother is openly abused for having insulted the gods, because it is in the nature of animals to beget more than one. On the very mention of the name "twin" the poor superstitious women generally whirl their hands over their heads and snap their fingers with horror, meaning, "This evil must not rest on me."

The missionaries realized that an attack must be made on this shocking custom, the national superstition with its attendant miseries. So the Bishop took up the subject in the King's courts, in the presence of the chiefs, and quietly but firmly exposed the foolishness and evil of such practices. They had their answer ready, however, "It is our country's fashion." On the following Sunday the Bishop preached from Genesis XXV. 23: "And the Lord said unto her, Two nations are in thy womb." After this very explicit discourse the crusade against the custom began in right earnest. Everywhere, in meetings, visitations, prayers, pulpit, social talks, this evil was roundly denounced. At last, in answer to many fervent and effectual prayers to God, a great event occurred. The King and chiefs one day held a solemn council upon the question, and passed a law that as the national constitution will never recognize the existence of twins in the town, any one hereafter happening to be so unfortunate should call the missionaries to take the children away to the mission station, about a quarter of a mile distant, where they shall make themselves solely responsible for the vengeance of the offended gods. This amiable piece of legislation, which adroitly kept the custom, but transferred the penalty for its disregard, was a bit of mother-wit on the part of these African sages. But the missionaries did not mind; they were not scared by the thunderbolts of these deities, and they gladly sent for their watchers to be on the spot and ready when the double blessing visited any house. The juju priest, however, disagreeing with the enactment, had his pickets posted too, and managed to achieve a massacre of the innocents like a little Herod before the rescuers came. The following instance will show with what difficulty this legal act of mercy could be made operative.

One morning about five o'clock there came a rap at the mission house door, and two converts had come to give the information that in a certain house a woman had just given birth to twins. The mission party at once sallied forth; two pastors were sent indoors to protect the infants, while the son of the Bishop, the present Archdeacon, ran to the most influential chief, Oko Jumbo, and told him how he had come to take charge of twins born that morning, according to the new legal arrangement. The old chief was not, however, to be hurried, and took time to consult with his fellow-senators, and finally gave permission, sending an aged and extremely nervous woman to assist. The secret had been well kept up to now, but at seven o'clock, while the hapless little waifs were being prepared for the journey, a wild mob of fifty men, armed with clubs and cutlasses, led by this particular juju priest, began to belabour the door. Not a moment was to be lost. The pastors seized the babies and jumped through a back window, while the future Archdeacon stood by the frightened mother, and met pluckily the inrush of the rioters. Baulked of their prey, and afraid to tackle this stalwart defender of the weak, they rushed out again, and gave chase; but by this time the rescuers had reached home, and after howling round the mission fence, which they dare not pass, they departed, leaving the infants in the care of Mrs. Crowther, the wife of the mother's valiant champion. It is good to know that at night the poor horrified mother was also brought into the mission premises to look after her own offspring, one of which had died, chiefly through the trembling carelessness of the nervous old woman, but the other grew up a well-favoured little maiden, baptized by the name of Theodora Kezia Powell, and afterwards, in brighter and safer days, returned with her mother to Bonny, heartily welcomed by both Christians and heathen.

For by degrees the leaven of this humane influence began to leaven the whole lump of Bonny society. The next occasion gave no trouble, as both children were brought safely to the mission, and presently the now happy event took place in the household of an influential chief, and he, with the spirit of a father in him, refused either to have them destroyed or even taken to the mission station. So that in due time the thing once denounced became a popular privilege, and no home or clan without twins was looked upon as having a full share of heavenly blessing!

But the best of the story is in its sequel. This cruel juju priest became himself a baptized convert and full communicant, and through his influence a brother priest, whose duty it was to take care of the national house of skulls, threw up his priestly office, and position too, and accepted Christianity. Other priests joined them, and the Archdeacon makes a note in narrating these facts: "Such are some of 'the Lord's doings, and they are marvellous in our eyes.' We give God the praise, and pray that we, who are the privileged servants in the field, may recognize more and more the influencing power of the Holy Spirit, and may have grace to keep us humble, knowing that it is not by might, nor by power, but by the Spirit of the Lord."

A few years later, during one of his journeys up the Niger, the Bishop left Rabbah and crossed on foot to Ilorin, and on leaving he halted for the night at a village called Ogbomosho. A very interesting incident occurred here, of which the Bishop makes a point of specially noting in his journal. It appears that ten years before some Baptist missionaries from America started a work in this place, but the Civil War in their own country compelled them to give it up and return. Doubtless these good men, who had so little time in which to sow the good seed, would afterwards grieve over a fruitless effort of failure. This is what the Bishop says:

As soon as we were lodged one of our party, who had visited this place some years ago and was acquainted with the American missionaries, was anxious to see what had become of their station, that he might be able to say from actual knowledge at his return to the coast; so he went to see. He soon returned to our lodging with surprise at what he had seen and observed: the station was in total ruins, but in a corner of the premises a hut was erected and screened with mats, in the verandah of which he observed a small group of people with books in hand, as if they were holding divine worship. As he could not speak with them (because of the language), he returned to tell me what he had discovered. He was followed by a few of the men at prayers to our lodging, who told me that they were converts of the American Baptist Missionary Society; that since they had been left to themselves they had been in the habit of meeting together on the Lord's Day to keep prayers, as they were met that morning; so I promised to be with them in the afternoon if they would send someone to conduct me to the ruined station, which they did, when the gentleman who was there in the morning accompanied me. On my arrival I found the dwelling-house and chapel gone to ruins, but some of the doors and window shutters, and such other building materials as might be of use, were collected together under a shed, together with such household utensils as tables, chairs, pots, saucepans, etc., which stood the weather, were carefully packed under the shed, with as many benches as were not in use.

In the meantime a large group of spectators gathered while the converts were placing the benches in order to sit on. Having taken my seat, I asked for any book they were possessed of, when the first edition of St. Luke, with Acts and Romans in Yoruba, was handed to me; so I addressed them from Romans i. 9–13, as expressing the wishes of their missionaries and Christian friends at large on their behalf that they were not forgotten, but hoped that God would remove the obstacles in the way of fresh access to them in due time.

There were some young persons among them who had been taught to read, who always read portions of God's Word when, in turn, the elder ones engaged in prayer. Wishing to know how many they were, I took their names in my pocket-book—fifteen males and seven females. Of all, only three females had been baptized; but all determined to adhere to the religion which they found to be the truth, which they would not change for any other. Having given them some word of counsel and advice, I encouraged them to be steadfast in their Christian profession.

I provided them with some cloth to enable them to make a better shed for a safer keeping of those building materials saved from the ruins, hoping in some future days we may be able to make some use of them. Here we began to meet traces of Christian missionaries in the interior among heathen population.

It is now some ten years since the missionaries had visited this town ; their houses and chapel have gone to ruins, but their spiritual work survives the wreck. Here they are, like good plants, struggling to recover their vitality in the midst of choking thorns and bramble bushes, yet they are not overgrown. Twenty native Christians among a large population of about fifty thousand maintain their stand in the very ruins of their missionaries' station. Is it credible ? Come and see. They were discovered this Sunday morning by one of our fellow-travellers, himself a sceptic in the results of missionary work among the heathen. He first brought me the news of having seen a praying people. He accompanied me back to the place, and was a witness when I addressed and prayed with them, when these solitary converts resolved to hold fast their Christian profession in the midst of all disadvantages. I should like objectors to Christian missions to the African heathen to say what could have been the worldly inducements held out to these converts, since left by their missionaries for a period of ten years, which made them stand steadfast to the doctrine which they had been taught. They had weathered the shock of persecution from relatives and former associates in idolatry from which they had separated themselves ; no missionaries to comfort, encourage, or support them in those trying hours ; no superior buildings to boast of, but instead of which they struggle to maintain their new faith in an humble shed among the very ruins. Can all these things be ? The facts speak for themselves. The member of the sceptic school, who has witnessed the sight in the interior, must set his seal to the truthfulness of these results of missionaries' operations, which he has seen in the course of his travels.

It is no worldly inducement, but the power of the Spirit by the preached Word.

" My Word shall not return unto Me void, it shall accomplish that which I please, it shall prosper in the thing whereto I sent it."

Fifteen years after this visit of the Bishop a Wesleyan missionary, the Rev. J. T. F. Halligey, also came to Ogbomosho, and had a very interesting interview with the chief relative to establishing a mission station, and asking for the favour of a plot of ground. He told the missionary that he would think over it all through the night, and see him in the morning to give his decision. When the time came it was pointed out to him how much better it would be for him to give up his idols and accept Christ as his Saviour; but he shook his head. He lifted his hand to his crisp iron-grey hair, and said:

"When we get old we do not care to change our religion, and I shall die believing in the gods my fathers trusted. But my children and my people, they are young, and will like a new religion, and will do as you say. Let them follow the white man." He then took the missionary, attended by much noise of horn and tomtoms, to a point where the country could be seen, and directing his finger to a hill, quite a mile long, gave it for the mission. He was thanked for such great liberality, and being assured that only a small piece of land was requisite, he answered, "When my people trust your Christ they will want to come and live near the missionary."

It is rare for an old chief to change his religion, but one who lived at Ilesa is an instance of what the gospel can do. This old chief died in 1891, having for some considerable time embraced Christianity, and in his last illness requested the native minister to attend him, so that he might hear the Bible and pray.

Five days before he breathed his last he said: "A few days more and I shall be with God, through Christ, who has washed away my sins in His blood." He then thanked the minister for his reading and talk, and died a most triumphant death, surrounded by his believing children.

CHAPTER VIII

IN LABOURS MORE ABUNDANT

THE difficulties which beset the path of missions among the heathen are manifold, and especially do they hinder where pioneer work is concerned. To those who enter into other men's labours and build upon foundations already laid, the work, however praiseworthy, is not so difficult, for the neck is broken of opposition and persecution. It is quite possible, of course, that fresh hindrances may crop up, and there are trials in the work of consolidating not to be ignored. But in the first instance the brunt is borne. There is the solid barrier of long-established customs, a religion which touches every detail of human life and the vested interests of its priests and witch-doctor, who raise again the old cry of "Great is Diana of the Ephesians" in another language and with another title of the god. Then there is the secular power, represented by kings and chiefs, dressed in a little brief but very despotic authority, interlocked at all points with native customs and regard for guardian or opposing deities, mixed with the human vices of jealousy, envy, and greed of gain and power. It is obvious that the former obstacle admits of no compromise, and the latter is an uncertain quantity to depend upon, and demands the greatest tact on the part of the missionary. Then there are the inevitable complications which appear in the wake of the march of purely commercial interests, when perchance the flag is insulted, traders suffer, and severe and necessary reprisals are made by the white man's Government. Many other difficulties might easily be quoted, but these, closely affiliated, were always much in evidence in the history of the Niger mission, which the Bishop built up with such patience and pains.

He was no mean diplomatist, and again and again his presence saved the situation, not only for the present, but as regards the safety and success of the future. He found himself often standing between contending tribes, trying to act as peacemaker, when they would let him, facing frequently some bloodthirsty chief, and, like another Elijah, denouncing the barbarities of this African Ahab, and warning him of Divine wrath and judgment. On other occasions, as we have seen, the Bishop found it very difficult to explain that he was not associated for personal profit with commerce, and this became still more necessary because he was so much in sympathy with anything which would develop the material prosperity of his country. In his journals, with their picturesque statement of facts, he has little to say of his own feelings and struggles, but between the lines it is not difficult to discern that indomitable perseverance, scrupulous rectitude of character, and utter disregard of self which made up the man. The Bishop seemed to have no idle moments, and he always had a knack of knowing what to do in an emergency. Singularly free from fear, he was patient and tender to the utmost. He never seemed to lose heart, though few men had more reason to despair. He knew his converts as none other did, and, like a true shepherd, cared for and did his best for his flock, many of them very weak and tender sheep, needing the crook to preserve them from perilous pastures.

We see him in anxiety for Lokoja, fearing it might have to be abandoned, for Masaba was in an unfriendly mood, and this note is made in his journals: "The silent ejaculation of Nehemiah before Artaxerxes, 'Grant him mercy in the sight of this man' (Neh. I. 11), was most applicable in my case, and was frequently offered." Then after visiting Egga, with its pestilential filthiness and many disagreeable experiences, the Bishop reaches Bida, and finds to his joy that the King has adopted quite another attitude, and has himself suggested that the mission should remain at Lokoja, where better order amongst the people shall be established.

We were agreeably surprised to hear this difficult subject solved by the King himself before we had time to broach it. Thus the dark gloom which overshadowed the prospects of Lokoja was blown away as the morning fog before the rising sun, even before we had opened our lips to protest against the order. Thus we have been relieved of our anxieties and doubts. This is an instance of an answer to prayer: "Before they call I will answer; and while they are yet speaking, I will hear." The Lord has graciously interposed in behalf of

His own cause. The clouds we so much dreaded have broken in blessings on our heads. "The king's heart is in the hand of the Lord, as the rivers of water. He turneth it whithersoever He will." How often has this His prerogative been pleaded at the throne of grace in this case! He has shown His readiness to help in every time of need, yet we need again and again to pray: "Lord, increase our faith."

The element of the ridiculous frequently enters where the question of gifts to royal persons in Africa is concerned, and when some presents were made by Lieutenant Molyneaux, who landed from his vessel, the *Pioneer*, on behalf of the Government and the West Africa Company, the sable monarch was dumbfounded by their variety and value. A huge looking-glass, five feet by four feet, which must have had miraculous escapes in transit, was exposed at the gate of the palace, and reflected hundreds of countenances grinning with wonder and delight. But the thing which captivated the king's fancy and interest was a plan on paper of the Suez Canal, which the naval officer did his best, through the intervention of the Bishop, to explain. The principal advantage gained by this gift was to impress upon the King's mind that the Viceroy of Egypt, a Mohammedan of eminence, should be actually working with a great Christian power, and asking it to execute this great work for the benefit of his country and the commerce of the world. The Bishop writes:

This people, being shut up in the interior of Africa, knowing little more of their religion than scraps of the Korân, which they repeat by rote as they perform their ablutions and say their prayers, look down with bigoted pride and contempt on all those who do not conform with them in these holy acts;

but the fact of the Mohammedan and Christian powers combining to promote the general interest of the world in the centre of Mohammedanism and seat of learning, has tended very much to disarm this poor ignorant people of their pride and contempt and to cool down their bigotry, which has led them to regard themselves as the holiest people in the world.

The Bishop's presents from the Church Missionary Society comprised some oval meat dishes, with highly polished covers, and he was at much pains to explain to the royal recipient thereof how the gentlemen in the white man's land use them, and that the covers kept the flies from the meat, and this would be an advantage, seeing that Bida swarmed with these insects. The King nodded his head, but said his idea about the use of the cover was different. He coolly screwed off the handle from the back, then set it upside down, saying: "I shall have the holes of the screws stopped up, and inside this cover, which is deep and wide, I shall put my food, and eat out of it; the dish may take place of the cover."

"We could not help laughing," said the Bishop, "at this inversion of the uses of the covers and dishes; but as he would enjoy them better that way, we said he was perfectly at liberty to suit his own idea about their uses." The picture of this black King, sitting on the ground before his big looking-glass, eating out of an inverted dish cover, while studying the plans of the Suez Canal, is comical beyond words.

When the Bishop returned to Lokoja he found the Christian converts very dispirited, but he cheered their hearts by telling them what had taken place, and how the King had promised not to disturb the mission, and intended to prevent any more outrages of his soldiers. Such good news greatly heartened the flock.

I preached in the church on the mission premises from Psalm l. 15: "Call upon Me in the day of trouble," etc. Some of the Mohammedans who were present remained till our little preaching place began to be full. As some poor heathens, whom they despised, were taking their seats near them they began to be uneasy, as much as to say: "Come not near unto us, for we are holier than you." On a sudden they started out and went away, but, however, a few remained to the end. An elderly looking man was particularly attentive throughout the service. This self-righteous people would be glad to have separate seats assigned them, but this cannot be allowed in a Christian church, where all are one in Christ Jesus, through whom we have access by one Spirit unto the Father. We rejoiced to see them enter our places of worship and lend an ear to our preaching, but we are forbidden to feed their pride by indulging their erroneous notion of holiness. In the afternoon I preached in the out-station, where there was a congregation of fifty people, some of the deserters being returned. I then directed their minds to the Lamb of God which taketh away the sin of the world. These were strangers from the interior who had never attended any place of worship before, with whom I had interesting conversation on the folly of idolatrous worship after service. Though I was looked upon as an extraordinary person, who could have such an influence with the King to restore their companions who had deserted without any further apprehension. I endeavoured to convince them that we were instruments in the hand of God, through whom He was pleased to work. "Not unto us, O Lord, not unto us; but unto Thy name give praise, for Thy mercy and Thy truth's sake." The heathen have not been able to say in this instance, "Where is now thy God?" for He has manifested His power among them.

The Bishop gives us, in visiting Onitsha station, some interesting details respecting the rules and customs which hedge about the dignity of a king. He arrived on a great holiday, when the King made his annual appearance amongst his people, amid great merriment and unlimited consumption of yams. His Majesty is never allowed to pass beyond a certain limit from the date of his coronation till his death, otherwise a human sacrifice would be necessary to propitiate the gods. This prescribed area extends to 4950 square yards of ground, on which his rickety mud hovel, called his palace, and the equally miserable huts of his many wives are erected. As the Bishop humorously points out, he is like a harmless animal in a zoological garden, roaming inside his fences at pleasure, but no further. After he is crowned no attempt is made to instruct him as to his country and people; he knows absolutely nothing beyond his fence. Although the station had been established for over thirteen years at Onitsha, the King had never seen any of the premises, neither house, church, store, nor steamer. It is against the law that he should see the river, or a boat or canoe, which may resemble a coffin, lest it should hasten his death. Those immediately near him make him the dupe of their slanders and designs, and often influence him quite easily against the work of the mission. But some of the chief ladies of the palace, including the King's own daughter, having been converted and baptized, an opportunity was given for the Bishop to preach the Gospel in the royal apartments. He took the opportunity to store the King's mind with Bible truths, upon which he would have plenty of time to meditate afterwards. He also opened the new church at Ouitsha. It was simplicity itself, and would have disarmed the most captious critic by its plain frugality. The temporary bamboo mat roof screened the floor of mud, a plain wooden rail divided the chancel from the body of the church, two side seats were fixed up by slips of boards nailed to bamboo sticks, rows of low mud walls served for seating the worshippers, and some iron cask hoops with bits of candle stuck thereon made a brilliant illumination at the evening service. The collection from the faithful consisted of a small piece of leaf tobacco, a bunch of trade beads, a reel of cotton, some fish-hooks, and a silk pocket-handkerchief. Within these mud walls, by the light of those twinkling candles, the Bishop, in his surplice, preaches and prays, and the hymn, "Arm of the Lord, awake, awake!" in a strange language, is sung without any musical accompaniment. It seems a little thing and insignificant, but it is a little light shining in a very dark place, for within a few yards of it a day or two afterwards an innocent girl was dragged to death by the feet, for two miles of agony, to atone for the sins of the people. This was done at dead of night, but the Bishop's son, Dandeson, with a lantern, discovered the outrage, and saw the poor child just dying from her wounds. The Bishop writes:

I was afterwards told that the King was afraid lest I should witness the deed and spread a bad report of him; that he changed the time, which was usually daylight, into the dark hours of the night. I hope the time is not far distant when the fear of man, who is only a servant, will be changed to the fear of Him who has employed man to proclaim from His Word that God Jehovah alone is to be feared and to be had in reverence of all His reasonable creatures.

At this time the Franco-German War was in progress, and the echoes of that dire conflict were heard in far Africa. But it is curious to note in the correspondence of the Bishop that a quite mistaken idea prevailed. Whether the news was purposely distorted, in the first instance, to diminish British prestige, it is impossible to say; but these chiefs had everywhere given out to the people that it was the English who were being defeated by the French armies, and as a consequence that anti-slavery natives would now be powerless to interfere, and under the flag of the all-victorious French the slave trade would revive and gain its old ascendancy. This information, of course, greatly excited the tribes of the interior, and was easily credited by some to whom the wish was father to the thought, and spies were sent down to the coast at Lagos to have the tidings confirmed. Wherever the Bishop travelled up the Niger he was beset with a crowd of anxious inquirers, to whom he had to give the assurance of the truth of the war.

On the death of one of his native helpers the Bishop felt that a character like that of Francis Langley should have more than a passing reference, not only because he was such a devout Christian and faithful worker, but as an instance of the efficiency of the negro in the work of preaching the Gospel. Langley, like the Bishop, was a liberated slave, landed at Sierra Leone, where, as an apprentice, he worked hard for a trading merchant, instructing himself in his spare time in reading and writing, until he had, with the additional aid of the Sunday-school and evening classes, gained a fair education. He then secured a good and rising position in Government service at Freetown. Then came his call to the Niger mission. The need of workers there much impressed him, and, in spite of the Governor having pointed out that he was giving up what might become a lucrative post for one of personal peril among the uncivilized heathen, the young man made his choice for the service of God, and in due time, with his wife and family, was the solitary representative of the mission at Onitsha. When that station was at its worst stage of persecution his life was attempted one dark night, and for a long time he had to watch sleeplessly lest he should be secretly murdered. But his pluck and faithfulness to duty won over even his enemies. A terrible epidemic broke out while he was working at an out-station, and every one fled to Onitsha; but Langley and his family stuck to their post, exposed to enraged cannibals, and for ten weary months he gave instruction and help to the many inquirers who sought his door as their only friend. In spite of impaired health, he had kept on working with a consecrated persistency, which will bear comparison with some of the bravest and best records of the mission field. As the Bishop said of him, though perhaps he had but one talent, he traded therewith and gained another for the Lord's treasury. Can any one doubt the fitness and spirit of such a man, negro though he was? The Bishop writes thus respecting his fellow-worker:

Through faith in Him whom he believed to be the only Friend of sinners he trusted for pardon and forgiveness. From

Him whom he so faithfully served here on earth we may hereby express our belief that Francis Langley has received the approbation : "Well done, good and faithful servant: thou hast been faithful over very little things: enter thou into the joy of thy Lord." Oh, that this were the ardent desire of us all labouring in this mission, to spend and be spent for the salvation of the souls of our heathen countrymen! Half a dozen men of like mind as that of our dear departed Francis Langley would be inestimable boons to missionaries among our heathen brethren according to the flesh.

While the Bishop is giving such a good testimony of this native worker, it is not out of place to mention here the opinion which an English naval officer formed of the Bishop and his work. Captain East, R.N., of H.M.S. *Lynx*, had orders to go up the Niger, and he here met the Bishop, and had opportunities of observing him and his conduct of the diocese.

At Lagos (he says) I first met Bishop Crowther, to whom I had written offering him a passage in the *Lynx* to the Niger. I had often heard of him, and years ago he had preached for my father at Bath. He called on me, and, as most people are who meet him, I was much impressed with his simple unaffected manner and his almost perfect pronunciation of English, so that in speaking to him you could scarcely realize that you are speaking to a black man. On returning his call I found the Bishop packing up with his own hands the books and slates intended for the Niger Mission. . . .

The native town of Akassa is at some little distance to the east. This station was in charge of a native catechist, and he told me that he had a good hope that ten of the natives were earnest, sincere Christians, were baptized and communicants. He had also sixty others who continually came to these services, and many of them were anxious to be baptized, but the Bishop was very careful in all these matters not to go too fast.

Having arrived at Lokoja, he goes on to describe a service which he attended, the first ordination service in that part of Africa :

At 10.20, accompanied by four of the officers of the *Lynx*, I went to the Church Missionary Society's church, and after morning prayers witnessed the ordination of three black native catechists (Messrs. Paul, Romaine, and Langley) by Bishop Crowther, who conducted the service in a quiet but most impressive manner. He was attended by his chaplain and the native clergy of Lokoja and Onitsha. His text was Acts xiii. 46, on which he preached a short sermon, and concluded by addressing the candidates for ordination, who, having taken the oaths, had the office of deacon conferred upon them.

It was an impressive sight. There was the Bishop —now an elderly man, once a slave, but rescued by the British cruisers—dressed in the usual robes of the English Bench and surrounded by his clergy, seated within the rails of as primitive a Communion Table as ever was seen ; in front, the candidates for Holy Orders ; Bishop and all *black*, the only white men being myself, four officers of H.M.S. *Lynx*, and my coxswain, who occupied a pew close to the Communion rails. In the congregation, numbering some two hundred (as many as the church would hold) were some fifty native and Sierra Leone Christians, and the children of the school, about twenty in number. The rest consisted of the Mohammedan and Pagan natives, who had come from curiosity ; and among others was our passenger, the Arab sheikh, who, at all events, could see the simple earnestness of the Bishop and his clergy. This sheikh is most regular in the performance of his devotions on board and whenever he goes on shore. After the service the Bishop and his clergy partook of the Sacrament. . . . I will here just mention a little incident indicative of the esteem in which Bishop Crowther is held. Having to try to arrange a dispute between the King and the merchants about trading matters, the King expected me to send for the Bishop, "for," he said, "I know he is a man of truth and will know what is right ! " Poor Masaba ! The Bishop, indeed, would have been only too glad to have imparted to him that truth which could make him wise unto salvation had he been willing to receive it.

Reference has already been made to Dandeson Coates Crowther, the son of the Bishop, who was with him when a prisoner through the treachery of Abokko, and was the constant and capable companion of his father in his missionary journeys. He is now well known as the Archdeacon of the Niger. On 19 June, 1870, he received ordination at the hands of the Bishop in St. Mary's Parish Church, Islington. The event was of unique interest, it being the first time that a black Bishop had ordained his black son. A large crowd filled the church, and the service was followed with the deepest attention. It was by a happy coincidence the day on which the annual sermon was preached in aid of the Church Missionary Society. The Bishop took for his text 2 Timothy II. 23, and in forcible language drew a parallel between the temporal and spiritual conflict, and solemnly committed to his son the responsibility and yet privilege of waging a brave warfare against sin under the banner of the cross. The subsequent service of ordination was a touching spectacle. The venerable Bishop, already growing grey under many experiences; the tall, capable figure of his son, led up and presented by the Rev. T. Green, Principal of the Church Missionary College; and inside the altar rails the Rev. Daniel Wilson, the aged vicar, assisting in the ceremony. When all was over, in the heart of not a few was a sense of gratitude that here was another sign and promise that "Ethiopia shall stretch her hands unto God." This young minister who was ordained that day was destined to be his father's capable right hand in the work of the diocese, and to take up the sacred inheritance of his labours as well as his name when the old Bishop was no more.

In his visitations to different stations on the Niger the Bishop frequently experienced that the prevalence of sickness was a serious check to the mission prosperity, because of the superstition of the people. During his stay at Onitsha in 1874 a plague of small-pox carried off some of the most promising converts. Several of the children of the native missionaries also died, and the sorrow which visited the town was shared by the Christian teachers. But the native doctors and juju priests made the most of the calamity to advance their own ends, and naturally attributed the disaster to the anger of the offended gods. When the king Idiari died of the malady his opponent, the pretender to the throne, greatly rejoiced; but his exultation was cut short rather abruptly when the chiefs and people accused him of bringing the disease into the country to kill their king. In their summary fashion they started a new theory, and explained that the disease had come because a well had been dug on the mission compound fourteen fathoms deep, and the displeased deities would only be satisfied by a human sacrifice being made, and the body thrown into the well. This was averted by argument and persuasion; then the chiefs expressed themselves willing to compromise, if a sort of indemnity be paid by the missionaries by being permitted to charge them with goods which they had never received. A young convert, however, stood up between the parties, and said to his people: "My friends, I have listened to all that you have been saying about the well at the mission compound. I will join you in filling it up, if you can promise me that, after it is done, there shall be no more death at Onitsha." This challenge they could not accept, and so happily the question of the well was dropped. But they turned their attention from the mission to the elderly women in the town, whom they accused of having bewitched the people, and thus brought sickness among them. They seized upon twenty of these poor old creatures, and made them prove their innocence by drinking draughts of poison, with the sad result that half their number died in agony. This dreadful ordeal by drinking dangerous liquids was a common test among the natives.

In spite, however, of these measures, the sickness did not abate, and even the sudden destruction of their sheep and pigs did not prevent the spread of the fell disease. The meetings for worship were deserted, which possibly was not without its advantages, until one man announced that he had had a dream in which their old pastor Mr. Langley appeared to him, and seriously warned him that if he continued to slight the offer of mercy now made to him and to all the people of Onitsha, they would all go to hell after death. This set the tide flowing in another direction, and the public services were soon full to overflowing. After a time the plague was stayed, but its ravages were great.

One of the characteristics of the Bishop's mind was its absolutely fair and dispassionate way of judging men and their circumstances. Although allied to the negro by blood relationship, he recognized their limitations, and was never afraid to speak plainly and act firmly when they were proved to be in error. He had, as we have seen, a great desire to improve the position of the people on the Niger by encouraging trade, as they were thereby brought into contact with white men, and it gave them other interests, which would work out well, not only in the matter of material prosperity, but also in strengthening their character. Here are some comments upon that love of money which was getting a hold upon the people :

> Their indifference to the means of grace is to be attributed to this in a great measure. It appears this people cannot bear prosperity—from abject poverty they have been improved to what they are now ; but the more trade is brought among them the more unbearable they are becoming in their demands to lessen the measures by which produce is brought from them, and to increase goods for payment to nearly double the former quantity ; and because this would not be consented to trade has been stopped ever so many times for weeks, as if to compel the merchants to comply with their terms. But, strange to say, some of the merchants have tried to implicate our mission agents by suspecting some of them, and even complaining to me of an individual as putting the natives up to all this dissatisfaction with the state of trade. How groundless such a charge ! Here we are between two evils, the unjust suspicions of the merchants—as if the mission agents were instigating the natives against them, which creates ill-feeling and distrust on their part—and the evil influences of the mercantile agents, which we of necessity are compelled to expose, to their disgrace and confusion. Thus we are situated in heathen lands, conflicting with civilized evil influences, as well as the barbarous heathen practices, all which militate against the holy religion of our Lord Jesus Christ.

How much the political as well as the commercial interests on the Niger owed to the Bishop! He was always ready to place at the disposal of the representatives of British authority his popular personality and experience in language and native ideas. In 1874 we find him accompanying the merchants to Bida, introducing them to King Omoru, and, as their interpreter, enabling them to hold a long conversation with his Majesty, and make some definite and profitable arrangements as regards future trading. He also took the opportunity of reading the letter from Governor Berkeley, which accompanied the Queen's presents and congratulations on the accession of King Omoru to the throne of Masaba. Here is his own account of the scene:

> Amongst other things, I informed the King of the visit of the Shah of Persia to England, his kingly reception, and the impressions made on his mind so favourable that he could not express them in words, but in ardent request that England would be kind enough to consent to construct railroads in his dominions for the facility of communication and commerce; that while such a mighty Mohammedan monarch did not spare himself the trouble of such a visit, nor did he think his kingdom was beyond improvement, how much more should African kings desire a foreign power to improve their countries by their wealth and skill. I then showed him a lump of coal, which Captain Croft had kindly given me on asking, as the fuel with which steam work is done in England, and that he should show it to his subjects; perhaps they might come across such a thing as that in the country one day, to report it to him. This was a piece of curiosity.

These interviews with native dignities were sometimes attended with a little risk, and two little accidents attended this particular ceremonial. The King had gathered for review a large force of cavalry and a crowd of footmen to make the visit of the foreign gentlemen more distinguished; but as the party were going out, one of these dusky warriors, a little hilarious with palm wine, discharged a revolver, without any idea of doing harm, but the bullet narrowly missed the Bishop and struck one of the bystanders, who died almost immediately. The King at once prohibited any further reckless use of firearms. But another misadventure from a different cause occurred shortly afterwards. When he returned to the town, after a prolonged palaver with the Bishop and his other visitors, some of his horsemen started to gallop through the narrow streets, when the horse of Captain Croft, one of the merchants, took fright, and thrust its rider against the wall, breaking his leg just above the ankle. Two native doctors speedily came to the rescue with their original first-aid appliances, pulling the parts till the bone was set, then making splints of the hard bark of the bamboo tree, and tightly binding round it the native calico bandages. It is not to be wondered at that they added to these fairly common-sense and effective remedies some superstitious ceremonies, prayers muttered to the gods, and the application outside of a sacred ointment of ostrich marrow and hen's fat. When a messenger fetched the medicine-chest from the steamer, and the Bishop carefully explained the uses of the various things therein comprised, the King was deeply interested and not a little astonished at the woodcuts in the book, showing the different parts of the body, with directions how to treat them. "You were well prepared before leaving home for a foreign country," was his comment. The Bishop spoke highly of this intelligent King of Nupé. Well read as he was in Arabic books which had come to him across the desert, he was a man of considerable knowledge, open-minded and reasonable to deal with. He was able to write a very sensible letter to the English Governor, sending his thanks to the Queen for the presents, and giving a strong assurance that while he remains in authority, all English subjects shall have his protection and interest. The Bishop accompanied this letter with one from his own pen, in which he says:

King Umoru is an educated Mohammedan, and is well read on subjects relating to civilized nations in the north; the quickness with which he entered into the idea of any information on such subjects at once proved his superior intelligence to his late predecessor. Taking all these into consideration, together with his own express wishes to be led and advised by wiser minds, and also the extent of countries over which his influence is felt, I feel persuaded that if Her Majesty's Government would continue to show their recognition of his earnest wishes to promote the interest of trade and more extensive cultivation of produce suitable for European markets by a moderate annual remuneration, I believe good benefits will accrue from it both to commerce and Christian civilization of this extensive portion of interior Africa.

This letter was a business epistle. The Bishop subsequently visited New Calabar, where he discovered in the otherwise muddy and miserable surroundings of the town a bit of dry and firm sandy beach, unexpectedly suitable for a mission station.

We could scarcely believe our own eyes till we entered the jungle and examined it to some depth, which proved satisfactory. We walked along the beach to some distance, where I could fancy a fine playground for a shoal of school children. When let out of the schoolroom in which they have been confined at their lessons for a few hours, how they would skip about and amuse themselves with their many antics!

He secured the land by a written agreement under the signatures of the King and himself, whereby they each undertook to pay half the expenses of the mission premises being built and even the school fee, for every child is carefully stipulated for at £2 per annum.

The news which reached him at this time of the position of affairs at Idda gave him much concern. Since the death of the old Atta, who was not a very reliable factor as regards either commercial or religious undertakings, very little progress had been made by his successor Akaia. This man was the murderer of a faithful friend and adviser, Okoro, an old retainer, who had stood by the young ruler in many times of hardship and peril. The people therefore were much divided in their allegiance, and, as the Bishop put it, "Under this circumstance, what friend of humanity and of the oppressed would not wish and pray that such a weak, rotten, and powerless government might one day fall into the hands of another power, which could defend the poor and justly punish the wrongdoer?"

This wretched and unreliable King was very anxious for the Bishop to open a missionary establishment at Idda, not possibly from any particular love for the Gospel, but because it would bring the merchants and stimulate trade. But the Bishop would have none of it unless the Atta should proclaim a law that the river passage was free and safe in open boat or canoe for the mission agents to pass from one station to another, and that the King would hold himself and his chiefs responsible for any molestation, if such should occur. Here we get also a final reference to that wretched chief who betrayed the Bishop into captivity, but who does not seem to have prospered much by his treachery:

> The covetous Abokko (says the Bishop), who had done the mischief in 1867, has since returned to Idda after the death of the late offended Atta, though reduced to beggary for his daily subsistence. Neither myself, I am thankful to say, nor few of my fellow-labourers now in the mission care much for any amount of work we may have to do, or exposure to endure in travelling by land, river, or creek in the pursuit of our duty, nor are we careful for what the Lord may permit to befall us, as the results of a faithful preaching of the Gospel, when the rage of Satan may be roused against us; but when a meditated treachery, prompted by covetousness, well disguised under pretended friendship, with the avowed intention to extort money, entraps one into difficulties in order to get it, this is more difficult to endure with feelings of resignation than suffering in the cause of the Gospel. But we must remember "The Lord reigneth; clouds and darkness are round about Him; righteousness and judgment are the habitation of His throne."

While the Bishop was busy with his work, founding his mission in Western Africa, the thoughts of the English people were wistfully turned towards the eastern side of the Continent, from which news of Livingstone had been brought by Stanley. The tension of many years of suspense had been at last relieved, and the great traveller and missionary had been found alive and well in the deep forests of that land for whose sake he died. The touching story of his passing away soon followed the tidings of his discovery, and the nation wept for the loss of one so brave, so unselfish, so loyal to his God and duty. It is supposed that his death occurred in either April or May, 1873, but a few months afterwards the Bishop met with news of him, while staying at Egga, above the Confluence of the Niger. The tidings were already two years old, and although no name was mentioned, but only a brief description could be relied upon, he felt it might be Livingstone, and therefore wrote the following letter to travel back into the far east of the continent, as he said, "just for experiment; it matters not into whose hands the letter may fall":

Egga, River Niger, West Africa,
28 September, 1873.

Having met with an ivory trader by the name of Abudulai, who reported having seen a white man in the far east country about two years ago, whom he described as an old man with white whiskers, who wore long boots, red shirt, and a cap, at a place called Kàkade Binà, at a large body of water called Kàdai, paddled in a large canoe called Bàya, who wore head-bands of cowries and bedaubed themselves with oil, who are also cannibals.

Suspecting this white man may be Dr. Livingstone, I write these lines in hope, if so they may verify the statements, should Abudulai go that way again and may come across the traveller.

S. A. CROWTHER,
Bishop, Niger Territory.

One wonders what became of this precious missive, passing, perhaps, from hand to hand in the mysterious heart of Africa, written by one of her greatest sons about one of her most steadfast friends. When the Bishop was writing these words at Egga, the famous missionary explorer had passed to his rest at least four months. The sacred burden of his poor worn-out body was being at this very time carried through swamp and forest, in peril of hostile and superstitious tribes, with infinite difficulty by his faithful servants, Susi, Chuma, and Jacob Wainwright, to the coast. How it was borne to his native land and buried with honours in Westminster Abbey is a page of history which no true lover of Africa can recall without stirrings of heart to all time. Although his explorations were in another region of the Dark Continent, and he touched other tribes, still we can imagine what a pleasure it would have been to Livingstone could he have met the Bishop before he died. For he, too, believed in the possibilities latent in the African native, and he would have rejoiced to greet as a fellow-worker in the missionary field one who so conspicuously fulfilled that promise and destiny.

Trade had begun to flourish on the western coast, and the natives in the Gulf of Biafra welcomed the erection of factories at the different places on the shore. As the Bishop foresaw, this introduction of the trading element did not advantage the people from a moral standpoint. The Bishop took pains to show the people of England that bringing the native in contact with civilization must not necessarily make him a better man. In many cases it was only sharpening his wits and developing characteristics which were not good for himself or the white man, with whom he was now called to strike a bargain. In a ten years' retrospect of work among these degraded people he adverted to some comments from time to time in the English Press, oftener prompted by ignorance of than by hostility to the work of Christian missions, in which it had been assumed that there was little necessity for anything but the commercial association with Europeans to improve the native character. Indeed, if the missionary counts for nothing, the only hope for the heathen is in the trader and possibly the schoolmaster, although the latter generally is brought in with the Bible. The Bishop does not shrink from plain speaking; he sketches the unconverted native of the Delta with perfect frankness, and shows that he will do his best to overreach the white man.

They are very shrewd, artful, and cunning, watchful of strangers, whom they sound to ascertain the extent of their knowledge of native character and the state of business, so that they may deal with them accordingly. A stranger just entering the country is really an object of pity, on account of the imposition he is exposed to in buying provisions or building materials, such as sticks, bamboo for roof covering, etc.; he will be expected to pay a hundred per cent more than the ordinary price articles are sold at amongst themselves. All being brokers, you can scarcely get anyone to put you on your guard, unless he be a foreigner who has himself gone through the same ordeal and has, after a time, arrived at a better knowledge of things by a dearly bought experience. For instance, building materials, which may be got from the bush at the end of one's own new ground close at hand for little or nothing, are charged for most extravagantly, and are even dearer than planks brought from England; nor will you be told that such may be got close by unless a person happens to find it out for himself. When these impositions are discovered, they are never ashamed of themselves as long as they have gained their object for the time being—the strangers being considered their lawful prey.

The Bishop gives instances of this to show their cleverness and cupidity. In building mission premises, and in even providing the necessary food for their inmates, he has had to battle with them against extortion.

Deceitfulness and self-interest, again, are traits in their character. No sooner was the new mission station occupied at New Calabar than one of the petty chiefs brought his son to one of the mission agents to be received and educated for him on his private account till the boarding-school was opened. When he was asked, "What about his board?" the father promised to pay one goat and three fowls monthly as an equivalent. The boy was with the mission agent for six weeks, but not a chicken was given towards his food. Meanwhile the father came and asked permission to take his son with him to join in some great amusement which was then going on in the town. After two weeks' absence the son was sent back by a messenger to the mission agent, but nothing was brought in payment. I knew from the beginning what the arrangement was, but I wished our new friends to prove it by their experience. No such agreement was ever yet fulfilled by private arrangement, to my knowledge, at Okassa, Brass, or yet even Bonny. I ordered the boy to be sent back to his father to make good his promise; if he was in earnest about his education, he was to send him to the boarding-school through the King, who makes every one responsible for the boarding of their children at the price agreed upon. I told the King of the fraud which was practised on us, and asked him to tell me candidly whether he thought that that chief ever meant to pay for the maintenance of his son. He was surprised at my discovery of the cheat and significantly shook his head, which meant "No." . . .

Keenness in trade is conspicuous amongst them; they are shrewd, calculating, and hard bargainers. Before an understanding is come to the buyer's patience is well-nigh exhausted. Time is to them of no value; after the seller has wasted about five hours in holding on to see whether you would call him back and accept his terms, he will come back and offer to accept your terms as a particular favour to you. . . . When there is any suspicion of an individual or a people beware of treachery; among your visitors are treacherous men, who watch your words and proceedings and draw you out in a cunning manner, reporting to their employers.

They are passionate and revengeful; hence there is a great

DELTA SCHOOL AND NATIVE TEACHER

To face page 264

difficulty in reconciling them. Nothing satisfies one who imagines himself wronged, unless retaliation. The propensity to theft may be classed as an instinct. When a stranger is robbed, it is considered as a matter of course; by mutual agreement nothing is revealed by anyone privy to the theft, old or young. . . .

Church building materials have been robbed from us. Although the thief was well known—a person of note in the town—yet because the planks had not marks on them by which we could identify them, we could not accuse the thief. Some months elapsed after the robbery when the very planks were brought and sold to us, which we repurchased. . . . Even places of worship do not escape them. The velvet coverings of the cushions on the seats at St. Clement's Church were torn off at night and carried away. At St. Stephen's Church the benches for seats, the coverings for the reading-desk and pulpit, the black school board, and even the church bell were stolen.

And yet the Bishop points out that these people, judged from an intellectual standpoint, rank high. They show great aptitude for acquiring knowledge, will study intelligently, have retentive memories, and will often aspire to superior attainments. In fact, that King William Pepple and his son George had been to England gave an incentive to the advantages of a European education. Some of the chiefs, therefore, sent their sons to England for this purpose, but the experiment was hardly a success. The motive in sending them was sometimes wrong to begin with, and then they were not altogether fortunate in their location on this side. An instance is given of a little girl who was sent by her father, the chief, with the one idea that she might afterwards be her father's private secretary in the oil business, and when, after three years, she came back with only the rudiments of learning and little knowledge of accounts, she was packed off again back to England for two or three more years with again disappointing results on her return. The chief was enraged, as indeed he might reasonably be, for he had spent £1200 on this education experiment. There must have been something radically wrong on this side the water.

A school was established at Bonny by the Bishop, where a good education might be imparted without the necessity for these unsatisfactory and expensive voyages abroad. It was a step in the right direction, and in some cases the pupils, after being well grounded there, were sent to England, where their intelligence and their parents' means warranted this course. The rage for education increased. So anxious were the parents that their children should learn quickly, that they would bring them to the mission school with instructions that the poor little black wights should be kept at study day and night, and they could not easily be brought to see that relaxation and sleep were necessary to young people. Sometimes the Bishop was frankly told that all that was wanted was that the children should be able to gauge palm oil and add up the books correctly. But in other cases ambition and vanity formed the driving power to get these girls and boys to bring lustre upon their name by displaying superior attainments in the presence of less fortunate families.

Vanity and a love of show are never very far away from the negro mind. On a Sunday there used to be always a display of extraordinary costumes at a church parade, which, for colour and variety, if not for strict æsthetic taste, would surpass a European boulevard. But the egregious vanity of the people reached its maximum when a general holiday came round, and everybody put on bunting galore. The Bishop, with his observant eye, gives us a little glimpse of such a scene at New Calabar:

On these days every one appeared in his or her best dress, the males in long shirts like nightshirts, but made of the best Manchester goods they could obtain, such as rich silks, silk velvets, damasks, etc., their under wrappings being of the same materials. The head coverings are black or straw hats or caps, decorated with coral beads of the best quality obtainable. The females appeared in the same rich drapery, but their dresses are cut into lengths of cloths about the size of a moderate table cover. Many such are passed round in layers on the waists and bent in the front until they become a large pile of goods, which make their gait awkward. In addition to all this rich drapery, strings of large, expensive, real coral beads are suspended on the necks of both males and females, at the lowest rate to the amount of £50 or £60 on the body of an individual. The necks of some females are quite weighed down with them. These coral beads are of very large grains, which are much preferred to small grains, mostly long pipe, round, or drum shape. During the late amusements a new ornament has been introduced in addition to corals as jewels, viz. coins. Gold sovereigns, silver dollars, florins, shillings, and sixpenny pieces are bored through and strung up with coral beads for the neck, wrists, or ankles to the amount of as many pounds as each one was able to purchase. These are exhibitions of greatness and the test of superiority in riches. In consequence of this English gold sovereigns and silver coins have become articles of great demand in the palm oil trade, for ornamental dresses as above stated. One of the native chiefs at New Calabar was said to have purchased coins for his own ornaments, wives', and children's to the amount of £500, paid for in palm oil. It was estimated by gentlemen competent to judge that the hat of another chief was valued at forty puncheons of palm oil, which at £12 per puncheon, as oil was rated in the river, was equal to the value of £480, of coral beads, gold and silver coins, with which the hat was decorated.

This being one of the chief objects of their emulation, one may guess how eager each one must be to make as much by trade as possible, and even to increase their accumulated stores by enormous overcharges on their native produce or materials, and how wasteful it must appear to some of these ignorant people to pay £2 a year school fee for the education of a child, because education is not a visible appendage for exhibition as an ornament, as two sovereigns, twenty florins, forty shillings, or eighty sixpenny pieces would have been on their persons.

This picture of native character as drawn so faithfully by the Bishop is intended as a commentary on the native as blessed by commerce and civilization. What have these European influences done for these people? It is clear that the innate love of money has been only exaggerated into developments of avaricious deceit. Even education in the eyes of the chiefs meant only more opportunities of making a fortune, making a son or daughter a trade asset or a glorification of family pride. And to what purposes is this acquired money used? The Bishop draws a veil upon the sensuality which is so often the curse of the unconverted and prosperous African. These brute passions, sometimes beneath even the respectable brute, are unchecked by European contact, and indeed the success of trade often fans the embers of iniquity into a flame. The Bishop makes no charges against the moral character of the European trader, though doubtless then, as now, and perhaps more so, the reputation of the Christianity of the white man in some cases is wounded in the house of its friends. But the picture he portrays of the childish vanity, the reckless extravagance of dress and ornaments, while quite consistent with the native character, demonstrates that neither a smattering of education, nor the acquisition of money, teaches these poor foolish people a wiser and more excellent way. It is a dark but truthful view of heathenism minus the grace of God. Incidentally it is not difficult to see how the repudiation of all this by the Christian standard created a barrier to the progress and popularity of Christianity, and was a continual stumbling-block in the path of new converts to the faith.

On the Niger, as indeed in every mission field, with varying intensity, the sale of intoxicating liquors has been from the beginning a terrible hindrance to Christianity. The Bible has been followed by the beer, and what the missionary has accomplished has been by the merchant undone. This is an old and painful story, the jarring chord in many a song of praise, a black stain, one might call it a crimson wound, in the history of missionary endeavour. In West Africa the sale of spirits became such a menace to the moral character of the people that some official action was forced on the Church Missionary Society. On 18 December, 1884, an influential deputation waited upon the Foreign Office to lay before the Government of that day the crying wrongs which this vile business was inflicting upon the African people, and the injury which was done to the mission work of the Society in that part of the continent. The immediate and urgent necessity for action was stated to be the conclusions of the Berlin Conference, as reported in the " Times " of 8 December, in which it was stated that the suggestions of the British representative had been overruled, and the Niger and other parts of the West Coast of Africa were to become the licensed sphere of this degrading traffic. It was pointed out that there were grave reasons for anticipating that this sale of alcoholic drink would ruin the missions and irreparably demoralize the natives, undoing all the patient and faithful work of missions in the past and present of that important field. Some startling personal testimonies were given. The Secretary of the Society stated that when on a visit to the Niger he saw with his own eyes vessels laden with nothing else, in one instance carrying 25,000 cases of gin, introducing the fire water to these poor, half-delirious and drunken natives. So considerable had the traffic become that the African towns were disgraced with evidences of frightful drunkenness, and that the importance of some of these villages was reckoned by the huge piles of gin bottles stacked up at the gate. No language could express the miserable condition of these poor natives, who have been deceived and drugged by Hamburg spirit so vile that the most drunken European sailor would not touch it. Like a demoniac possession, the whole being of the native was afire with it, every moral quality was destroyed, and the worst instincts of the savage were brought back anew.

The African kings themselves foresaw the ruin of their country, and implored the missionaries to save their people from this scourge. A notable instance of this was a letter which Maliki, the Emir of Nupé, addressed to one of the native pastors, to be placed in the hands of Bishop Crowther. This man was not a Christian, but he dreaded the approach of the white man's drink, having seen what havoc it had already wrought amongst his people. It is most pathetic to read these words, wrung from the very heart of a native king, coupled with an almost childlike affection for the Bishop, in whom he had such confidence. The original letter and its translation by the Bishop are still happily preserved:

Maliki, Emir of Nupé.

Salute Crowther, the great Christian minister. After salutation please tell him he is a father to us in this land; anything he sees will injure us in all this land, he would not like it. This he knew perfectly well.

The matter about which I am speaking with my mouth, write it; it is as if it is done by my hand; it is not a long matter, it is about Barasa (rum or gin), Barasa, Barasa, Barasa—my God, it has ruined my country, it has ruined our people very much, it has made our people become mad! I have given a law that no one dares buy or sell it, and anyone who is found selling it his house is to be eaten up (plundered), anyone found drunk will be killed. I have told all the Christian traders that I agree to everything for trade except Barasa. I have told Mr. McIntosh's people to-day the Barasa remaining with them must be returned down the river. Tell Crowther, the great Christian minister, that he is our father. I beg you, Mallam Kipo (Rev. C. Paul, native missionary), don't forget the writing, because we all beg that he (Bishop Crowther) should beg the great priests (committee of C.M.S.) that they should beg the English Queen to prevent bringing Barasa to this land.

For God and the prophet's sake, for God and the prophet His messenger's sake, he (Crowther) must help us in this matter, that of Barasa. We all have confidence in him; we must not have our country to become spoiled by Barasa. Tell him may God bless him and his work. This is the mouth word from Maliki, the Emir of Nupé.

Years have passed since this old African king uttered this touching and fervent appeal, and it would be an agreeable task to record a substantial result of that appeal. But the time of the emancipation of West Africa from the slavery of European imported drink is not yet. It is still desolating these people. If the Bishop were still with us he would be the first to uplift an earnest remonstrance, and appeal against the continuance of this curse upon his beloved land. Whatever evidence may be adduced as to the injurious effect of alcohol upon other native races, the evil seems to reach its maximum in extent and intensity in West Africa. It is, or ought to be, unnecessary to affirm our responsibility in this matter, especially as regards our new Nigerian dependency, with its enormous possibilities in the future. Lord Avebury said long ago that "the partition of Africa can only be justified if the nations of Europe regard their possessions as a sacred trust," and still more important is the opinion of Sir George Taubman Goldie, the founder of Nigeria, when he has said:

> I speak from sixteen years' experience . . . and to say confidently that unless immediate steps be taken to stop this traffic—not by higher duties, but by absolute prohibition—a state of things will soon be brought about that must ultimately lead to the entire abandonment of the country. . . . I cannot believe that the conscience of Europe will long allow that the vast populous regions of tropical Africa should be used only as a cesspool of European alcohol.

Those who have the right to speak with a personal knowledge of what their eyes have seen in West

Africa declare that the present duty on spirits is no bar to the evil, and that an increase would be insufficient to arrest the progress of demoralization among the natives. Bishop Johnson, one of its able native bishops, declared that "European commerce, weighted as this commerce has been for many years with the liquor traffic, has been as great a curse to Africa, and greater than the oceanic slave trade." Even still more effective was a statement made by a Christian negro speaking to an audience in England, when he brought out of a bag an ugly idol and said, "This repulsive object is what we worshipped in times past," and then he added, "now I will show you what England has sent to be our god to-day," and produced an empty gin bottle. Then he solemnly affirmed that, judging from what he had seen of the degradation of his people through drink, he would have preferred that they had kept to the idol of their forefathers. Perhaps the highest authority and the one most immediately concerned in this question is Bishop Tugwell, who has an accurate knowledge of things as they are on this question in his huge diocese, combined with a passionate love for the native millions for whose welfare he is responsible. He has drawn public attention to the drunkenness of Lagos having lifted the death-rate to shocking excess; that the people are killing themselves with drink in their own homes and in clubs formed for the very purpose; that the Kroo boy, who was famous for his physique and character, has been demoralized; that so great is this mad craze for alcohol, that the natives will only receive payment in trade transactions in gin, and that nothing but immediate and absolute prohibition will save the country from ruin.

As an obstacle to missionary progress it is terrible beyond words. We speak of facing Mohammedanism in West Africa, but we carry in our train a traitor which will do its best to blot out every blessing Christianity may bring, and precede us with a new vice which the Moslem in his darkness did hitherto avoid. The white man's religion is checkmated by the white man's drink.

CHAPTER IX

CORRESPONDENCE AND COUNSELS

IT will have been observed that the journals of the Bishop, speaking generally, exhibit him as a man of action, dealing more with incident than opinion, and for his inner thoughts on things we must look elsewhere. In a sense, of course, the facts he graphically records are self-revealing; unconsciously he displays his characteristics of modesty, fidelity, tact, and courage. What a spirit of compassion this man had! How hot was his indignation against wrongdoing, especially if it was the oppression of the weak by the brutal and strong! Possibly these scenes may also have shown his limitations: he made no pretension of being anything but very human. Mistakes he doubtless made, was at times possibly taken advantage of, as the truly meek often are; as he grew older wisdom increased. There was no arrest in his development, that flaw which so often stiffens and contracts a man.

But the Bishop did not carry his heart upon his sleeve, and to find it we must seek him when alone writing a letter, or, better still, seek a corner in which to listen while he delivers a charge to his native clergy.

Here we see him in his fatherly aspect, giving wise counsels, warning them off the rocks upon which they may make shipwreck, inculcating sound doctrine, and feeding them with the strong meat of Scripture, the imperishable principles of the faith once delivered to the saints, and stimulating their zeal to good works. Besides which the Bishop, with his practical turn of mind, would discuss industrial work in detail, and urge the social development of his people, so that the people might be diligent in business, as well as otherwise serving the Lord.

As regards difficulties, he had to deal with a state of things widely different from any English diocese. Around every little church and station was a dark zone of superstition and practices, such as, for instance, polygamy, and he had to teach them what attitude they should assume towards such an ingrained system of African life. If this has proved a hard nut to crack in the councils of experienced European missionaries, how much more perplexing would the position be to a native clergyman in the shallows of his training and experience. Upon the subject of slavery he had naturally very strong opinions, and it would have been useless for any philosophic apologist for this evil to dispute long in his presence thereon. Root and branch, in his opinion, it was of the evil one, and was responsible for the blight and misery of his country. Like Livingstone, the Bishop was not afraid to speak his mind, and to denounce because he knew. And lastly, and perhaps especially, he felt that he and his clergy were face to face with

Mohammedanism, and he was particularly careful in giving his advice as regards this, one of the greatest hindrances in the way of Christianity in Africa. On this point he took a decided stand, and maintained it to the finish. It has been already seen how he treated the Mohammedans as individuals, and that wherever he came in contact with their rulers they accepted him as a wise and righteous man. We shall now pass in review his spoken or written views upon these and other questions, apart from which some of the letters will disclose many deeply interesting personal touches.

In his first charge, delivered in 1867, the Bishop very properly reviewed the work from the beginning, in order "to know what has been done, in what way it has been done, to detect our errors and correct them, so as to be able to start with fresh vigour and earnestness in the strength of the Lord in this good work." He laments the breakdown of the Expedition of 1841, and the consequent blow of disappointment it gave to those who had projected it, and not less to the natives, who had been encouraged to believe that a bright era of light and prosperity had come to Africa.

> It appeared as if the Niger was doomed to remain in perpetual seclusion and its mighty waters destined to float down only human cargoes, aggravating the miseries of the country and her people, as if, instead of becoming a highway through which to convey light, life, and liberty into the heart of the country, it should present, as it were, an impassable barrier to their introduction, and thus keep the people and country still in the darkness of superstition, ignorance, and vice, in a most servile and abject degradation and slavery, and in a state of spiritual death, in trespasses and sins.

He then recounts the subsequent history of the mission, through what difficulties it has had to fight its way and how, by a mysterious Providence, they have had to lose by death some of their most valued native helpers at a time when, in their human judgment, they were most indispensable. But they have cause for thankfulness:

When we look back to the results of these feeble attempts to plant the banner of the Cross among our benighted countrymen, and that too under many disadvantageous circumstances, one of which has been a want of regular communication and supplies—though we have not much to speak of—yet we have cause to give thanks unto the Lord of the vineyard that, under peculiar trying circumstances, He has not left Himself without a witness. His Word, preached by faith in His name, has not returned unto Him void; marked changes have been perceptibly observed and felt and publicly acknowledged by both chiefs and people. The worship of idols is being duly reflected upon by a large number of the population, as far as our influence, or rather the influence of our preaching, has been felt; the system of idol worship is being looked upon by such persons to be of no value, and the fears of receiving injury from their imaginary deities are gradually losing their hold upon the minds of the people.

Like the late Sir Fowell Buxton, the Bishop was a firm believer in "the Gospel and the Plough"; in other words, the combination of Christianity and industry. He tells his hearers that when he arrived at Onitsha, in 1857, the people were in a state of downright idleness; they were scantily and filthily clothed, the old crops were insufficient and they were too lazy to grow more, though the soil was so exceedingly fertile. So when they had months of semi-starvation they were content to live on wild fruits and edible plants. But the mission introduced the cultivation of the cassava plants and other fruit trees, and one of their pastors took great pains to teach them to raise a second crop of Indian corn, and to make more of their yams. Now, as a result, they are cleanly and orderly, and so the effort of the workers in this respect has not been altogether without success.

I regard industry (says the Bishop) as a necessary though a secondary part of missionary labours; it is a direct command of the apostle Paul to the converts at Thessalonica: "For even when we were with you, this we commanded you, that if any would not work, neither should he eat. For we hear that there are some which walk among you disorderly, not working at all, but are busy-bodies. Now them that are such we command and exhort by our Lord Jesus Christ, that with quietness they work, and eat their own bread" (2 Thess. iii. 10–12). Those who were already made converts are commanded and urged to habits of industry. I have enlarged upon this head thus much to show that we have acted consistently with our profession by introducing the Gospel and the plough, or Christianity and industry; both have worked hand in hand—the Gospel primarily, industry as the handmaid to the Gospel.

But in these days it is necessary to guard such a statement as I have now made from being misunderstood. Beware of those who propose to suspend, at the beginning, teaching the people by preaching, and first to teach them mechanical arts and industrial habits to better their temporal condition; and then afterwards to introduce Christianity among the people as a secondary thing; then, say these men of reason, the heathen will believe your preaching, because they will say these men, who have taught us to make our houses better, to cultivate our lands, and to better our temporal condition, must be true in what they tell us of their new religion. I have been positively told by one of these reasonable advisers that unless I put aside teaching the natives the art of reading and writing, and teach them carpentry, coopery, cookery, etc., he would never subscribe a farthing towards my missionary work to convert the heathen.

But, my dear brethren, to set aside these futile reasonings

we need not go as far as the Chinese or to the Hindoos in the East, who have been notable for ages for skill in works of art or for a state of affluence, and who are not behind in the literature of the East. Let us look at home, and make our advisers themselves our witnesses, who not only have the honour of being the sons of the first nation in the world, the country which is the seat of health and of arts and sciences, in their present perfection, but also the sons of the nation which is the mainspring of the world, through her wealth putting all in motion both by land and water, through the invention of steam, and who can communicate their minds from one country to another with the quickness of the lightning through electricity. Surely our advisers cannot deny this wonderful pre-eminence attained by their nation above all others. Let us ask them what favourable effects have these wonderful advantages had upon their minds towards the reception of the Gospel? Do they so much as pay the smallest tribute to the Bible and the religion which it teaches as being the *source* from which all these blessings flow? I fear there are no such effects. Neither themselves nor many who maintain such an opinion are found near the doors of the places where the Gospel is preached; it is to them foolishness. Would their plan be more favourable among the heathens? Painful experience belies this.

The weapons of our warfare are not carnal, but mighty, through God, to the pulling down of strongholds; it is the faithful preaching of the Gospel, which is the power of God unto salvation to every one that believeth; it is that alone which can work a change in *hearts* both at home and abroad.

While appreciating all agencies which would tend to the civilization and betterment of his countrymen, the Bishop always made a great point of keeping first things first. He always accounted it the primary duty of every missionary to preach the Gospel, and he begged his clergy to maintain the simple efficacy of the way of salvation. Let them not be led aside by the counsels of men, nor make as their model in conduct and service any but the Great Pattern, asking in every time of perplexity "What would Jesus do in my place?" He pleaded for a message that even a child might take in:

Whether we hope to make converts from among the heathen or from the followers of Mohammed, our aim should always be to preach to all as to needy and helpless sinners who must be pardoned through the atoning blood of Christ alone. Preach without a prejudiced mind; the hearts into which the seed is sown belong to the Lord, who owns both the seed and the hearts. The growth of the seed cast into such a heart is in His power, just as we sow our natural seed both morning and evening, and know not whether this or that shall prosper, or whether both should be alike good. So must we preach the Gospel to a mixed congregation of heathen and Mohammedan, thus sowing by prayer and faith; we must leave the results to the Disposer of all hearts, who can influence them by the inspiration of His Holy Spirit.

Again, in preaching divest yourself of a disposition with Mohammedans or to censure heathens; rather be possessed with the feelings of sympathy with all classes of hearers. Whenever there is an opportunity of preaching to or speaking with Mohammedans, unfold the truth of the Gospel of Christ in its fulness, commending the truth to their consciences in the sight of God. It was not always that Christ made severe rebukes upon the Scribes and Pharisees, as hypocrites, in His discourses, though some were always probably present to hear Him, though not with the intention to profit, but to watch and catch something from His mouth, that they might accuse Him. Though He knew this, yet generally He preached as if He knew not their wicked intentions. The effects on them we are told thus: "Among the chief rulers also many believed on Him; but because of the Pharisees they did not confess Him, lest they should be put out of the synagogue: for they loved the praise of men more than the praise of God." Even the officers who were sent on one occasion to apprehend Him were disarmed by His powerful and resistless preaching, and returned without Him with this conviction and frank confession of His heart-searching sermon: "Never man spake like this Man." Aim at supplying the hearts of the heathen with the infallible truth of the Gospel of Christ, in the room of the doctrines and commandments of men.

With the heathen population we have mostly and chiefly to do; them you must not censure as ignorant, stupid, and foolish idolaters; your dealing with them must be that of sympathy and love, as you would deal with the blind who errs out of the way. Surely he would not have wittingly gone out of the way but for want of sight. Thus the Bible tells us: "He [Satan] hath shut their eyes that they cannot see, and their hearts that they cannot understand."

When we first introduce the Gospel to any people we should take advantage of any principles which they themselves admit. Thus, though the heathen in this part of Africa possess no written legends, yet wherever we turn our eyes we find among them, in their animal sacrifices, a text which is the mainspring of Christian faith: "Without shedding of blood there is no remission." Therefore we may with propriety say: "That which ye ignorantly practise, declare we unto you." "The blood of Jesus Christ the Son of God cleanseth from all sin."

No man appreciated intellectual culture more than the Bishop, and he frequently pointed out the disadvantage under which the African labours through having no written language, and therefore no literature. He assured his clergy that, apart from gifts of tongues, of healing and miracles, which God gave as credentials of their Divine mission, the Apostles found it a great advantage that the age in which Christianity was introduced into the world was that of literature. Both the Greeks and the Romans were men of letters, with an imperishable treasure of writings, the Jews were versed in the oracles of God, the Thessalonians and Bereans searched the Scriptures, and when those who used curious gifts were converted, they brought out their books and burned them before all men. In dealing with such a people, the Bishop declares, you could get them to compare one writing with another, to search and prove for themselves, not depending only upon the uttered word of the Apostles. And this, he urges, is the advantage to-day, where the missionary goes to a people who read for themselves. But the African never had books, and is not a reader. With this disadvantage, then, the missionary must make a written language from the lips of the natives, and then teach them the use of it in books. And he shows that by patient effort they have in this Niger mission succeeded in getting over this difficulty :

> This great drawback must be gradually overcome by a steady and persevering labour in places where we have to establish new missions. Where this great difficulty has been overcome, the hitherto ignorant natives, who had never known how to desire information from the thoughts of others through the medium of books, nor how to communicate their own thoughts to others through that channel, have betaken themselves, with all diligence, to acquire the art of reading ; and it may be witnessed in those who have mastered this new and mysterious acquirement what is their estimate of the art of reading by their attachment to portions of God's Holy Word translated into their native tongue, which they value as a pearl of great price. They, having nothing here, like the Vedas of the Hindoos, from which to argue for the antiquity of their mythology, and nothing, like the Korân of the Mohammedans, to stiffen them in arguing for the superiority of the religion of Mohammed to that of Christ, receive the translated portions of the Bible which we put into their hands with the eagerness and simplicity of children, even the engrafted Word which is able to save their souls. Thus God is overruling the very great obstacle in the way of the rapid progress of Christian missions, wherever it has been overcome, by persevering labour and faith to a permanent establishment of the knowledge of His Gospel among the heathen.

But one of the most serious problems of the African mission field was then, and is now, the universal system of polygamy. It is not easy, sitting by an English fireside or enjoying the stimulating atmosphere of a missionary meeting, for home-staying Christians to understand what a difficulty lies here. It is not sufficient to waive its discussion aside as a foregone conclusion of illegality; polygamy has such an inherited hold upon the African character, its roots go so far down, and spread out so widely, that its treatment from a missionary point of view is not so easy as might be imagined. It has also its discreet apologists within Christian borders. Travellers have come from explorations which have brought them into intimate contact with the native at home, and they have written pages in their travel books in which the system is declared to be a necessity, and indeed as a beneficial arrangement of family life in Africa. This, however, has been more especially the case where the writer has held a sort of watching brief for Mohammedanism, because it is associated with and sanctioned by the ruling professors of that creed. English missionaries have been confronted with this difficulty, and turned their faces homeward for the best advice; in some cases there seemed such possibilities of success, if on this point things might be left undisturbed, while to insist upon a man having one wife and dismissing a dozen as an essential qualification for church membership meant mountains of failure. Upon one point, however, there could be no considerable divergence of opinion, and that was that a polygamist could not there, any more than here, be a satisfactory Christian convert. The principle of more wives than one is so clearly at variance with Christian teaching and rule that no Church would venture upon a compromise to circumstances, however difficult, or practice, however ancient.

The position of the Bishop on such a question has a special claim to our serious consideration. He was a negro, had been brought up in touch with this common system of his superiors; he knew, if any man could, its ramifications in tribal life, and he saw, as a Bishop, that whatever stand he took upon the subject would be assumed also by his clergy with implicit confidence. The clarion gave forth no uncertain sound. Fearlessly grappling with the subject, before a native audience living in the midst of it, he instructed his pastors what to think and do:

> Many would place it prominently above all other obstacles in the way of Christian missions in Africa, but perhaps I do not go to the same extent as they do in ranking it as the greatest hindrance in the way of the heathen embracing Christianity, though it is the most common. The system prevails throughout the country; it insinuates itself into the corrupt and unsubdued will of the children of Adam; it has become a second nature, to break off from it is to part with the right eye, the right hand, or the right foot; it is such a darling system to depraved nature that it does not only enslave the practisers of it themselves, but it presses thousands of unwilling victims into its service. So the song of the women of Israel in honour of David after his successive victories over the Philistines may be well applied to this system: "Saul has slain his thousands, and David his ten thousands." Other obstacles, taken separately, have kept back each its thousands, but the system of polygamy its ten thousands. The system is a *web* of the *lust* of the *flesh*, which is the parent evil. . . . But when once the old man is crucified the meshes of polygamy will give way, and the wrongly oppressed victims enclosed therein will easily be set at liberty and the system abolished.

" For the law of the Spirit of Life in Christ Jesus hath made me free from the law of sin and death " (Rom. viii. 2).

But as some have in this day advocated the admission of polygamists into the Christian Church, let us honestly view this subject in its various bearings and inquire into the lawfulness and unlawfulness of the system from God's own Word and acts and from its effect upon our social state and happiness.

The Bishop then took his listening clergy step by step through the teaching of Holy Scripture on the subject, showing that from the beginning, when God put the first man into Eden and gave him a helpmeet, right along to the Christian teaching of the New Testament, it is the Divine law that a man shall have one wife, and that to her he should cleave without rivalry or dishonour. He has been stirred up by reading reviews of recent books in the English papers, in which polygamy is presented in rosy colours, but he tells the naked truth about its evil effects on his country-women :

It has enslaved the female population of the countries where it prevails, and made many to be miserable victims to the cruel lust and depraved appetite of one man. It has wrenched from them the right of nature which God has implanted in each for her own social happiness. Let us stand above the level and take a view of this social evil. We are in the midst of it, and are in no danger of misrepresentation. . . . It is impossible for every polygamist in this country to support from two to half a dozen wives out of his own scanty resources, and when this is the case there is no alternative but that every wife must enter into a life of labour and drudgery and shift for herself the best way she can. Hence to earn her own livelihood she must become a carrier of loads from one market town to another, or she must be a trader to neighbouring towns and tribes, which involves an absence of days and weeks and months from home, and on her return it has not unfrequently happened that she provides for the husband out of her earnings in addition to providing for herself and her children, if she has any, for the chief care of the children devolves on the mother and her relatives. The occasional gift of a few cowries from the father to the children for their morning gruel, and perhaps occasional share of yams to the mother, constitute mainly the support of the father. . . . It has been often remarked by the men themselves that when a man had but one wife there was that degree of love and affection between them as might be observed in a married state in civilized countries—they were one in everything. But no sooner was a second wife added than the cord of union and affection was broken, and domestic evils immediately showed themselves. Hence arose this memorable proverb among the Yoruba females: *Obiri kò rubo ki o li orogun* ("No woman would ever undergo the expenses of a sacrifice to procure a rival"); that is, that her husband may have an additional wife. These are the feelings of the female population on the subject. The proverb is their own; it is their watchword, showing the repugnance of their feelings against the system, and may be heard among them to-day; but it is generally suppressed like their other proper rights, which they forego for fear of being reproached with jealousy.

After denouncing the system of the harem of the chief, often a walled enclosure like a prison, he strikes at the roots of the evil of polygamy as consisting, not for any useful purpose, but as an instrument of sin. It must be remembered that these words were spoken at a time when the system had found defenders in England:

The system of polygamy will not check the evil of sensuality, or else we would not have occasion so often to witness the accusation of one polygamist against another for intrusion into his right. And if the principle be such as has been stated, whether we look at it, on the one hand, from the personal wrong done to the female sex, or, on the other hand, the injustice and oppression of which the man is guilty, who, I may ask, correctly knowing this state of things, can conscientiously recommend its continuance? Captain Burton, referring to this common practice of polygamy in his book on "Abeokuta and the Cameroons," says: "Polygamy is the foundation-stone of Yoruba Society. I can assure these missionaries that had less objection been made to polygamy on their part, the heathen would have found fewer obstacles to conversion. Those who hold it their duty to save souls should seriously consider whether they are justified in placing such stumbling blocks upon the path of improvement."

It has been suggested by some that the present polygamists could be received into the Church by the Sacrament of baptism on the condition that such persons promise not to add to their already possessed wives; but who can guarantee that young persons will not purposely hold back till they have possessed as many wives as their hearts desire before they offer themselves to be admitted into the Church by the same rite as the example of their fathers? The human heart is so deceitful and desperately wicked that it will ever find a loophole to gratify its carnal propensity. Once establish a precedent, you cannot easily change it.

Having adverted to the system of polygamy as being a great hindrance in the way of the male population to embrace Christianity, it remains also to ask what hinders the female population from a readier profession of religion. Whether their husbands be polygamists or not, as long as a woman remains faithful to her husband, upon her profession of faith in Christ as the all-sufficient Saviour of sinners, after a course of instruction she is received into the Church by baptism; her husband's fault cannot be imputed to her, and if her will were consulted she would rather be the only helpmeet for him.

In his charge on 8 October, 1885, the Bishop drew special attention to Mohammedanism, and in this instance also he was moved to plainer speaking, because certain travellers who had spent a comparatively short time in Africa had returned to England to eulogize, by speech and written word, the religion of the False Prophet. He evidently feared lest in the minds of Christian people at home some mistaken ideas might exist as to the real meaning of Mohammedanism as a menace to the spread of Christianity, especially in Africa. To many Islam is only a word, without a ripple of interest, to others it is a force which terrifies in its possibilities ; others, however, regard it as a beneficent factor in the lives of millions. What Crowther thought will be gathered from these words to his brethren :

Mohammedanism arms the hearts of its professors with deadly weapons against Christianity, by denying its fundamental doctrine, the Sonship of Christ, and His Divinity as one with God the Father to be blasphemy according to the teaching of the Korân. Thus their hearts are hardened with prejudices, self-conceit, self-righteous spirit, and self-confidence in their meritorious religious performances, especially in prayer and fasting and the works of supererogation, which they believe they can make over for the benefit of others who are deficient.

They are freely allowed the indulgence of the sinful lust of the flesh ; they do not scruple to commit acts of cruelty and oppression on those who are not professors of their faith. Slave-holding and trading is fully sanctioned, to carry out which slave wars are waged against the heathen with great cruelty, in order to enslave them with oppression and violence without remorse, contrary to the law of Christ: "Do to others as you would they should do to you." Hence slave wars have desolated the lands of populous heathen tribes and nations, whose inhabitants were carried away captives and sold into slavery ; and those who are reserved in the country are doomed to perpetual servitude—hewers of wood and drawers of water, and most oppressive tributaries. This is a faint description of the soil of the minds of the professors of Islam, in which the seed of the Gospel of Jesus Christ is being attempted to be sown by preaching repentance of sin and a renewed change of heart through faith in Jesus Christ the Son of God, who is the way, the truth, and the life, without whom none can come to the Father. But for all his earnestness the preacher is looked upon with horrified contempt as a blasphemer, because God never had a Son. "There is no God but God, and Mohammed is His prophet."

The Bishop subsequently pointed out how great was the belief of these poor people in charms, and that he was continually being asked for scraps of the Bible to wear as a means of preventing sickness. He tells a curious story of an old chief who paid him a visit while at Bida, bringing with him a present of two fowls ; but it soon transpired that this generosity was only to get from him in return a few sheets of the white man's paper. On being pressed to disclose what use he intended to make of it, the chief admitted that he had lost twelve horses, and was anxious to keep the remaining one by tying protective charms about its body. The Bishop, however, reasoned with him, telling him that bits of paper with scraps of writing, either from the Korân or the Bible, could never charm away evil. He told him, moreover, that for twelve years he had ridden the same horse in his missionary journeys, without wearing a single charm. What he did was to wash and currycomb the horse regularly, never expose him to the sun at midday, and always feed him well. This chief must have been an open-minded man, for he thanked the Bishop for his good advice, and said he would not want any paper after that.

The Bishop, however, declared that the women were really more under the spell of superstition than the men. They were more addicted to idolatrous worship, and so mixed up with their priestesses, that it was very difficult to get over the barriers. The position seemed different from that of other lands and in other ages, when women were always the first to believe. In this respect they are very much under the influence of their grandmothers, who form one

THE BISHOP AND HIS NATIVE CLERGY

of the most serious hindrances to the spread of the Gospel. They very much encourage and foster the faith of children in that subtle system of charms which the Mohammedans adopt to enslave the native mind. They write short sentences of the Korân in Arabic on bits of parchment, and sell these at a price to suit all cases to the people. Some of these, the Bishop pointed out, were used as protective charms, making the wearer safe against any danger at home or abroad, sickness, witchcraft, or the evil eye; warding off arms in war, blunting the edges of swords, etc.; also vanishing charms to enable him to disappear from the clutch of an enemy, and, to mention no others, there are the confounding charms, which are supposed to enchant others, so that they cannot stir.

The Bishop truly said on this subject, "Can we be surprised that the foolish heathen, who are thus worked up by a man looking into a book and writing out such scraps from it in the name of God and Mohammed His prophet, are more easily made converts to Mohammedanism than to Christianity? But Christian missionaries cannot have recourse to such deceits to recommend the way of salvation to the heathen."

In the course of a noteworthy speech delivered at Exeter Hall at the May meeting in 1873, the Bishop told his audience how Moslem converts are made, and showed the superficial and superstitious character of the native profession of that creed.

If it be said that Mohammedanism makes more converts than Christianity, I say it is true. Mohammedanism makes converts because it finds the native mind in a fit state to receive its teaching. The whole country was heathen some two hundred years ago, when Mohammedanism made inroads into the interior; and through slave wars they made conquests, and those who were conquered must become Mohammedan or be sold into foreign slavery. Of the two alternatives, certainly it is better to become a Mohammedan than to be sold away and to be transported across the Atlantic. When I went to the banks of the Niger I saw Mohammedans opening their schools, and men and women went to them. What did they go for? To receive scraps of the Korân. When a man goes to the market he will go to the priest and ask for success in his trade, and a mother will go and ask for prosperity in her household. The Mohammedan priest issues scraps of paper to these people. He tells the man who goes to market to tie one of these scraps round his neck and he will be successful; and he tells the mother who goes to ask for prosperity in her household that it shall be well with her. And the poor superstitious people receive these papers, and when anything happens as was foretold the child becomes a Mohammedan. I was applied to by heathens to give them scraps of paper the same as the Mohammedan priests did, and I refused. Even some of our friends, the Europeans, would say: "Give them papers, it does no harm." But I said it does a great deal of harm. If I would have given them scraps of paper, I could have given them scraps of the Lord's Prayer, and have got them to come to me. But these papers would have led them into error, and we do not make our converts that way. God forbid. I would rather let the Mohammedans take possession of the field, and that we should be without any converts at all, than that we should use cunningly devised frauds to deceive souls, leading them into hell.

Upon the practical question of how to deal with Mohammedans the Bishop had something to say to his clergy. His advice will probably commend itself to missionaries even at this present time. He indicates a course of courtesy, and demonstrates how much evil in the past has accrued from ignorance of the Moslem, and consequent mistakes in managing him. On this subject extracts from three letters written by the Bishop will be of interest. In the first he is insisting on the value of a knowledge of Arabic in work among Moslems; in the second he shows their willingness to receive the word of testimony; and in the third, written thirty-five years later, we see even the mallams paying due respect to the Christian Scriptures:

To the Rev. Hy. Venn.

Fernando Po, 22 June, 1857.

It is very useful to be exercised in Greek and Latin, and if possible, in Hebrew characters and inflections, but I think Arabic ought to have the first place in these classic studies. All our Mohammedan population with whom we came in daily contact, both in Sierra Leone, in Yoruba, and up the Niger, have more or less knowledge of the use of Arabic characters. As our labours are now extending among this class of people, it is necessary that the ordained native missionaries should know also the use of these characters. It will have fresh effect to meet these Mohammedans with their own weapons, not so much by argument and vexatious disputations, but by the Christian minister being able simply to point out from his Arabic Bible the important truths of Christianity. Though they may not believe, yet they will be humbled at the superior knowledge of their own book.

To the Rev. Hy. Venn.

Rabba, 8 Feb., 1859.

In spite of misrepresentations from the enemies of Christianity, the mission huts are frequently visited by very large numbers of caravans from the interior. Abbeja is very useful here; last Sunday there were several groups of visitors around him, with whom he spoke on religious subjects and read to them portions of the Word of God from the New Testament in Hausa.

I have instructed him to tell the people who Christ is and what He teaches in His Gospel, and leave them to judge for themselves, leaving Mohammed and his doctrine alone, for we have only to deliver our message and that from the Word of

God. We have always had listening ears, and confession of self-condemnation was made by many hearers. If we can do nothing more for the present at Rabbah than spread the truth of the Gospel among the thousands of the interior in this way, ought we not to be thankful?

To the Rev. R. LANG.

Kipo Hill Station, 19 Nov., 1883.

There are two Arabic readers about the village who assume the title of priests, also attendants of services at Katsa, who listened attentively to the preaching of the Gospel; but, not content with what they heard only, are desirous of reading the same from the Arabic Bible at the station, and have since attended the Sunday-school for this purpose to read passages of Scripture; though they could not give a correct translation in the native language of what they read in Arabic, yet Mr. Paul always gave them a correct translation from the English Bible translated into the native language. At Mr. Paul's visit to Katsa, Sunday the 11th, a Mohammedan hearer from the interior was disposed to argue a point against Christianity, but the priest Atikù, a Foulah, one of the Arabic Sunday-school attendants, immediately cautioned the stranger of his ignorance, for they knew nothing in comparison to what the Anasara knew as regards their religions. This at once shut the stranger up, who remained during the service to hear what was preached.

On 13 October, 1874, the Bishop addressed a gathering of his clergy at Onitsha. Many changes had taken place during the past five years. Death had been busy; they were mourning the loss of two native pastors, the Rev. F. Langley and Mr. O. E. Cole, and also of Mrs. Johnson, a faithful worker in the Brass mission. The old King of Onitsha, who had welcomed the mission so far back as 1857, had died of a good old age; his son, Idiari, a very promising successor, had been carried off by an epidemic, and now the country was without a ruler, and plunged in anarchy. About the same time Masaba, the famous old King of Nupé, had breathed his last, and his nephew, Umoru Shiaba, had stepped into the throne, and was doing well. Times of violent persecution had swept over the Christians, but God had kept the infant churches alive, and there was much cause for thankfulness. The Bishop had pointed out the white fields of need, and now exhorts his fellow-labourers to brace themselves up for the reaping, and seeks to inspire their hearts with courage, bidding them look up and fear not. It is the appeal of a leader of brave, good men :

But who is sufficient for this work ? We are ready to despair as the spies did who viewed the land of Canaan, when they returned and said : " The cities are walled up to heaven, and the trenches are deep to the bowels of the earth ; the people are tall, strong, and numerous ; we appeared as feeble kids before them : we shall not be able to overcome them."

The statement of their great strength was perfectly correct —they were emblems of the castles of Satan in human hearts which St. Paul calls strongholds. If we confer with flesh and blood, if our weapons are carnal, if we have to use cunningly devised fables, seeking our own glory ; if we make use of the name of Jesus to answer our end and object amongst those whom Satan has so long strongly possessed and fortified with idolatry, superstition, and darkness of ignorance—blindly prejudiced in favour of the customs of their forefathers—we cannot expect otherwise but a reaction upon ourselves, the like results upon the seven sons of Sceva, to whom the evil spirit answered : " Jesus I know, and Paul I know ; but who are you ? "—a disappointment and a total failure.

But when we go out at the command of Jesus to preach the Gospel to the heathens as Christ's faithful soldiers and servants, having no other objects in view but the glory of God and the salvation of souls, we need not fear. Even the devils will be made subject unto us through His name ; the castle of Satan will fall flat before us like the walls of Jericho before the Ark of the Covenant by the seven priests merely blowing the seven trumpets before it, at the command of the Lord. If we have faith even as small as a grain of mustard seed, whatsoever we ask in prayer, believing, we shall have from the Captain of an army, who is always with us and will be unto the end of the world.

But, thanks be to God, I trust we can sincerely say we are not of them which corrupt the word of God; but as we are put in trust of the Gospel, so we speak, not as pleasing men, but God, who trieth the hearts. His sure precepts are our encouragement; His ability to accomplish His purposes of man's redemption is our hope of success; His willingness to save all who come to Him in the name of Jesus Christ His Son is a stimulus to labour, to preach to and invite those who are dead in trespasses and sins to awake and arise from the dead, and Christ shall give them light. I believe that we have not been left to ourselves; this the review of our five years' service will show. Though we have been assailed with the usual weapons of Satan—persecutions, false accusations, slanders, hatred—yet we have been upheld till now; though sorely wounded, yet not mortally; though sorely tried, yet not above what we are able to bear; and by the supporting grace of the great Head of the Church we are what we are—still His witnesses, both to the wise and unwise, both to bond and free.

In touching upon the state of the various stations of the mission the Bishop displays his characteristic frankness. As an instance of this, as regards Bonny, he reminds his hearers that for buildings, school-chapels, boarding-house, and dwelling-houses, with galvanized roofs, this place has had the reputation of being the first and most successful.

"But this is an empty show, the shell without kernel, the leafy fig tree without fruit. It verifies the truth, 'Every kingdom divided against itself is brought to desolation, and every city or house divided against itself shall not stand.'" He speaks of the internal condition of the country, the hostility of the ruling chiefs, once so favourable, and how the division of the population consequent on the civil war has half emptied the church, and brought Bonny as a mission station very low indeed. Christian slaves had refused to paddle the canoes on Sundays, and from a spirit of spite their masters were secretly and severely punishing them for not joining in idolatrous worship. The Bishop had intervened and used his own judgment in putting things right.

At Brass, too, they had suffered much persecution. A secret plot to ensnare the Christian chiefs and set their town and mission premises at Tuwon in flames at midnight was providentially discovered in time. The matter was referred to the King, who was a traitor in disguise, and while the agents of the mission were promised safety, the native converts were fined heavily.

In face of these chequered experiences the good Bishop gives them some final counsels, as to the value of example, of study, and of a faithful heart. His fatherly words were listened to in breathless silence, and many hearts were deeply stirred:

My dear brethren, we ourselves must be equipped for the fight; we must therefore put on the whole armour of God that we may be able to stand against the wiles of the devil. First, unblemished character. "In all things showing thyself a pattern of good works: in doctrine showing uncorruptedness, gravity, sincerity, sound speech, that cannot be condemned; that he that is of the contrary part may be ashamed, having no evil thing to say of you." This emboldens Christian teachers to face the enemy.

Secondly, in order to our attainment of uncorrupt doctrine, we must implore the teaching of God's Holy Spirit, for He was particularly promised to the disciples to this end. "But the Comforter, which is the Holy Ghost, whom the Father will send in My name, He shall teach you all things, and bring all things to your remembrance, whatsoever I have said unto you." Yet this promise does not preclude personal application in habit of reading and studying. In regard to this we have the injunction of St. Paul to Timothy: "Till I come give attendance to reading, to exhortation, and to doctrine." Neither did the apostle himself, with all his miraculous gifts and abundant revelations, slight the privilege of book reading. In his imprisonment he felt the want of such ordinary source of information, as well as the use of his cloak to shelter him from the cold. "The cloak that I left at Troas with Carpus, when thou comest, bring with thee, and the books, but especially the parchments."

Although some of you have had a few years' advantage of college education at Sierra Leone, to discipline your minds and prepare you for a future usefulness, yet you must not consider these advantages as the foundation on which you have to build your knowledge of missionary life and labour; you must have some one still to guide you to attain right doctrine, you must still sit at the feet of a Gamaliel in the capacity of some standing books, written by the fathers of the Protestant faith of riper years and mature extensive experience and of deep research into divine things. The Homilies of the United Church of England and Ireland well read, and their Divine Spirit and sound principles imbibed, cannot fail to enlarge your knowledge of the Holy Scriptures and settle your faith in the sound doctrines of the Christian religion The same is applicable to the standard works of other evangelical fathers of the Protestant faith, who had devoted the best part of their lives in digging deep into the unfathomable mines of God's revelation as far as they could go, and committed the results of as much of their deep research and discovery into writing for the help and information of succeeding generations, of the hidden treasures, of the mysteries of God's plan for the salvation of men.

These are left on record, which will ever be invaluable helps to young students in diversity who are willing to be led by them till their own thoughts are formed, and, being guided by the unerring spirit of truth, they may be able to descend deeper into the mines of those deep mysteries without making use of the ladders of others, to search for themselves the impenetrable purposes of God for the salvation of mankind. We are but a Church in embryo; we must derive nourishment from the mother. If we thus build upon the foundation of the apostles and prophets, Jesus Christ Himself being the chief corner-stone, we need not fear any test when trial of our work is come to be made. Let us bear this important truth in mind, and more so as we are not introducing Christianity among the superstitious heathen only, but are gradually advancing among bigoted Mohammedans also, some of whom are inquiring of the reason of the hope which is in us in Christ Jesus, that we may be able to give it with meekness and reverence.

At first sight it would seem quite superfluous for the Bishop to warn his clergy against losing sight of their nationality, and not taking sufficient heed of the native customs and ideas which they met round about them. But he knew his people well. These native pastors would be specially liable to the adoption of European ideas without stint; their outward dress and their inward thought would be quite soon enough and sufficiently after the pattern of the white man. He warned them against expecting too much from their converts, and not to force them to abandon what is perfectly natural and becoming in their life for a merely artificial imitation of the English.

Christianity has come into the world (he says) to abolish and supersede all false religions, to direct mankind to the only way of obtaining peace and reconciliation with their offended God. It condemns all vices, reforms the morals, and recommends virtues as laid down in the Gospel of Christ, the great Law-giver of the New Covenant. These we must impress upon the minds of our converts from heathenism, and point out to them from the Word of God. But it should be borne in mind that Christianity does not undertake to destroy national assimilation; where there are any degrading superstitious defects, it corrects them; where they are connected with politics, such connections should be introduced with due caution and with all meekness of wisdom, that there may be good and perfecting understanding between us and the powers that be; that, while we render to all their dues, we may regard it as our bounden duty to stand firm in rendering to God the things that are God's.

Their native mutual aid clubs should not be despised, but where there is any connection with superstitions they should be corrected and improved after a Christian model. Amusements are acknowledged on all hands to relieve the mind and sharpen the intellect. If any such is not immoral or indecent, tending to corrupt the mind, but merely an innocent play for amusement, it should not be checked because of its being native and of a heathen origin. Of this kind of amusements are fables, story telling, proverbs, and songs, which may be regarded as stores of their national education, in which the heathen exercise their power of thinking ; such will be improved upon and enriched from foreign stocks as civilization advances. Their religious terms and ceremonies should be carefully noticed ; a wrong use made of such terms does not depreciate their real value, but renders them more valuable when we adopt them in expressing scriptural terms in their right senses and places, though they have been misapplied for want of better knowledge.

I hope these few hints will guard you against the common prejudices which are apt to prevail in your minds against native usages in general because they have their origin from a heathen state. If judicious use be made of native ideas, the minds of the heathen will be better reached than by attempting to introduce new ones quite foreign to their way of thinking. Improved habits will keep pace with the Christian civilization of the rising generation, whose education should be properly attended to as early as children can possibly be collected. Many awkward native habits may gradually be dropped and other more comfortable ones be introduced in their stead as matters of conscience ; and thus the state of Society will be imperceptibly improved without forcing it. When once Christianity has taken a firm hold among the people then will follow in its train many attendant blessings.

The presence of the Bishop on a public platform was always an interesting feature, and especially when his theme was some phase of missionary work in his own country. At a great missionary gathering in London, in bidding some workers farewell on going to their post of duty in the field, he drew attention to the special difficulties which they would have to face; when leaving the sphere of British influence and protection, they would find themselves where heathenism was in unrestrained activity. These new surroundings made it necessary to walk carefully, lest by an act of indiscretion they might prejudice the future freedom and success of the mission. He stood there also to vindicate the courage and faith of the converts, and show his hearers that whatever persecution might essay, it could not extinguish that Divine lamp of truth which God had lit in dark Africa. And before sitting down he enforced the value of simple and scriptural teaching among the heathen :

In such places we are in the hands and under the control of a heathen Government. And how do we proceed ? We do not carry with us any inducement to the chiefs to allow us to remain in their country or to introduce our religion ; we go with nothing but the Bible in our hands, and we simply declare that we are messengers sent to proclaim a doctrine from heaven for the salvation of mankind. At first the people do not know what this doctrine can be. Many of them seem to suppose that it is some new religion which may be added to their own, for there is a great multiplicity of gods in heathen countries. The people are always ready to adopt the gods of other nations. When they hear of a god who is very powerful, whether for affording protection or for granting wealth, or for giving some other advantage to his worshippers, they are ready to add this new false god to their own gods. Well, in like manner when these Africans in the interior heard of the God of the white man they thought at first that He would probably bring them some great worldly advantage ; but when we preached to them the doctrines of the Christian religion, when we repeated to them the commandment, " Thou shalt have none other gods but Me," or the declaration,

"There is no other name given under heaven whereby men must be saved except Jesus Christ and Him crucified," they began to look up and say, "This is a very strange religion." When we preached in their streets children came, and at first listened suspiciously; but the result was that some of the listeners refused to bow down to the false gods of their fathers and mothers, and then a spirit of opposition was excited. It was gradually perceived by persons of influence that the missionaries are inducing numbers of the natives to forsake idol worship; and when the priests and priestesses began to complain to the native authorities, they saw that their religion was in danger, and hence arose persecution. There was no Government interference to suppress that persecution. Those who had for some time been watching for an opportunity of attack were glad when it arrived, and the result was that a persecution arose against the missionaries, and the Christians were all driven out of the country.

But do you call that a failure? In travelling along the road I have been asked: "What about the Abeokuta Christians?" "What about the Abeokuta missions?" "Well," I have replied, "they are all scattered; but though it is night with us now daylight shall come." I have told those who questioned me that we were bound to be prepared for such events from the very fact that we were the aggressors and not the natives. It was me, and not they, who demanded that the gods of their fathers should be set aside. We demanded in the name of Jesus Christ that they should cast their idols to the moles and to the bats; in the name of our Master we preached to them repentance towards God and faith towards Jesus Christ, and called upon them to forsake their sins and lead, by the help of God's grace, a life of holiness. It was we who were the aggressors, and it was not natural that Satan, whose kingdom we attacked, should sit still and make no struggle to regain what he had lost. I told those to whom I have alluded that although we were "persecuted," yet we were not "cast down." In connection with the persecution of Abeokuta I must take this opportunity of vindicating the Christian character, the zeal, the energy, and the courage of the missionaries who were then labouring in the town.

Almost at the very time when the attack was made at Abeokuta, and the people seemed determined, as it were, to pull down Christianity, an attack was made upon myself on the banks of the Niger, as if the two nations were in correspondence with each other as regards the time of attack, though I think they had hardly ever heard of each other.

As regards our mission work at Abeokuta, what has been done resembles what occurred when St. Paul was at Ephesus, and when Demetrius called a meeting of men of like occupation with himself and represented to them that their craft was in danger. When Paul was persuading the people everywhere that they be no gods which are made with hands, Demetrius and his friends cried out publicly, not in the name of their craft or their wealth—that motive had been carefully concealed—but they cried out in the name of religion, and for two hours there was heard the cry: "Great is Diana of the Ephesians!" It was in that way that a mob was created. A dozen people may by that means get two thousand people to join them. Something like the scene of Ephesus occurred at Abeokuta; the cry then resembled that of Ephesus: "Great is Diana of the Ephesians!" and the result was that the mission houses were attacked, the mission property was plundered, and the mission churches were spoiled. On a Sunday morning, when the native converts were ready to go to church and their children to attend the Sunday-schools, they were attacked without any notice, and before the afternoon they were all stripped, even to the caps on their heads and almost the shirts on their backs, and there they were left friendless, houseless, and penniless.

Happily they met with the protection of a certain chief. This man had been urged to join in the persecution, but in God's providence he refused to do so. The man who thus refused to become a persecutor was one of the most wicked men in Abeokuta, and it seems astonishing that such men should be raised up by God to protect His people and His cause. This man, I say, refused to join in the persecution, and it was owing to that cause alone that the missionaries' lives were preserved.

Before sitting down I wish to allude to Onitsha, on the banks of the Niger. There were on one occasion nine European persons assembled there from Her Majesty's ships and merchant vessels, paying a visit to the sovereign, when some chiefs took an occasion to make an attack upon Christianity, no doubt wanting to feel their way and see what materials we were made of. When these gentlemen had talked about the object of their visit, the King of the place said: "Yes, we heard what you say, but we wish to know what presents the missionaries have to give." Our reply was that we had no presents to give. What was especially desired in this case was that I, as the headman, to use their expression, over the native Christians in that neighbourhood, should make a law that all the converts should return to heathenism. The chiefs wanted me to give a law to the Christians of Onitsha that they should join their fathers and mothers in offering sacrifices, and also wanted me to prohibit the Christians from eating certain fish in the river which they deemed sacred, and to do various other things of the same kind. I called to one of my catechists to give me my Bible, and holding it in my hand I said: "This is the message I have to deliver: to command these converts to return to idolatry is out of my power. I cannot do it, and I dare not do it. If I had power to prevent the soul of any of those converts from leaving the body I might have power to give them permission to return to idolatry; but they will not and should not return to it!" One of the converts then came forward and said: "Do you know me?" He belonged to a good family, and at once arrested the attention of the King. "I was a wicked one," he went on to say, "a notorious character, a great troubler of the town before Christianity came to this country, but since it came it has made the country what it is, and particularly it has made me what I am. What can have made me so different from what I was? It is the Christian religion, and that religion I will never give up; you shall rather take my life than make me give up that religion, which is the power of God to my salvation."

The Bishop never addressed his fellow-workers in these charges without taking the opportunity of discussing every phase of the subject of a native ministry, which at the time was uppermost in their thoughts. Just at this stage of the work many educated Africans were discussing, not only the advantage of native agency in missionary labour in their country, but whether Africans could regenerate their own people without outside aid. The remark had been made, "Africa for the Africans, the rest of the world for the rest of mankind."

The Bishop was therefore quite ready to discuss this patriotic standpoint of view:

I myself, being an African and a missionary, must be allowed to be somewhat qualified to answer the question from personal experience. The author of the remark about "Africa for the Africans" no doubt had his own views on the subject, and may have used the phrase either in a political, commercial, or evangelical sense. It will be quite foreign to my purpose to meddle with either of the first two senses, if they were meant; but inasmuch as the latter—the evangelization of Africa—may be implied in the idea, I may say a few words on that head. The question which we have to ask is: Are the Africans yet able to regenerate Africa without foreign aid?

The Bishop proceeded to give two reasons why this was not possible; viz. the absolute necessity of men and money. While speaking in words of warm appreciation of the work done at the training centres, the Fourah Bay College and the Freetown Grammar School, in providing such well-equipped and efficient men, not only for the mission work, but for the departments of the civil service, he pointed out how unequal the supply of men was to the demand:

We must remember that those already mentioned are employed and at work at their posts; we must not forget that the ranks of the soldiers must be thinned by death; and if advanced posts are to be taken and occupied, we must have men in reserve to fill up vacancies as well as to occupy advanced posts. They must be qualified men, well versed in scriptural knowledge, and, above all, sound in Christian character; they must "have a good report of them that are without," "full of faith and of the Holy Ghost," self-denying in the service of their divine Master.

Dealing with the necessity of accepting the generous gifts of friends in England, the Bishop said that it would be impossible for the infant Church in West

Africa to keep its feet or enlarge its borders. He spoke of the willingness of the native Christians to do all in their power for the support of Christianity, and how much the Mother Church appreciated this evidence of their zeal and practical interest in the work of the Gospel. But they are still too young and feeble to bear responsibility without outside assistance. It must be remembered that the Bishop is speaking these words in the year 1869, when the idea of a purely native Church on the Niger was as yet on the dim horizon of the future. With rare prescience he foresaw the possibility of such a development, and while carefully guarding against any wild or imprudent ambitions in that direction, which would forestall and perhaps injure the prospects of the native Church of years to come, he has in this charge given a clear note of hope which is significant and worthy of record. It is evident that the cry "Africa for the Africans" had been foolishly used as regards the evangelization of the whole continent:

If it were possible (says the Bishop) to go out now in the simple character and spirit of the primitive missionaries and preach the Gospel, "providing neither gold, nor silver, or brass in our purses," etc., on the principle of faith that God will provide our daily food, shall we find the men among ourselves ready to go out in the name of Christ and do so? . . . No one can desire our self-support and independent action more than the Mother Church, whose offspring we are. The timid and anxious trial she is now and then making by a gradual withdrawal of foreign influence, by leaving the superintendence of entire parishes and training schools to the native agents which now constitute the native pastorate, is a clear evidence that no one would rejoice more than she to see the largest portion of West Africa entirely worked by African pastors and missionaries on a self-supporting system if they are so circumstanced as to be able to do so. . . . The small spots occupied as mission stations on the line of coast, at great distances of some hundreds of miles apart, which are touched at by Royal Mail steamers, do not constitute the whole continent of Africa to be evangelized. These places are mere ports, occupied only as starting points to work the main continent teeming with population, of the immense number of which we have no correct idea until we actually enter among them.

What has been done to evangelize the one hundred tribes represented by the liberated Africans in the colony of Sierra Leone, such as the kingdoms of Ashantee, Dahomey, Yoruba, Benin, Nupé, Hausa, Bornu, and Ibo on this part of the continent? By the side of one of these kingdoms all the spots occupied on the line of coast put together will appear as a very little speck, without saying a word of those on the north, south, and east of the continent. "Africa for the Africans," the rest of the world for the rest of mankind! Can the idea thus expressed and widely circulated be applied to the evangelization of Africa? If so, and it be adopted as a watchword, let us rise up and be doing. The land is before us; let us enter the length and the breadth of it and bring the nations to Christ. "Now is the accepted time, now is the day of salvation." If we delay, thousands on thousands will continue to pass away into eternity without the knowledge of Christ, without hope, and without God in the world. Woe be unto us if we preach not unto them the Gospel of salvation in due time! . . .

When we think of the wealth and the advanced civilization and enlightenment of Europe, Asia, and America—three great quarters of the globe—when we reflect that, notwithstanding their great advancement, yet Christians from one quarter go into the others to evangelize the heathen portions of these quarters, when we consider the vast population of China and India—both wealthy and skilful in arts and sciences, and yet into these countries Christian missionaries are sent by scores from other nations to evangelize the heathen, and their help is hailed with inexpressible joy by the sons of the soil—is it not an act of great ignorance, not to say unpardonable selfishness, on the part of any man to claim "Africa for the Africans alone," when she is neither wealthy, skilful, nor enlightened, to the exclusion of others from other quarters of the globe?

Africa has neither knowledge nor skill to devise plans to bring out her vast resources for her own improvement, and, from want of Christian enlightenment, cruelty and barbarity overspread the land to an incredible degree. Therefore to claim "Africa for the Africans alone" is to claim for her the right of continued ignorance to practise cruelty and acts of barbarity as her perpetual inheritance. For it is certain, unless help came from without, a nation can never rise much above its present state. "Hath a nation changed their gods which are yet no gods?" No, "for all people will walk every one in the name of his God."

But we must pass on to quote from a few of his letters, gleaned selections from hundreds which are happily carefully preserved. In nothing, perhaps, so much as his correspondence does the Bishop show his clear, exact, and methodical style. He did naught in a flurry. It was his habit to write a careful draft of every letter from his pen, and these he preserved, as well as copies of all he received, generally also in his own handwriting. Up to the last few months of his life his script was neat, and deserving of the encomium of copperplate, a treat to read.

As to a missionary soiling his hands by merely secular work the Bishop gives his views in a letter written from Lagos on 12 January, 1875:

But some may question the propriety of missionaries employing a portion of their time to such secular occupation whilst they are exclusively employed to preach the Gospel. True, they are sent to preach the Gospel as their chief work among the heathens—it may be in the market places, under shady trees, or in a compound—and return home satisfied that their work is done. But is that all among uncultivated savage heathen?

This is applicable to countries where Christianity has been previously established and people somewhat civilized, where the time of preliminary work is past; in that case other men laboured, and their successors have entered into their labours solely to preach the Gospel. A real missionary life among the heathen is widely different from this. A man of true mission ary experience sees difficulty from this, as he has, like St. Paul, often to labour with his own hands when it comes to the push, for his own support and those who might be with him; he will become an example in all things to all men that he might gain them for Christ; he has to labour to construct his own abode, and erect preaching places in an improved state, different from native idea of building, although he is not a common labourer; he must attend the sick and wounded, although he is not a physician; when at the same time he will not neglect his proper work to attend to reading and preaching of the Word. A missionary must be a living example, known and to be imitated by all men, especially in Africa, where all hard labours are entailed on the females, and the males pass their time in idleness and selfishness. We have not far to go to prove this.

One of his dearest friends was the Rev. Henry Venn, the secretary of his earlier days, so deeply interested in the ideal of a West African native Church, and always an inspiration to Crowther. Here is an extract from a letter written from Lagos on 8 February, 1860, to acknowledge some expressions of sympathy recently sent from Salisbury Square:

To H. Venn.

Lagos, 8 February, 1860.

Your kind letter of December last was really as a soothing cordial to my heart; there is nothing that ministers so much comfort to the drooping heart and desponding spirits like sympathy which springs from a truly experienced Christian heart; the very fact that others share with us in all our trouble, and bear a part with us in the slanders and aspersions which unprincipled people are ready to cast upon us, is sufficient to make one forget and pass them over little noticed, and to pity those who try to do us evil instead of seeking to resent. I have since the last few years been taught to know that one of the most difficult things to learn to know in the world is *man*. I have not known before that man, who at one time is confided in as the best of friends, and to whom one can open his heart and mind without reserve, can upon a different circumstance prove like a broken reed, which not only gives way, but wounds and pierces. This is a painful fact. Many years ago I would not have believed it could be acted concerning myself, but I have experienced it, and but through God's protection I should have severely suffered from it. But the Lord reigneth.

It is not often that a Bishop is credited with a business faculty, because few realize how much of this department engrosses their time and energies, but Crowther was always keenly alive to the material well-being of his country. He kept his accounts with scrupulous care and method, and as regards the commercial development of the Niger, the following letter shows that at the earliest stage of cotton export he took the initiative. He is writing from Lagos in March, 1860:

To H. Venn.

Lagos, 7 March, 1860.

It will be a new piece of information to you to know that I commenced it at my station at Igbein with a deaf and dumb boy whose name is Thomas Craig, who seemed to be delighted in the working of the saw gin, when every one ran away from it as being too laborious to turn all day, and, being a strong lad, it was he who chiefly worked the 500 lb. of clean cotton which was first produced from Abeokuta in 1851. This same lad, now a young man, continues to work in connection with the Industrial Institution to the present time. From this small beginning, with a deaf and dumb boy, the work has gained the interest of the chiefs and people of Abeokuta. . . . They are consigning their cotton to merchants in England of their own choice, being taught by the Industrial Institution to develop the resources of their own country, for which a market was shown them. Thus I consider the first object of the Society has been fully answered.

The following extract from a letter written on 3 February, 1868, will give an idea of the Bishop's difficulties in travelling on the Niger before the *Henry Venn* was sent out :

To H. VENN.

Lagos, 3 February, 1868.

As long as I shall have to depend upon an annual trip of a trading ship or of a gunboat to visit the stations, so that when either one or the other of the ships appear I am seen in her as hitherto, it will take a very long time to dissuade the natives from the old belief that I am interested in those ships. To avoid this I tried to sever myself from trading ships as much as possible, so as to be independent, quietly moving to and fro, revisiting the stations in my own boat ; then I was exposed to an outrageous attack from a covetous chief. Of two evils I must choose the least for safety's sake, and must either move in a trading steamer or in a gunboat whenever an opportunity presents itself, whether I be called the proprietor—though I do not own a pennyworth of her—or be called a warrior from being associated with the ship—although I may not fire a blank shot. One thing I am sure of, that if the mercantile part of the Treaties of 1841 had been properly attended to as they were made with the native chiefs no such trouble as the present would have been experienced. Though the last year was closed with a chapter of most painful events in connection with our mission, yet I look above to the Hand which has ever overruled similar affairs which had happened in times past to His honour and the advancement of His own cause. May He give us more faith to trust Him.

A rather pensive epistle, penned evidently by the bedside of his sick wife, lies before us. He is writing in 1880, and the flight of time impresses him :

Lagos, 1880.

" Give an account of thy stewardship, for thou mayest be no longer steward." Whether we are willing or reluctant to hear, the truth stands unchangeable ; every day's occurrences which we are called to witness, by the removal of our companions and friends to give their accounts, are solemn proofs of the fact of the shortness of time. This night our souls may be required of us; may we learn to redeem the remaining days of our life.

During the last eighteen months my mind has been more or less exercised in these ways at the bedside of my dear sick wife. How watchful I had been for her speedy restoration to health, that I might be able to go out in my annual visitation to the Niger Mission; but the favourable change was long and tardy in coming. As the time for my preparation was rapidly approaching, I could neither hasten the one nor retard the other, till I was obliged to give in under the circumstances. Mental struggles, to choose the preference between two great responsibilities, are weighty; it was a natural duty to attend my sick wife, apparently in a dying state, which could not be avoided; and the cares of the mission, especially at a time when it was disorganized in various ways which threatened its prosperity, could not be easily quitted; so I was obliged to perform the first duty of charity at its proper place, for "charity begins at home." But God, in whose hand our life is, has not seemed to be ready to relieve the patient sufferer, but rather to continue to use the application as a rod in the Father's hand to correct and cure the soul. To Him be all the praise.

"Better to wear out" is the expressive sentence of a letter written from Onitsha on 12 January, 1885:

We have invitations from several heathen and Mohammedan authorities from various parts of the country to go and establish among their people; so that no less than three of the remaining experienced working agents have been proposed to be transferred from their limited but promising stations to others of most extensive spheres as centres, if practicable, in answer to their call.

It is better to wear out in running to and fro in conveying the Gospel invitation to such people, rough handed, than to spend one's days in weeping and lamenting over unwilling people to accept the message of the Gospel.

He has been giving a full description of the Obotsi tribe and their heathenish customs, and relates an interview which he has had with the King and chiefs, who did nothing but obstruct and criticize. He is writing in February, 1886:

> My reply was simply this. That in the Obotsis refusing the Christian religion and God's messengers in their town they refused God Himself and His message, sent not to them only, but also to all nations; hence they refuse His gracious offer of salvation to them through Jesus Christ. That God Himself heard all that we were talking about. He claims all souls as His, that none could refuse His messenger Death when it is sent to summon any soul before Him at any time.
>
> As regards their surprise that no case of gin was produced to open the meeting with, I told them plainly that it is against God's religion to give them poison to drink, therefore they must never expect any from me.

One of his last letters, written on board a ship off Bonny on 16 May, 1890, deals with the condition of the churches, the inevitable misery, and, after pleading for patience, as well as punishment, in dealing with the weaker brethren, he says:

> All which tends to show that the life of a Christian in this world is a life of constant warfare, of watchfulness, lest Satan take an advantage over us; it is a life of earnest prayer to the stronger man for support in time of trial and temptation, that we may not be ignorant of Satan's devices, though he may appear as an angel of light.
>
> We never feel satisfied with the external sign of Christian profession, when the converts brought to us their idols and other objects of worship in the service of Satan, until we have instructed them to apply to Christ to arm them with the whole armour of God, to stand in the evil day by Christ, and pray that He may not leave them to themselves to be drawn back to the bondage of Satan, from which He has already set them free; notwithstanding what allurements may be offered to draw them back or whatever may be the threat to their mortal bodies, even to death, that they may stand steadfast by faith that Christ is with them.

CHAPTER X

STORM CLOUDS AND SUNBEAMS

LIKE the ebb and flow of the tide, the progress, with intervals of retrogression, of the work on the Niger went on. The simile, however, is not quite fitting, for, little by little, ground was gained, and, in spite of many drawbacks, the revivifying waters of Christian teaching and influence were making the desert of heathenism to blossom as the rose. It was, of course, as all pioneer work must be, a constant contest with difficulty, the traditions of the fathers, the grip of priestly tyranny; these kept the armour of faith bright by valiant use. As the Bishop puts it:

When a change is about to take place from an old constitution to a new state of things there will ever be a conservative party to defend the retention of old time-honoured systems in opposition to those who desire a change from the old, unprofitable, and meaningless customs and superstitions received from the tradition of their fathers.

Heathenism is in Africa the old system which invests the old men and priests with power by which to rule, govern, and keep the population in awe under their control. The priests in particular, through whom the gods speak as their oracles, whose word must not and cannot be denied, are, in fact, the chief ruling power among many superstitious tribes; through them sacrifices, human and animal, are made to propitiate the gods; through them oaths are administered to bind the keeping of an agreement made between two parties in all matters of importance, commercial or political.

When the new and foreign element is introduced alarm is taken—the aggression must be opposed. Christianity is that silent but powerful aggressor which threatens the downfall of Paganism.

This fluctuation was most keenly felt at Bonny. In spite of the cruel edicts against the Christians, the services were attended with regularity, and the persecuting party could not understand how it was that whippings and irons, starvation, and even death itself, to say nothing of the allurements of worldly inducements, held out by the masters to their slaves, could not stamp out the faith. Converts were being baptized, and the Church roll increased, although the greatest care was taken to admit only those who maintained a sound practice as well as a good profession. But still the unsettled political state of the place was a perpetual hindrance. No one person had sufficient power to rule, and the work of God had nothing to gain from the anarchy of men.

The views of the few educated minds are at variance with those of the old men, who are the fathers and the leading men of the country. Unless both classes can be so tempered as to meet half-way with each other for the good of those under their controlling power and influence, the subjects are all the sufferers. Where an acknowledged leading head is not regarded there can be no order. When priests and priestesses of the gods take the lead in swaying the destiny of the nation, some of them acting the part of Ahab, and their wives, the priestesses, the part of Jezebel, stirring up their husbands against Christianity, as threatening the abolition of their idolatrous system, you may fairly conceive some idea of the state of things in this mission.

The converts were closely watched, and it was felt even a risk to be seen too much in the company of their own Bishop. One day the latter was going to preach at St. Clement's Church when he overtook a number of young men bent upon the same direction. One of them was pointed out as formerly a soldier in the Ashantee War, and the Bishop asked him to give his compliments to his master on his return home. The young fellow answered cautiously and in a low voice, "No, I no fit." He was asked why he was no fit to do this. He replied: "If I deliver your message, I report myself, because my master will say, 'Where did you see the Bishop? Ah, you have been to church!' therefore I must get punishment."

As might be expected, the Bishop was prompt and courageous in interceding for the liberty and safety of his flock, and on one occasion waited for hours under an old tree until the chiefs could or would assemble, so that he might lay before them the case of these poor suffering converts. When they did meet at last it was only to prevaricate and try to make out that the converts were disobedient to their masters, and therefore were worthy of punishment. But they were not going to put off the Bishop with these groundless and frivolous excuses. Fearless of their frowns and threats, he faced this shuffling Sanhedrim of paganism, and poured forth a stream of forcible language, which made them wince, especially as every bush in the vicinity was alive and awake with eager listeners. Might was all against him, but God was on his side.

CONGREGATION LEAVING ST. JAMES', BONNY

To face page 316

I struck at the root at once, and told them it was because the converts refused to join in the worship of the gods, in making sacrifices and eating offerings to the dead; that I could not be deceived in such a matter; that we were commanded to teach all men—they, the chiefs, not excepted—to abstain from sacrificing to dumb idols and eating the sacrifices to the dead, which provoked God to anger, confirming all these prohibitions by appropriate passages from Scripture, which were distinctly read by one or another of our party. The chiefs heard on this occasion more Scriptures against idol worship, with its unprofitableness and inability to do good or to do evil, than they had ever expected. The weakness of their superstitions was publicly exposed before them, which they could not defend.

The case, put so strongly by the Bishop, was confirmed by a quite unexpected and impartial witness. Captain Boler, a white merchant and a kindly-disposed man, being appealed to by the King to say whether this persecution of converts was true, stepped forward, and delivered his soul to this effect. He told them that this kind of thing had been tried and found to fail centuries ago, that persecution was never successful to check the progress of Christianity, instead of which it had roused the attention of even the most indifferent to inquire into its nature, and ultimately to adopt it. Probably this excellent man said much more to the point, but only this sentence has come down to us; still, such a testimony was of the greatest value at such a time.

At the Brass station the Bishop found things much more promising. Preaching to a crowded church, and afterwards holding a confirmation service, he was glad to notice in his audience, not only the chief, Thomas Spiff, who had endured so much for

Christ's sake, but just in front of him, sitting submissively, clothed literally and in his right mind, the chief Oruwari, the leader of the late persecutions. A great and wonderful change had taken place; he had put down his name for baptism, together with those of his wife and other persons of his household. Some time before this he had given permission to all his servants and retainers, about one hundred in all, to go to church and worship God, had delivered up his idols, and one of these discarded deities now adorns a niche in the mission house at Salisbury Square. The conversion of this man had been one of the trophies of the mission, for he was a standing terror to everybody. He was a trader in palm oil, and in his prosperity was the enemy of the faith; but trouble came, some old debts of his ancestors were demanded by merciless creditors, and in his distress and isolation he renounced his false friends, the priests and the chiefs, and turning from his insufficient deities, fled to the Saviour of the Christians, whom he had heretofore persecuted so relentlessly. He summed up the position in a shrewd if worldly-wise remark: "Those whom we persecuted and attempted to reduce to poverty are growing fat, while we who persecuted them in defence of the gods are growing lean."

Anyway, with whatever mixed motives in the first instance, this Saul was found among the prophets, and the wondering whisper went round the church that Sunday morning, "Is Chief Oruwari a churchgoer?"

When the Bishop reached Akassa he found some of the leading old chiefs much shaken in their confidence in their gods, because death had ruthlessly carried off recently both chiefs and priests, in spite of incantations. They were glad to welcome the Bishop again, and held a palaver with him about the preaching, and on other hands told him that the assurance given by the gods through their priests did not seem worth having. The Bishop showed them that these superstitions could not affect life and death:

God's Word declares (said he) that we must die sooner or later, therefore we must prepare and flee to Jesus Christ to fit us for it; whereas the gods assured them, through the priests, that if they offered prescribed sacrifices they need not fear death. I asked what was the cause of the loud cries and mournful lamentations and firing of guns which were echoing in our ears as we sat talking. They replied: "Ah! Depagara, the great medicine man, is dead! True alabo [i.e. gentleman], God be true, Juju be lie; we are all thinking what to do with Juju!" I asked whether any of them were ready to be with Depagara this evening, to accompany him into the world of spirits. "No," was the reply. "Why did not Depagara tell Death to wait till you were all ready to go together?" They replied: "He [Death] no will hear that." Then I impressed upon them the necessity of going to church now. "Go to God, each of you, as soon as possible; wait not one for another."

Once more he found that the inconsistency of the white man trader was a stumbling-block in the way of the Gospel among the natives. Of course these offending persons by their conduct at home could bring no discredit on Christianity, because they make no profession of it whatever, but the effect is so different among the heathen. Every sailor or soldier, merchant or traveller, by simple virtue of his colour and civilization, is at once accounted a Christian, and thus that title, which ought to mean so much, is dragged in the dust. The condition of the Church at Onitsha was a forcible illustration of this, and the observations of the Bishop thereon are well worth being reproduced. They will furnish another instance of his love of discipline and refusal to spare the rod for the sake of keeping up a numerical appearance of prosperity in the Church.

Civilized intercourse through trade has its advantages as well as its disadvantages. Very much depends upon the agents employed in the trading establishments; if they are right-minded persons—I do not go so far as to say real Christians; if they take some interest in the arduous efforts of missionaries to convert the heathen from gross idolatry and teach them Christian civilization—our work is very much facilitated; but when the agents have no spark of sympathy for missionary efforts, and care not whether the natives are Christianized or not—are ready, moreover, to accuse missionaries as meddlers in trade matters because they are reproached for trading on Sundays, while converts are prevented from attending church or class on pain of forfeiting their place on the factory—what can be expected but disorder and confusion when this opposition proceeds from a white man? Those who were doubting about the truth of their own heathenish religion since the introduction of Christianity are now hesitating to make a change to the new religion, which is opposed by those who ought to have supported it as true.

But this is not all the mischief that is done. Monogamy has been represented to this people as contrary to Scripture; Jacob, David, and Solomon have been quoted as examples of polygamists, and yet they were beloved, chosen people of God. The result has been that the female palm oil traders have prostituted their female slaves at the factories, and some of our female converts followed the example of their heathen companions by hiring out slaves also. Messrs. Perry and Buck, the young ministers in charge, had to combat these difficulties both with the female converts and the civilized nominal

Christians. They suspended from membership all the female converts known to prostitute their female slaves.

On my return to this place on 27 July the male converts got a long letter written to me, stating the unstable state of the Church through the ungodly example of civilized men employed at the factories.

It became therefore necessary to distinguish between nominal and ungodly Christians and those who are real Christians, whose walk was consistent with their profession. It was no easy matter to make these distinctions, and to make these men believe that characters could exist in Christian countries who are not regarded as true Christians. It was not a pleasant subject, but to protect the new Church just emerging out of gross heathenism it was most necessary. On the following Sunday, the first day of August, I made this the special subject of my sermon, many of the educated natives employed at the factories being present. I had to expose the ungodly conduct of some as most inconsistent with the religion they profess, by which they cast a stumbling-block before the heathen, and so weaken the faith of the new converts to Christianity. Truly there is a time and season for every purpose; this was a time to rebuke sharply, that they may be sound in faith: "their mouths must be stopped, who subvert whole houses, teaching things they ought not for filthy lucre's sake."

On Monday following the elderly female converts asked for a hearing; it lasted about three hours, when many questions were put to me on subjects they wished to be corrected in, among which was the prostitution of their slaves. Those who acknowledged their offence, expressing deep sorrow and promising amendment, were forgiven and readmitted; while others laid the whole blame upon the factory men who had enticed away their slaves, over whom they had no control; on showing that they never received payments for such an act, they were readmitted into class, for which they were thankful. It is a time of ordeal for the faith of Christian converts from heathenism. May the Lord bring them forth from this furnace purified seven times! A pleasing feature in the conduct of these converts was the desire to be corrected and guided aright; they were overcome by the influence of bad example of those from whom they had expected better things, but finding they had been misled they were ready to remend.

In the year 1875 the Bishop was able to make good progress with his work of translating the Scriptures, and gave special attention to the preparation of a grammar of the Ibo language. So far back as 1854 to 1857 he had begun this difficult task, and had sent the manuscripts to England by the hands of his old friend and comrade Mr. Schón. The great hindrance was the existence of so many dialects, each being naturally assumed by its speaker to be the only one of superiority, whereas in constructing a written grammar of Ibo it appeared that the Isu-ama was the only leading dialect of the nation. Onitsha was not recognized as the place of an original Ibo tribe; the people had come from the Ado country on the west side of the Niger, crossing to the east on the borders of the Ibo country, and becoming naturalized by intercourse and marriage. They retained their old customs, and their word of salutation, "Do!" is the same as in Ado, Benin, and the Ondo. Therefore the language of Onitsha was a corrupt dialect of the Ibo proper, Isa. Another difficulty the Bishop met with in this translational work was that a translator from Sierra Leone might be born of parents of different tribes; the father might be an Isu-ama and the mother an Elugu, so it was necessary to find a teacher who knew the pure Isu-ama dialect, and by his assistance construct the vocabulary. In this the Bishop was not altogether successful. He says:

Many of the original stock of the Ibos imported in Sierra Leone years ago have died off; others are so old and infirm that they cannot now leave the colony. Therefore teachers were sought out from among the colony-born men, whose parents were known to be good Ibo speakers. We commenced our work with every hope of success when, to my pain and grief, it was found out that the former habits of these men, uncultivated for mission work, totally unfitted them for a connection with the mission. Under these circumstances I was obliged to send them back to Sierra Leone without delay.

Like the typical marine, the Bishop was a handy man. He was as much at home in helping with building operations as constructing a grammatical language. We get a glimpse of him showing his people how to make bricks. On his return to Kipo Hill station from Bida he examined with the eye of an expert the red and white sandstone clay which formed the hill. He observed that after the heavy rains the action of the sun hardened the surface of the clay, but a little deeper down it still continued soft and moist. So he got a carpenter to make him a brick mould according to pattern seen in England, but probably the same as used in Egyptian buildings, and then after getting some men to work the clay into the proper consistency, he showed them by his own hands how to use the mould, and made twenty-five specimen bricks. He then constructed artificial arches of dried bricks for furnaces, and was soon able to produce, with his assistants, five hundred baked bricks, made as far as possible in the same way as in the white man's country. Of course this was before the introduction of machinery and other progressive inventions as regards kilns, etc.

Of these home-made materials the new mission house at Kipo Hill was built.

On 11 June, 1877, the Bishop, being in England, read an important paper upon the River Niger before the Royal Geographical Society, which attracted much interest. Apart altogether from the valuable geographical facts which he brought before the audience, the personality of the lecturer was an unusual feature. It had never been the case that a black man, once a slave and now a prelate, had come before them as an explorer and a well-read and cultured observer, and so distinguished. He went into minute and valuable details of this great and then almost unknown territory through which the River Niger flowed, giving vivid sketches of the various tribes, and the possibilities of trade developments in the future.

References were made to the various languages in vogue, and he ventured to give some sound practical advice which would be helpful to travellers and merchants entering the country. The origin of the Foulah race was an interesting section of his paper.

At the close, the President, Sir Rutherford Alcock, asked, as he had been much struck by the Bishop's remarks on the progress of Mohammedanism among the conquered nations, what was the real effect of their religion upon the races; did it purify and improve their social position? It seemed by its simplicity to recommend itself to the native mind, but it was a question how far it could be possible to convert tribes into peaceable natives.

The Bishop, in reply, admitted that Mohammedanism had done some good among the natives; in so far as they dared do it with safety they had abolished the worship of idols and offering of human sacrifices, but if they had mingled charity with their teaching, the natives would have more firmly adhered to them. They were, however, very oppressive. They were slave holders, and their object was not so much to proselytize as to enslave, and the populations under their sway disliked them exceedingly. When he first established a Christian mission at the Confluence of the Niger and the Binue the Mohammedans attended this place of worship, but though they had been masters of the country to his knowledge since 1841, no sooner did the Christian mission go there, than the heathen voluntarily erected a shed and invited him to preach the Gospel to them. Both this shed and a second one were accidentally burnt, but the natives rebuilt them, and worship was conducted there. Because the Yoruba country people dress in flowing toga, travellers had taken them for Mohammedans. Two years ago, in a village, it was found that out of a population of five hundred there had not been a single convert to Mohammedanism, the people remaining idolaters, though all taken for Mohammedans because of their clothing.

In proposing a vote of thanks the Dean of Lichfield "hoped that Bishop Crowther was the representative of a new race of African bishops, who with enlightened knowledge and judgment might be pioneers of those who should still further explore Africa."

Later on the Council of the Royal Geographical Society presented a gold watch, value forty pounds, to the Bishop, in recognition of his valuable services to geographical science.

The work on the Niger had already attracted a great deal of interest in England among the supporters of missionary enterprise, and it was felt that if a vessel could be built specially for his use in going to and fro, it would prove a great advantage. Subscriptions came in freely from his many friends at home, and as a result a trim little paddle steamer, able to do ten knots an hour, was built and launched on the Clyde, and suitably christened the *Henry Venn*, in memory of that faithful friend of West Africa. It was a temperance ship, with an efficient crew, and to ensure its safety it sailed off from Falmouth, escorted by H.M.S. *Forester*, on 2 March, 1878. This vessel became a valuable acquisition to the mission; but the most remarkable voyage was up the Binue, nearly eight hundred miles, the result of which Mr. Ashcroft, the newly-appointed secular agent, embodied in an interesting journal. It will be remembered that the second expedition of Dr. Baikie and Bishop Crowther in the *Pleiad* in 1854 reached a point not far from Hamaruwa, four hundred miles from the Confluence, and six hundred miles from the sea. Three years before that time Dr. Barth, in returning from his explorations in the Soudan, crossed near the same place, Ayola, seventy miles further up the Binue, but had not stayed to make any explorations either up or down the river. The *Henry Venn*, however, steamed one hundred and forty miles beyond this point, and discovered that further up the tributary the Mayo Kebi flows in, and from this the Binue gains its strong volume of water, above that being only a small stream. The valuable observations of this expedition were set forth in a paper contributed to the Royal Geographical Society, and read at one of their meetings on 22 March, 1879, by Mr. Hutchinson, the lay secretary of the Church Missionary Society. The Bishop was unfortunately unable to accompany this expedition, in consequence of the illness of Mrs. Crowther. His disappointment is expressed in one of his letters quoted on another page. This being the case, it is not within the province of this work to do more than record a few words from the journal of Mr. Ashcroft, describing his visit to the chief at the furthest point reached by the *Henry Venn*, and how he further pushed up the stream in an open boat to explore to the utmost this fascinating country before turning back. The water was falling rapidly, and it was clear that the river every day was growing more dangerous for navigation. They anchored in midstream, and sent a boat towards a crowd of naked natives assembled on the shore on the right bank of the river.

The people were not able to get to the edge of the main stream on account of the grass being overflowed about three feet; but they called for us to try higher up, and soon we found an opening in the thick grass and pulled the boat, the people coming up to their middle in water to help us and going before to show us the best way to get to the dry ground. We got the boat as far as we could, and then it had to be carried thirty or forty yards.

Mr. Kirk, Flegel, and myself then went to visit Garawara. The chief's name was Sufen. He informed me that the rocks near which we had anchored would soon be dry, for the water was going down, and he did not think it would rise again this year; also that when the river began to fall it fell very rapidly, and that we should see all the rocks in a few days. When asked, "How long are you able to use canoes?" he said, "Two or three moons only every year." The rest of the time they go by land, and can cross the river without canoes; but there were deep pools with plenty of alligators, etc. I asked the name of the mountain to which I had given the name of Burdett-Coutts, and was told it was "Ostuting-gading." I asked how far the Kebi was, and they said by canoe three and a half days, by land two and a half days. The town of Dengi was at the Confluence of the Binue and Kebi. "What is the Binue like past the Kebi?" "It is only a small river." "How far is it until you get to where you say the Binue comes over mountains in the Gumderi country?" "By land, fast walking, eight days; by canoe thirteen days." "Do you know the names of any towns on the way?" "Yes, a few. Reborn, Duli, Drugi, and Golumbi." But our informant had not been beyond Golumbi, three days distant from here. They said that where the Binue rises the name of the people is the Bum people. No one that we came across knew anything of the Belle or Shary or of any great river or lake hereabouts.

In the afternoon we took the *Winifred* and steamed about eight miles up the river to the town of Reborn, on the right bank, a beautiful situation and about a mile from the Burdett range, magnificent mountains, and at the distance they looked like a large palace, with the centre part of the building higher than the rest. The finest scene of the whole river was just about here. I was exceedingly sorry to have to turn back, the country being so beautiful; and the people just received us like old friends, not the least alarmed when we approached with the steamer; they were also Bornu people, speaking Fula.

We had only time to climb a hill and look at the mountains in the distance before it was time to turn back. I asked if they would like white men to come and live with them at this and other towns, and the people and her chiefs would like it much, for white men would make their country good. That appears to be the belief of all of them whenever you ask. It was getting dusk as we very reluctantly got into the launch to run back to the *Henry Venn*, distant about eight or nine miles. We bid the people good-bye and they wished us God speed, and hoped we should soon come again and visit them and be able to stay.

Although, as we have said, the Bishop had been debarred from seeing with his own eyes these new regions, and to make acquaintance with a people so interesting and accessible, he was keenly interested in this voyage of the *Henry Venn.* To him this seemed as another open door, and he yearned for the time when he would be able to carry the good tidings of Christianity up there.

In the meanwhile the progress of commerce on the Niger was unfortunately from time to time interrupted by the blind opposition and treachery of the natives. In 1878 two trading steamers at a narrow bend of the river found a stout hawser stretched across to bar their further progress homewards down the stream, and while thus arrested were fired upon from the banks, and one man killed on board. The motive for this outrage appears to have been pure jealousy of the palm oil trade on the river, and a determination to divert it by force into another channel for the advantage of other tribes. As a consequence the merchants appealed to Commodore Hewitt, who was blockading Dahomey, and two gunboats ascended the Nun branch of the Niger and destroyed the offending village. For a time peace was restored, and both traders and missionaries were undisturbed; but in October, 1879, a more serious outbreak occurred. Outrages had become insufferable upon British subjects in the pursuit of commerce, and as this was chiefly at Onitsha, the British Consul on board H.M.S. *Pioneer* anchored off the town, and sent for the chiefs to come and give guarantees that better order should be kept in future. At first they refused to show themselves, but when two of the mission agents, accompanied by some of the leading traders, went to persuade them, they came on board, and the Consul demanded that the ringleaders of the recent riots and outrages be given up. The chiefs said they must refer to their King, and the Consul gave them till noon the next day. In the meantime the robbers were actually raiding some houses, and a mob gathered and plundered the mission premises. To fill up the cup of their insolence to the brim, during the night the ships were fired on, and one of the captains wounded. Early in the morning the huts of the ringleaders were destroyed, and at the expiration of the time allowed, the vessel opened fire on the town, which was burnt and utterly destroyed. The lesson to these unscrupulous heathen was doubtless a salutary one, but it was a sad blow to the Christian work of this the first station founded by the Bishop. On the previous Sunday more than two hundred and sixty persons were present at church, and the Bible classes were largely attended. Now the place was a deserted and smoking ruin!

"Thus end," writes the Rev. S. Perry, the pastor, "our hopes and plans for the improvement of Onitsha." We now return to the Delta, and a notable person, Ockiya, the King of Brass, deserves a mention here. He appears to have been a man of intelligence, and was much impressed by what he saw of the industrial work which the Bishop had inaugurated in the mission compound. He was shown the sawyers at work, which was a surprise to him, and when he had visited the gardens where the fruits were growing so well and the little yams, recently planted, were giving such promise by their special cultivation, he naturally expressed a desire to see such yams growing in his own place. The Bishop, who displayed these things to the King, took the opportunity of pointing out the folly of juju worship, and he appeared thoughtful. About this time his daughter, who was a scholar in the Christian school, died suddenly, and Ockiya, instead of consulting his god for the reason of this sorrow, bore it very patiently, repeating what he had been taught, "God gave and God takes away." The Bishop later on reported that the King had broken through the laws of the gods which forbade the inhabitants of the Brass River to grow yams on their own soil, and to cut the stems of certain creepers or climbers, or large trees, on pain of punishment of paying a heavy fine of some casks of palm oil for the offence given to the gods. Ockiya, however, seems to have plucked up heart and dared these deities, for he ordered men to clear the jungles, to cut down the trailing creepers, and in place of these to plant yams. This was followed by a bolder step, when he sent three of his largest idols to the missionary by the hand of his daughter, and afterwards, in the face of his people, he carried his charms and other objects of his confidence, and threw them into the river.

On Advent Sunday, 1879, he was duly baptized, receiving the new Christian name of Josiah Constantine, having previously handed to the Bishop his remaining idols, cut down his sacred groves, and, last not least, dismissed all his wives save one. Two weeks after this the King died. It is reported that on his death-bed the juju priests tried hard to make him recant, but without success, being kept steadfast in the faith through the influence of the Christian woman of his household, who attended him in his last moments. He died "calling on Christ."

Many instances might be given of the power of the juju superstition. A new station had been opened by the Bishop at Okrika, and here a notorious chief, Atorodibo, and his wife were converted to the Christian faith. At a certain time of the year the women of the Okoni and the Okrika people visit a market for trade, midway between the two towns, and before crossing the stream the Okrika women offered sacrifices to gods for a favourable market, and every woman on crossing was chalked on the forehead by the juju priest. When it came to the turn of the wife of Atorodibo she refused to offer sacrifices or suffer her face to be daubed with chalk, and that night, in consequence of some offence given by the Okrika people, the Okoni men lay in ambush, and killed nearly all the women, except a few reserved for captivity. Amongst the latter was Atorodibo's wife. She implored her captor, "in the name of the God of heaven," not to injure her. She was told it was the Okoni juju, which was stronger than that of Okrika, which had delivered her into their hands. But the woman replied: "I do not believe in any juju; myself and my husband worship God, the God of heaven, and for that God's sake release me, and let me return home." This answer mystified the man, and he asked her to tell him about this "God of heaven," and what was His worship. The woman then, like her predecessor at Jacob's well, told him what wonderful things the Lord had done for her, and how her husband, too, had accepted Christ and worshipped idols no more.

The story strangely charmed the man, and dropping his voice to a whisper, he said: "Be quiet, do not let any one know that you are with me. At dead of night I shall take you over to Okrika, though we have sworn that not a soul shall return."

True to his promise, he woke up the distressed woman at midnight, led her through the bush to the riverside, and pulled her across in a small canoe to Okrika town. Of course all the place was astir, anxious for the return of the wives, sisters, and daughters who would come back no more. Preparations were at once set on foot to attack Okoni at daylight. Through the agitated town Atorodibo's wife quietly passed and knocked at the door of her house. Her appearance was like one from the dead. She told all the sad story, and also of the plans which she had overheard by the way in which the Okoni warriors were going to repel any attack. This guided her own people in their expedition, so that they were successful in rescuing the surviving Okrika women out of the hands of the enemy. This incident made a great impression at Okrika, for the people felt that her refusal to sacrifice or have her face chalked had saved her life and that of so many of her people, and that the Christian's God could preserve where the juju failed. Among a people prone to signs and wonders this event was wonderful and effective.

It is encouraging to note that some of those who had been the leaders of persecution in these Delta stations died in the faith, acknowledging their wrong-doing. One of these, a chief who had been a cruel opponent of the work, openly confessed the great change which had come over him, and described himself as "the Saul who became Paul, and took off his hat for Christ, whom he had fought and hoped to conquer, but who had conquered him." Indeed, he became valiant in defence of the truth he had once persecuted, and his dying message was, "Tell the minister when he comes that I die in Christ."

Some of these chiefs were ready to help in the building of churches, and even sent to England for their gifts. This was the case with Chief Squiss, who wished to show his friendliness in helping to furnish the newly-reopened Church of St. Stephen's in 1880, and obtained from London an elegant drawing-room clock, for which he paid nine pounds, and this rather unusual timepiece for such a purpose certainly gave a finish to the interior appearance of the sacred building. This was the offering of a man who had not accepted Christianity. The Bishop makes a point of drawing attention, in a letter from Bonny at this time, to the salutary effect of Christian influence even among people, like this chief, who have not become believers in its teaching :

> Contrary to custom, when canoes were got ready to go out on a war expedition, and sacrifices were made and the blood of the animal victims were spilt on the war canoes to propitiate the god of war, the converts, as one man, refused to perform juju or to eat of the sacrifices, on the ground that it is idolatrous, superstitious, and contrary to the law of God and the doctrines of the Christian religion which they had performed. Some of the head chiefs sided with them ; but one of the head chiefs, an opponent to Christianity, ordered a priest to offer an animal sacrifice to his own canoe, which the priest, though not yet professing Christianity, refused to do on the conviction of the folly of these practices. The head chief, being enraged, ordered one of his slaves to take a whip and chastise the priest to compel him to do his duty, but the servant declined doing so. He ordered another to execute his order on the priest, but he also declined. On the third refusing, he got up in a great rage, took up the whip himself, and spent the whole of his strength on the delinquent priest, when he was led away by some standers by who were witnessing the proceedings of the day. Thinking that the priest has received a salutary lesson from him, and that he would now be intimidated to refuse his order, he sent to call him at another time to go over and perform the required sacrifices, but the reply from the priest was to this effect, that had he intended to offer the sacrifice he would not have suffered himself to be so severely beaten and shamefully treated in public ; but it was too late, he would do no more sacrifices to the gods. Soon after this he enlisted himself as a candidate for baptism.

The reaction in favour of Christianity was largely due to the dying warnings of a notorious idolatrous chief known as Captain Hart, who had persecuted the converts, and had made a great show of his adherence to the tradition of his gods. It was through this man's wicked treatment of the poor converts that their sufferings were beyond expression, and often meant death. They, however, stood firm. Pardon, gifts, and promotion even were offered if they would only give up Christ, and as an alternative they were threatened with a fearful increase of suffering should they decline. But these poor black men, whose names are unknown save to the recording angel, were magnificent in their martyrdom. Here is the answer sent by one of them to such an offer: "Tell the master I thank him for his kindness. He himself knows that I never refused to perform duties required of me at home. But as regards turning back to heathen worship, *that* is out of my power, for Jesus has taken charge of my heart, and padlocked it. The key is with Him. So you see it is impossible for me to open it without Him."

Another, in the midst of excessive agony, was not prepared to purchase release by apostasy. They threatened him with keener pains and heavier burdens. He answered: "I have made up my mind, God helping me, to be in chains, should it so please the Lord, even till the coming of the judgment day."

No wonder that the author of such wrongs should strive to make some atonement, and to show how he himself had done with the worship of the gods. On his deathbed he told his people that he had found out that all these gods were lies, and warned them against putting any trust in such vanities. His orders that after his death every image and juju found in any house was to be destroyed were carried out to the letter.

Two young men converts came to the mission house

one day and asked the Bishop to sell them some books. He asked them where they had come from, and they answered, "The Land of Israel." What meant that strange reply ? They told him : "You do not know, sir, what changes are taking place at Bonny; that yonder village Ayambo is now named the Land of Israel, because no idol is to be found in it. Though you may walk through the village, you will not find a single idol in it as an object of worship."

This place might also have been styled a City of Refuge, for it was a place of security to which converts fled when persecuted by their enemies. In a later letter dated June, 1881, the Bishop speaks of a service held at Nembe, on the Brass River, when four old women, one too aged and infirm to totter to the altar rails, were duly confirmed in the presence of four hundred and eighty people. These old women had been a great stumbling-block in the way of Christianity; one was formerly a devoted priestess of the gods, and their humble and sincere consecration of themselves to Christ that day had a marked effect upon the people. It must be borne in mind that the old women, with their great influence and authority, are often a serious drawback to mission work in West Africa.

Passing to the work on the Upper Niger we have a description of the Onitsha native given in one of the reports of Archdeacon Johnson, which shows what a genuine savage he is. This is the material upon which the missionary has to work, and nothing short of Divine grace could transform such a creature into a convert worthy of the Christian name :

As he scruples not to do injury to his neighbour, so he is ever afraid of being injured himself; hence there is a general feeling of distrust. They are rarely seen about but with knives and guns—a sure proof of a prevailing sense of insecurity. The Onitsha increases his natural ferocity by making ghastly incisions about his body and fantastic marks on his face. He chalks his eyebrows for the same reason, and looks fierce indeed. Like the great Ibo tribe generally, he is quick to be in a passion, and while in that state can commit the most brutal crimes without the slightest hesitation; nor does he afterwards feel the smallest compunction in reflecting upon the sad effect of his passion. Nay, in certain cases he prides himself on having done these things and boasts of his conduct to others. The time has not much gone by, if at all, when a certain Onitsha in quarrelling with his companion would say to him in a tone of superiority: "What do you mean to tell me? I have killed about six men in my time. How many have you killed?" It is true; the feathers in his cap prove that the boast is not an idle one.

Still, while the Bishop was visiting the station, many incidents were told him of conversions which had occurred in the revival following the time of persecution. One of these stories is worthy of a brief record:

A woman named Ekubie gave up idol worship and brought her gods to the catechist. She was converted by means of a picture. Once, on entering the Mission House, she saw a picture on the wall. It was one of the cheap German sketches, a representation of Jesus sitting before a table in the attitude of blessing a loaf of bread which He held in His hand, and a cup before Him. The catechist patiently explained who Jesus Christ was: "The Saviour of men, who came into this world and died to take away sin." Gradually the woman became interested, and at length she asked: "Did He die for me too?" "Yes," was the immediate reply; "and if you believe in Him He will save you." So the conversation went on until at last the poor heathen woman resolved to give up heathenism and embrace Christianity. She became a regular attendant at church and a consistent believer.

There is something very admirable in the courage and constancy of these converts of Onitsha, quite worthy to be mentioned by the side of the Delta martyrs. After the bombardment and the transfer of the mission to Asaba on the other side, many still refused to go, and remained at great peril to their lives. The church and mission premises had been plundered and burnt, windows and doors carried off as loot, and when the shells came from the gunboats, the place became a pandemonium. But these few faithful Christians did not desert their faith in its peril, nor turn their backs upon their Saviour because of the reign of terror and violence. In spite of all this they assembled for prayer every Lord's Day, when a little black schoolboy read the Liturgy, and made what exposition he could of the Scriptures in place of a sermon! The church was a wreck and ready to tumble down, but they clung to it as the house of God, and had good times sitting on rubbish heaps in place of the seats already stolen away. Of course some fell away, and even relapsed into polygamy, as a kind of halfway house on the backward journey; but the majority stood firm, according to the light they possessed, and held the fort of faith.

The Bishop, on his visitation, found many opportunities for the exercise of discipline, and tells us that at Lokoja especially this was the case. There was a lack of true spirituality; many of the immigrants from Sierra Leone bringing a certain profession of Christianity with them, without much power, soon fell into a deplorably listless and formal way of worship. Some seemed to have no strength to resist the deep black current of immorality which flowed through the place. It is better to draw a veil over a condition of things which has been sufficiently referred to, the result, it must be confessed, to a large extent, of the introduction of a civilization minus Christianity.

But the African mind is constitutionally optimistic. As an example of the hopefulness of the native pastors when preaching to their flocks about the future redemption of Africa, here is a brief quotation from one of them, the Rev. D. G. Williams, of Trinity Church, Sierra Leone. He has taken for his text "Ethiopia shall stretch forth her hands to God," and has spoken of Philip and the eunuch. With intense earnestness he bewails the evils which beset his native land, its degradation and darkness:

> Brethren, I am aware of these evils. I am not ignorant of the fact that the enemies of Divine revelation make use of them to justify their unwarranted assumption that we were doomed to perpetual ignorance and blindness. And yet, taking my stand by the Scriptures of the inspired Word, and resting on the promises of God, which are as immovable as the everlasting hills, I maintain, without fear of opposition, that this land of pagan darkness shall yet be won for Christ.
>
> That these untutored heathen tribes,
> A dark, bewildered race,
> Shall sit down at Immanuel's feet,
> And have and feel His Grace.

For the hope of Africa's future regeneration rests on the living God. Hence exclaimed the sainted Latimer Neville, himself a pioneer missionary, to the Pongas heathen, notwithstanding the difficulties which stared him full in the face: "I am as certain of the conversion of Africa to God as I am of the rising of the sun to-morrow morning."

With similar confidence the Hon. William Grant declared

AKWETE CHAPEL AND PASTORATE BOAT

of the negro: "I believe in his restoration from barbarism and heathenism to Christianity and civilization."

That our Lord during His infancy should have found shelter in Egypt from the cruel edict of a relentless king might be favourably interpreted with regard to the land of Ham. Simon the Cyrenean, who aided the Saviour in bearing His cross, and Simeon that was called Niger, one of the dignitaries of the early Church in Antioch (being Africans), might also be viewed as representatives of innumerable persons, sons of Africa, who may yet bear the cross and despise the shame for Jesus' sake.

He then speaks of the inestimable value of Holy Scripture, and how God has at sundry times and in divers places spoken to the world by prophet and seer:

Equally important is the voice of the living missionary in the present day. From that voice sounds out the Word of the Lord to distant lands; to that voice the heathen listens to catch the sweet message of a Saviour's love; beneath that voice multitudes sit and find refreshment to their souls. Hence it is that missionary societies attach so much importance to the living agents they send abroad. It is because they feel that prayer alone would not suffice. Even the Bible and prayer, valuable and indispensable as they are, will not do. There must be the united agency of prayer, the Bible, and the preacher, like a threefold cord not easily broken. Well may we seek out properly qualified men for the work of the Lord in every land—teachers who are not only bathed in a stream of classic lore and are masters of the abstract sciences, but are also bathed in the fountain that flows from beneath the throne of God, and are masters of the science of salvation and the art of holy living, and adorned with the beauty of holiness. We indulge in no Utopian dream, we entertain no wild and visionary idea when we aver that Africa's future may yet be more glorious than the past if God will. The attention of the civilized world that is now being directed to it, the openings in the East, and the invitation in the centre may all be regarded as a voice from heaven, saying: "Arise, shine, for thy light is come." The time to save Africa; yea, the time is come!

On one occasion the Bishop, accompanied by his son, the present Archdeacon, visited a powerful chief named Alumi, who lived in a town seven miles up the river from Benin. The object of the journey was to secure some premises for a mission station, which buildings had been hitherto used for trading purposes. They had to paddle the native canoe through the narrow and dangerous creek in a heavy storm of rain and flashes of lightning, the thunder crashing above and echoing in the dark forest close by. Eventually, however, they reached the great man's hut, and as he boasted the luxury of a table they were entertained with a supper of "palm oil chop," and after this repast they squatted on the ground and commenced the palaver. The quick eye of the Bishop noticed how fitful the light was, now dull almost to darkness, then blazing up quite brightly. This he discovered was because the lamp was of a most primitive character, simply broken bits of calabashes used for years in carrying oil, and therefore well saturated therewith, cut into small pieces, and stuck on an arrangement resembling a saucepan lid. Several naked boys were told off to keep this illumination in good order, dipping the bits in fresh oil to awaken the light when it drooped. Sometimes these lads would forget their duty, and an elder chief would shout sharply, "Alupa," meaning lamp, with sundry dashes at the forgetful youngsters to administer chastisement.

After resting awhile and talking about everything else, according to African custom, the Bishop broached the subject of the premises, and then the chief called his visitors into an inner court, with one of his sons, who talked English pretty well. The Bishop reminded his host of certain promises he had made for a mission and a school where the children might be taught the white man's book. At the suggestion of books the chief showed a spirit of reluctance, saying: "Book palaver will not do for Sekeri people" (this is the proper name of the people inhabiting Benin River; Benin proper is some days' journey inland); "that they will not wish to get their hands dirty, will get lazy, and will not work after knowing book." The other younger son, sitting close by, added that their custom of kneeling before a father or elder will be done away with when book is taught, and shaking of hands will be substituted, while such an impertinent act from a younger to an elder is criminal in Sekeri, and is accompanied by death.

The Bishop listened patiently to this opposition to education, and then quietly took up their objections one by one. He wanted to know why the Sekeri people are supposed to be different from other folks in the world, as, for instance, Lagos, Niger, Brass, New Calabar, and Bonny people; for if the teaching of God's Word and the knowledge of book were good things for them, why not the same for those at Benin River? Trade, he observed, seemed in their opinion to be good for them, as for other nations and tribes. Then as to the charge of their being made lazy, the opposite is proved to be true; book knowledge makes men more active—as, for instance, the Bishop asked Chief Alumi who are those who manufacture cloths, silks, which are brought up these rivers for sale? Are they not made by the book people? Who are those who plant wheat and corn for bread, make biscuits, kill bullocks which are salted, and the various eatables brought here and to other rivers in great quantities, and sold to them? Who are the workers of all these but people of book knowledge, and are these things signs of a lazy people? Further, he went on to say that some of the richest people in England are farmers who had been toiling with sleeves rolled up and with dirty hands in working and turning up the ground. Then, by a happy thought, the Bishop suggested the English engineers in steamers, and asked the chief which Sekeri man is more dirty and as hard a workman as an engineer from the engine-room, with black, oily hands, and oftentimes face: and can an ignorant man "make ship move"?

Then turning to the younger son about shaking hands, the Bishop told him that the Bible taught the young obedience to elders, more than Sekeri people ever knew, and that the Bible will not interfere with such customs as those, that they will find in course of time that those who know what is in the Bible are sincere in their obedience inwardly, and not outwardly through fearing death.

The chief could not gainsay this reasoning, but found another excuse, explaining that "he did not exactly mean to say that Sekeri people were incapable of learning, but that those who had been sent to know book die away, and are never seen again." To support this extraordinary statement he gave instances of boys going to Liverpool and Portugal who never came back, so, said he, "if a mission be established to teach all Sekeri people, their time on earth will be limited, especially old men such as he is; that he had better wait after this generation of old men has passed, then the young people can do what they like."

In spite of all the Bishop could say, it was evident that a superstitious fear of death was at the bottom of the chief's objection. He stood firm, in spite of the fact that the visitors stayed far into the night, and afterwards in the darkness rowed back down the creek and river unsuccessful. "With a parting 'good night,' which ought rightly to be 'good morning,' we turned into bed, but not before asking the God of missions to open in His good time the dark eyes of the heathen, to bless and strengthen our weak effort of that night, to the extension and glory of the Redeemer's name."

The Bishop, in writing to his "brethren and fellow-labourers" from the mission house, Bonny, on 26 February, 1883, after speaking of the good way the Lord had brought him hitherto, tells what has been specially his prayer and heart's desire in the work on the Niger:

In addition to the above-mentioned advantages, I have been blessed with *unbroken health*; that I have not been laid aside any day, week, month, or year from pursuing my duty, which is a rare blessing, with many other privileges granted to me, for which I cannot feel that I have exerted myself enough to make adequate return by making myself more useful in God's service for the evangelization of my ignorant countrymen. Whatever success God has been pleased to grant to our feeble and imperfect efforts, you, my fellow-labourers in the mission, are eye-witnesses. To God be all the honour and praise. He is fulfilling His own promise: "The Gentiles shall come to the light, and kings to the brightness of Thy rising."

During my missionary labours in the Niger Mission I have often ventured to make two *timid requests* in prayer to the God of missions, which I sometimes fear may savour of selfishness. One is like to that of Caleb, made to Joshua for the mountainous countries of Palestine, but with *spiritual application*, when he said: "Thou knowest the thing that the Lord said unto Moses the man of God concerning me and thee in Kadesh-barnea. Forty years old was I when Moses the servant of the Lord sent me from Kadesh-barnea to espy out the land; and I brought him word again as it was in mine heart. . . . And Moses sware on that day, saying, Surely the land whereon thy feet have trodden shall be thine inheritance, and thy children's for ever, because thou hast wholly followed the Lord my God. . . ." (Joshua xiv. 6–13). I have quoted the passage at length to call your attention to it for reference.

The mountain prayed for to be given is the countries of the Niger territory, visited forty years ago, in 1841. The cities great and fenced are the strongholds of Mohammedanism and heathenism, fenced with deluding religions and strong shackles of slave system. If so be, the Lord will be with us; then we shall be able to possess the land for our Saviour Jesus Christ.

The second subject of prayer is that in all the stations already established good and substantial places of worship may be erected for the permanent uses of the converts before I be laid aside, that my successors may not be crippled on this head, to put into operation the most desirable system of self-support in the mission.

CHAPTER XI

IN THE CRUCIBLE AND AT REST

THE closing decade of the Bishop's long career was marked by turbulence and shadowed by suffering. It is sometimes granted to those who go down to the sea in ships, after battling with many storms, to return in fair weather, gliding along the familiar home waters in unruffled calm, beneath sunny skies. But it was not thus with the Bishop. He had faced many a tempest, steered clear of hidden and perilous reefs, and might have reasonably trusted that as the end of the voyage drew nearer he, too, might make the harbour on a tranquil day. The great Disposer of his life and ours had, however, otherwise ordained, and before the abundant entrance was vouchsafed to this brave veteran mariner, the clouds were to darken and billows of worry and disappointment threaten his peace.

He was already full of years and growing a little weary, although no one could detect any diminution in his incessant labours and selfless zeal. Across his immense diocese the mission stations on the Niger were dotted at wide distances, and before the little steamer, the *Henry Venn*, was dispatched from England for his service, he could only reach these places at such intervals as the passing trading ships would allow. This, too, as we have seen, was an intermittent quantity, for the accident of an outrage would cause a political isolation of the river for a considerable time. And even with the advantage of this little mission craft, which had to carry freight to pay expenses, he found the work of supervision exceedingly difficult with all his labours, his patience, and his pains. He said little about these troubles and difficulties, for he was not the man to wear his heart upon his sleeve, but the fact remains, as we have already seen in his history, that few men could more adequately realize the trials of the great Apostle to the Gentiles as regards tribulations, for he was literally in journeyings often, in perils of waters, in perils of his own countrymen, in perils of the heathen, in weariness and painfulness, in watchings often, in hunger and thirst, in fastings often, in cold and nakedness, and beside these things which are without that which came daily upon him, the care of all the churches. And apart from the shepherding of the flock, he had personal cares not a few.

One of the deepest sorrows of his life was the death of Mrs. Crowther, which occurred at Lagos on 19 October, 1880. In an earlier chapter of this book their happy courtship and marriage were duly recorded. It will be remembered how they were brought into touch as mere boy and girl; both had suffered slavery and tasted the sweets of liberation, and they had bloomed together in the genial atmosphere of the same Christian home. In the years of married life which followed they had been everything to each other. A missionary's wife has always to make many sacrifices, and during the time when her husband was on his long journeys as explorer and as Bishop, Mrs. Crowther felt her part was to spare him, and faithfully fulfil the not less sacred ministry of home and children. And so it happened that after celebrating their golden wedding day, she was taken ill during one of the Bishop's six months' visits in the *Henry Venn* to the Upper Niger. When he returned to Lagos it was to find his faithful helpmeet at the point of death. "It was," he said, "one of her earnest wishes, during her long illness, that she might die in my arms, and this was granted her, though she never knew it, for she lay unconscious till her death." The old survivor mourned her loss with secret tears, and went about his work again with his heart in heaven.

A few years later another blow came to the Bishop, when his venerable mother passed away at Lagos. She was a great age, reaching nearly a century, and had shared the shelter of her son's roof in these later years. The Bishop was absent when her call came, but one who stood by her deathbed afterwards assured him that she died full of joy to go to the Saviour. In a letter which the Bishop wrote while on board the s.s. *Qualaba*, on 6 February, 1884, he makes the following touching references to this sad event:

During my absence up the Niger my aged mother has been

called to her rest at the advanced age of ninety-seven years. We have much cause to be thankful that she was spared to us so long in the midst of so many adverse changes in her course of life and family circumstances, to be at last brought to know the Saviour in whom she placed her trust as her Good Shepherd to the end of her life.

When after twenty-five years of separation through the violence of slave war, and we were brought together again through God's good providence at Abeokuta in 1846, and I told her that she must not expect that I should be stationary at home with her as other members of the family would do, because I was a travelling public servant, her reply was: "You are no longer my son, but the servant of God, whose work you must attend unto without any anxiety for me; it is enough that I am permitted to see you once more in this world."

To this resolution she kept to the last.

When she was on her dying bed at Lagos in October last, 1883, she told Mrs. Macaulay, her granddaughter, who was attending her, as follows:

"Iya [mother] warned me not to write and tell you of her state then, for fear of perplexing your mind; she said to me: 'Will you not tell him what took place afterwards? Are you afraid?' I replied: 'I am not afraid.' Then she said to me: 'You are as good as your father's being at home; keep near to me, you have a great work to do.'" This was the last account I received of her about me, when not many days after she entered into her everlasting rest. I state this that you may know what value she placed on my missionary work among our heathen countrymen.

In recording these bereavements it would be the Bishop's wish that a word might be added about the loss he sustained by the death of his old friend and fellow-traveller, the Rev. J. F. Schön, in 1889. To him he owed his first recommendation to missionary work. He had been as a father to the young African when his friends were few. Apart from his association with the Bishop, Frederick Schön was a missionary of a very high order, with great attainments and wholehearted consecration to his work. His translations of the Scriptures would alone perpetuate his name, and those who knew him well will concur in Dr. Cust's estimate of his labours when he says, "The new Christians will know nothing of this good and holy man who paved the way for their salvation; but his name will be recorded in the Book of Life as the servant who only closed his labours for his Master when he ceased to breathe." When Frederick Schön passed, the Church Missionary Society placed on record that "he was called away in the very midst of his labours, having been occupied within a few days of his death in the correction of proof sheets of his own translation in Hausa, of the Book of Common Prayer."

Besides these personal losses there lay upon the Bishop's heart the shadow of increasing care and anxiety about the state of his diocese. As the demoralization of native character on the Niger at this time became a topic of sufficient importance to demand an inquiry, it is only just to draw attention again to the powerful agencies which were at work, and may be in some degree responsible for this declension. In a previous chapter attention has been drawn to the frightful desolation caused by the introduction into West Africa of strong drink. Drunkenness was one of the counts of the indictment brought against these native Christians, a sin not to be palliated either in Lokoja or London, but it is not surprising that amongst these weaker brethren, fresh from heathenism, facing for the first time the white man's conquering enemy, some should stumble. Then on the score of immorality, have the natives been altogether to blame? There are Europeans, doubtless of unimpeachable character, who in the walks of commerce, civil and military life, are a credit to the Christian country from which they have come. But others do not set a good example, and the character and fair name of Christianity is blasted by the inconsistency of men, who, free from the controlling influence of public opinion, make the natives feel, not only in West Africa either, that the white man in some respects is quite as much a heathen as themselves. Any missionary will confirm this, although it is not a difficulty which takes the prominence it deserves, in justice to the native races.

Another injurious element affecting the Niger Mission, although not an evil in any way comparable to those already referred to, was the inordinate love of trading, which became indeed a passion with the native coming fresh in touch with the outside market of the world. In this respect the African is no better or worse than any other human being, given the same environment. The Bishop has shown us in his frank manner how cunningly the native can battle in competition for commodities, not in themselves harmful, and how easily he gets into the current of smart bargaining. Possibly practice with European adepts in the art of good business has sharpened his wits a little, and he has learnt his lesson only too well. With wise foresight the Church Missionary Society bound over all their agents and preachers not to engage in trading of any sort, a very necessary stipulation which required something more than moral courage to respect and obey in the face of lucrative chances of doing this *sub rosa*. And in this direction, as far as his knowledge and control extended, the Bishop kept his clergy well within the four corners of their bond. Any infraction of this rule would clearly be detrimental to the true interests of the work, and also provoke jealousy among the trading community, as creating an unfair competition in the sphere of business. These, then, were some of the perils which beset the mission, and in varying degrees of complicity led to strong measures of discipline in some cases.

The stormy weather which was in store for the devoted Niger mission began to manifest itself by disquieting rumours which reached the ears of the committee in Salisbury Square from travellers and traders who had visited those regions. These became so serious that it was impossible to disregard them, and it was therefore arranged that a committee, composed of the Bishop, three European missionaries, the two native Archdeacons, and others, should meet at Lagos to discuss the situation. Their report, written by the Rev. J. B. Wood, a missionary of experience and judgment, showed an unfavourable state of affairs, and soon after its receipt in London it was naturally referred back to the Bishop for his consideration and comments. It was quite an unforeseen and pathetic coincidence that it reached Lagos at the time of Mrs. Crowther's death in October, 1880.

When in the following year the lay secretary of the Society and the Rev. J. Bradford Whiting were sent out to Madeira to meet the Bishop and others there, the various allegations against the native agents were carefully discussed. It was then resolved that it would be a great advantage to the work on the Niger if an English clergyman could come out to assist the Bishop as secretary to the mission, and the Rev. T. Phillips, who had received ordination at his hands, entered upon this arduous duty; but in nine months he returned home again, and upon his recommendation several of the native agents on the Niger were dismissed. It is not difficult to realize how all these changes and acts of necessary discipline upset the mind of the Bishop, especially feeling that so much inconsistency on the part of the native agents reflected upon the supervision which he, as Bishop, had striven so hard to maintain. He had done his best, but he was conscious that it was a physical impossibility for him, apart altogether from the question of his advancing years, to visit the stations of the Upper Niger more frequently.

The trouble which was exercising the minds of the workers and supporters, both at home and on the Niger, was immensely aggravated at this juncture by the publication in English journals, copied from native sources, of a shocking scandal—nothing short of murder, under brutal circumstances, of a girl by two native agents of the Society at Onitsha. The central secretary, Mr. Sutton, wrote immediately a public disclaimer, explaining that the persons implicated were not then connected with the work, one having been dismissed by the Bishop three years before, and the other had since withdrawn. As a matter of fact, the offence, grave as it was, had been committed five years before, and its reappearance at this time was due to the firm action of the Rev. J. B. Wood, who having discovered the offence insisted, at any cost, upon the guilty parties being punished. A tempest of criticism and blame had, however, been evoked at home, and the opportunity well served some individuals to make an attack upon missions generally, and the Niger mission in particular. The secretary, however, put the case effectively in the following words, which deserve quotation, as they refer to the difficulties on the Niger, apart from the specific charge:

> A case like this, we need hardly say, is in reality no argument against missions. On the contrary, it is an additional proof, if proof were needed, of the necessity of missions and of working them vigorously and without stint. Christianity at home does not prevent crime, nor is Christianity in Africa likely to do so in the present dispensation. But individuals may be saved from falling, and if the means at the committee's disposal had enabled them to give more support to Bishop Crowther in his arduous undertaking, and in particular if the *Henry Venn* steamer, which has made frequent inspection of the stations so much easier, had been provided some years earlier, it may be that individual agents might have been rescued in time from the temptations with which the great enemy has so persistently beset them.

Much on the same lines was a strong article in the "African Times," published in England, but simply a trade journal, without any association with missionary societies. The concluding words of this journalistic defender of Christian missions are these :

> Finally, we would say to the Church Missionary Society : " Be not discouraged because human wisdom is fallible. You have in the ranks of your native teachers men who are working as zealously and as purely for their Lord and Master as any, even the most faithful, of the ministry in the favoured kingdom of Great Britain and Ireland. You have scattered seed in Western Africa which will, by the continual blessing of the great Head of the Church, produce a glorious harvest.

The value of such a testimony at a time of trial like this may be appreciated when it is remembered that on 12 April, 1883, the Duke of Somerset made the incident the occasion for a violent attack upon the Church Missionary Society in the House of Lords, which drew from Earl Cairns and Dr. Benson, the newly-elected Archbishop of Canterbury, a defence which will be memorable.

While these contrary winds of criticism and cross currents of difficulty were giving so much anxiety at home, it is not surprising that at the scene of operations on the banks of the Niger the trouble was equally distressing. The Bishop had been in England the year before, conferring with the committee and labouring hard to settle on a satisfactory basis the perplexing problems of his diocese. And now, back again at his work, with this fresh clamour in his ears, and a burdened heart, he hurried from station to station, cheering, admonishing, and blessing his little flock. Archdeacon Henry Johnson meanwhile was hard at work on the Upper Niger, sometimes at Lokoja preaching to a crowd of mixed nationalities, with four different interpreters at his side. His remarkable facility in mastering the various languages proved a great advantage to the mission.

It was felt that his hands would be much strengthened if a medical mission could be established at or near Lokoja, and a young qualified man, Dr. Percy Brown, came out from England and started a dispensary, doing good service in this direction. But the healing ministry of this young missionary of so much promise was destined to be short-lived. The African fever laid him low; around his prostrate form stood a crowd of natives, his own patients, watching with pity and wonderment the white man, who could heal others, so sick and overcome with weakness himself.

He was lifted on board the next vessel sailing for England, but died on his way home, and was committed to the watery deep until that great day when the sea shall give up its dead. The sweet simplicity of this young doctor's manner had endeared him to his sorrowing patients. One of them was a convert at Ghebe, and continued for years a consistent member of the church at Lokoja. Upon this man Dr. Percy Brown had performed a difficult but quite successful operation, and had personally nursed him afterwards, until he was able to resume his usual work. In token of his gratitude he used to come every morning to the doctor's door, bringing fresh water and firewood. On hearing of the death of his benefactor and friend this poor man was heart-broken. This pathetic failure of a brave attempt to start a needed branch of the mission was a misfortune to workers and natives alike.

The Bishop was much cheered when the Rev. James Hamilton consented, under these trying circumstances, to go out to the Niger and act in place of Mr. Phillips, who had been invalided home. The new secretary was an old and valued Sierra Leone missionary, who understood the nature of the native work, and had retired for a time, working as Association Secretary in England. He entered upon his duties with tact and delicacy of feeling, travelled with his old friend the Bishop from place to place, holding courts of inquiry, and, where necessary, dismissing any agents against whom the evidence was sufficient to warrant such acts of discipline. He seems to have grasped the difficulties, and found the Bishop always ready to concur in any suggestion for improvement and the better supervision of the work. For a time all things were working well; a new *Henry Venn* was built and sent out to take the place of the old vessel, which had ceased to be of any value, and an English builder had also brought out to the Niger some valuable practical experience in that line.

Archdeacon Henry Johnson being in England in 1885, the University of Cambridge conferred upon him the honorary degree of M.A., in recognition of his linguistic attainments. Before returning to his work on the Niger he confirmed a report he had sent on the state of things there, pointing out how very difficult it was to conduct its operations with any measure of success with such a weakened and diminished staff of workers. Still he said he was sanguine of the ultimate result.

"If the mission," said he, "was established by the will of God, if the work is His, as we have no doubt that it is, if it is His desire that it should continue to be carried on for the benefit of the tribes along the banks of the Niger, as we may conclude from what He is now achieving by His weakest instruments, then surely we are bound to believe that without doubt He will thrust forth labourers into this His own harvest field."

On the appointment of the Rev. James Hamilton to be Archdeacon of Lagos, in 1887, he was succeeded by the Rev. J. A. Robinson as new English secretary, who subsequently joined Mr. Graham Wilmot Brooke and others in a new departure, whereby an attempt was to be made to reach the Hausas. The scheme was an original one, as it involved the missionary wearing the flowing robe and turban of the Mohammedan, and both Brooke and Robinson wished it to be understood that they renounced all the privileges of their British nationality: "If they imprison us, the British Government is not to interfere; if they kill us, no reparation must be demanded."

Never, perhaps, did any missionary party go away under such enthusiastic and hopeful circumstances. At the crowded valedictory meeting in Exeter Hall on 20 January, 1890, the Bishop was present, and gave them his blessing. The courage and devotion of these missionaries, the noble and ambitious project to which they had committed themselves, and possibly the fact of the Niger having caused so much anxiety hitherto, all combined to raise the highest hopes of success. It must not, however, be thought that this was the first attempt to bring the Gospel to the Hausas, for the Bishop had for years past taken every opportunity of exploring their country, having undertaken, as we have seen, several journeys to Bida, and his desire had always been to push on as far as Kano, and establish an outpost of the mission there. His special interest in the Mohammedans marked the growth and progress of all his work on the Niger.

But this new venture was a definite enterprise, with the aim of reaching them on new lines and methods. The journals of these missionaries are full of interest, and the story of their experiences, especially among the Moslems, is a striking page of missionary history. At a public discussion held in the open air at Lokoja, where a mixed party of Mohammedans, comprising Hausa, Fulahi from Sokoto, Yorubas from Ilorin, and Hausa traders living on the spot, the missionary, clad in flowing white, and wearing the turban, sat to receive them in Oriental fashion, and as each native visitor arrived a respectful salutation was made to the Englishman, sinking down upon one knee with the words, "Greeting, scribe."

The adoption of native costume raised many questions among the Mohammedans and some suspicions. The Governor of Egga, upon whom the missionaries called, was by no means satisfied, and demanded to know what secret purpose was underlying this strange and unusual practice for a white man. The answer given explains the position taken up by these new missionaries :

> We came into the country (they replied) to make known the work of our Lord Jesus, the Messiah, whom God sent down from heaven for the sake of the whole world six hundred years before Mohammed began writing his Korân. We quickly found that a great misconception was quite universal. It was supposed that we preach the white man's religion for the benefit of heathen tribes, but that Islam was the proper religion for Hausas and Nupés. It is not so ; we ourselves are but disciples, and you must obey the message of God as well as we—it cannot be annulled. Therefore, after consultation, we have resolved to put off our own dress and our own customs, which are in no wise a part of our religion, and to adopt yours, in order that when you see us pass along the streets dressed as Hausa you may remember that it is you—*you* we summon to submit to our blessed Lord, who is coming again from heaven to reign over the whole earth.

The Governor listened, and politely said good-bye, but did not return the call of his visitors. Whether this black official continued to care for none of these things, except presents, history does not relate.

This mission, inaugurated amid so much enthusiasm, watched by home friends with such interest and hopefulness, was doomed to failure. After a manful struggle against attacks of fever, one by one the workers were invalided home, death entered the ranks, and, finally, both the leading spirits and pioneers of the expedition, Mr. Robinson and Mr. Graham Wilmot Brooke, died.

The division of the work into two distinct parts, the Upper Niger and Soudan and the Lower Niger, represented by the Delta, which had taken place, although nominally under the supervision of the Bishop, was not an unmixed advantage. Very drastic measures of reform adopted by the local committee at Lokoja involved the dismissal of several native agents, and the continual strain of these discussions as to the justice of this in some cases began to tell upon the strength, if not the patient endurance, of the old Bishop. It is needless and inexpedient after this lapse of time to awaken the echoes of that time of trial; it is enough to affirm, on the one hand, that the condition of the work fully justified prompt and efficient action to enforce discipline and remove the reproach which the inconsistency of some agents had brought upon the mission. At the same time, no blame was attached to the Bishop personally, for he had done his utmost to keep his under-shepherds and their flocks in order, and with great fairness and judgment he presided over these committees, whose function it was to deal with such matters. Nothing became the man so well as the dignity and Christian forbearance he displayed. But it must be added that his feelings were much wounded by what he felt was a lack of consideration and even interference with his proper province as Bishop of the diocese. He never objected to the introduction of European missionaries; indeed, he always felt that their co-operation and help were most valuable; but he was quite naturally jealous of that native ministry which had been created by his labours and prayers during a lifetime, and which he firmly believed to be a necessity and blessing to the work. As the first African Bishop he honoured and loved his native clergy. He was no fanatic on the subject of a native ministry, but he was patriotic to the core, and rejoiced to see his own country being evangelized by her own sons. It must also be borne in mind that the great ideal of a native Church with a native ministry, self-supporting, was first advocated by that venerable and honoured secretary of the Church Missionary Society, the Rev. Henry Venn, for whom the Bishop had the greatest respect and affection.

As regards the consistency of the members of these native churches, which had been so strongly, and in some cases justifiably criticized, it is only just to take into consideration that they had emerged from heathenism but a few years before, and had not had the advantage, as is the case with the converts in England, of a Christian parentage and a favourable environment. They could not fairly be measured by European standards, and their backslidings, regrettable as they were, might be largely due to the pressure of peculiar temptations and of surroundings of which they recently formed a part, and might easily entangle them again. The native Christians, however, knew how to suffer for the faith, and endured with patience and fidelity trials which would be impossible for the white man to bear. As we have seen, the slaves who had trusted in Christ were the prey of their Mohammedan masters, and made to suffer indignities and penalties which would not have been their portion if they had not chosen the Gospel brought by the missionary. Some had suffered the pains of slavery, but their liberty had been assured under the British flag. Now, however, as the willing slaves of Jesus Christ, they, like St. Paul, were ready to endure all things. When a leading chief passed through their towns and villages these poor people were the specially selected victims of their hate and rapacity.

An instance of this occurred at Lokoja. One of the relatives of a passing chief exercised their privilege of robbing these hapless natives, and if they dared to resist they were made to suffer for their remonstrance. One of the Christian converts having ventured to draw attention to the simple fact that his sheep was stolen, was tied up, together with his wife, and exposed to the heat of the burning sun, while three thieves went to his house and barn and carried away everything they could lay their hands on. Even then the suffering was not over, for the chief fined the poor man fifty bags of cowries, and slavery for three of his household. Utterly ruined and half-dead, he had to escape into the bush, and after hiding for three days, crossed over to Ghebe, and waited patiently till this tyranny was overpast. Disappointed of their victim, these ruffians fell upon the house of his neighbour, and carried off some of its inmates to be sold as slaves. This incident will give some idea of the lawlessness of a town which had a certain importance as a trading station, and what the Christian converts had to bear. In what spirit did these converts regard their enemies? One instance

Photo, Turner]

ARCHDEACON DANDESON C. CROWTHER

To face page 364

will suffice. The persecutions at Bonny have been already depicted. If ever a people exercised the "charity which suffereth long and is kind," these poor black, ill-treated Christians did; gathered in a prayer meeting when the fiery furnace of their afflictions and woes was at its hottest, one of them is heard praying: "We beseech Thee not to rain down fire and brimstone on these stiff-necked people, as in the case of Sodom and Gomorrah, but we pray Thee to rain down *Thy love* on them, as in the case of Saul, so that the persecutors may be arrested on their way to ask, 'Lord, what wilt Thou have me to do?'"

Is it any wonder that for such as these, his children in the faith, the old Bishop had most tender affection? Every missionary has a peculiar love for his converts, and looks at them with eyes altogether unlike, and impossible to, even the best friend of the heathen at home. They have seen the horror of great darkness which preceded their conversion, against many difficulties and disappointments faith and prayer have struggled, and now that the Divine light shines on these black faces, there is joy as of a battle won. Still more so was this the case with the Bishop, for he had the additional interest of being one of themselves, raised up to be a leader and commander of his people.

For this reason the backsliding of his flock was all the more keenly felt; love always suffers most. But there was no weakness in the Bishop. He was not afraid to exercise discipline, and was vigilant to detect its necessity, as far as human discernment could allow:

> Surely (says he) I think these facts must show that I did not shut mine eyes to the faults of the agents of the Niger Mission during a period of now over twenty-five years.

Just one letter shall be quoted to show his spirit in dealing with delinquents. He has discovered one of the tutors of his Institution guilty of a breach of the seventh Commandment, though otherwise a capable and apparently respectable man. He is writing about it from Lokoja, 23 October, 1884:

> This is another proof that we are apt to be misled by the outward appearance or intellectual qualifications of men; whereas the Lord looks into the heart which has imbibed the disposition of our Lord and Saviour Jesus Christ, learning daily to be meek and lowly, to be pure and holy, according to the dictates of the Holy Spirit, which He has promised to give us as an indwelling Teacher.

And again, after discussing the inconsistency of the native converts, and lamenting the backsliding which has given such occasion for their suspension and exclusion from membership, he shows that due care has been taken in accepting such. He is writing from Bonny on 16 May, 1890:

> All which tends to show that the life of a Christian in this world is a life of constant warfare, of watchfulness, lest Satan take an advantage over us; it is a life of earnest prayer to the strong man for support in time of trial and temptation, that he may not be ignorant of his devices though he may appear as an angel of light.
>
> We never feel satisfied with the external sign of Christian profession. When the converts brought to us their idols and other objects of worship in the service of Satan, until we have instructed them, with the whole armour of God, to stand in

the evil day, and pray that He may not leave them to themselves to be drawn back to the bondage of Satan from which He has already set them free, notwithstanding what allurements may be offered to draw them back or whatever may be the threat to their mortal bodies, even to death ; that they may stand steadfast by faith that Christ is with them.

In some cases the Bishop asks that judgment may be withheld before utterly condemning some of these natives, who as slaves perhaps in the midst of heathen customs cannot so entirely avoid being, at any rate, spectators of these rites. He is writing from Onitsha on 12 August, 1885 :

> We firmly demand and insist upon entire separation of all Christian converts from having a hand or voice in any such acts of violence, injustice, or brutality in the future. But when we make such a stand against the future we must not be overbearing in punishing what has been done against the will of those who were involved in such acts, who would have willingly got out of it if they could find a way to do so, they being under the influence of the heathen authorities, whom they could not contradict. In cases of these our severe punishment to maintain Christian discipline must be moderated with sympathy and guided by due allowance for the measure of knowledge and experienced Christian principle which the converts possessed to guide and govern them under such perplexing circumstances, they having scarcely emerged out of these rooted barbarous practices of their forefathers.

Through all these trials and resettlements of the mission the Bishop never wavered in his confidence in the value of native agency. His ideal never forsook him, and to his mind the lesson to be learned from these painful experiences was that not only the selection, but the training of the agents should be more carefully considered and safeguarded. He pointed out that in breaking up the hard ground work of the Niger Mission he was very glad in the years gone by to have the co-operation of agents whose education was slight, but being of ripe Christian experience, and having the spirit and perseverance of pioneers, they well answered the needs of that time. They were superior to the chiefs by having a knowledge of the Christian religion, and able to hold their own in argument. As an instance of this, old King Ockiya once asked for a teacher, adding, "I do not want a boy, but a man," meaning not age, but the capacity to discuss and take a superior stand among the chiefs and headmen. These agents were not from an intellectual standpoint ideal teachers, but they did their duty. The Bishop observes:

> Though I do not advocate their ordination now, as I was compelled to do some years past, yet I would most seriously advise the committee not to overlook the usefulness of such Christian men. . . . It is now and then the will of the Great Shepherd to employ the services of such men to call hundreds of wandering sheep into the fold.

But in writing from the mission station at Bonny on 11 July, 1884, he gives, with his usual humility, a word of advice upon a subject upon which he was perhaps the best qualified to render any counsel. He is so anxious that the character of the native agents should be maintained, that they should be well equipped, all-round, capable men of God:

> In adverting to the agents to be employed in the mission hereafter, I hope I shall not be considered as a persistent conservative in my ideas on this subject, in spite of any improved plan, which may have been adapted to be followed hereafter. I am as liberal, open, and favourable to improved and well-qualified agents as any well-wisher of the mission

can be—namely, that none but the *best* and *well qualified* of the sons of the African churches—*whose hearts are fired with ardent zeal, whose bowels yearned with love and longing desire* for the salvation of their countrymen—should be employed as mission agents. That they should be decided spiritual men, because *spiritual men* can only teach spiritual things. That interpreters are only crutches, especially if they are not spiritual men, and should be got rid of as soon as possible.

Standing in the midst of his flock, yearning over the fearful ones, weeping over the wandering, his heart still full of gratitude for what God had done for and through him in the past, the old grey-headed shepherd of souls is wistfully looking towards a future in which he can no longer take a part. These troubles have cut him deeply, but his heart bleeds in secret, and only here and there in his letters, and then more between the lines than along the written words, do we see something of what he feels. Here is the fragment of a letter written to the secretary in London on 30 January, 1884:

I know my place as negro, but I have ever paid my respects to Europeans, whether old or young, missionaries or those in secular occupations, as the race of our benefactors, to whom we owe our bodily freedom and the spiritual privileges of the glorious liberty of the Christian religion. . . . I have never left undone anything which I thought might conduce to the health and welfare of a white man in this country of Africa. . . . My intention is to show clearly the present state of things and to urge the Parent Committee to supply the Niger Mission with as many European missionaries as they can, to be the chief workers under the superintendence of the European secretary. . . . The Europeans are better managers, their actions and report will be better confided in both out here and in England. We shall be content to work under their direction as in former years. This impediment will not be removed from the way of the extension of the mission.

His one absorbing thought was his work; while under Divine guidance he could be of any service he was ready and willing to go on; but if any better way or wiser worker could be found, the Bishop was quite willing to stand aside. All who knew him personally will confirm this. But it is not surprising that at times the old man grew sad and depressed; worry began to wear even where hard work had told little as yet. Just a week after sending the foregoing letter he writes another, the very penmanship here and there vibrant with the throbbing of his heart:

After long prayerful and mature consideration, I have thought it advisable to write out the impression which the present state of the Niger Mission has made upon my mind. If others are delicate to tell me of my incompetency in the superintendence of the Niger Mission, it is my duty to relieve their minds of that delicacy. I am ready to yield place to others to act as leading managers of the Niger Mission. I am willing, as long as my health lasts, to labour as a pioneer in opening fresh grounds, while the already established stations can be worked by superior intellects and better managers.

The work is a public one and of great importance, and should by no means be allowed to suffer for want of proper management, strictness of discipline, and firmness of principles.

It is needless to say that the Society, true to its great traditions, would not consent to the step suggested by the Bishop. Amid all the clamour and criticism of their own administration, with its conflicting reports, resignations, personalities, and misunderstandings, the committee did their utmost to hold blameless that venerable figure. To his labours, life, and unique personality the work on the Niger had owed its very existence. His stainless name was associated with every step of its advancement, and when the storm of trial came, and it seemed as if shipwreck was inevitable, his courage and loyalty were not counted on in vain. Never possibly had any society such a sorrow to undergo ; it was a decade of care and burden under the strain of which the health of many responsible for affairs was impaired, and some precious lives never survived. It was one of those experiences which teach the human heart its infinite need, and that the wisest judgments sometimes are at fault. When discipline had purged the native churches, dismissed the agents who were adjudged unsatisfactory, and reorganized the entire work under European direction, one of the firstfruits was the expressed desire of the native churches of the Delta to form themselves into a separate and self-supporting mission. The idea was not a new one. So far back as 1881 the Bishop drew attention to a plan whereby the chiefs (and particularly when in 1864, after King Pepple's death) might subscribe and share at any rate a part of the expense of establishing a Christian mission in the Delta. The subject did not at the time receive much attention, but the native churches were constantly encouraged to do their utmost for the support of the work. But under the circumstances which had transpired it was not surprising that the converts felt the time had arrived when they should make an effort to put in practice that hope expressed by the late Henry Venn, "that in course of time the churches in the Niger Mission shall become self-supporting, as those in the Colonies are." After taking the sense of the members of the churches, a formal application was placed in the hands of the Bishop, who sent it to Salisbury Square, with his personal approval and support. His closing words were:

> When the extensive openings in the oil rivers in God's good providence are taken into consideration, and the unhealthiness of the muddy Delta region as a natural impediment to European health and life is weighed, I feel convinced that the suggestion of the churches of the native pastorates of Lagos and Sierra Leone is providential that the Delta district should be made a native pastorate to be worked entirely through native agency, towards the expenses of which they resolved to contribute a supplement.

And now at last the Bishop broke down. He had always been so uncomplaining, and his energy never failed him, for he had a constitution which carried him through toils and hardships to which others younger, to right and left of him, succumbed. Nobody expected him to fall; even those who were with him, and knew him best, marvelled that he kept up so bravely, in spite of unremitting toil and anxiety. But it came at last. In a letter written to Salisbury Square in August, 1891, came tidings of sudden indisposition, which made his many English friends greatly grieved. Still, in his quiet, cheerful way he made little of it, said the trouble was only the result of a cold after enduring the excessive rains of two months' wet season, but it was really much more serious. In a letter addressed to General Hutchinson, dated 16 October, 1891, and thanking him for some words of sympathy, he gives some details :

I was laid aside by a sudden attack of paralysis, as I got up from my desk, which paralyzed my right hand and leg and affected my speech for many days, so that I could not speak audibly. The doctor thought a change of place would improve me, and therefore ordered me to this place, for which I left Bonny on the 25th September and got here on the 28th. I am thankful to say that I am improving, hoping to be all right again in a few weeks. I sincerely thank the many kind friends who sympathize with me in my affliction, from which I never suffered before. Wishing soon to recover my health, to spend the remainder of my days in the service of our Divine Master, I remain,

Sincerely yours,

SAMUEL A. CROWTHER.

To his dear friend, Rev. J. Bradford Whiting, he writes to the same effect, and a fortnight afterwards he is more hopeful in his letter to the secretary, and says :

I am glad to say it has done me good, and if it continues so I shall soon be fit to resume work.

A touching reference is made by way of apology for his shaky handwriting ; the clear, precise regularity of his pen is certainly missed. When the Rev. H. Dobinson called to see him one day he found the old Bishop slowly recovering, but not at all himself. For hours he would sit, deep in thought, gazing across the sea.

Every life has its stormy weather, and every bit of work for God and humanity has its day of cold grey sky. These are the times when clouds of misgiving, much bigger than a man's hand, creep up from the horizon to mock us, and every gust that blows wafts a wailing requiem to our ears. The song of the birds ceases, the face of nature seems strangely full of pity, our need may be the plea of many prayers, but we feel somehow that the burden on our heart is being borne by ourselves alone—and God. It may be that our confidence in man, like thin ice, is breaking at every step, for where help was expected trouble has come; we have been misjudged, perhaps we too in part have also misunderstood. Then like the disciples on the Emmaus road, with our plaintive "But we trusted," we look into the face of Divine compassion, and ere long, when our eyes are no longer holden, the sunshine of His presence turns our sorrow into wondering joy.

Possibly such an experience dwelt in the Bishop's heart as he watched the dawn and sunset on that Lagos shore. He seems to have kept it very much to himself. He was half in heaven. His wife was there, and his mother and a multitude of beloved friends. He told his own heart that his work was done, and he doubtless felt, as all the aged do, the intimations of the end. In the watchful hours of the lonely nights he heard the music of a far-off land, as would a mariner in sight of home. And when the day came back, and he went forth in the morning slowly towards the sea, the crisp hair on his brow looked a little greyer, and the lines were deepening in his face; those bright, pathetic eyes shone with a pleasing sadness, like sunshine after rain.

When Archdeacon Hamilton landed at Lagos on one of the last days of December, he spent an hour with the Bishop, and afterwards took him on his arm to a dismissal meeting of seven schoolmasters going out from the training institution. At the close the old man stood up and gave his blessing, tenderly, fatherly, with slow and faltering speech, his last act of public service. So much had he brightened up with the change of air and scene that he spent a good part of the next day in diocesan business with his visitors, at which time, with evident effort, he rallied his forces of memory and mind to the important matters under discussion. He even spoke of leaving for Bonny the first week of January, and sent a letter to Major Macdonald, the Consul from the Oil Rivers, now Sir Claude Macdonald, of Japan, who happened to be at Lagos, asking if he could give him a passage in his steamer. On Christmas morning he walked to Christ Church, and this was his last attendance at the house of God. A week passed, and the last day of the old year was reached. It was his custom to write out in draft form any correspondence of importance, and in an old Letts's Diary there is a feebly written letter which he had attempted to compose in acknowledgment of a kindly expressed letter from Salisbury Square. This letter was never sent, and has a very pathetic interest as being scrawled by a dying hand. It was possibly the very last writing he penned before he passed away. There is a pencil note to the effect that the doctor in attendance on the Bishop forbade him to write any more :

My dear Sir,—You will see by my handwriting that I had been sick since these four weeks, sick by—on my right hand and foot and affecting my speech, so the doctor forbid my doing anything, but I am getting better.

But, sir, your two accompanying documents brought to my memory my visit to the Archbishop of Canterbury about two archdeacons. It is possible I was accompanied by a secretary, by whom (explained) the matter to the Archbishop, to which he gave his assent, or he assented to the secretary. I thought it was right, I being a novice and not knowing the difference. I apologize for my ignorance. Your memorandum of my character before (and after) my call to the ministry in 1843, and after my call to the episcopacy in 1864, to this day was in answer to my prayer that the God who called me first from among my people to the important post in His service, may give me grace to set a good example for others to follow.

Since my appointment to the superintendent of the Niger Mission in 1857 to the present I never refuse any suggestion made by the committee for the improvement of the Niger Mission. Though I am single-handed, I like to be improved by the ideas of others.

His daughter, Mrs. Macaulay, at whose house he spent the last days, has kindly supplied a recital, in simple and touching words, of what took place on this final and never-to-be-forgotten day of his life:

He was up as usual on the morning of the 31st, dressed, and went through the morning devotions as he did every day; then had his tea after seven o'clock. About eight o'clock he sent to call me to read a letter to him. I took the letter and read it, and said: "Father, I have read this letter to you several times." He said: "I have read it too." (This was the last letter he got from the Secretary of the C.M.S., Salisbury Square.)

I then said: "If you want any more letters read to you, father, call for Charles [a grandson of his]; he will read them to you. I am going to be busy with your breakfast." He smiled, and I left him sitting at the table, with his Prayer Book and hymn-book and some papers.

About nine o'clock or so an old Christian woman, Emma Taiwo, called to see the Bishop. I told her she could go and have a chat with him; he is not busy, and will be leaving in a day or two for Bonny. She went into the parlour and returned in haste, and told me his head was not properly on the sofa. I ran in just in time to take hold of him, to save him from dropping from the sofa, and I called: "Father! father!"

He answered me. I said: "What is the matter?" He made no reply, but when I asked if he was cold he nodded, and said: "Yes." I ran for some brandy and water, which he drank, and sent for Dr. I. Baudle, as Dr. O. Johnson was away from home.

After the attack he did not speak much, but answered when spoken to.

At two o'clock in the afternoon the doctor said he should go into his bedroom, as the wind was blowing cold. He walked to the room supported. I had not the least thought there was anything serious, although I kept all the time with him. The doctor was in and out constantly; his last visit was at seven o'clock. He took the medicine patiently, sitting. I said something about his coughing; he said, "No pain."

At midnight when I came in to give him his medicine he sat up and said he hoped it was the last dose. He lay down, and as I covered him I said, "Good night, father," and he said, "Good night." Half an hour later I heard movements in his room and saw father just lying down, and I jumped on the bed, for I saw he was dying. "Father! father!" I cried. He heaved a sigh, and all was over. He passed away at a quarter to one in the morning.

So the end had come at last! To that little room God's messenger had brought the mandate for His beloved to come Home.

"The Master calls for thee," and at that word
  The servant rose and passed the Gate of Life,
Whose janitor is Death, and, listening, heard
  The song triumphant o'er the end of strife.

Into the sunlight, after darkness drear,
  Out of long travail, into perfect rest,
This side, the wreath of cypress and the tear,
  Beyond, the Rose of Sharon and the blest.

No breath of change can ruffle thy sweet calm,
  Nor cloud of care break in upon thy peace.
Thine the white raiment and the victor's palm,
  The joys unspeakable that never cease.

We, still in conflict, for a little space,
Would strive and bear and do, with faith like thine,
If haply His poor wandering sheep may trace
The path of mercy to the Love Divine.

He was buried next day, 1 January, 1892, the funeral service being held at Christ Church, and a solemn address was given by the Rev. James (now Bishop) Johnson to a large congregation, including the Governor and most of the chief European officials. Ten clergymen, European and native, including his two nephews, preceded the coffin, strewn with ferns and frangipani, to the grave, the Rev. E. Pearse taking the first part of the service, and Archdeacon Hamilton the committal. He was laid by the side of his wife and mother, and the mourners sang together, "Hush, blessed are the dead."

Something, however, more enduring than these sweet but fading flowers was destined to mark the resting-place of the late Bishop. His many friends in England and West Africa gladly subscribed, and as a result a beautiful monument in white marble was erected, and this was unveiled with much ceremony on 4 August, 1898. A large crowd of people of all classes gathered in the cemetery. On every hand there were signs of the deepest respect for the one whose memory they came to honour. Several hymns were sung, and prayer offered by the clergy. His Excellency the Governor then spoke of the virtues of the Bishop, and unveiled the monument. An address was afterwards delivered in Yoruba by the Rev. James (now Bishop) Johnson, and after the choir had sung the recessional hymn following the Benediction,

CHRIST CHURCH, LAGOS

To face page 378

a large number of the spectators lingered behind to read the inscription, which is as follows:

SACRED TO THE MEMORY OF

The Right Rev. Samuel Ajayi Crowther, D.D.,

A NATIVE OF OSÔGÚN, IN THE YORUBA COUNTRY;
A RECAPTURED AND LIBERATED SLAVE;
THE FIRST STUDENT IN THE CHURCH MISSIONARY SOCIETY'S COLLEGE,
AT FOURAH BAY, SIERRA LEONE;
ORDAINED IN ENGLAND BY THE BISHOP OF LONDON, JUNE 11TH, 1843;
THE FIRST NATIVE CLERGYMAN OF THE CHURCH OF ENGLAND IN WEST AFRICA,
CONSECRATED BISHOP JUNE 29TH, 1864.
A FAITHFUL, EARNEST AND DEVOTED MISSIONARY IN CONNECTION WITH
THE CHURCH MISSIONARY SOCIETY FOR 62 YEARS,
AT SIERRA LEONE, IN THE TIMINI AND YORUBA COUNTRIES,
AND IN THE NIGER TERRITORY;
HE ACCOMPANIED THE FIRST ROYAL NIGER EXPEDITION IN 1841;
WAS A JOINT FOUNDER WITH OTHERS OF THE YORUBA MISSION IN 1845,
AND FOUNDER OF THE NIGER MISSION IN 1857;
AND OF THE SELF-SUPPORTING NIGER DELTA PASTORATE IN 1891;
HE FELL ASLEEP IN JESUS AT LAGOS, ON THE 31ST DECEMBER, 1891,
AGED ABOUT 89 YEARS.

"*Well done, thou good and faithful servant. . . . . Enter thou into the joy of thy Lord.*"—Matt. xxv. 21.

"REDEEMED BY HIS BLOOD."

It is scarcely necessary to sum up at any length the striking characteristics of Bishop Crowther in these closing words. Through the foregoing pages it has been the sincere aim of the biographer to allow this wonderful personality to reveal itself, not only that those who knew him should, as from a phonograph, hear his voice again, but that a wider sphere of thousands to whom he has been but an honoured name should realize the manner of man he was, and learn to respect and love him too. And from time to time an endeavour has been made to point out traits of his character which have been in his own words or actions exemplified. And these marks of a noble mind and a faithful and devout spirit will be confirmed by all who had the privilege of knowing him. Wherever he has visited and preached in England he has left behind memories which any man might envy, and it is needless to say that in his own land and among his own people thousands rise up and call him blessed as the father of his country.

It only remains to glean some particulars of his home life, the man as he was at his fireside, or rather to say, in such a climate, in his family circle, that sacred idyll which we carry in our hearts till it ceases to beat, the memory of which is precious beyond price to him who hath, and he who hath it not is poor indeed. By special request, therefore, the Bishop's son, the Ven. Archdeacon Dandeson C. Crowther, has kindly supplied some personal details of his honoured father which will be scanned with deepest interest. No member of the family is more qualified to render this great service to his father's memory; as we have seen, he was his secretary and companion from his boyhood, shared his vicissitudes and sufferings, drank deep of his spirit while trained in his company for future service, and upon whom his mantle rests, and the noble heritage of his work and name. It is the simplest meed of praise to say of a very modest man that he is a worthy successor of a father so honoured and beloved.

He tells us that in his home life his father was conspicuously a consistent Christian. He was not a great man abroad and insignificant at home. Those who were visitors to the family, and knew the Bishop in his private life, admired the reality and practical value of his piety in this inner sphere. A European writer who had no particular sympathy with African superintendence said: "The late Bishop Crowther was as remarkable and worthy a man as it would be possible to find anywhere, combined with the most transparent sincerity and earnestness."

We are told at home he was very strict in discipline and in the observance of religious truths, which may be said to be bordering on a puritanic method. No one in the household missed services on Sundays, class, prayer meetings, or any religious exercise within reach on weekdays without giving an explanation for their absence. One of his sons disobeyed his schoolmaster one day, and accordingly received punishment. Relying on sympathy at home, the son left the school and came in with tears and bitter lamentations, while the schoolmaster stood trembling, and awaiting the consequences from the father, who was the minister of the station. Finding out that the son had been disobedient, the father (who was the future Bishop) took him back himself to school, and after further inquiry into the case, he ordered the schoolmaster to give him a dozen strokes with the birch before all the other pupils; and after a lecture that his schoolmaster is to be obeyed in all things lawful and right, he left the school. After this example the schoolmaster had an easy time with his pupils, and the son ever after learnt the grace of obedience.

And yet with all this good old-fashioned discipline he was a bright and entertaining father among his children. In the evenings they used to gather round his knees to hear stories of his early days, of the life he lived as a boy at Oshôgún, stories of monkeys and rats, and of adventures when he accompanied his father to the towns. He sketched pictures of the large farm they had then, and how he used to be up early in the morning, go to the farm with his hoe, and working hard would throw up his allotted heaps of earth to plant with the yams, and then sit under a tree enjoying the fun, and laughing at the slothful companions still toiling hard under the heat of the sun. Then he taught his children many Yoruba proverbs, and those amusing fables with which their language abounds. But nothing delighted them more than to hear the story of how he put on his first shoes, which he illustrated with actions which made them clap their hands and shout with glee. Here are the very words of the story; it was of the time when he was a pupil at college:

There were four of us who were promoted to the position of monitors; one called Attara was the cleverest among us. This was at Fourah Bay College, under Mr. Haensel, a kind German tutor at that time, between 1834 and 1840. To give effect to our position we were allowed to wear shoes. Four strong, stout shoes with very thick soles were procured and given to us from the soldiers' barracks; they were called "Blucher shoes." On a Saturday afternoon we were called, presented with a pair each, and told to put them on every Sunday to church at St. George's Cathedral, a distance of about three miles. Never having had shoes on before, we began practising in our dormitory that evening; none of us could move a step after lacing up on our feet these unwieldy articles, and consequently we were objects of laughter by our pupils. An idea struck me at once, which I put into execution. Crawling to a corner of the room, I first knelt down, then holding on to the wall for support I stood up, and, still being supported by the wall, I stepped round the room many times, the others following my example, till we were able to leave the wall, stand alone, or move about without support. You can well imagine what a burden this was to us, and after losing sight of the college we sat on the grass, took off the shoes, walked barefoot, and only put them on at the porch of the church; we did the same on returning to college. After some months' practice we were able to move better in them, but complained how they hurt our feet so and would rather be without them. But after some months we invested in the purchase of boots ourselves, and were careful to buy those that made noise and creaked as we stepped with them, to our great delight and the admiration of our pupils.

If ever a man had the grace of humility, not a popular virtue, it was the Bishop. His son has supplied some instances of a purely personal character, which throw a fresh light upon a distinguished incident of his life, a veritable peep behind the scenes. The much-revered Rev. Henry Venn, the honorary secretary of the Church Missionary Society in 1864, found a hard task in persuading Crowther, for whom he had such a personal regard, to accept the office of Bishop. Without knowing why he was sent for the latter left for England only a week after his return from the Niger, and so urgent was the instruction that he should attend the General Committee on a certain day that he had no time to get a new suit of clothes made, and consequently entered the committee-room in his Niger travelling dress—a heavy old shabby pilot coat with a row of large shining brass buttons in front, which on his appearance set the whole of the members into a roar of laughter. He could not make out what was the cause of the fun, and it took him some time before he knew that something was amiss in his appearance, and apologized for it. At this committee meeting, after asking him about the welfare of the work on the Niger, he was told that he had been sent for on a very important matter, which the honorary secretary would communicate to him in his office after the close of the meeting. At this private interview he was told that it was the desire of the committee to recommend him for the Bishopric. He rose and said, "I am not worthy," and after a pause continued, "See the European missionaries, as Rev. H. Townsend and others, who have been labouring for the cause of Africa these so many years. Why should they be left, and I am asked to take up such an office? No, sir, I am their servant in the field; I cannot accept it." The Rev. Henry Venn quietly replied, "True, but we saw them all; we know and appreciate their work, before asking you to take this office." Still standing in deep humility, Crowther refused to comply with the request, and Mr. Venn knelt down and prayed with him. Then he bade him good-bye, told him to go to New Brompton and spend a quiet time with his old friend, the Rev. J. F. Schón. Here he stayed two days, and Mr. Schón tried to show him by every argument in his power the issue of usefulness to the Gospel and the Negro race, if he would make up his mind to yield to Mr.

Venn's wishes. Still unshaken, however, he returned to Salisbury Square, and entering Mr. Venn's room, the latter rose, made him sit down, put his hands on his shoulders and said, " I hope you have brought me good news to-day." Seeing no signs of good tidings, he took hold of both his hands in his, and looking straight into his eyes, he said solemnly: "Samuel Adjai, my son, will you deny me my last wish asked of you before I die?" This broke Crowther down altogether, and with tears in his eyes he answered, "It is the Lord; let Him do what seemeth Him good." They both knelt down, and prayed together, Mr. Venn sobbing with gratitude. This was the way he was led to become a Bishop, and he never related this story to his son without the deepest emotion.

Afterwards I was his secretary for a long time, and when written to as "My Lord" my father used to tell me, in reply, to put a postscript thus: "Please address me Right Reverend Bishop, and never as My Lord." If there was only one seat and a schoolmaster came in, he would rise and offer him his chair. Once I asked my father why he did so, and his reply was: "People, seeing me standing, will very soon go and get me another seat, but will not be so quick, if ever they did think of getting one for a schoolmaster." It may be added that for Europeans of all conditions and under any circumstances his humility and reverence were marked, as he often said, in explanation of this: "I owe so much to their fathers."

What shall be said of the unwearied patience of the Bishop? Some might think he bore things, suffering long, almost to a fault. For the exercise of this grace he had no lack of opportunity, and it dignified and ennobled him. This is not one of those heroic virtues which enlist the commendation of men, but it has more of the Divine likeness than we perhaps imagine. Patience makes no noise and is not always wiping its sword with grim satisfaction; it is satisfied to be infinitely tender, quietly waiting, its face flushed with the mercy of God. From this good Bishop's life we take one or two personal memories of this. The Rev. J. C. Taylor makes a note in his journal, under date 23 December, 1861, of this incident:

At the first opening of the Sunday-school at Akassa, Mr. Crowther took the first class at the head of the table, and with his venerable silver-bound spectacles on, a pointer in his hands, pointing to the alphabet characters, calling out loudly, "A, B, C, D," while the Akassans stood mute, not knowing what to do. As soon as he could make them understand the words for "repeat together," they at once broke out in hearty laughter, one going out and another coming in, and others coming against the table; but there was this good man, patiently waiting till the uproar ceases, and then commencing again to point out A, B, C, D to them. His heart was full of great and broad plans for the good of all Africa, and yet did not count it waste of time to give his whole mind to the simple work of teaching the alphabet to a rowdy Sunday-school class.

One more instance must be given, this time by the Rev. J. Boyle, his faithful friend and co-worker:

An instance of it is quite fresh in my mind. As far back as the year 1874, when the New Calabar Mission was first started on the old site, the late Rev. W. E. Carew was stationed there as a pioneer missionary with Mr. J. D. Garrick, then a catechist, as his assistant, but now a clergyman in the Sierra Leone pastorate. The Bishop has a by no means easy task to deal with the king and chiefs in connection with the work of the boarding school established there, especially with regard to the payment of fees incurred for the maintenance of the pupils. On one occasion the Bishop determined to call on the king and chiefs to speak on this particular subject among them. After a long pull in the mission gig boat, the town, which was nine miles from the station, was reached, and, led by trusty guides, we wended our way to the king's quarters. Although the king and chiefs were previously notified of the intended visit, yet to our great surprise and astonishment no one came out to meet the Bishop, but we were simply directed to a verandah, where we had to wait for a good while ere the king made his appearance. During the interval of waiting my brother missionary and myself, fresh from college, with very little or no experience of life in these parts, did not fail to express our indignant feelings to the Bishop that he should be so treated, although timely notice of his visit had been given. The Bishop, instead of sharing in our indignation, in a quiet, calm, and collected manner said: "My young friends, you have to bear and forbear with these people, because at best in some of their actions they are nothing better than children. In dealing with them you have to be armed with a threefold coat of mail called Patience."

Another leading trait in his character was his sense of gratitude. He always taught his children to say "Thank you" for the smallest favours, and they had before them not only precept but example in this respect. He always spoke to them about Mrs. Weeks so gratefully because she taught him his first letters. When he first came to their house he acted as pantry-boy, and this lady one day saw him with a paper in his hand trying to read, and he asked her to teach him. So she promised if he would be quick and good in washing up things and keeping his pantry in order she would give him half an hour every evening to teach him. How thankfully he recalled this little service rendered to him! After his consecration at Canterbury, on his return to London, the first people he called on were Mrs. Weeks and Admiral

Leeke, who rescued him on the *Myrmidon* in 1822. His gratitude to the Rev. Henry Venn was unbounded; he taught his children always to call him "The good father of Africa."

Much might be added on the score of his unwearied diligence. The Bishop had a grand capacity for work. His pen was ever in his hand, on his voyages, in brief delayings in his journeyings, in his brief home stayings, during meetings, his writing never seemed to cease. He never let his correspondence go behind, a virtue which only the elect can dare to claim. Every letter, however trivial, he answered forthwith and by his own hand. Looking up from a pile of such letters with which he was carefully and laboriously dealing he said, "These sort of letters should be carefully answered to lead the writers to a higher aim and nobler thoughts." It seems incredible for one whose life was so full and strenuous, but his mass of papers evidence the fact that he copied with his own hand not only the letters he wrote, but most of those he received. So he toiled on, preaching, praying, working, an apostolic life in modern times.

His work, like his name, remains an imperishable monument of all his faith and labour. Whatever achievement in the path of Christian enterprise lies on the Niger, it will never be forgotten that he broke the hard and fallow ground. It was his brave heart and strong hand that cut the first path through the dense undergrowth of superstition; it was he, as a wise master builder, who laid the foundations of the work of God that was to be. Like Washington, he was the father of his country; but he did more, for he proved in his own person the capacity of the African to serve his own people and his God. His life has silenced many who made us to differ, and in the advancement and development of the native, not only in spiritual but in civil responsibilities, he will be remembered as the forerunner of a potential race to be. Above all, this man walked with God, and he was not, for He took him, full of years and honour, laying down a sickle which in the great day of harvest shall not fail to fill his arms with golden sheaves.

CHAPTER XII

THE FIELD—TO-DAY AND TO-MORROW

NO true life ends at the open grave. It may be a fine fancy to hearken to the heart beating its funeral march thither, but of the great and good this is not, can never be, the case. The music of their pulsing blood is victorious, with one clear note of faith and hope in unison, a strain of rejoicing in that divine and deathless energy which kindles other lives and repeats itself in power, not only to-day but in the to-morrow of the world. So we who mourn, turning slowly homeward over the grass, brush away our tears, feeling that we have not lost our heart's treasures; they are but sunbeams lifted higher, and we are satisfied that whatever may be their celestial service yonder, they have left something much more than a memory here. Freed from the tense limitations of mortal life, they can now serve a nobler sphere, and their influence, in ever widening waves of blessing, does more than when we could look into their faces and listen to the voices we so miss to-day.

This is true of Bishop Crowther, who has left the print of his character upon his people, and is, even now, an inspiration in the work he left behind.

One of the most important incidents in the later

years of his life was, as we have seen, the formation of the Delta Pastorate Church. This ideal never faded from the horizon of his hopes, through all those years of patient and faithful toil; his prayer was that he might be permitted to see an African church, self-supporting, and ministered to by a purely native pastorate for the evangelization of West Africa. The idea did not, of course, originate with him, the credit for its origin is justly due to that wise and devoted secretary of the Church Missionary Society, the Rev. Henry Venn, who treated Crowther as his dear son in the faith and greeted him as a happy augury of the possible fulfilment of his heart's desire. In that fine classic of missionary history, which preserves for all time the interesting record of this great Society, Mr. Eugene Stock truly remarks:

> Preparation for the euthanasia of missions, that is, self-supporting, self-governing, and self-extending native churches, was perhaps the most important work of Mr. Venn's life. The subject had never been touched when he took it up. There is no sign in the first half of the last century that anyone, either in the Church of England or outside of it, had given a thought to the matter. Henry Venn led the way, and, with no experience or precedents to guide him, gradually formed conclusions and worked out plans, which have since been adopted in substance by most missionary societies sufficiently advanced to have Christian communities to think about.

An incident occurred in those early days which accelerated this impulse in the mind of Mr. Venn. A native merchant from Sierra Leone was taking tea with him one day. The visitor had brought his wife and children with him to England, and, apparently regardless of expense, it was his intention to go up to

Scotland, and even pay a visit to Paris before he and his family turned homewards. Mr. Venn said to him, "If you can afford to spend so much money in travelling for your pleasure, why don't you contribute something for the support of your own clergy, instead of leaving it all to us in England?" The answer was significant enough. "Mr. Venn, treat us like men, and we shall behave like men; but so long as you treat us like children, we shall behave like children." The result of that tea-table talk has been felt in the missionary field in every land ever since. It is not surprising that on these lines Crowther proved himself an apt and most sympathetic pupil. So far back as 1864 we find him discussing with King William Pepple an arrangement whereby he, as native leader, should contribute a moiety of the expense of building mission premises, and again and again Crowther reported in his letters home the advantages and rightful claims of his fellow-countrymen in this matter.

The crisis which so seriously dislocated the operations of the Niger Mission during the closing years of the Bishop's work was, without doubt, an incentive, prompting the native pastors and their converts to make a specific and earnest appeal to him, as their Chief Shepherd, to establish a self-supporting native church on the Delta. There was, however, no anxiety on their part to sever themselves from the doctrines and discipline of the Church of England. This long-anticipated stage was received with a little natural regret on the part of the authorities of the Church Missionary Society that the suggestion should come at a time when some misunderstanding was felt on the Niger. The Bishop had strongly supported the appeal, and on a matter of so much moment the counsel of the Archbishop of Canterbury was asked, and in a most fatherly and sympathetic spirit given.

It was a great day of rejoicing at Bonny when, on 29 April, 1892, the Delta Pastorate was inaugurated with special services of thanksgiving at St. Stephen's Cathedral and St. Clement's, the sermons being preached by the Rev. J. Boyle and Archdeacon D. C. Crowther. The latter spoke hopefully of the future and said:

> I am feeling more and more convinced that God wishes in these latter days to extend the name and knowledge of His beloved Son by simple, inexpensive means, using local instruments to carry it into the interior, and by the formation of this pastorate the people make the religion their own, and are already feeling the responsibility of taking the Gospel with them everywhere they go, and preach it to their countrymen in the interior, where we, with our hamperings, cannot so easily get to. It may be said that they are weak, yet they act as pioneers for us, and do impart the good instruction they receive, preparing the minds of the people for the time when missionaries (I trust steady, godly young men from our churches) will be located among them. This is our aim, and may God grant it may come to pass.

It was not, however, until the year 1896, when, after mutual conference in London and Lagos, that a formal constitution was drawn up for the self-government of the work in the Delta, and signed by all parties, that the Niger Delta Pastorate Church became an accomplished fact. This set forth its ecclesiastical basis as a branch of the Church of England, and provided for its administration as a self-supporting organization by

Church Councils and Committees under the jurisdiction of a Bishop. Such a happy result was largely due to the patient and loving influence of the late Bishop Hill and of the present Bishop Tugwell, with the co-operation of Archdeacon D. C. Crowther, the present Bishop James Johnson, and other representatives of the native ministry. Since then the work has progressed, new churches have been built, and boarding schools established for boys and girls.

One of the needs of the Delta Pastorate is trained natives of that district to undertake the pastoral and evangelizing work among the heathen in the hinterland. Hitherto it has been dependent upon Sierra Leone or the Gold Coast for its ministerial material, and at the present time a special effort is being made to establish a training institution or college for native students in the service of God. It is intended very appropriately to call this a memorial to the late Bishop Crowther. Nothing could be more appropriate to his memory or more in accordance with his own wishes if he could be consulted. Archdeacon Crowther has already visited England to urge the claims of this project upon the churches at home. When this is done men will go from its doors, not only with a zeal for extending the blessings of Christianity to the tribes of heathen to which it is as yet a stranger, but by proper qualification they will be able to exercise a wise development of the churches already established in the Delta Pastorate. The Church is from time to time stimulated by seasons of genuine revival, when, as in the Okrika Church,

DEDICATION OF ST. STEPHEN'S, BONNY

To face page 394

in 1906, there is a quickening of spiritual life, which becomes a permanent blessing. There is a bright outlook in the mission districts of the Delta, and there is much need for more translation work. The claims of the coming generation are not forgotten, and special interest attaches to the important work among young native girls undertaken by Mrs. Crowther, the wife of the Archdeacon. In one of the villages in the Ora district, in the care of a native evangelist, a recent report stated that the greater number of the young people were turning towards Christianity, and some have learnt to read the Bible in the Yoruba language. From time to time some of the converts from Opobo make excursions into the interior to carry the Gospel and establish outposts among the heathen, who are still living in dense darkness and superstition. The Delta Pastorate Church has a great work before it, and many difficulties to overcome; but it is going forward, wisely directed by its leaders, and trusting in God for ultimate success and blessing.

Other missions, which mostly owe their origin to the faith and work of Bishop Crowther, are the Yoruba Mission, the Niger Mission, which has of recent years been divided into Northern and Southern divisions, comprising the work of the Church Missionary Society in Nigeria. In many parts self-supporting, with African pastors, under the direction of European missionaries, having the oversight of the churches, with district councils for local management.

Wherever the native missionaries go the old chiefs

repeat the common observation that they are too old to give up their religion, even if their gods are but dumb idols; the coming generation may perhaps take with profit the Christian religion. But in other instances those who came under the power of the Gospel were not afraid of going all the way in putting away their idols. At a place called Abo Fowole, in the neighbourhood of Ibadan, the missionary gives a case in point, where an old Shango worshipper, accepting Christianity, said he would destroy his gods. He sent his children to bring them out, but they dared not venture, so he went into the idol house himself and brought them to the missionary—a calabash full of innocent-looking stones, which were supposed to be thunderbolts, also a curious thing like a bowler hat, with a rim top and bottom, which was his *odufa* to hold his *ifá* nuts and charms. Then he went to the village and began to clear away the devil stones, but a woman remonstrated, as she said one of the devils belonged to her husband. But the old man straightway assured her that if her man wanted a devil he must place it somewhere else, for he was master of this compound, and would have no more of that rubbish there.

Every missionary has to contend with the secret societies which are such a terror to the people. There is a fraternity among the heathen priests called Oqunegba, which is mainly responsible for many of the religious observances, and arranges the ordeal of poison. Another is the Ijamo, about which one of the missionaries says: "This council of aged senators meets every nine days, but all their agenda and proceedings are kept secret. They are looked upon as the conservators of their country's original integrity. All laws made by them are implicitly obeyed throughout the country, however objectionable or ruinous is their effect upon the nation. Many of the frightful abominations, stamped out of other countries by British influences, are still practised among the Ijamos, especially in connection with the burial of their members. All responsible chiefs of the land, to become accredited, must join the famous Ijamo fraternity as members."

The Southern division of the Niger mission before mentioned deals chiefly with the Ibo and the Ijo tribes. Three-fourths of the whole Protectorate, including Yoruba, speak the tongue of the first-mentioned people. In 1857 Crowther opened a station at Onitsha, and its jubilee has been recently celebrated under the very tamarisk tree which he planted. Great changes have taken place since he came as pioneer there on his journeys up the Niger. It is now a populous town, and the trading factories are a feature of its river front. An excellent work is being done amongst the native girls by training schools and homes, but it is difficult sometimes to get them in, as they are betrothed at an early age to men for a monetary consideration. And a child of ten will give as a reason for not coming to school that her husband objects! Heathenism is never far away. A few miles from Onitsha it is still possible to find a sick man with a large idol over his head, its feet tied, and a bandage over its mouth to prevent it from killing him. At Asaba, on the other side of the Niger, there is a useful station doing good work, although having in the past to struggle against many difficulties. At the back of this lies the Benin country, which stretches across to the Yoruba district, a very dark land, with a people still joined to their idols. The native pastor at Idumuje Ugboko speaks hopefully of the work among the young, but laments that many of the old men give up going to church when they find it involves loss. In this district the native probationers find a useful sphere of work.

The course of the Niger is partly through the Ibo country, and the lower portion of this comprises the Delta Pastorate sphere of action ; but the interior has not yet been occupied for missionary work. It is perhaps the most interesting portion of Southern Nigeria. At one time, too, it was well populated, but the ravages of the slave trade have swept away many of its people and reduced its busy towns to small and insignificant villages. For a long time a portion of this country, the Bende district, was as inaccessible to Europeans as Tibet, the motive being possibly lest the slave trade, its staple industry, should be interfered with, and also to preserve the fearful power and authority of the Aro-Chuku or Long Juju, at whose shrine thousands of deluded human victims had been sacrificed. At last the enormity of this wickedness reached its limit, and the British Government sent an expedition into the country and avenged the inhuman slaughter of eight hundred women and children by Abams and Arons. Then followed the destruction of this horrid shrine, with its cave of divination and pools of sacred fish. And when Bishop James Johnson visited the place in 1903 he found little left but the dense bush at the foot of a declivity to mark the spot where for generations human life had been wantonly sacrificed. So great was this dread of a bloodthirsty divinity that even as far as Benin and Dahomey reverence was duly paid to it. Its priests, a set of cruel cut-throats, were promptly deported by Government to Calabar. So here again in this fine country the oft-quoted line is true, and "only man is vile." There is plenty of water, the villages nestle under the graceful branches of the palm and banana trees, the cocoanut palms offering everywhere an abundance of refreshment; and when the rainy season is over sweet water can be obtained by tapping the tree known in Yoruba as *aga*. The people are wild and savage; their dress a handkerchief cloth, the boys and girls nothing at all; the women painting the skin of each other's bodies with strange devices; and both sexes are fond of tattooing their foreheads. In one respect amongst many there is urgent need of the uplifting power of Christianity, for the men are lazy drones, quite content to see the women do all the work. Where nature provides the daily commissariat free of charge or exertion, the menkind of the nation are all of the unemployed class, and like some of their brethren elsewhere of whiter complexions, they prefer to remain so, and it is said that often the British Government have considerable difficulty to engage them for service as porters.

One of their curious customs is to live in compounds, comprising households of from fifty to five hundred persons, relatives and domestic slaves. Within these walls there is some idea of order, a chief, when necessary assisted by sub-chiefs, acting as authority, and there is always a reception-room set apart for visitors, and a club-house garnished with as much ornamentation as the means or fancy will allow, where the male members of the community assemble from time to time to discuss and perhaps quarrel over their various family and national affairs. For these people are too cruel in their customs to keep anything like peace within their borders. They are fond of a fight, and British officers who have had to face them say that they never seem to know when they are beaten. In spite of our Protectorate there is no doubt that cannibalism still prevails in many districts. It is part of their war usage. They consider their triumph over their enemies is only complete when they have eaten them. They glory in their power to take human life, and hang up the skulls of their victims as trophies of honour. Here the practice of twin infanticide prevails to a frightful degree. Not only are such unhappy little ones killed outright, but the mother for the offence is driven away, never allowed to visit a market, or walk a road used by the public. Bishop James Johnson when in this district paid a visit to one of the hamlets of such miserable women in the Azurim neighbourhood and found five poor creatures who had been twin mothers, and had suffered banishment with the loss of their little ones. He tells us a very pathetic story: "There was an old and very grey-headed woman among them. She did not remember how long she had lived in that hamlet, but she knew that she was a young twin mother when she was driven away from her home and sent there, and that she had lived there all her life since under these conditions. They were all very sad. Tears fell from the eyes of one of them as I endeavoured to comfort them in their disconsolate state and hold out to them some hope of a change for the better by and by, especially as the country was gradually coming under active British protection. This seemed to them impossible, and their looks asked the question despairingly, "Will this ever be?"

There is only space left to record some features of the religious belief of these people, for after the fashion of the heathen they form a combination of cruelty and piety. The Bishop already quoted has taken pains to ascertain in what direction and how far their native worship extends. They have a clear idea of a Supreme Being, to Whom all their prayers are directed, and to Whom, looking towards the sky, they offer their sacrifices with open hands. His name is "Chineke," from *Chi*, the Supreme Being, and *eke*, a market day, and *neke*, to divide; that is, the Great Being Who divides unto us our lots in life. There are, of course, subordinate divinities, as "Njoku," the god of the yams, and many evil spirits who have to be conciliated. It is remarkable that of this great Deity they have no image or idol. The Bishop says: "When, as I noticed at the entrance of one of their villages a large collection of offerings, some on the ground, others on erections, and a very young chicken suspended alive on a rope that bound a small tree to another at some distance from it, I asked some of the villagers what their object of worship was, and to whom these offerings were made, they replied, with evident surprise at the question, 'Whom should we worship but the Being Who has made us, and Who owns the world?' striking the earth with the palms of their hands out of reverence for the great Being, and pointing their fingers to the sky as the place of his special residence." It only remains to add that these people believe in a future state of blessedness, called "Eligwe," and another of misery for the wicked. Under these circumstances it seems obvious that with all their wickedness they are not far from a true conception of God, and therefore the missionary has something to work on when he takes to them the illuminating and saving truths of Christianity. It is fifty years since Bishop Crowther first preached the Gospel to the Ibos, and left Taylor at Onitsha to translate the Bible and instruct the converts.

Now there are thirty stations near, eight churches are included in the Ibo Pastorate, supporting their own ministers, while three or four churches have their "own missionary" to the regions beyond. Figures are not always the best estimate of success, but in this comparison of past and present we note that 37 native pastors are preaching in the Ibo language, that 1700 are professed Christians, and 438 are regular communicants; last, not least, in the 28 schools about 2000 scholars are being trained and taught for the life present and the life to come. In the opinion of a thoughtful C.M.S. missionary, to whom we are indebted for much valuable data on this subject, while these results are very encouraging, there is much still to be done among the Ibos, and he does not fear difficulties from those quarters and for those reasons commonly adduced. His judgment is of service as that of an eye-witness, and deserves a permanent record in these pages.

As regards the future of the Gospel (he says) amongst these interesting people we have good reason to believe that the time is ripe for widespread sowing, in the strong hopeful expectation of an abundant harvest speedily. I do not think it is polygamy or the drink question, mighty evils though they be, that hinders the growth, nor do I think it is the influx of Mohammedanism and the domestic slavery so closely associated with it which are given as reasons why Christianity makes headway so slowly. Still less would I accept the reason of slow progress given that Christianity is unsuitable for the needs of the African as affected by the physical, social, and climatic conditions of his mind and environment. Certainly none of these reasons apply to the Ibos. Moreover, all these theories limit the efficacy of the Gospel and the healing and recreative power of Jesus Christ, whereas we have seen with our eyes and can testify that the Gospel is "the power of God unto salvation" amongst these people. Rather is the slow rate of expansion due to paucity of workers. It must always be remembered that one-third of the European staff are always on furlough or sick leave, and thus the continuity of the work is sadly interrupted. From the results of the last ten years or so one is almost prepared to say that given the same number of workers actually in the field, with the same continuity of service we should see almost as great results on the Lower Niger as we see in Uganda, provided, of course, that there be earnest and unceasing prayer "that the same Spirit be outpoured in all abundance, operating to the conversion of the heathen, to be followed by real consecrative and enthusiastic service."

As regards Northern Nigeria the work has many difficulties, but the missionaries are valiantly holding on. It would have gladdened the heart of the old Bishop to have seen the celebration last year of the fifth year of the Lokoja Native Pastorate Church, and to note the efforts at Bida and elsewhere being made to teach the boys. At Mokwa, the last new station of the Nupé country, the Sunday services are well attended, and the Sunday-school is making slow but sure progress. Household slavery is not yet abolished in Northern Nigeria, and this is a hindrance to the work. But the greatest difficulty is Mohammedanism, and this prevents progress among the Hausas, who are so intelligent. This fine race, superior in many respects to the tribes inhabiting other parts of Nigeria, and capable of so much discipline — making excellent soldiers and policemen—are still a difficult and disappointing ground for Christian work. This is chiefly owing to the power of Islam, and even medical agency, which rarely fails to find some appreciation on the part of the natives, cannot get a constituency here. The natives are quite satisfied with the prescriptions given by their mallams, consisting of strips of parchment with words from the Korân, as charms when they are taken sick. They also cling tenaciously to primitive and old-fashioned ideas, and it is amazing to think that they will deliberately refuse the skill of trained Christian doctors, preferring to have their teeth drawn by the village blacksmith with the aid of red-hot skewers, and have great faith in the native barbers, who bleed or tattoo their patients according to their choice and means of payment. It must be admitted that the results of the work in Northern Nigeria are disappointing. What is to be done in this fine country, among a people of such capacity and promise, is a problem not to be solved without patient and persevering effort. One statement made by a missionary as to the religious position at Kutigi and Mokwa, within easy reach of Bida, is worth quoting. These natives, like many others, possess a very mixed religion of Mohammedanism and heathenism, which can hardly be a credit to the former, with its pretensions to elevating the heathen. "The people," he says, "with few exceptions are farmers, and although all take part in Mohammedan rites and festivals, fully one-third join in heathen feasts. About one-third regularly go through the Mohammedan daily prayers, the remainder doing nothing except at festival seasons, when they join in with whatever is going on, either heathen or otherwise; they are quite willing to join in our Christian rejoicings also. Beer and palm wine drinking are indulged in to excess by all at times, the latter by the Mohammedans."

Another, writing from Bida, says: "The work among these Mohammedans is terribly difficult; there is no open opposition, no argument, nothing but sheer indifference." It is something much more in the Ijebu country behind Lagos, as the missionary tells us "there have not been for some years past such accessions from heathenism to Christianity as formerly, because the people all flock to Mohammedanism, which has become the popular and predominant religion." A native pastor draws attention to the advance of Islam from the north with some concern. "The force gathers," he says, "it behoves us to be on the watch that we may keep the foe at bay." A distinguished observer, conversant with Nigeria past and present, is of opinion that Islam and not heathenism is the force to be reckoned with by the missionaries in that country. Missionaries returning to their old fields of labour in Nigeria are startled by the rapid increase of the religion of the False Prophet, not only in the interior, but at the ports on the coastline.

"The Propaganda of Islam" was one of the subjects discussed at the great Pan-Anglican Conference held in London in 1908. And it has been elsewhere stated that unless some special effort is made to repel this quiet but sweeping attack of the emissaries of Islam, the native conscience and loyalty will be almost entirely captured by the Crescent instead of the Cross. What shall we say then of this difficulty of the Mohammedan progress among the heathen? It goes without saying that the conquest of the heathen by Christianity is by no means achieved in this country. After all the labours of weary and incessant years, it must be admitted that only the fringe of the dark multitude of these natives has been touched or even brought into earshot of the merciful tidings of salvation. The wheels of the chariot move slowly, the ground is heavy and obstructive, and no true missionary boasts of easy progress. Millions in Nigeria know less of the Cross than of the British flag. As a nation we govern them by a rule of which the majority have never heard.

As a Church we have brought the light of Divine liberty here and there, but for the great hinterland of superstition we have done little more than pray. The field, from a purely pagan point of view, is ripening unto the harvest.

On the other hand, especially as regards Northern Nigeria, it is Islam blocks the way. Comparatively speaking there is little improvement in the position during recent years. Many things have happened since the days of Bishop Crowther, and the difficulty of dealing with the Mohammedans is even more acute than when he, and other pioneers, worked so zealously and with such patience for their welfare. He may not have done much, but he succeeded at any rate in establishing an *entente cordiale* with the royal and religious leaders of Islam, who were willing to listen to the Arabic Bible, and even discuss the great truths of Christianity without provocation. His aim, as we have seen, was to win their respect and attention, and then lead them through Holy Scripture and public services to the acceptance of the truth. He proposed no weak compromises, he gave no quarter to polygamy and other practices, and recognized to his native clergy the immense difficulty of success.

In the past history of the work on the Niger, in spite of many disadvantages, there was evidently a more willing spirit on the part of the Moslems to listen to the missionary than to-day. Conferences were held, at which a very serious spirit of inquiry was manifested. One instance of this may be recalled at this point. At Lokoja a Christian missionary was sitting in the midst of a number of Moslems, discussing very earnestly one afternoon the insufficiency of the Korân as compared with the Bible. The missionary laid down his Arabic Bible and proceeded to say:

Well, if what we have told you is the law of God, which He says must be fulfilled if we are to enter heaven, what are you going to do, you who do not profess to have kept the laws of heaven? "Ah! we trust in the mercy of God." Not so. You call it His mercy, but you are really trusting to the untruthfulness of God. You are hoping that at the Judgment Day God will rise up before all men and say: "O men, I have indeed made a mistake. I said by the mouth of My prophets that it was absolutely necessary that all who should enter My home should keep certain laws, should render a certain amount of service to Me and their fellow-men. I find now that My law was too strict. I find that many persons who refused to obey it are nevertheless very good people to put into heaven. So I take away My law; I made a mistake in making it at the first." So you hope God will say.

The Yorubas were silent for a moment, and the Hausas pressed them for an answer, and seemed somewhat impressed at no answer being forthcoming. Their leader then said: "Let all keep silence. I have a weighty question to ask. If all the prophets, as you have told, need that the Messiah should do their service for them and should take their punishment, what is to be done for us who are worthless to God as the grass of the field?"

The missionary answered:

"Was not the slaying of the Messiah a great enough thing to teach all heaven and earth how God hates sin? Would your being destroyed teach men any more about the wickedness of sin than they know already, when they have heard that the Great Messiah died for it? His death covers the past; the road to heaven is now open to you too."

The Hausa paused, for he was thinking very solemnly upon the matter, and then, looking up, he quietly said:

"Now, I want a straight answer to a straight question. The Messiah has done all this for men. What can *we* do to become saved?"

This was the missionary's opportunity, and with a full heart he answered:

"Trust yourself to Him, become His people, go down to the town; tell them you thank God for the Messiah who has opened heaven to you, that they too must submit to Him and become His people."

All was silence for a few moments, the Mohammedans were slowly weighing these words in the balance. Presently their leading speaker exclaimed:

"Now, tell where do these two roads of the Messiah and Mohammed meet?"

"They never, never meet. If one leads into the light, it is equally certain the other leads to darkness."

All rose together, and, leading the missionary to the corner of the verandah, whence a straight road led to the town, the chief Hausa said:

"We love you for the words you tell us; it is as though you stood here on a height and saw the straight road, and watched all of us wandering in the long grass on either side and you shout to us, saying: 'Turn back! turn back! You are straying from the path; there it is leading straight to the town!' Thus you are doing to us every day."

This conversation exhibits the mental attitude of both teacher and taught, and one can readily join in the expressed desire of the missionary at the close of the interview: "God grant that these first early signs of hope may quickly ripen into believing and being baptized, which we tell them is an essential part of our commission."

The issue is of perennial interest, and perhaps deserves even more attention to-day than it obtains in missionary circles. One might safely affirm that in any meeting it is easier to excite enthusiasm over a naked savage with his idol and his fetish than the white-robed Moslem with his praying carpet. It may be easily urged that the latter is obviously more enlightened than the former, but it is equally true that the creed of Islam is insufficient and unsatisfactory, and is, moreover, the sworn enemy of Christianity. Of course it has its able apologists among those who argue that one religion is as good as another, and that this for practical purposes is better, and who are also anxious to protect it from interference on grounds of political expediency.

In one particular at least, as regards Nigeria, Islam has not the advantage she once possessed in making converts—the weapon of force can no longer be used. Under the British flag full liberty is allowed for any religion which does not menace the laws of order and humanity. Therefore no tyranny of cruel compulsion or ill treatment in retaliation or punishment is permitted. It is the fashion in some quarters to-day to conveniently forget that the propagation of Islam has been a reign of terror, but the history of this fateful creed is the story of ruthless bloodshed, extermination and conversion by the scimitar. Even in the annals of West African mission work we have adduced evidence enough of persecution endured to the death by Christian natives from the hands of their Mohammedan masters. It is unnecessary to go further back to record the unparalleled atrocities which mark the subjugation of the Hausa race by the fanatical *jehads* of the Fulanis.

All this state of things is over now, and the natives walk no longer in fear of Mohammedans, although, where Christianity has not revealed something better, they still regard them as persons of superior knowledge, which is true. But though the sword is sheathed and cannot reap its thousands as of old, Islam is not neglecting the milder method of persuasion. Among the sects of Islam that of the Quadriyah order of missionaries holds a very important place. It was founded in the eleventh century, and introduced into West Africa as far back as the fifteenth century. They might be termed the Jesuits of Islam. It is their practice to come as peaceful strangers to pagan towns and villages, to gain influence, render themselves of service as possessing education, and make a special point of securing the favour of the king, chief, or any ruling authority. Missionaries refer to these visits to-day, and indicate how from the northern districts streams of Moslem influence are quietly but surely affecting the natives of the Delta. They describe how at first the Moslem missionary begins by marking his prayer place with stones, and later on replaces these with strips of split bamboo. But the best description of one of these missionaries is given in Mr. Morel's valuable work, "Affairs of West Africa," which we venture to quote on this page. He states that Dr. Blyden told him the story when relating how one of the large pagan towns was proselytized to Mohammedanism.

On a certain day the inhabitants of the town observed a man, black like themselves, but clad in a white garment, advancing down the main street. Suddenly the stranger prostrated himself and prayed to Allah. The natives stoned him and he departed. In a little while he returned and prostrated himself as before. This time he was not stoned, but the men gathered about him with mockery and reviling. The men spat upon him and the women hurled insults and abuse. His prayer ended, the stranger went away in silence, grave and austere, seemingly oblivious to his unsympathetic surroundings. For a space he did not renew his visit, and in the interval the people began to regret their rudeness. The demeanour of the stranger under trying circumstances had gained their respect. A third time he came, and with him two boys, also clothed in white garments. Together they knelt and offered prayer. The natives watched and forbore to jeer. At the conclusion of the prayer a woman came timidly forward and pushed her young son towards the holy man, then as rapidly retreated. The Moslem rose, took the boy by the hand, and, followed by his acolytes, left the village in silence as before. When he came again he was accompanied by three boys, two of them those who had been with him before, the third the woman's son, clad like the rest. All four fell upon their knees, the holy man reciting the prayer in a voice that spoke of triumph and success. He never left the town again, for the people crowded round him, beseeching him to teach their children. In a short time the entire population of that town, which for three centuries had beaten back the assaults of would-be Moslem converters by the sword, had voluntarily embraced Islam !

It has been said in explanation of the easy conquest of such a people by Islam that it must be borne in mind that the natives of the lower parts of Nigeria follow Animism as their religion, and that they have therefore a strong inclination of mind towards any teaching which deals with spiritual and supernatural affairs. The appearance of this holy man in their midst, although in the first instance greeted with ridicule and even contempt, soon affects them as they hear him praying to his God, one who seems to have a knowledge of the suppliant, which their deities do not pretend to possess, and who is evidently brought into personal relation with this kneeling man in white raiment. This grows upon them, their imagination is excited, they are hungry for more knowledge, and eventually are captivated by a religion which they willingly accept in preference to their own.

There is no need to disguise the serious character of such a wholesale success of Islam as in the case mentioned, or to doubt that this is occurring in many parts of Nigeria, and will, if not checked, in time absorb the greater part of the thirty or forty millions of natives under the British rule. This prospect is based not only upon the statements of writers who are avowedly friendly to the Moslem creed, but from independent testimony, and the invaluable evidence of the missionaries themselves. If this be so, are we prepared to accept the responsibility of the conversion of Nigeria to this religion under our own eyes? Stripped of its romance, the glamour which veils so much in Oriental life and story, dare we hand over these missions to a creed which is condemned by the judgment of history and violently opposed to the most sacred principles of the Christian faith? Is it likely to elevate the negro and develop him morally, intellectually, and spiritually, as Christianity can do? Is it not true, as Wuttke has affirmed in his system of ethics, "Islam is to be regarded as an attempt of *heathenism* to maintain itself erect under an outward monotheistic form against Christianity"?

In fact this is the practical issue, and it must be tested by the evidence of history and present-day experience. What is commonly advanced as arguments in favour of Islam within West African borders?

It is declared to be a vital, living, and progressive force, in contradiction of that famous passage in Palgrave's "Arabia," which affirms: "Islamism is in itself stationary, and was framed thus to remain;

sterile like its god, lifeless like its first principle in all that constitutes life—for life is love, participation and progress, and of these the Coranic deity has none." It claims to have imparted to the negro "an energy, a dignity and self-respect which is all too rarely found in their pagan or their Christian countrymen." We are told that it is a valuable asset in the political settlement of Nigeria, everywhere knitting the conquerors and the conquered into an harmonious whole, and that contrary to reputation it encourages instruction and even promotes chastity. A great point is made of the prohibition of strong drink and encouragement of personal cleanliness, hospitality, and the inculcation of chastity as one of the highest virtues. It is even affirmed that it is the teaching of Islam develops in the African character that rather neglected grace of industry, and creates a thirst for knowledge. If this could be safely regarded as a fair and impartial picture of the possibilities and promise of Islam, then it is a veritable evangel for the West African people. One might even then think there would be some little ground for the contention that Mohammedanism is a benefit to Africa, and that, compared with Christianity, she has done more for the well-being of that land.

But is this so? What is the testimony of those on the spot to-day? We are told that the religious standard of the followers of Islam is not a very high one, and from a point of intelligence it is not much in advance of the heathen. And this is a very moderate statement of the case. It has no mosques south of the Niger-Binue Confluence. There seems to be no place of worship, and the utmost is the place of prayer marked out, as we have seen, by stones and pegs of split bamboo. The majority of these easily enclosed converts to the Prophet's fold are perfectly satisfied to follow the dictates of the mallams; they do not exercise their reasoning faculties, or are, indeed, asked so to do, and the religion they have taken over largely consists of repeating the Arabic prayers at the appointed hours. They do not understand. They cannot read or write. The Korân to them is a sealed book, except so far as it is represented by the verses they have been taught to commit to memory, or the scraps which are written on strips of parchment and sold as charms. This is not to be wondered at, seeing that the mallams themselves are not very well instructed. They are strict in the letter of ceremonial, but ignorant of some of the tenets of their faith. These men make cheap sport of the superstition of the people, and scorn them for their fetish worship, but there are few Mohammedans who are not wearing some charm, in the shape of an amulet of Korân texts, round either the neck or the waist.

As to the moral elevation of the negro by accepting Islam there is grave reason for doubt. In the nature of its teaching the Korân cannot be held as a model of morals. It allows polygamy and concubinage; its system of easy divorce is subversive of domestic happiness. It degrades woman, reducing her to a chattel, and with such a pernicious treatment of the sex it brings no new element of happiness in the home life of the native, to whom, amid all his faults, wife and mother, sister and daughter, had some sense of respect and even sacredness.

Lord Cromer, in his "Modern Egypt," contrasts the teaching of the Korân with its depreciation of woman with her elevation and sanctity in Christian lands.

"The Moslem, on the other hand, despises women; both his religion and the example of his Prophet, the history of whose private life has been handed down to him, tend to lower them in his eyes. Save in exceptional cases, the Christian fulfils the vow which he has made to his wedded wife for life. The Moslem, when his passion is sated, can if he likes throw off his wife like an old glove."

But this distinguished authority states that the present enlightened Egyptians are growing more inclined to monogamy through education, contact with Europeans, and its evident happiness.

What is the testimony of Dr. Miller on this point, from his personal association with Moslem influence in Hausaland, where, up to the present, it has had its own way, undisturbed by Christian missions? The quotation is from a paper read at the First Missionary Conference on behalf of the Mohammedan world, held at Cairo in April, 1906.

The lack of home life, the utter prostitution of virtue, the total disregard of morals, all these have brought a moral ruin to the people, and made West Africa a seething sink of gross iniquity. Woman, although allowed much more freedom than in North Africa, is nevertheless the "thing" of men. Polygamy, of course, is the law; only lack of wealth prevents men from having four wives and as many concubines as

FOUR NIGER BISHOPS OF TO-DAY

BISHOP JAMES JOHNSON (*Photo, Russell & Sons*) BISHOP OLUWOLE (*Photo, Russell & Sons*)
THE LATE BISHOP PHILLIPS (*Photo, Russell & Sons*) BISHOP TUGWELL (*Photo, Elliot & Fry*)

To face page 416

possible. Divorce for anything is possible—a quarrel, sickness, infirmity, poverty, or worse. The youngest girls are taught the worst vices; no one is innocent, none pure. Boys and girls grow up in the densest atmosphere of sin, where there is hardly a redeeming feature, and this all under the strictest adherence to the outward laws of Islam.

The whited sepulchre is full of bones. Immorality of every sort is rife, and there is little shame. Adultery and fornication are not reduced through men having many wives. It is rare to find a woman past the prime of life living with her husband. One would therefore expect to find that progress is ruled out, and that the glance is backward, not forward, to "the things our fathers knew and did." The inevitable fruits of a slave-ridden land—laziness, oppression, dirt—have fallen upon West Africa, and only where Christianity, as in Sierra Leone, Lagos, etc., has had a long time to affect the character and condition, do we see progress. Islam has not, and will not, in West Africa do anything for progress.

One of the strongest points urged in favour of Islam in West Africa is its legal abstinence from strong drink. Undoubtedly this condition of the creed places the Mohammedan far in advance of the native of West Africa, who is not naturally a drunkard, but to whom the importation of alcohol has proved such a curse. It is stated that in Southern Nigeria the Mohammedans and the Christians are the only people who restrain themselves from this fateful habit. But it is reported that this vow of total abstinence which the Korân enjoins is not kept so consistently as it might be.

There is little doubt that the influence of the Mohammedans has tended to sharpen the wits of the natives. We are told that in the matter of honesty there is little to choose between them. In his original condition, before the outside world had reached him, the native was not difficult to deal with, but since then he has become a better hand at settling a good bargain. The Mohammedan, of course, considers himself superior in both knowledge and ability, which is quite excusable, and is apt to take advantage in business matters, which is not so defensible. Undoubtedly this superior position affects his chances of success in trade. Without being more industrious than the natives he can make a better show and reap a larger profit than they do. The natives, for instance, in Northern Nigeria make excellent leather goods. But while they are busy manufacturing, or working hard upon their farms, or cheerfully toiling as porters and bearers of burdens at the ports, the Mohammedan can devote himself to trade and has the faculty of going from place to place to pick up bargains and discover the best market for his goods. He may not have the physical strength or even energy of the natives, but making money being his one object in life, he can soon outstrip his native competitors. Every Mohammedan in West Africa is engaged in trade in some form or other, and therefore they are numerically in possession of the field, whereas only a certain number of the natives give themselves to this business. It must be borne in mind that one of the attractions of Islam is that when a native accepts this creed he becomes part of a widespread fraternity, with many advantages as regards commerce amongst other things. And the difference between his choice of Christianity or Islam is that the former involves isolation from his own people and bitter persecution from the all-pervading

Moslem class, whereas in the latter case he makes friends, gains status and importance.

But is the African the better for it ? In his valuable volume, " Hansaland," Canon Robinson quotes Major Lugard to the following effect as referring in his day to that district of Nigeria and the country behind Lagos:

> In that part of the continent there are teeming populations, eager to purchase our cottons and our hardware. But there, too, the barrier of exclusion, due in this case to Mohammedanism, has to be broken down. Over vast areas of West Africa it (Mohammedanism) has become so deteriorated by an admixture of pagan superstitions and by intemperance that its influence for good has been largely discounted. The Mohammedan negro is inflated with a sense of his superiority, which has taught him a supreme contempt for human life outside the pale of his own creed. The pagan is to him as a beast of the field, fit only for slaughter or slavery. His religion has not taught him to condemn deceit, treachery, or cruelty. Having raised him somewhat above the chaos and the superstition of the pagan it has left him with no brighter aspirations, the victim of bigotry and exclusion, the scourge of non-Mohammedan humanity.

This indictment, severe as it may seem, is justified by facts, although it may not coincide with the curious partiality which is often shown towards Mohammedans by Europeans, both as travellers and merchants. An African bishop has said that it is quite an unfounded slight upon the Christian negro to say, as it is common to do, that he is a less dependable servant than the Mohammedan. It is not an unusual thing for a European governor of a province, even when a Christian himself, to promise every assistance to missionaries while they confine their efforts to the conversion of the heathen, but any attempt to proselytize the Mohammedans will be discouraged. What are the reasons for this attitude? Possibly from its political side it springs from an unexpressed fear of Moslem discontent, an unrest which might seriously embarrass the administration of a province. And yet as far as West Africa is concerned there does not seem to have been any ground for this alarm; no outbreak has arisen, and no special objection has been raised by the Africans against the introduction of Christianity. Possibly the position taken up is not so much a political one or even influenced to any great extent by local circumstances. It is much the same at home, and many who have, without examination, been satisfied to consider Mohammedanism as an amiable variant from Christianity are not unprepared to think the best of it when face to face with it abroad. Indeed, there is in all who are not absolute scoffers a sense of respect for the native in his religious aspect: his rigid observances, penances, and prayers, especially the way in which his religion finds a place in his daily life, an experience not so common in Christian home circles, all impress the onlooker, especially if he be a traveller of the tourist type. It is not his business or his desire to peer into the dark nether world of cruelty, corruption, and death, which underlies these external devotions. That is the missionary's affair, and when he discloses things as they are it often awakens more of a shudder than a sympathetic interest, even in Christian minds. Human nature dislikes the disagreeable, except in novels and on the stage. The amazing indifference of Christian people generally to the progress of Islam is sometimes difficult to account for. It is much easier to credit the superficial admiration of a man of the world, whose principle of toleration is quite consistently summed up in the question, "What *does* it matter?"

It would, however, be interesting to explore the grounds of this indifference to Mohammedanism to-day. Islam is not in evidence in England; the dome of the mosque at Woking, or its place of worship at Liverpool, is practically a negligible quantity. Except at an exhibition the Mohammedan is little seen elsewhere than at the docks, which is an unknown land to the majority. So it must be chiefly through travel, and more through books, which bring its results to our easy chair, that we know anything of the Moslem, apart, of course, from the missionaries, who are not at this moment giving evidence in the case. Able writers, mostly after their journeyings, have recorded their impressions, and though sometimes mistaken in their special pleading for that creed which has been and still is the deadliest foe of Christianity, their opinions are deserving of the best consideration of the reader. It carries the greater weight, for Islam is thereby not urging her own claims, she is content with the generous and unasked recommendation of her enemies. It does not detract from the sincerity and value of all that has been said in favour of Islam, but the fact should be borne in mind that the love is all on one side. We may think that it does not much matter for time or eternity whether a man follows the

Bible or the Korân, believes in Christ or Mohammed, but the Moslem thinks differently. There is nothing of Laodicea about his view of the position. As far as he knows the tenets of his own religion—and sometimes that is not much—he always recognizes his duty to hold Christianity at arm's length, to call its believers infidels, and have contempt for every one of them. If he be an instructed mallam he will tell you that your Bible is not a genuine word of God, that the Korân has superseded its authority, that such Christian doctrines as the Trinity and the Divinity of Christ as the Son of God are unreasonable, and even blasphemous. There is nothing backward about the Moslem, his religion is a continuous profession; he spreads his praying carpet in the market place, and is a missionary everywhere and at any time. The only compromises he makes are with the heathen, meeting them half-way with indulgence in both wives and charms; but towards the Christian he shows no sign of truce. He can quote a passage from the Korân about *Sirát*, a bridge over the midst of hell, with an edge sharper than a sword, over which all must pass barefoot. The infidel Christian will slip and fall into eternal flame, but the Moslem, with firm footstep, will walk over unhurt into Paradise. He will tell you that the Korân, or inspired word of God, was sent down to lowest heaven complete, and there revealed to the prophet Mohammed by the angel Gabriel piecemeal, without a wince of unbelief. He has no qualms on the score of tradition, for he has accepted his Bokhari of 7275 apocryphal stories which Abu Abdullah Muhammed ibu-i-Ismail selected from 600,000, uttering a pious *Rikát* over every choice he made. Still it may be said that his religion does not make as much demand upon his credulity or even self-sacrifice as if he were a Buddhist or a Hindu. And with it all he is a good fellow, a faithful servant, as his British masters everywhere will agree, an obedient and brave soldier, as his officers will attest. Bishop Crowther always admitted the advantages which Islam brought to a people living in pure paganism. To a certain extent it introduces reform, stops cannibalism, and abolishes idolatry, though as regards fetishism it only may be said to supplant the practice by its own charms. And to-day there is not much danger of the virtues of Islam being overlooked, either as a creed or as applied to the personal character of its individual believers. The question is what is the relative position of Christianity to Mohammedanism, and whether it is not our bounden duty and service to send missionaries to show them the way of life. This point Canon Robinson has ably argued by showing that when Christianity went forth as a missionary religion the people of the known world were living in dense darkness, except in Greece and Italy, where, in the days of St. Paul, philosophers like Epictetus taught a high conception of God and duty, and Seneca with his school of wise disciples. It is quite possible that these argued with St. Paul that he had better go to the heathen and leave them, with their light and advancement of religious thought, alone. But this he would not do; he went first to the philosophers and preached Christ to the most enlightened.

Therefore when we are told that the Moslems have a good religion and believe in God, we are not ashamed to follow the example of St. Paul and treat them as needing salvation and the message of mercy in Jesus Christ.

To many the fact that Islam denies the doctrine of the Trinity is not the serious disadvantage which it ought to be. It is not only a deliberate refusal of what God has revealed of Himself, but it replaces the Deity of the Bible with an insufficient Divinity without His glorious attributes. There is much force in the opinion of the venerable Dr. Alexander Maclaren in his sermon on John XIX. 1, where he says :

> Historically a pure theism is all but impotent. There is only one example of it on a large scale in the world, and that is a kind of bastard Christianity—Mohammedanism—and we all know what good that is as a religion. There are plenty of people who call themselves Theists and not Christians. Well, I venture to say that is a phase which will not last. There is little substance in it. The God whom men know outside of Jesus Christ is a poor nebulous thing, an idea and not a reality. You will have to get something more substantial than the far-off god of an un-Christian theism if you mean to sway the world and satisfy men's hearts.

In the Allah of Islam there is no attribute of love, and the divinity and eternal Sonship of Jesus Christ are explicitly denied. " Infidels are they who say, Verily God is the Messiah, the Son of Mary. Say, who has any hold on God if He wished to destroy the Messiah, the Son of Mary, and his mother, and those who are on the earth together ? " (Surah v. 19). The atonement, with its solution of the mystery of sin, is absent, the sign of the Cross is abhorrent, and an object of contempt even to Moslem children. In a very able paper on "Strategic Problems," prepared by the Rev. W. H. T. Gairdner, a C.M.S. missionary at Cairo, for the consideration of the Pan-Anglican Congress, there are some profound observations on the moral results of such a denial of the Trinity. He points out that the Moslem God is a mere negation.

With them the infinite is equivalent only to the negative of the Finite, and in reality their god is utterly unintelligible. . . . Islam is philosophically agnostic. . . . The solitary, inscrutable, characterless sultan of heaven is, I need hardly say, a passionless being. An analysis of the ninety-nine epithets or names wherewith he is characterized can really be reduced to the unethical categories of Being, Understanding, Will, and Force. Epithets which seem to fall within the ethical category are really explained away by Moslems themselves, who say of the attributes of *Love* and *Wrath* that they are respectively aspects of favour and disfavour, which of course are simply names for arbitrary will, and who, as in the case of the attribute of *Justice*, wholeheartedly endorse the profound conclusion of Caliban philosophizing on Cetebos, and thus reduce it, too, to will. I need hardly stop to draw out the miserable jejunency of the ethical fruit which such theological soil as this must always produce—what low views of holiness, what callousness towards sin, what absence of tenderness and truth!

If it is pleaded that Islam does well for the nations now, which is subject to contradiction, what guarantee have we of the future? Judging from her history in the past, and how everywhere she has deteriorated and sterilized the country and people under her influence and government, we should hesitate to bind other nations with the same blighting power. What of Arabia, the cradle of her creed, where for thirteen hundred years she has had a free hand, undisturbed by Christian invasion and interference, political or religious? Look at Palestine, Syria, Egypt, Morocco, or any country which has lain under her blighting shadow. Wherever the Crescent reigns is decay, neglect, corruption, arrest of all development, and misery. Her history is against her. If Africa is her chosen child, the sphere of her greatest exploits, it is at the same time a living indictment against her rule. She has failed to uplift the nations which have been spared by her sword and slave market. If it be a sin to persecute the saints her cup is filled to the brim with guiltiness; if to be the wolf that came down on the Christian fold, sparing neither shepherd nor flock, is sin before high heaven, the skirts of Islam are defiled and blood-red.

Of late years Islam has made some effort to set her house in order. Ten years ago a conference was held in Mecca to discuss the causes of its failure, and no less than fifty-six reasons were adduced by these pious Moslems for this want of success. It was then recognized that the doctrine of fatalism was paralyzing the energy of Islam, and she was also losing ground by her ascetic attitude towards the gains and honours of the world. The spirit of the age seems to have pervaded the atmosphere of this conclave, for strong regrets were expressed that Islam restricted religious liberty, possibly with stricter truth a stronger phrase might have been employed, for her history past and present, as far as she is able to act, is despotic and oppressive in regard to every religion but her own. No practical effect seems to have ensued from this learned and really earnest conference, at which the various nations of the world were each represented. We are greatly indebted to Professor Margoliouth for bringing this remarkable incident under the notice of Christian people in England, and in the pages of "East and West" are some conclusions which will meet with the concurrence of all serious thinkers on the subject.

Has Islam any golden age to look back on, except in the sense that at one time Mohammedan sultans were a terror to their neighbours, whereas now their neighbours are safe from their raids? There is no real abuse current in Mohammedan states from which they have ever been free, except by accident for a limited time; on the other hand reforms, whether forced upon the people from outside or not, have been introduced—it is sufficient to point to the abolition of slavery—at least over the greater area of Islam. The days of the pious Caliphs, could they be reproduced, would mean no progress, even in the most backward of Islamic countries. The strengthening of Islam, if it is not to be a calamity to the whole world, is not to be effected by the reproduction of a barbarous past, but by an attempt to utilize the vast force which Islam represents, as a factor in real progress, the civilizing and ennobling of the race. And whether this can be done and the whole of that huge capital must be "written off," is the question which reformers have to solve.

Why should we send missionaries to convert the Mohammedans? This is another form of the old question, why preach to people who have a religion of their own, instead of going to the unenlightened heathen? But it must be admitted that the heathen also have a religion, and therefore it comes to this, we must either ignore the distinct command to "preach the Gospel to every creature," or prove ourselves justified in making a distinction between the various religions of the world as to which is most deserving of the tidings of salvation. The probable course would be to strike off those who were, in our opinion, in no special need of Christianity, either on the ground of the antiquity of their religion, its philosophic excellence, or practical utility. In this case not Islam only would be excluded, but Buddhism, Confucianism, Hinduism, and others, which represent the conscience of millions of the world's family. But have we any right to withhold the Gospel from the votaries of such religions, and to assume that Christianity is only for the darkest and most ignorant pagans?

Another ground taken up in the argument is that, judging by results, it is almost an impossibility to convert a Mohammedan to Christianity. The same reasoning is often used as regards missions to the Jews, as though difficulties excuse effort, and that the soul of a man is not worth all means and expenditure to save.

It is for the missionaries in the fighting line to decide what are the best weapons for the conquest of Islam in Nigeria. But before anything can be attempted, the public opinion of the Church at home must be aroused to the right conception of its duty, and then we shall see a movement of men and money and the might of united prayer for the conversion of the Moslem as a sinner in the dark, and needing salvation through Jesus Christ as much as the heathen. Briefly put, the constituents of success involve missionaries specially trained, with a knowledge of the Korân and all phases of Moslem belief, the circulation of copies of the Bible in Arabic and the languages of the native races, medical missions combining faith and skill, educational work, teaching the natives to think for themselves and giving them subjects for their reason to digest ; and, above all, a clear faithful proclamation, at all risks, of Christian faith and doctrine. The African who has accepted Islam has undergone no conversion of character ; he is still the same man at heart, and needs as much as ever the grace which can make all things new in Christ. This, too, is the condition of his instructors, for the mallam, with a little more knowledge, is still in the dark.

We can make no truce with Islam, except to own humiliating defeat ; it is ours rather to take the offensive, and storm her ramparts in the name of God. Difficulties ought not to unnerve or deter us ; the victories of the Cross are testimony of the power of the Gospel over heathenism all over the world, and the same grace and truth can lift this shadow from the face of millions in West Africa and the East. As Mr. J. R. Mott has said, "We should lay siege to the Port Arthurs of the non-Christian world with the undiscourageable purpose to capture them. We should not shrink or falter before such apparently impregnable fortresses as the Mohammedan world." In dealing with Nigeria we must claim the right to urge the cause of Christianity among Moslems with as much freedom, at any rate, as Islam is allowed to propagate her religion among the heathen. The native pastors, upon whom so much of the hopeful future of Nigeria depends, must be instructed in the history and character of this religion, which is the wolf of their sheepfolds.

This is a season of golden opportunity. As Dr. Zwemer points out in his striking book, "Islam, a Challenge to Faith": "Over one-half of the Moslem world is now under Christian rule or protection. Christian rule has not always been favourable for the spread of Christianity, yet it means generally a free Press, free speech, and liberty to confess Christ. Pure Mohammedan rule means an enslaved Press, no freedom of speech, and death for the apostate from Islam. The keys to every gateway in the Moslem world are in the political grasp of Christian powers, with the exception of Mecca and Constantinople."

Controversy has its place in dealing with Moslems, and for this the Christian missionary must be fully qualified by knowledge of the Korân, armed by such an excellent guide as Dr. Tisdell's "Manual of the Leading Mohammedan Objections to Christianity," and watchful tact and unruffled good temper. But the necessity for a mediator and an atonement for sin must be kept in view, and as to a man, not merely a Moslem, Jesus Christ, as the only Saviour of the world, must be proclaimed. It is a crusade of righteousness and peace against darkness, error, and distress holding in fetters the souls of millions.

> "Through the promise on God's pages,
> Through His work in history's stages,
> Through His cross that crowns the ages,
> Show His *love* to them."

*

We have watched the reaper at his toil from the rising of the sun to the going down thereof at the end of a very long day. Our eyes through all these pages have never left the field, its wide plains dotted with native towns and villages, forests dark and alive with mystery, the silver sheen of the mighty river hastening to the sea, losing itself in thick swamps of mangrove trees, whose grey-white roots at the ebb stick out of the black slime, and at the flood the stream, struggling through a mass of decaying vegetable life, through which the crocodile glides and flies in myriads swarm. We have heard the cries of wild creatures prowling in the darkness in search of food, and the buzz and flutter of wings in the feverish air. But we have listened to other voices—the groans of fettered men, the shrieks of driven women, the wail of the dying dropping down unpitied and alone. Then the raiders came no more, and the crying ceased, the sun shone again upon a people standing safely at their doors or clustered with a babble of tongues in the markets. We have drawn nearer and looked into their faces, and saw they were not yet really free; the fetter had gone, but the fetish remained. Cowering with dread, they sought to propitiate a hundred vengeful deities, or danced with plaintive wails at feasts of shame. And we forgot the scenery then, the fronded palms, the glitter of water, and the blue mountains beyond, and only regarded these poor wandering ones—millions with hearts dark enough under that cloudless African sky, and we were gladdened by the first streaks of daybreak in these souls of men. This was the field, white in its ripeness, black in its need, unto the harvest.

And lo! in the early morning of a great life a boy is seen in the field, tasting its heartbreak, and growing up to look across its waving human pastures with eyes aglow with love, going forth sickle in hand to do God service there. Through the long hot day he works on, sometimes lost to sight amid a thicket of difficulties, ever hopeful, unwearied, cutting ways for others' feet to travel, reaping possibilities, gathering sheaves of immortal souls. Then the day deepens, the sun, just sinking over the horizon, flings a glow on the brave, tear-stained face, the voice of the great Husbandman calls his name, with a smile of satisfaction he lays his sickle down and is gone. Work is over, the reaper is at home now, resting for evermore.

But though the reaper is a memory, the field is there still to-day. The sickle has passed to other hands; many who thus follow in his steps are themselves the spiritual harvest of his patient, prayerful toil. From this time the land of the Niger will be ever fragrant with the memory of a worker who in earth or heaven "needeth not to be ashamed," and to us he has left the heritage of his country and its children for our prayers, our succour, and our love.

INDEX

WM. BRENDON AND SON, LTD., PRINTERS, PLYMOUTH

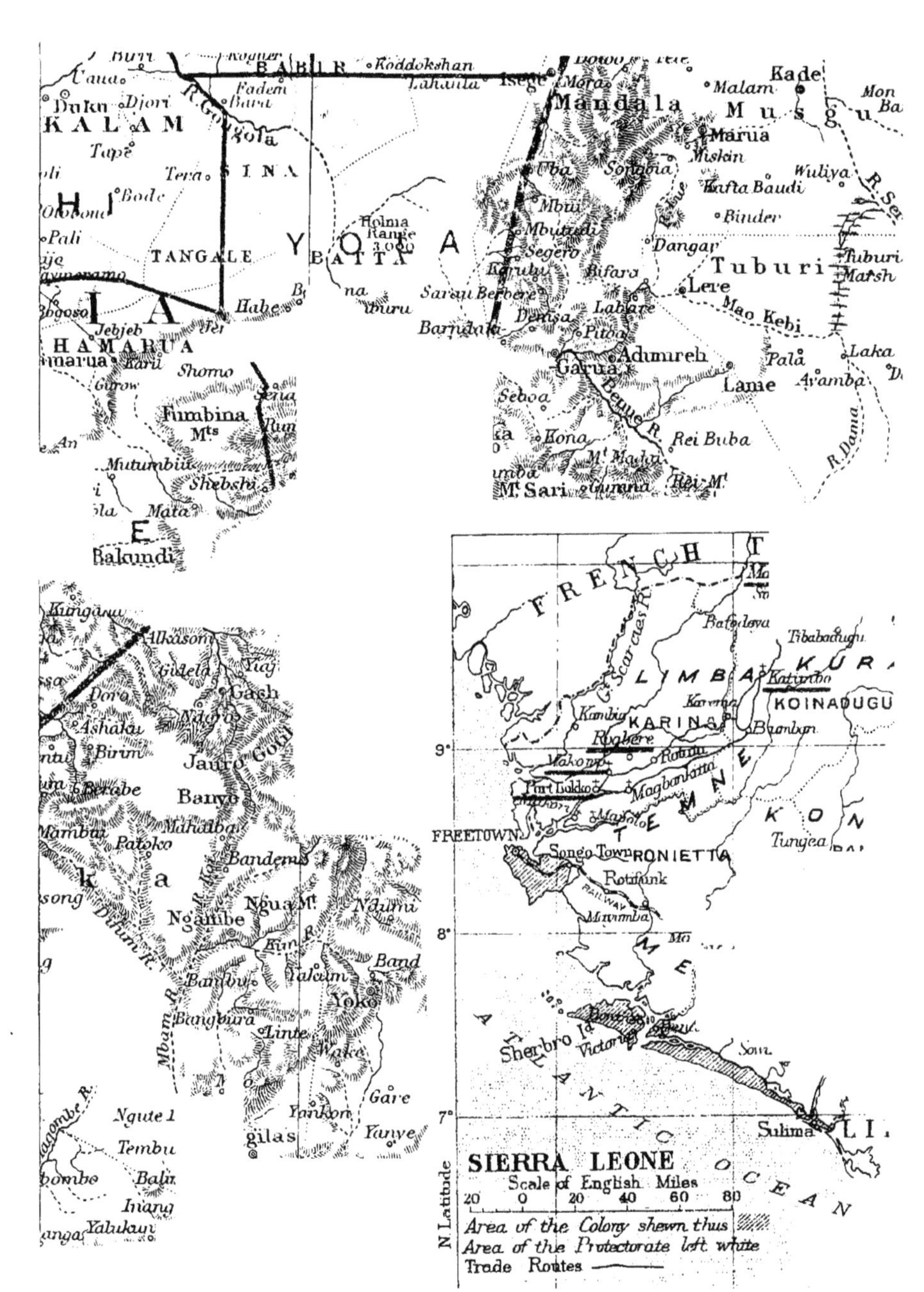

Stanford's Geogl. Estabt.

WEST AFRICA SSIONS

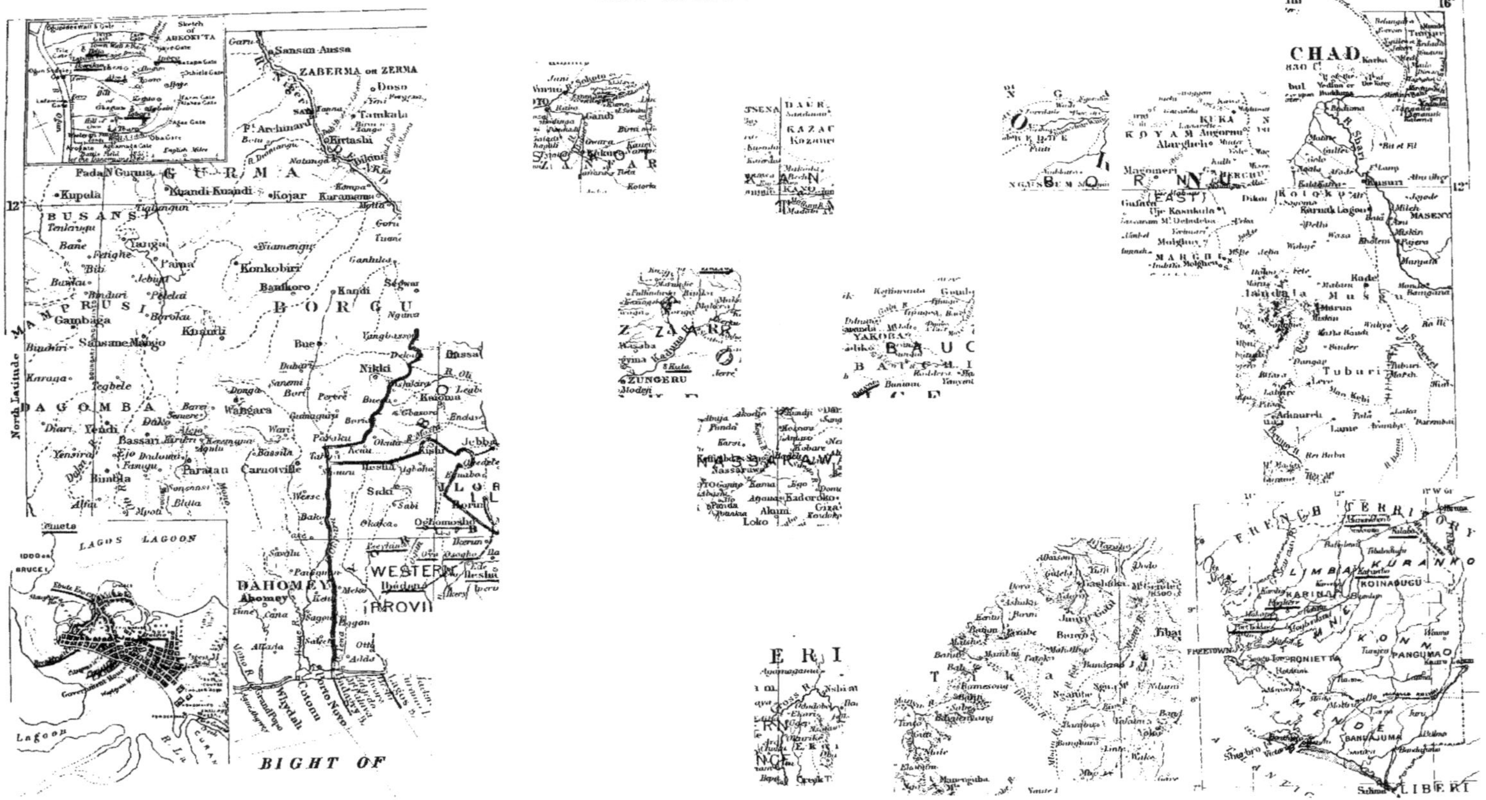

UC SOUTHERN REGIONAL LIBRARY FACILITY
AA 000 811 112 2

Lightning Source UK Ltd.
Milton Keynes UK
UKHW010400181218
334173UK00009B/182/P

9 781331 499480